PRAISE FOR

The Politics of Jesus

"Jesus was one of the Jewish people's most revolutionary prophetic voices, and Obery Hendricks shows in *The Politics of Jesus* that Jesus' teachings are as powerfully relevant for us today as they were in his own day. A powerful thinker and inspiring teacher, Hendricks presents a rereading of the New Testament and contemporary politics that will challenge, enlighten, and help to transform the burning debate about religion's role in American society and politics."

  —Rabbi Michael Lerner, editor of *Tikkun* and author of *The Left Hand of God: Taking Back Our Country from the Religious Right*

"Professor Obery Hendricks does a needed service to the Christian and non-Christian communities by reminding us of the challenge of the Ministry of Jesus to all earthly kingdoms in the name and service of the Kingdom of God. *The Politics of Jesus* is a sobering and needed perspective from which to inform our faith understanding."

  —William J. Shaw, president, National Baptist Convention, USA, Inc.

"*The Politics of Jesus* is an explosive and courageous prophetic work that calls us to revisit the life and words of Jesus to discern the true nature of his politics and his message for our time."

  —David C. Korten, author of *The Great Turning: From Empire to Earth* and *When Corporations Rule the World*

"Obery Hendricks's new book, *The Politics of Jesus*, is a gift in a time that is out of joint, with its radical portrayal of a radical Jesus, and the promise of freedom in an age of tyranny."

  —Gary Percesepe, Ph.D., coordinating director, Baptist Peace Fellowship of North America

THE POLITICS OF JESUS

Rediscovering the True Revolutionary Nature of the Teachings of Jesus and How They Have Been Corrupted

OBERY M. HENDRICKS, JR.

THREE LEAVES PRESS

Doubleday · New York

THREE
LEAVES
PRESS

PUBLISHED BY THREE LEAVES PRESS

A hardcover edition of this book was originally published in 2006 by
Doubleday.

Published in the United States by Three Leaves Press, an imprint of
The Doubleday Broadway Publishing Group, a division of
Random House, Inc., New York.

www.doubleday.com

THREE LEAVES PRESS and its colophon are trademarks of Random House, Inc., and
DOUBLEDAY and its colophon are registered trademarks of Random House, Inc.
Biblical quotations are from the New Revised Standard Version (NRSV)
unless otherwise attributed to the New International Version (NIV),
Revised Standard Version (RSV), New American Bible (NAB),
King James Version (KJV), or the author's translation.

BOOK DESIGN BY AMANDA DEWEY

Library of Congress Cataloging-in-Publication Data
Hendricks, Obery M. (Obery Mack), 1953–
The politics of Jesus : rediscovering the true revolutionary nature of the
teachings of Jesus and how they have been corrupted /
Obery M. Hendricks, Jr.—1st ed.
p. cm.
Includes bibliographical references.
1. Jesus Christ—Teachings. I. Title.
BS2415.H39 2006
2005056003

ISBN 978-0-385-51665-5

PRINTED IN THE UNITED STATES OF AMERICA

9   10

For Mariam and Diata,
my wonderful granddaughters,
at whose births I swore a holy oath to make a better world

And for Rochelle, who has never stopped believing

"The Spirit of the Lord is upon me,
because he has anointed me . . .
to let the oppressed go free."

THE GOSPEL OF LUKE 4:18

Take no part in the unfruitful works of darkness,
but instead expose them.

THE LETTER TO THE EPHESIANS 5:11

CONTENTS

STRATEGY FOUR: CALL THE DEMON BY NAME

STRATEGY FIVE: SAVE YOUR ANGER FOR THE MISTREATMENT

OF OTHERS

STRATEGY SIX: TAKE BLOWS WITHOUT RETURNING THEM

STRATEGY SEVEN: DON'T JUST EXPLAIN THE ALTERNATIVE, SHOW IT

PART THREE

ACKNOWLEDGMENTS

MANY THANKS to the scholars whose ideas and insights have so influenced my own: Howard Thurman, whose 1949 classic, *Jesus and the Disinherited*, prefigured liberation theology and the liberationist readings of the Gospels that have followed; Clarice Martin, the wonderfully insightful seminary professor who convinced me to pursue doctoral studies when my internalization of America's historical estimation of those of my race and class had convinced me that I could not; Richard Horsley, Ched Myers, and Walter Wink, groundbreaking biblical scholars and dedicated social activists all, who opened my eyes to the politicality of Jesus and whose work I humbly build upon; the late J. Christiaan Beker, the "Mad Dutchman" of Princeton Theological Seminary, my dear friend and mentor, who taught me that biblical scholarship is, indeed, a ministry; my brilliant friends and doctoral advisors John Gager and Elaine Pagels, who continue to model what it means to be a gracious teacher; James H. Cone, whose *God of the Oppressed* taught me that God does indeed take sides; Toni Morrison, whose kind words ("you write well, Obery") unleashed my pen; and Cornel West, whose seminal book *Prophecy Deliverance!* continues to influence my work, and whose deep humanity and revolutionary Christianity have exemplified for me and so many others what it means to treat the people's needs as holy.

My Personal Journey:
How I Came to Know Jesus
the Political Revolutionary

I T SEEMS THAT all my life I have been on a quest to understand Jesus. I am a son of the Christian Church. Raised in the Church. Nurtured in the Church. I joined the children's choir at the age of five. Offered my life to Christ when I was ten. My maternal grandfather was a Presbyterian elder, two uncles were Baptist preachers, three were deacons. My devout father was a longtime church trustee and my mother's Christian witness was so respected that in her later years my childhood church bestowed upon her the honored title of "Mother." My family never missed a Sunday service unless my sister or I was sick or we were on one of our regular pilgrimages Down South (the only trip my family ever took).

I was raised on the bland Jesus of Sunday school and of my mother's gentle retellings, the meek, mild Jesus who told us, in a nice, passive, sentimental way, to love our enemies, and who assured us that we need not worry about our troubles, just bring them to him. He was a gentle, serene, nonthreatening Jesus whose only concern was getting believers into heaven, and whose only "transgression" was to claim sonship with God—a fact so obvious to my family that we were sure even a blind man could see its truth.

That was the Jesus I knew. Reinforcing that perception were the renderings of him in my church, in my own home and the homes of relatives and friends, even in the images adorning the little cardboard fans we used to swat away the sweltering heat at the height of worship: Jesus with his head meekly tilted, soft hands bent limply at the wrist or clasped tightly in prayer, eyes downcast or beatifically turned upward, but never so bold as to look anyone in the eye. Then there was the famous blue-eyed Jesus by Warner Sallman, the most popular and most fanciful image of him (which I, like most folks I knew, thought to be the exact likeness of the Lord). The Scandinavian features and the clipped beard and carefully coiffed blond curls—not to mention the piercing blue eyes—gave Sallman's Jesus a nobility that assured all who gazed upon him that the last thing he would do was cause trouble or upset anyone's day. Anyone except a few mean, greedy Pharisees (whom we children hated without having a clue to what a Pharisee was) and evil priests who certainly deserved it anyway. I prayed to that Jesus daily, called out his name in times of trouble, loved him because he first loved me and because he gave his life so the devil would not get my soul.

Yet for all my trust and love and fervor, something in the portrayals of Jesus and his message did not seem quite right; something just didn't make sense. Was this meek, mild Jesus the same Jesus who defiantly called the Pharisees "a brood of vipers" and described them as "whitewashed tombs full of every unclean thing"? Was this the same outraged Jesus who, swinging a fearsome stick, set the Temple money changers to flight? And if he was so meek and mild, how could he get anyone's interest in the first place, much less hold the attention of thousands at a time and effortlessly get tough guys to follow him, like the apostle James, who was so rough and blustery that he was nicknamed "Son of Thunder"? And what did Jesus mean by sayings like "I have come not to bring peace, but a sword"? I tried my best to understand, although questions like these were frowned on by my parents and every believer I knew as evidence of weak faith or, worse, of the devil's confusion.

As I arrived at puberty and was allowed to wander my neighborhood more freely, I began to hear of a more assertive Jesus. I don't mean the scary, vengeful Book of Revelation Jesus who the fire-and-brimstone preachers claim will burn up everyone except the Elect—that is, *them* and the other fanatics who think like them. Rather, it was the brave, bold Jesus that was proclaimed by the lofty old Garveyites I encountered in the barbershop; or by scary-looking men with huge Bibles dressed like ancient Hebrews; or by unsmiling exhorters beneath stiff red fezzes with black tassles, pontificating on street corners; or by self-taught scholars in white shirts and narrow ties selling furiously annotated self-published books claiming that Jesus' divinity was nurtured in a childhood spent not in Nazareth but in Africa or Tibet. All those sincere zealots proclaimed another Jesus. In their various ways they spoke of a courageous Jesus who was executed not because of bowed-head, clasped-hands religious pronouncements, but because he stood ramrod straight against the oppressive political forces of his day.

But black Christians can be some of the most religiously conservative people in America. My parents certainly were. Like everyone else in my world, it seemed, they knew only a long-suffering Jesus who was concerned with the things of heaven, with little thought for the matters of this world, matters like social injustice, racial and gender inequities, or the systematic oppression of the poor. Not even my parents' wholehearted support of the civil rights movement and its calls for biblical justice affected their traditional view of Jesus. So when I began to voice my questions and to repeat the things I'd heard, my parents, worried that this "new" Jesus would befuddle me and undermine my faith, explained to me that those passionate, unorthodox preachers *just didn't know Jesus.*

Well, that was that, because in those days, to have it said that you did not know Jesus was the ultimate dismissal. At best, it meant that you could not be trusted. At worst, it meant that you were irretrievably traveling down the road to damnation. I certainly didn't want to burn in hell.

And, to be honest, some of those preachers' claims did seem a bit fantastic, and still do today, like one group's belief that Jesus survived the cross to quietly live to a ripe old age in Tibet. So although my questions remained, I pushed them to the back of my mind.

Yet my quest and my questions never went away. The more I wondered, the less a passive, politically uninvolved Jesus made sense. If he loved his people so much, I mused, wouldn't he stand against their oppression? Could a truly loving Jesus worry only about saving souls while the flesh of his people was raked and torn beneath the sharp heel of imperial subjugation?

My parents saw my struggle, my rising skepticism, the strange books I read, and they became more and more concerned. "Why can't you be like other boys?" my worried father asked. I had no answer. I only knew there must be more to Jesus than the meek, mild persona extolled by every Christian voice I heard; there must be a Jesus who loves us so fully that he wants the same liberation from fear and oppression and exploitation for us on earth as he promised awaits us in heaven. I just couldn't reconcile this growing realization with the fact that nowhere in the Church did I hear this Jesus preached about, a Jesus who cared not only about our souls but about our earthly circumstances, too. I was torn and confused, apprehensive about questioning the foundational teachings of my life, yet unable not to. Finally the struggle and the contradictions became too great. In my early teens I left the Church altogether, vowing never to return. Famous last words.

TODAY I AM a seminary graduate, an ordained minister, a trained scholar of the Bible, former president of a historic theological seminary, a teacher and professor to aspiring ministers and an advisor to seasoned ones.

I have earned an Ivy League Ph.D. in religion and have preached and taught all over America and in Africa, too. I have worshiped with European Christians, Asian Christians, Middle Eastern Christians, African Christians, rich Christians, poor Christians. Called God's name in drafty one-room backwoods churches, in sweltering urban storefronts, in sprawling compounds that could be mistaken for college campuses, and in structures so ornate and opulent that they embarrassed me and made me wonder if they wouldn't embarrass Jesus. In these years I have been blessed to experience the adoration and worship of Jesus in every aspect of his person and his grandeur, from the Lamb of God to the warrior Christ of Armageddon, from the son of Joseph and Mary to the Son of Man to the Son of God.

All of them. Except one: Jesus the political revolutionary, the Jesus who is as concerned about liberating us from the kingdoms of earth as about getting us into the kingdom of heaven. Yet the Gospels tell us that is who Jesus is, too. And what he was crucified for. This is the Jesus that called me back to the Church—the revolutionary Jesus.

Jesus the Political Revolutionary

Yes, Jesus of Nazareth was a political revolutionary. Now, to say that he was "political" doesn't mean that he sought to start yet another protest party in Galilee. Nor does it mean that he was "involved in politics" in the sense that we know it today, with its bargaining and compromises and power plays and partisanship. And it certainly doesn't mean that he wanted to wage war or overthrow the Roman Empire by force.

To say that Jesus was a political revolutionary is to say that the message he proclaimed not only called for change in individual hearts but also demanded sweeping and comprehensive change in the political, social, and economic structures in his setting in life: colonized Israel. It means that if Jesus had had his way, the Roman Empire and the ruling elites among his own people either would no longer have held their positions of power, or if they did, would have had to conduct themselves very, very differently. It means that an important goal of his ministry was to radically change the distribution of authority and power, goods and resources, so all people—particularly the little people, or "the least of these," as Jesus called them—might have lives free of political repression, enforced hunger and poverty, and undue insecurity. It means that Jesus sought not only to heal people's pain but also to inspire and empower people to remove the unjust social and political structures that too often were the cause of their pain. It means that Jesus had a clear and unambiguous vision of the healthy world that God intended and that he addressed any issue—social, economic, or political—that violated that vision.

Now, I know that doesn't square with what most Christians believe. In fact, it's my experience that, on the one hand, many Christians will actually bridle, even become angry, at the very thought of calling their Lord and Savior a political revolutionary. On the other hand, those who do recognize anything revolutionary about Jesus regard him simply as a *spiritual* revolutionary who sought only to bring the world to a new *spiritual* relationship with God. They might even grant that Jesus was a *social* revolutionary, but only in the narrow relational sense that he sought to transform society by changing people's individual relationships without concern for transforming the institutions and structures that so callously dominated people's lives and so ruthlessly circumscribed their life chances. This despite the fact that the Gospels give little or no attention to the salvation of individual souls, instead focusing chiefly on the welfare and salvation of the entire community, as in Luke's account of the devout old Simeon, who spent the last days of his life in prayer, not for personal salvation, but for the comfort and salvation of his people (Luke 2:25–35).

Most Christians would probably grant these limited notions of revolution, albeit grudgingly. But as to calling Jesus a political revolutionary who sought to change the power structures of his time—that's where most Christians draw the line. "Christianity is spiritual, not political," they say dismissively, as to a wayward child, although they have readily supported any number of political issues and initiatives, even unabashedly political organizations. Like Jerry Falwell's Moral Majority, for instance. Or Pat Robertson's quixotic "Christian" campaign for president of the United States. Or the Christian Coalition, Robertson's well-financed, thinly disguised partisan political organizing and lobbying enterprise that at times seems to be joined at the hip with the elitist political factions that have waged virtual war against the most vulnerable in our society—the very ones whose welfare concerned Jesus most. And often these are the same

Christians who publicly demonstrate—and sometimes kill—for the rights of the *un*born, while all too often giving short shrift to the rights and welfare of the *already* born, especially those not of European heritage.

The reality, then, is that most Christians *do* recognize a political dimension to the message of Jesus, in some shape or form. Moreover, by the very fact of their involvement in politics and political matters, as well as by their certainty of Jesus' approval of their efforts, these Christians demonstrate to the world their unquestioned conviction that political activities really are consistent with the message and ministry of Jesus.

So what is at issue for most Christians is not whether the message of Jesus has a political dimension. What they reject is the notion that Jesus was a political *revolutionary*, that he not only sought to address the *symptoms* of the people's suffering, but also—and here's the rub—that he sought to alleviate the systemic *causes* of their suffering. They reject that Jesus advocated revolutionary changes in a political order that militated against the happiness and wholeness of the people he came to serve. In other words, most Christians will tolerate imputing radical spiritual and relational intentions to Jesus, but when you go past the realm of individual piety and say that he actively opposed the oppressive political structures of his time—and counseled others to do the same—you've gone too far. The tragic result of this perspective is that the crucial guiding implications of Jesus' actions for confronting the political issues of today's world are lost.

But the biblical evidence says something very different. Consider just a few examples from the Gospels.

In what the Gospel of Luke portrays as the inaugural sermon of Jesus' ministry, Jesus announces that the reason for his anointing by God and the purpose of his mission in the world are one and the same—to proclaim radical economic, social, and political change: "The spirit of the Lord is upon me,/because he has anointed me/to bring good news to the poor./He has sent me to proclaim release to the captives/and recovery of sight to the blind,/to let the oppressed go free,/to proclaim the year of the Lord's favor" (Luke 4:18–19).

In this passage, Luke's Jesus leaves no doubt as to the radicality of his calling. First, he heralded *good news to the poor* (*ptochois*, the Greek word for "poor" here, indicates a collective or class identity). That is, he announced that the reason for his ministry was to struggle for radical change in the circumstances and the institutions that kept people downtrodden and impoverished. Yes, *radical* change, because only *radical* change could make a real difference in their plight.

He also announced *release* to the captives—that is, *to those unjustly imprisoned*—which was a declaration of major proportions, because Roman jails were full of political prisoners and those reduced to penury by economic exploitation.

Then he made the ultimate political pronouncement: he announced *liberation to those who were oppressed* by the crushing weight of empire. Not "bruised," as some translations render it, but "oppressed," from the Greek word *thrawo*, "oppress, crush." Jesus ended his inaugural sermon by proclaiming "the acceptable year of the Lord," an allusion to the year of Jubilee (Leviticus 25:8–10), the end of a fifty-year cycle, when all land that had been confiscated or otherwise unjustly acquired was to be returned to its original owners. When read in the context of his times, Jesus' sermon has the ring of a manifesto. It is the pronouncement of his divine appointment to struggle for—to "bring"—economic, political, and social justice to his people. It is difficult to make a more radical political statement than this.

Or consider the "Lord's Prayer," in which Jesus instructs his disciples that whenever they pray, their first concern should be that Caesar's unjust governance and unjust will (as manifested in imperial policies and laws) be replaced by the just governance and the just will of God ("*thy* kingdom come, *thy* will be done"). And to make sure that these instructions were not misunderstood as mere abstract notions, Jesus carefully added, "*on earth as in heaven.*" These sentiments were so politically radical that under Roman law they fully constituted treason against the state—the very crime for which Jesus was executed.

Or consider Jesus' statement "Blessed are the peacemakers." He did not say, "Blessed are the peace*keepers*"; he did not bless those whose primary goal was to *keep* the peace, to maintain the status quo without regard for justice or equity. No. The ones that Jesus explicitly blessed were the peace-

makers, those who actively strove to cleanse the world of oppression and exploitation in order to make a reality where true peace can reign for all.

Or consider one point more. For all of his moral and ethical teachings in the Beatitudes and the parables and in his instructions to his disciples and others, Jesus gave just one criterion for judging the righteousness of our lives:

> Then he will say to those at his left hand, "You that are accursed, depart from me . . . for I was hungry and you gave me no food, I was thirsty and you gave me nothing to drink, I was a stranger and you did not welcome me, naked and you did not give me clothing, sick and in prison and you did not visit me." Then they . . . will answer, "Lord, when was it that we saw you hungry or thirsty or a stranger or naked or sick or in prison, and did not take care of you?" Then he will answer them, "Truly I tell you, just as you did not do it to one of the least of these, you did not do it to me." And these will go away into eternal punishment, but the righteous into eternal life. (Matthew 25:41–46)

By the measure Jesus gives us here, it is not religious practice, or memorization of scriptures, or even faithful attendance at church or temple by which our lives are judged. It is simply this: whether we have tried to relieve the plight of the hungry and dispossessed and those stripped of their freedom; whether we have tried to change this war-torn world to a world free from oppression and exploitation, so that all of God's children might have life, and that more abundantly. In fact, Jesus identified so completely with the oppressed that he made an astonishing declaration that today's political leaders—and religious leaders, too—would do well to remember: "as you have not done it to the least of these, you have not done it to me."

THE BIBLICAL EVIDENCE is clear: the Gospel of Jesus Christ has a dimension of meaning that is undisputably political, which means that the worldview of Jesus himself also had a crucial political dimension. The primary purpose of this book is to explore the powerful yet little-known personage of Jesus the political revolutionary. The book's most basic premise is that Jesus Christ was "made flesh and dwelled among us," as John's Gospel puts it, to model and set into inexorable motion the way of liberation of mind, body, and soul from the tyranny of principalities and powers and unjust rulers in high places.

In numerous Gospel passages, Jesus employs various tactics to address the social, economic, and political conditions of his day and their terrible effects upon the lives of his people. By focusing on the words and deeds of Jesus, we will consider these tactics as strategic models. We will begin by examining the issues and conditions and religious ideals that helped to shape his earthly political consciousness and that he embodied in his ministry. From there, we will identify the political principles that were so integral to his message. That will lead us to consider one of the most crucial questions in today's political culture: Which leaders or political factions, if any, are practicing the politics of Jesus? Finally, we will suggest ways Jesus' political principles can be applied strategically to today's political realities, both in this country and on the world political stage.

What differentiates this work from others, even the relative few that recognize his radicality, is that Jesus is studied not only as a political activist, but also as a master political strategist who continually sought to increase the effectiveness of his outreach by taking different courses of action. Yet this is not a dry historical study. It is not a book about politics. It is a book about the courageously loving humanity of Jesus of Nazareth. What I seek is to present a new Christian manifesto, an empowering and inspirational resource for actions and policies that will transform our society—and the world—into a kingdom of justice in which all of God's children, regardless of color, creed, or national origin, can have life, and that in abundance, in every sphere of living. For, as the Gospel of John reminds us, Jesus came not to condemn the world, but to save it.

PART

ONE

ONE

❦

From the Red Sea to the Jordan River: The Roots of Jesus' Political Consciousness

*"Do not think that I have come to abolish the law or the prophets;
I have come not to abolish, but to fulfill."*
MATTHEW 5:17

I F JESUS WAS a political revolutionary, what were the political issues and conditions of the world of his birth that he was responding to and that he sought so fervently to change? To fully appreciate the politics of Jesus we must begin with the most basic factor in his worldview and social identity: his Jewishness. We will briefly survey the major historical moments in the development of the religion of Jesus and note how the influence of each is reflected in his message and ministry. In other words, we must begin with an understanding of the legacy of the Judaism into which Jesus was born and its influence on his life and his every pronouncement.

JESUS OF NAZARETH was a Jew. Not only was Jesus a Jew, but he was an observant Jew who never disavowed his Jewishness. We see this in his consistent observance of Jewish customs and holy days, in his frequent references to Moses, and in his acceptance of the Torah as holy writ. All of

Jesus' major teachings either were consistent with the tenets of traditional Judaism or were expansions or elaborations of it, as in Matthew 5:17–48, in which Jesus intensifies the moral ethics of Judaism with the refrain "you have heard it said . . . but *I* say . . ."*

However, the major implication of Jesus' Jewishness for our understanding of the political setting of his life and ministry goes beyond the liturgical and doctrinal aspects of Judaism. Rather, it lies in one fact in particular: that the root event from which the foundational meaning of Judaism and the entire Judeo-Christian faith tradition flows is a *political* event—the liberation event that was the Exodus.

THE EXODUS

The Bible begins with the Book of Genesis, which includes the stories of increasingly faithful individuals like Joseph, Abraham, and Lot. The next book, Exodus, recounts the struggle of the Hebrew people to escape from their painful bondage under the Pharaoh, the Egyptian ruler. With the Hebrews' exit from Egypt, the emphasis of the Bible turns from individual deliverance to collective deliverance. It is in this sense that the Exodus event is a political event: it is about the collective deliverance of a subjugated class of people from political oppression and economic exploitation.

The political nature of the Exodus is epitomized in Exodus 3:7–8, which narrates God's liberating response to the cries of the oppressed: "I have observed the misery of my people who are in Egypt; I have heard their cry on account of their taskmasters. Indeed, I know their sufferings, and I have come down to deliver them."

What we are told here is that it was not the Hebrews' religious sensibilities, nor was it their worship pieties, that accounted for God's intervention in their desperate predicament. Rather, according to God's own testimony, *it was their political plight.* In fact, the book of Exodus tells us that

---

*Throughout this book, the author has italicized words and phrases in quoted Bible passages to emphasize their relevance to the material under discussion.

when it came to worshiping God, the Hebrews were not particularly commendable. As a group, they seem not even to have been monotheistic; that is, they seem not to have fully accepted belief in one God alone. Apparently they were what we call henotheistic, which means that even if they did worship only one God, they still acknowledged the existence of other deities. This is reflected in the first commandment, in which the Hebrews are specifically commanded to worship no other gods, a commandment that would have been meaningless if they had already believed in the existence of only one God. Thus, the liberating action of God in the Exodus was not in response to the worship pieties of the Hebrews. It was to their political plight.

The term "Hebrews" itself confirms this, in that it is primarily a sociopolitical identity—specifically a class identity—rather than a religious identity. In the Hebrew language, the term *'ibri*, or "Hebrew," means literally "he crossed over," which reflects the Hebrews' status as "outsiders" to Egyptian society. Moreover, the use of "Hebrew" as a term of social or class description seems to be related to the early Semitic term *hapiru*, which most scholars believe also connoted outsider class status in the ancient Near East. This sense of "outsider" is reflected by the Exodus narrative in its own presentation of the Hebrews as in every way outcasts and aliens to the social and political mainstream of Egypt. Indeed, the Book of Exodus graphically portrays the Hebrews as a despised and socially marginalized class. The ethic of compassion for the *ger*, or "alien stranger," that permeates the Hebrew Bible from this point has much to do with the Hebrews' treatment in Egypt.

Thus, in effect, the testimony of the Exodus is that the defining root event from which Israel sprang was God's act of taking the side of the oppressed. In the final analysis, the seminal importance of the Exodus event is that in God's response to the class oppression of the Hebrews, God firmly posited justice and liberation as the very foundation of biblical faith.

From the moment of the Hebrews' final deliverance from the murderous grasp of Pharaoh, the Exodus liberation event loomed large in their collective consciousness. In fact, the people of Israel have recalled their oppression and their emancipation from it during the annual Passover seder, or feast, for some five thousand years with these words: "We were slaves to Pharaoh in Egypt, but the Lord our God brought us forth with a mighty hand and with an outstretched arm."

The Significance of the Exodus for the Ministry of Jesus

As the root event of Judaism, the Exodus liberation experience is also the root event of Jesus' faith and his message. Jesus evokes the memory of the Exodus often in the Gospels by repeatedly invoking Moses' name. And just as God declared the oppression of the Hebrews as the motive for divine intervention, Jesus cites the oppression of his people as the focus of his own intervention—his ministry—by choosing the liberation text of Isaiah 61:1–2 as his manifesto: "The Spirit of the Lord . . . has anointed me . . . to bring good news to the poor" (Luke 4:18). Mark's account of Jesus' liberation of a young man possessed by "an unclean spirit" named "Legion" even evokes the image of Pharaoh's defeat at the Red Sea: "And the unclean spirits . . . numbering about two thousand . . . rushed down the steep bank into the sea, and were drowned in the sea" (Mark 5:13).

THE BIBLICAL JUDGES

As a class rather than a group sharing an ethnic or religious identity, the Hebrews consisted of a number of different tribes. The Song of Deborah in Judges 5:14–18 lists ten tribes. After their deliverance from Egypt they spent years wandering in the desert, during which time other tribes apparently united with them, eventually increasing their number to twelve.

When they finally settled in Canaan, for generations the painful memory of their experience under Egypt's hereditary monarchy helped the Hebrews withstand the temptation to institute a monarchy among themselves. Though the prophet Samuel actually represents a later historical moment than that recounted in the Book of Judges, the fears behind the Hebrews' rejection of a monarchy can be heard nonetheless in Samuel's warning that a king would "take the best of your fields and vineyards and olive orchards and give them to his courtiers . . . And in that day you will cry out because of your king" (1 Samuel 8:14, 18).

Instead of instituting a monarchy, the tribes of the Hebrews developed an egalitarian form of governance by a confederacy, or governing council, made up of representatives of all their tribes and factions. The united tribes came to be called collectively "Israel." Their confederate form of governance is seen at work in Joshua 24:1: "Joshua gathered all the tribes of Israel to Shechem, and summoned the elders, the heads, the judges, and the officers of Israel" to jointly confer.

This era of egalitarian governance without the oversight of a king came to be known as the period of the "judges" (*shophetim* in Hebrew, i.e., "those who do justice," from *mishpat*, "justice"), as leaders who fought to preserve the Israelites' freedom were called. Their story is told in the appropriately named Book of Judges.

The Book of Judges consists of a series of popular tales that tell the story of the free tribes of Israel resisting foreign oppression. These accounts include the story of Othniel of the tribe of Caleb, who led a peasant militia that freed Israel from the oppression of the Canaanite king Cushanrishathaim (Judges 3:7–11); of Ehud the Benjaminite, who successfully led a revolt against Eglon, king of Moab (Judges 3:15–30); and of the judge Deborah's defeat of Sisera, general of the Canaanite king Jabin (Judges 4 and 5).

What all these judges had in common was their role of freedom fighter. They were individuals who rose to temporarily assume the political leadership of Israel when the freedom of the Hebrew people was threatened. The Book of Judges itself says as much: "Then the Lord raised up judges, who delivered them out of the power of those who plundered them" (Judges 2:16).

As with the earlier Hebrews, the outstanding characteristic of the biblical judges was not religiosity. Rather, the main qualification for biblical judges was a willingness to fight for their people's freedom. For instance, the Bible characterizes Samson, the best known of the judges, as driven more by his ultimately disastrous romance with Delilah than by religious concerns. Yet despite a life of dissipation, Samson maintains a place of honor in the biblical memory because his dying act was to strike a blow against the enemies of his fellow Hebrews.

In addition to the rise of individual freedom fighters as de facto generals in periods of military threat, there is another significant aspect of the period of the judges that influenced the development of the political and ethical structure of Israel: by selecting individuals as temporary leaders to rule only in times of crisis, Israel decisively rejected the idea of a king or even a centralized government. Instead, it chose to be a free and independent people with no ruling class to lord over it. In that time and place, the choice to bow to no king and to pay tribute only to God was truly revolutionary.

The Significance of the Judges for the Ministry of Jesus

The primary lesson of the biblical judges is that fighting for the liberation of those who are oppressed is as important a responsibility of our faith as developing sound personal piety. It appears that this principle has largely been forgotten in Christendom. Yet it is repeatedly echoed by Jesus in his insistence that in addition to striving to better know the will of God in their personal lives and conduct, his hearers should also do justice in the world. Jesus stressed this point in such sayings as "Blessed are those who hunger and thirst after *justice*" (Matthew 5:6) and "Seek first God's kingdom and God's *justice*" (Matthew 6:33).

You'll note that I have rendered the Greek word *dikaiosune* in these verses as "justice" rather than the usual "righteousness." As students of biblical Greek know, the term can be translated either way. However, unlike "righteousness," with its strictly one-dimensional personal moral implications, "justice" connotes more than individual piety. It also means holistic, collective—that is, *social*—righteousness. Because of Jesus' holistic spirituality, his use of *dikaiosune* in these and many of the other sayings in which it is found should be understood as encompassing both of the term's meanings, that is, personal righteousness and social justice.

Jesus' embrace of the uncompromising egalitarianism of the biblical judges is reflected in his admonition to his disciples: "You know that the rulers of the Gentiles lord it over them, and their great ones are tyrants over them. It will not be so among you" (Matthew 20:25–26). It is also seen in his unwavering recognition of God alone as sovereign king. When offered "all the kingdoms of the world" by Satan, Jesus made clear his conviction that no kingship but God's is legitimate by quoting the unequivocal declaration of God's sovereignty in Deuteronomy 6:13: "Away with you, Satan! for it is written, / 'Worship the Lord your God, / and serve only him' " (Matthew 4:10).

THE JUDGES AND THE KINGDOM OF GOD

The reason underlying the Hebrews' remarkable decision to select judges from among themselves as occasional leaders, rather than have a king as most societies around them did, is precisely the legacy of liberative justice bequeathed to the Hebrews by the Exodus. This attitude of radical political equality—that is, the refusal to accept the domination of anyone except God—is exemplified by the refusal of the biblical judge Gideon of Manasseh to become the hereditary king of Israel: "Then the Israelites said to Gideon, 'Rule over us, you and your son and your grandson also . . .' Gideon said to them, 'I will not rule over you, and my son will not rule over you; the LORD will rule over you' " (Judges 8:22–23).

Gideon's refusal reflects the pivotal Israelite notion of *malkuth shamayim*, that is, belief in "the sole sovereignty of God," the recognition that God alone has the right to rule and dominate the life and affairs of Israel in particular, and the rest of the world by extension. This was a fundamental tenet of Judaism, based on no less than the first commandment to Moses at Sinai: "[Y]ou shall have no other gods before me" (Exodus 20:3).

Three streams of meaning can be discerned in the idea of *malkuth shamayim*:

1. God as king of the universe (Psalms 22; 29; 47; 93; 96–99; also Jeremiah 10:7, 10 ff.; Malachi 1:14)
2. God as the sole king of Israel (Numbers 23:21; Deuteronomy 33:5; Isaiah 41:21; Jeremiah 8:19)

3. God as king in the *eschatological,* that is, *future* sense (1 Samuel 8:19, 12:12)

Each strand of belief in the right of God alone to rule was significant and widely held. Observant Jews reaffirmed this belief every day, however they understood it, in their daily recitation of the prayer in Deuteronomy 6:4 known as the Shema (from *shemayah,* "hear"): "Hear O Israel, the Lord your God, the Lord is *ahad*" (i.e., singular, without peer).

Despite the various ways *malkuth shamayim* could be understood, its first stream of meaning—God as universal king—became the basis for all the resistance movements in Israel to come. The radicality of this notion lay in its rejection of all human domination. Its impeccable logic was that if God is the sole king of the universe, no other claim to kingship is legitimate. For common people to declare that they would bow before no earthly king was a dangerous and radical political statement in the ancient world, and they knew it.

The roots of this revolutionary belief run deep in the history of Israel. Time after time, belief in *malkuth shamayim* inspired and empowered Israel's fighters for freedom. A particularly poignant example is found in a Jewish religious book of the first century B.C. called First Maccabees, which can be found in the Catholic Bible and the collection of ancient Jewish religious texts known as the Apocrypha.

First Maccabees recounts the history of the Israelites' rebellion against their Greek occupiers that began about 167 B.C. The conflict was triggered by an edict that all Jews must recognize the Greek king Antiochus IV as *Epiphanes* (God manifest) and swear fealty to him and his own deity, Zeus. When Antiochus' soldiers came to his village to enforce the order, an outraged peasant named Mattathias invoked the sole kingship of God: "Even if all the nations that live under the rule of the king obey him, . . . abandoning the religion of their ancestors . . [w]e *will not obey the king's words*" (1 Maccabees 2:19, 22).

First Maccabees goes on to recount instance after instance of widespread and uncompromising resistance to Antiochus' rule in the name of *malkuth shamayim,* the sole sovereignty of God. In a particularly moving account, it relates that one group of rebels, including women and children, chose to die in their wilderness camp rather than submit to Antiochus' sovereignty. To his command they replied, "We will not come out, nor will we do what the king commands" (1 Maccabees 2:34).

The courageous obedience to *malkuth shamayim* of those who waged the Maccabean Revolt was deeply seared into the collective memory of the people of Israel. It is reaffirmed yearly by the festival of Hanukkah ("rededication"), which commemorates the Maccabees' liberation of the Jerusalem Temple from the Greeks' control and its reconsecration to the God of Israel.

Malkuth shamayim also fueled resistance movements in the decades before and after Jesus' ministry. Judas the Galilean, who is mentioned in Acts 5:37, led an uprising in A.D. 6, of which the historian Flavius Josephus (c. A.D. 37–c. 100) remarked, "Judas the Galilean [and his followers] have a passion for liberty that is almost unquenchable, since they are convinced that God alone is their leader and master."

In the fourth decade of the first century A.D., *malkuth shamayim* fueled the revolutionary fervor of the Sicarii (dagger men), whose leader was Judas' son, Menahem. In the sixth decade it inspired the Zealots, Jewish nationalists who waged full-fledged warfare against Rome. In the Jewish War (A.D. 68–70) it fueled the fervor of such rebels as Saddok the Pharisee and another rebel named Eleazar ben Ari, who was the rebel leader at the besieged desert stronghold at Masada. Josephus relates that Eleazar ben Ari invoked *malkuth shamayim* when explaining to the men, women, and children holed up with him why they should prefer death to surrender: "A long time ago, brave comrades, we firmly resolved to be subject neither to the Romans nor to any other person, but only to God."

Malkuth shamayim continued as a call to freedom at least as late as the early second century, most notably in the unsuccessful rebellion against Roman oppression in A.D. 132–135 that was led by the insurgent Bar Kochba. It is said that "*malkuth shamayim!*" was the actual cry of Bar Kochba and his fellow freedom fighters as they marched into battle.

Thus *malkuth shamayim*, the sole sovereignty of God, was both a religious principle and a political principle. It was religious in that it was a fundamental statement of the uncompromising monotheistic faith of Israel. It was political because it insisted upon complete freedom from every form of human domination.

The Significance of the Maccabean Rebellion for the Ministry of Jesus

The Gospels portray *malkuth shamayim*, rendered in its Greek forms *basileia ton ouranon* ("kingdom of heaven") and *basileia tou Theou* ("kingdom of God"), as Jesus' central proclamation. Although the translation of these terms from Greek to English seems to imply that God's kingdom is a physical place, in actuality both terms have the same underlying meaning as their Hebrew counterpart: recognition of God alone as sovereign.

Nevertheless, at times Jesus does appear to nuance the kingdom of God as a spiritual or otherworldly reality. In fact, Jesus seems to conclusively deny any social or political meaning of the term when he says to Pontius Pilate, "My kingdom is not from this world" (John 18:36). And the apostle Paul seems to confirm the kingdom of God as a future spiritual reality: "flesh and blood cannot inherit the kingdom of God, nor does the perishable inherit the imperishable" (1 Corinthians 15:50).

However, on closer examination of the John 18:36 passage it becomes clear that it is in no way a denial of a political dimension to the kingdom of God. Rather, it affirms it. John 18:36 is Jesus' testimony that true sovereignty comes not from Caesar or any other worldly ruler or regime, but from God alone. And with regard to Paul's claim about God's kingdom, as we shall see in chapter 3, Paul's mistaken expectation that the world would end in his lifetime renders his understanding of the kingdom of God very different from the understanding expressed by Jesus.

In fact, the vast majority of Jesus' pronouncements in the Gospels characterize the kingdom of God as an entirely earthly reality. Jesus proclaims that God's kingdom will transform economic arrangements, as in his statement of class reversal in Matthew 20, "the first will be last." He makes the same point in the Lord's Prayer when he links the kingdom of God with refusal to participate in the onerous debt system in Israel: "we also have forgiven [or "released"] those indebted to us" (Matthew 6:12, my translation).

In Matthew 11:12 Jesus laments the unrelenting opposition to the establishment of God's sovereignty: "From the days of John the Baptist until now the kingdom of heaven has suffered violence." But it is in the Lord's Prayer that we see that Jesus understood *malkuth shamayim*, the sole sovereignty or kingdom of God, in the same way that it was understood by freedom fighters throughout Israel's history: as a call to replace earthly kingdoms, which are so inevitably colored by injustice, with God's kingdom of unending freedom and justice: "Your kingdom come./Your will be done,/on earth as in heaven" (Matthew 6:10; also see Luke 11:2).

The Messiah

Following the period of the judges, some ten centuries before the birth of Jesus, the people of Israel abandoned the judges' radical egalitarianism and asked the prophet Samuel to anoint a king for them, "to govern us, like other nations" (1 Samuel 8:5). Samuel strenuously warned that "the ways of the king who shall reign over them" (1 Samuel 8:9) will be so oppressive that "you will cry out because of your king, whom you have chosen for yourselves; but the LORD will not answer you in that day" (1 Samuel 8:18).

However, because of Israel's mounting insecurity in the face of its better-organized enemies with their standing armies and permanent leaders, the era of the judges and its egalitarian model of governance eventually gave way to what Samuel feared most: a monarchy, in the form of an anointed leader, or *messiah*. Like the biblical judges, the messiah was a commander in chief chosen by the Israelites to defend them against their enemies. But unlike the judges, who were temporary leaders, the messiah was a permanent sovereign.

"Messiah" comes from the Hebrew term *mashiach*, "anointed," that is, anointed with oil to signify the assumption of political and military leadership. In the Greek of the New Testament, *mashiach* becomes "Christos," or "Christ."

It is true that in some cases, such as Leviticus 4:3–16, *mashiach* refers to a holder of a priestly office. Other passages indicate that some prophets were anointed, such as Elijah in 1 Kings 19:16. Psalm 105:15 calls the entire people of Israel "God's anointed." However, the original purpose of the messianic office is seen in the selection of the first messiah of Israel, Saul the Benjaminite. When he anointed Saul in response to the people's call for a permanent military leader to "go out before us and fight our battles," the prophet Samuel charged him in this way: "The LORD has anointed you ruler over his people Israel. You shall reign over the people of the LORD and *you will save them from the hand of their enemies all around*" (1 Samuel 10:1).

In other words, Saul the messiah was to be led by the spirit of God to be the savior of his people and their deliverer from those who would oppress them (1 Samuel 11:6). Saul fulfilled this charge by defeating the enemies of Israel, including the Ammonites, ruthless foes known for gouging out the right eyes of their defeated enemies (1 Samuel 10:28–11:15). The overarching meaning of "messiah" thereafter was liberator or deliverer, as demonstrated by Isaiah's pronouncement that Cyrus, ruler of Persia, was a messiah because he freed the Jews from their Babylonian exile (Isaiah 45:1).

David succeeded Saul as messiah as the eventual result of a particularly heroic act: his single-handed defeat of the powerful Philistine army by slaying Goliath, the Philistines' champion. The liberated Israel so flourished under David's leadership that when Israel fell into imperial hands the people prayed for "a messiah like unto David." From then on, David the warrior king and liberator remained the prime historical model of the messiah.

In subsequent centuries the Israelites did not fare as well as under Saul and David's military leadership. They found themselves conquered by one imperial power after another—the Assyrians in 721 B.C., then the Babylonians, then the Persians, eventually the Greeks, and finally the Romans. After so many successive losses and subjugations, some Israelites quite understandably came to wonder if their oppressors could ever be defeated. They began to lose faith that their people would ever again know freedom in this world. Yet they couldn't give up on the expectation of the Messiah altogether—it was an essential hope of their faith. So the notion evolved that the office of messiah was really a spiritual office, and that *malkuth shamayim,* the sole sovereignty of God, was really a heavenly destination reached only through the diligent practice of personal piety. This idea came to be embraced by many in Israel and is held in many quarters of Judaism and Christianity even today.

Despite the various conceptualizations of messiahship as a spiritual office, however, from the time of Saul to that of Jesus, and several centuries beyond, there remained an expectation of many that the Messiah was to be the savior and liberator of Israel. This is reflected in the messianic statement in the book of Isaiah: "Here is my servant, whom I uphold,/my chosen, in whom my soul delights;/I have put my spirit upon him;/he will bring forth justice to the nations . . . /He will not grow faint or be crushed/until he has established justice in the earth" (Isaiah 42:1, 4a)

One of the most dramatic articulations of the expectation of the Messiah as liberator is seen in the Psalms of Solomon, a Jewish text composed between 50 and 30 B.C.

> *See, Lord, and raise up for them their king, the son of David . . .*
> *Undergird him with the strength to destroy the unrighteous rulers, to purge*
>   *Jerusalem from gentiles [i.e., Romans] . . .*
> *To shatter all their substance with an iron rod; to destroy the unlawful nations with*
>   *the word of his mouth . . .*
> *He will gather a holy people whom he will lead in righteousness . . .*
> *And he will have gentile nations serving under his yoke . . .*
> *And he will purge Jerusalem and make it as holy as it was even from the*
>   *beginning . . .*
> *And there will be no unrighteousness among them in his days, for all shall be holy,*
>   <u>*and their king shall be the Lord Messiah.*</u>
>
>   (Psalms of Solomon 17:21–32)

In fact, there were several roles that the Messiah was expected to play. Three of these roles are articulated in the Dead Sea Scrolls, a diverse group of Jewish religious texts found at Qumran, near the Dead Sea, that date from roughly the time of Jesus. They are (1) the Lay King–Messiah, who was to usher in the "Kingdom of his people," as reflected in the verses from the Psalms of Solomon above; (2) the Prophetic Messiah, who was to proclaim the truths revealed on the eve of the establishment of God's kingdom; and (3) the Priest-Messiah, who was to be the final and ultimate teacher of Israel.

The Significance of the Office of Messiah for the Ministry of Jesus

There is little question that the earliest generations of believers considered Jesus the long-awaited Messiah. For instance, the Gospel of Mark, which most scholars consider the oldest of the four Gospels, opens by explicitly calling Jesus the Messiah: "[B]eginning of the good news of Jesus Christ" (Messiah). Although Paul the apostle seems to infuse the word with mystical meaning, he saw "Christ" as so fundamental to the identity of Jesus that for Paul it was almost a proper name: "Jesus Christ" or "Christ Jesus," that is, "Jesus the Messiah."

The perception of Jesus as Messiah was buttressed by many of the actions and pronouncements of Jesus himself. Jesus' Palm Sunday entry into Jerusalem seated on a donkey seemed to fulfill Zechariah's prophecy of a messiah-like figure's arrival in the holy city (Zechariah 9:9). On another occasion, Jesus asked the disciple Peter, "Who do you think I am?" Without hesitation, Peter answered, "You are the Messiah" (Mark 8:29). Not only did Jesus not dispute Peter's response, he elaborated on the persecution his messiahship would bring upon him. And Jesus' public demonstration in the Temple against those who were profiting from the faith of the people (Mark 11:15–19) is evocative of the "Lord Messiah" in the Psalms of Solomon who would "purge Jerusalem and make it as holy as it was from the beginning."

And consider Jesus' response to John the Baptist in Matthew 3:15 when John shows himself reluctant to baptize him. "It is proper to fulfill all righteousness/justice," Jesus tells John. What Jesus seems to indicate is that his baptism at the hands of John, a revolutionary in his own right, will anoint Jesus into his messianic role of justice maker.

The understanding of the Messiah's role of political liberator is also reflected in the heartbroken lament of Jesus' disciples in the immediate aftermath of his crucifixion, "[W]e had hoped that he was the one to redeem Israel" (Luke 24:21), and especially in their question to the resurrected Messiah, "Lord, is this the time when you will restore the kingdom to Israel?" (Acts 1:6).

THE PROPHETS

Another important factor in the evolving political nature of the religion of Israel and the formation of Jesus' social consciousness was the vocation of the eighth-century biblical prophets and the prophetic tradition.

The eighth century B.C. was a time of great prosperity for Israel. However, it was also the time in which the gap between rich and poor was the greatest that Israel had ever experienced. Those in Israel who prospered were those who were already rich. The poor now suffered like never before. It was in this context that the major prophets of Israel arose.

Today, prophecy is thought to be solely synonymous with foretelling the future. Speak of prophecy, and what comes to mind for many is images of Nostradamus, the Psychic Friends Network, crystal balls, and tarot cards. The purpose of prophecy seems to be to offer predictions about love, money, career promotions, and other personal concerns. In fact, some of the early terms used to describe prophets, like *roeh* ("seer," 1 Samuel 9:9) and *hozeh* ("discerner," 2 Samuel 24:11), do seem to stress the clairvoyant dimension of prophecy.

However, the most common term for a prophet in the Old Testament is *nabi*, which means "one called" or "one commissioned." *Nabi* corresponds to the Greek *prophetes* ("spokesperson"), from which we get the English word "prophet." What all this indicates is that the primary task of the biblical prophets was not *fore*telling in the name of God, but *forth*-telling in

God's name. As forth-tellers, prophets functioned as spokespersons for God who were commissioned to oppose the oppression and collective unrighteousness—that is, injustice—of those in positions of power and authority. Foretelling is an integral part of biblical prophecy, but it is the lesser part. It articulates the events, including punishments, that are destined to occur if the truths of *forth*-telling are ignored and social injustices continue unchecked.

Prophetic speech is characterized by two elements: an overwhelming sense of an encounter with God and a message of moral and political judgment that the prophet feels divinely compelled to proclaim, particularly to those in political authority.

The role of the prophet apparently goes back to Moses, who accepted God's commission to speak out against the injustices of the Egyptian social order. In the period of the judges, Deborah was called "the prophetess" because she rallied the northern tribes of Israel against their enemies. Gideon the judge received divine commission to lead the resistance against the Midianites. In the later years of the period, there arose groups called *bene nebi'im*, "sons [or disciples] of the prophets," whose major function seems to have been supporting the work of prophets like Elijah and Elisha, who took great risks by making prophetic pronouncements and engaging in bold prophetic actions.

The prophetic actions were often interventionist in nature. For instance, Elijah intervened in the unlawful seizure of Naboth's vineyard by Ahab and Jezebel (1 Kings 21). Elisha sent one of his *bene nebi'im* to anoint Jehu as king, for the purpose of setting in motion the overthrow of the unjust King Joram (2 Kings 9).

Thus the primary purpose of biblical prophecy is to effect social and political change in a society. Prophets never uncritically support the status quo. Rather, their role is to challenge it. In our time, when many seem to think that Christianity goes hand in hand with right-wing visions of the world, it is important to remember that *there has never been a conservative prophet*. Prophets have never been called to *conserve* social orders that have stratified inequities of power and privilege and wealth; prophets have always been called to *change* them so all can have access to the fullest fruits of life. In fact, it was the conservative forces—those who wanted to keep things as they were—that in every instance were the most bitter opponents of the prophets and their missions for justice.

The prophets' call to transform the social orders under which they lived is reflected in the pronouncements of the prophets themselves. For instance, Isaiah prophesied to those who ruled in his time, "[C]ease to do evil,/learn to do good;/seek justice,/rescue the oppressed" (Isaiah 1:16–17).

Jeremiah prophesied in his time, "But your eyes and heart/are only on your dishonest gain,/for shedding innocent blood,/and for practicing oppression and violence" (Jeremiah 22:17).

In his own time, Micah prophesied to those in power, "Alas for those who devise wickedness/and evil deeds on their beds! . . . /because it is in their power./They covet fields, and seize them;/houses, and take them away;/they oppress householder and house,/people and their inheritance" (Micah 2:1–5).

Amos, in many ways the prototypical prophet, prophesied to the rulers of his day, "For thus says the Lord God:/ . . . I know how many are your transgressions,/and how great are your sins—/you who afflict the righteous, who take a bribe,/and push aside the needy" (Amos 5:12).

It is Amos who summarizes the prophetic imperative for all time, intoning in words searing and timeless, "But let justice roll down like waters,/and righteousness like an ever-flowing stream" (Amos 5:24).

The courageous proclamations of these prophets of the God of the Exodus left few unjust practices unscathed. They prophesied against the unfair use of laws that "with a word make a man out to be guilty . . . and with false testimony deprive the innocent of justice" (Isaiah 29:21 [NIV]).

They stormed against corrupt economic policies: "Woe to him who builds his house by unrighteousness,/and his upper rooms by injustice;/who makes his neighbors work for nothing/and does not give them their wages . . . /But your eyes and heart/are only on your dishonest gain" (Jeremiah 22:13, 17).

They were outraged by gross dishonesty in the marketplace and the seeking of profits regardless of the human cost: "Hear this, you that trample on the needy,/and bring to ruin the poor of the land,/saying, . . . 'We will make the ephah small and the shekel great,/and practice deceit with false balances' " (Amos 8:4–5).

They even issued denunciations of political corruption and warmongering that could be spoken in our day: "Your princes are rebels/and companions of thieves./Everyone loves a bribe/and runs after gifts" (Isaiah 1:23) and "Its officials within it are like wolves tearing the prey, shedding blood, destroying lives to get dishonest gain" (Ezekiel 22:27).

The timelessness of these prophetic critiques is striking. Jeremiah 22:13 ("Woe to him . . . who makes his neighbors work for nothing,/and does not give them their wages") might have been written to protest the jobs and pensions destroyed by the corruption of corporate officials in recent years. Ezekiel 22:27 ("shedding blood, destroying lives to get dishonest gain") could refer to unprovoked wars and military incursions. Amos 8:4–5 ("Hear this, you that trample the needy,/and practice deceit with false balances") might speak to deceptive corporate accounting practices and stock market fraud. That we have not heeded the prophets' words is clear. That our world would be better if we did is clear, too.

Yet not only did these courageous prophets issue scathing critiques of the injustice that militated against the loving edicts of God, they also affirmed the workings of justice: "Wash yourselves; make yourselves clean;/remove the evil of your doings/from before my eyes;/cease to do evil,/learn to do good;/seek justice,/rescue the oppressed,/defend the orphan,/plead for the widow" (Isaiah 1:16–17).

Moreover, they assured their people that justice would one day prevail over injustice: "The meek shall obtain fresh joy in the LORD,/and the neediest people shall exult in the Holy One of Israel./For the tyrant shall be no more,/and the scoffer shall cease to be;/all those alert to do evil shall be cut off" (Isaiah 29:19–20) and "A shoot shall come out from the stump of Jesse,/and a branch shall grow out of his roots./The spirit of the LORD shall rest upon him,/the spirit of wisdom and understanding . . . /He shall not judge by what his eyes see,/or decide by what his ears hear;/but with righteousness he shall judge the poor,/and decide with equity for the meek of the earth" (Isaiah 11:1–4).

It is significant that Amos, Jeremiah, Isaiah, and Ezekiel, the biblical prophets who were the boldest advocates of social justice for all, apparently were people of significant financial means. Although they themselves were not poor, these prophets were so moved by the plight of the poor among them that they risked conflict and ostracism from members of their own socioeconomic class by standing up for their needier brothers and sisters. The strength and passion of their unselfish prophetic witness has modeled for all time an important dimension of what it means to "love your neighbor as yourself," a lesson that much of Christendom in our time seems to have forgotten or never to have learned.

The uncompromising example of the biblical prophets demonstrates that the purpose of biblical prophecy is never personal comfort or self-aggrandizement. Nor were the prophets' proclamations ever directed solely against the personal habits of rulers; their primary targets were always the practices and policies that exploited and oppressed those the rulers were supposed to serve. In a word, prophets took their stand against abuses of power, not personal missteps or weaknesses. Nevertheless, in too many churches today dramatic predictions about individuals' unique personal concerns are presented as God-inspired "prophecies" by clergy who have never spoken out against social injustice, never uttered a word of political critique, yet still call themselves prophets. Some even charge fees or request financial "love-offerings" for their "prophetic" services.

Despite their claims to prophetic powers, these men and women must be considered false prophets. Yet this is not a new phenomenon; there have been false prophets throughout history, and there are many today. How can a false prophet be identified? There are two telltale criteria: (1) they are silent about issues of social justice, and (2) they function as uncritical supporters of rulers and politicians, rather than as their moral conscience and dedicated arbiters of biblical justice. Instead of challenging political regimes—and all earthly regimes need to be continually challenged to do right—false prophets either align themselves with them or say nothing at all.

In 1 Kings 18 we learn of the prophet Elijah's confrontation with the false prophets of the unjust King Ahab. These "prophets" supported the king and told him what he wanted to hear. That is what made them false prophets: they did not serve the God of the Exodus, the God of the poor and oppressed; they served Baal, the god that those in power invoked to justify their own self-serving actions. Ultimately, the people of Israel rejected Baal, because as the god of the ruling regime it cared not for the plight of the many, but only about maintaining the privileges of a few. As 1 Kings 18:36–40 reports, when the power and legitimacy of the rulers' god Baal was discredited by the prophets of God, the false prophets who enriched themselves in the name of Baal were rejected as well.

The Significance of Prophecy for the Ministry of Jesus

Jesus embodied the prophets' tradition of speaking out against the oppression and mistreatment of the people of Israel in his own scathing critiques of the ruling class of his day. Scholar William R. Herzog II explains: "Jesus the prophet interpreted what was happening to the people of Galilee who were being increasingly squeezed by colonial domination and internal exploitation. He taught them to read their distressing situation not as God's will but as the consequence of the violations of God's covenant [of justice]."

When Jesus issued his critique of the priestly aristocracy in Matthew 23:1–36, decrying their hypocrisy and corruption, he was continuing the prophetic tradition. When in Mark 5:1–10 he characterized the presence of the Roman military—the unclean spirit tellingly called "Legion"—as a destructive, demonic force in Israel, Jesus was continuing the prophetic tradition. When he indicted Herod's political machinations and institutionalized thievery by characterizing him as "that fox" in Luke 13:32 and elsewhere, Jesus was continuing the prophetic tradition.

Like Jeremiah, Jesus stood in the midst of Jerusalem and challenged the religious establishment for exploiting and misleading the very people God had called them to serve. Like Elijah, Jesus opposed religious leaders who claimed to be prophets yet ignored their responsibility to speak truth to power. And most of all, when he defied the entire Roman Empire, choosing to die on the cross rather than submit to Rome's unjust authority, Jesus embodied the very best of the courageous prophetic tradition of risking one's life and sometimes dying a gruesome death to utter the truth of

God. The description of Jesus in Luke 24:19 is fitting: "a prophet mighty in deed and word."

It is Jesus' continuation of the prophets' legacy of speaking against injustice that gives us insight into his denunciation of the financially rich in Israel, in such sayings as "Woe to you who are rich" (Luke 6:24). Like the prophets, Jesus does not condemn the rich per se, but rather those who gain or maintain their riches through unjust means: theft, subterfuge, exploitation, greed, stinginess, and especially violence.

The uncompromising example of Jesus Christ places upon every Christian minister the responsibility to withstand the temptation to align oneself with the secular ruling powers. It is true that it is part of every minister's calling to be a pastor to his or her parishioners, to be a spiritual leader and teacher and a comforter of the sick at heart and those afflicted in mind, soul, spirit, or body. Ministers of the Gospel must comfort the afflicted, but they also have the prophet's duty to afflict the comfortable. It is every shepherd's charge to stand against anything that would harm his or her flocks, be it by direct assaults on their well-being or by willful neglect. Every minister's prophetic duty as a servant of the God of the Exodus is to bring good news to the poor and deliverance to the oppressed, not to bow to the desires of those in power simply because they are in power. One witnesses the chumminess of today's religious leaders with those in authority and wonders if these leaders realize that by catering to the powers that be they compromise their solemn prophetic responsibility and assume the role of false prophets. Their unwillingness to speak truth to power or to empower others to do so represents a refusal to prophesy for justice and a betrayal of their sacred calling. Moreover, ministers who are cozy with those in power run the abiding risk of becoming servants of Baal, the god of the privileged few. That is why a conservative prophet, a prophet aligned with the ruling regime, in reality is no prophet at all.

THE EXILE

In 597 B.C. the Babylonian army invaded Judah, the southern kingdom
of biblical Israel. They destroyed the Temple at Jerusalem and began a period of colonial domination that lasted six decades. Jeremiah 52:28 seems
to indicate that between 597 B.C. and 582 B.C. the Babylonians deported
some forty-six hundred Jews to Babylon, apparently to utilize them as
functionaries in the Babylonian bureaucracy. Because Jeremiah probably
only counted males, as was the custom at that time, the total number of
deportees was possibly as many as eighteen thousand. Though this still
constituted a relatively small number, the deportees represented Judah's
economic, political, and religious elites, who essentially were one and the
same.

In 539 B.C. the Persians invaded Babylon and vanquished the Babylonian empire. In a strange turn of events, Persia resettled the Jewish exiles
in an enclave around Jerusalem of some twelve hundred square miles, and
then did something equally surprising: they fully financed the rebuilding
of the Jerusalem Temple (Nehemiah 2:7–8; Ezra 1–4). Although this was a
much welcome development for the former exiles, the reason for the Persians' seeming largesse was not altruism. Almost certainly its purpose was
to establish a cadre of grateful returnees to represent Persian political interests in Judah and to assist with imperial bureaucratic functions just as
they had for the Babylonians.

It was at this time that the office of high priest of the people of Israel
was established with the sponsorship and the blessing of the Persians. Although the Bible indicates that the term "high priest" (in Hebrew, *kohen
gadol*) was used prior to the Exile, the term was not used specifically to indicate one authoritative head of the priesthood until Israel was under
Persian rule. What made this new development significant was that the
high priest was now considered the ultimate intercessor between Israel
and God. Apparently Jeshua, the son of Jozadak, was the first high priest
under the Persians. The Book of Zechariah, which recounts events of that

period, specifically refers to Jeshua as "high priest" in 3:1 (it calls him Joshua, son of Jehozadak). Zechariah 6:9–13 describes Jeshua's coronation as head of the priesthood and states, "he shall bear royal honor, and shall sit upon his throne and rule" (6:13). The Persians' recognition of Jeshua's position along with their appointee as governor, Zerubbabel, is attested by the two men's unmolested leadership in the rebuilding of the Jerusalem Temple.

Only the high priest was allowed in the Holy of Holies—the inner chamber of the Temple in which God was believed to dwell—to ask for God's forgiveness of Israel on the Day of Atonement. But in addition to being the intercessor between his people and God, the high priest was the intermediary between Israel and its imperial overseers. In that the Persians were the high priest's patrons, it was a relationship fraught with conflicts of interest that too often were resolved to the high priest's benefit, but to his people's detriment. The high priesthood would endure in this form and in this same relationship with Israel's various foreign rulers until the Jerusalem Temple was once again destroyed in A.D. 70, almost four decades after the execution of Jesus.

Although for Israel the high priesthood was a religious office, apparently the Persians' intention in establishing it was the same as its reason for repatriating the exiles: to bring Israel in line with the interests of the Persian Empire. This seems to be borne out by the high priest's practice of offering daily prayers and sacrifices for the Persian king, a practice that was begun immediately after the rebuilding of the Jerusalem Temple (Ezra 6:10). This was an extraordinary turn of affairs: a high priest praying for the well-being of the oppressors of his own people. Josephus reports that the practice was continued by every high priest for each subsequent colonial occupier of Israel, from the Persian occupation until Rome's final destruction of the Jerusalem Temple in A.D. 70 (*History of the Jewish War* 2:197).

Because the high priesthood derived its power from its association with the colonial oppressors of Israel, it was as much a political office as a religious one. In actuality and in practice the high priest answered to his imperial sponsors and had to serve their interests in order to maintain his office. This situation was highlighted in the years immediately preceding the birth of Jesus by Herod's habit of appointing and deposing high priests at his whim and will, a practice that will be discussed in the next chapter.

The overt politicality of the high priesthood, as well as the fact that "the people of the land"—the non-elites that had remained in Israel during the Exile—were not allowed to participate in the rebuilding of the Temple, the physical center of their own faith and culture, caused many to question the high priesthood's legitimacy. And in many quarters the high priest was reviled as a traitor because his office was sponsored by the oppressors of Israel. As a result, many Jews resented the high priesthood and, by extension, the entire hereditary priesthood. In fact, large numbers of Jews, particularly the poor, actually questioned the loyalty of the priests to Israel from Nehemiah's day through the time of Jesus right up until the destruction of the Temple and the dispersal of the hereditary Temple priesthood in A.D. 70.

The Significance of the Exile for the Ministry of Jesus

Each of the four Gospels depicts Jesus in contentious and often bitter confrontation with the priests. Jesus' opposition to them reflects the schism that began between the hereditary priestly class and the common people during the Exile. On a number of occasions Jesus does more than criticize the priests; he is shown going so far as to reject the priesthood's legitimacy altogether. For instance, in John 15:1–3 Jesus claims for himself the priests' defining role of facilitating ritual purity for supplicants through the offering of biblically prescribed sacrifices, then emphatically rejects the necessity of both the sacrifices and the priests by declaring: "*I am the true vine* . . . You have already been cleansed by the word that I have spoken to you." He also usurps the priests' role in Mark 1:40–44, when he pronounces a leper clean before any sacrifice has been made.

Even more bold were his public challenges to the priests at the Jerusalem Temple, the very seat of their power, on Passover and on other holy days when the city was full of pilgrims. The Gospel of John paints the most radical picture of Jesus in this regard. John recounts that Jesus journeyed to Jerusalem at least three times (John 2:13; 7:14; 10:22). At every visit he scathingly denounced the priests, in one instance even declaring to them, "You are from your father the devil" (8:44).

The twenty-third chapter of Matthew's Gospel tells us that Jesus went so far as to call the priests "blind guides," a "brood of vipers," and "white-washed tombs . . . full of the bones of the dead and of all kinds of filth."

These very public challenges to their status and authority go far in explaining the priests' murderous opposition to Jesus.

THE MACCABEAN REVOLT

In 330 B.C. Alexander the Macedonian defeated the forces of the Persian Empire, thereby consolidating his power over most of Asia Minor. He suddenly died soon thereafter. After much contention and warfare among his generals, Alexander's empire was divided among them, with Israel and Syria falling under the control of the Greek general Seleucus. It was the Seleucid regime that eventually instituted the onerous system of taxation that made the lives of the people of Israel so difficult and that was continued in modified form by the Romans. The Seleucid tax system took as much as 33 percent—a disastrous amount—from each farmer's production as the empire's due.

It was in 167 B.C. that Antiochus IV, a descendant of Seleucus and king of Syria and Palestine, declared himself *Epiphanes*, "God manifest," a declaration that greatly offended Israel's foundational belief in *malkuth shamayim*, expressed in the seminal biblical commandment "you shall have no other gods before me" (Exodus 20:3).

Anthiochus' claim to be divine was bad enough. Worse was the subsequent decree that forbade observance of the Torah, the practice of circumcision, the observance of the dietary laws, and the enactment of the traditional sacrifices. But the crowning outrage was Antiochus' order that all the Israelites must abandon their worship of the Lord God of Israel and instead worship Antiochus and his god, Zeus.

To ensure that these sacrifices would be both a real declaration of loy-

alty to Antiochus and his god, Zeus, and a true disavowal of their fealty to
the God of Israel, Antiochus ordered that each Jewish male was to participate in the sacrifice of a pig upon a holy altar—a terrible abomination in
the sight of Jews.

Greek soldiers were dispatched throughout Israel to force compliance
with Antiochus' edict. When the soldiers ordered the residents of Modein,
a small village in the Judean hills, to make the desecrating sacrifice, a peasant named Mattathias and his six sons attacked the soldiers with righteous
fury and led their fellow villagers in routing them. This began what became the Maccabean Revolt, which took its name from Mattathias' oldest
son, Judas, who became the revolt's leader. Judas was called "Maccabeus,"
which scholars believe meant "hammer."

In 164 B.C., after three years of fierce fighting, the Maccabees liberated
Jerusalem and reconsecrated the Temple to the God of Israel. Finally, in
142 B.C., after more than a generation of guerrilla warfare, the last of the
Greek occupiers of Israel were driven out of the country in a stunning victory for the Jews.

Parenthetically, Antiochus' edict ordering the worship of Zeus re-
newed the rupture between the hereditary priestly class and the common
people. The average Jew was incensed by Antiochus' action. But rather
than oppose the depredations of the Greeks, many of the priests sought to
assimilate into Greek culture instead. According to 1 Maccabees 1:14–15,
so ardently did the aristocratic priests seek to emulate the Greeks that they
attempted to remove their own marks of circumcision—without anes-
thesia!—so as not to appear different from the Greeks in the open naked-
ness of the *gymnasion*, or gymnasium, the elite institution of Greek culture
and education.

The Significance of the Maccabean Revolt
for the Ministry of Jesus

An indication of the importance of the Maccabean Revolt to the political consciousness of the people of Israel, and the depth to which the revolt's liberation sensibilities were seared into their collective memory, is

seen in the honor paid to the Maccabean leaders in succeeding generations by the naming of large numbers of male Jewish children after Mattathias (Matthew) and Judas.

It was no different in Jesus' setting. The Gospels and the Book of Acts tell us that in Jesus' small band of disciples alone there were at least two men named Matthew: the son of Alphaeus (Matthew 9:9; Luke 5:27) and the disciple chosen by lot to succeed Judas as one of the Twelve, who is referred to as Matthias (Mattathias, Matthew, and Matthias all translate the Greek *Matthian*) (Acts 1:23, 26).

There also were at least two Judases: Iscariot (Matthew 10:4) and another Judas (John 14:22). Mark 6:3 tells us that one of Jesus' six siblings was a brother named Judas, whom the New Testament Book of Jude claims as its author. The Book of Acts mentions three more Judases: two in relation to Paul (Acts 9:11; 15:22, 27), and Judas the Galilean (5:37), the historical figure who led a major revolt against the Romans during the childhood of Jesus, in A.D. 6.

In addition, the courage of the Maccabean freedom fighters was celebrated at the Temple annually at the Hanukkah festivities, the commemoration of the Maccabees' defeat of the Greek army at Jerusalem and their victorious rededication of the Temple to the God of Israel. The heroism of the Maccabean nationalists was also extolled on Nicanor's Day, an annual observance that celebrated the defeat and subsequent decapitation of the Syrian general Nicanor by the Maccabees. Although observance of Nicanor's Day was eventually discontinued, Josephus explicitly speaks of it as still being celebrated a generation after Jesus' death.

In these ways the memory of the Maccabean liberation event and its heroes was kept very much alive in Israel. The event remained a touchstone for the power of faith and the abiding hopes for liberation that were deeply embedded in the collective consciousness of the people of Israel.

As a Jew, Jesus was a direct heir to the profoundly compelling Maccabean legacy and its celebrated freedom sensibilities. The centrality of *malkuth shamayim*, the sole sovereignty of God, to his own ministry points to this.

THE HERODIAN REGIME

With the complete Maccabean victory in 142 B.C., the Jews of Israel were free of colonial oppression for the first time since 597 B.C. They instituted their own government, which became known as the Hasmonean regime, from Hasmon, the family name of Mattathias and Judas Maccabeus. The Hasmonean dynasty flourished for three generations. In territorial terms, the Jewish state the Hasmoneans established eventually exceeded even the holdings of David and Solomon at the height of their power.

Unlike their idealistic and self-sacrificing Maccabean forebears, however, the Hasmoneans proved to be so morally corrupt and so exploitative of their own people that when the Roman general Pompey entered Israel in 63 B.C., some Jews actually welcomed him. Most, however, did not. So in their initial foray into Israel and in subsequent campaigns, the Romans resorted to their typical ruthlessness to force the Jewish people to submit to their sovereignty.

Pompey laid a severe siege upon Jerusalem. The Jerusalemites kept the Romans at bay as long as they could, but the beleaguered city finally surrendered. Unfortunately Pompey was vicious in victory. In addition to the carnage and looting he allowed his troops, Pompey desecrated the Holy of Holies, the most sacred precinct of the Temple to underscore the totality of Rome's power over Israel.

After subduing Jerusalem and the southern province of Judea, Pompey then marched throughout Israel conquering the more hellenized cities, freeing them from Jewish law and custom. At the point of the sword he subjected the remaining territories of Judea, Galilee, Perea, and Idumea to rigorous economic tribute. Josephus informs us that especially during the initial decades of the occupation, the Roman army destroyed complete towns and slaughtered, crucified, or enslaved their entire populations. For instance, in 43 B.C. the general Cassius conquered Taricheae in Galilee and enslaved thirty thousand of its inhabitants, then later enslaved the residents of other major towns, in one case because they were slow in raising an additional levy of taxes.

To add insult to injury, the Romans did not depose the corrupt Hasmoneans, but instead installed another Hasmonean, Hycanus II, as their handpicked high priest to administer Roman interests. Rival Hasmonean factions arose in jealousy. For almost a generation thereafter, there was much intrigue and factional violence against the Roman-backed Hasmoneans. So fierce was the fighting that at one point even the Parthians, a tribe from the region southeast of the Caspian Sea in Persia, were called in to aid a rival Hasmonean party.

Eventually the Hasmoneans' importance to the Romans waned. Hasmonean influence was eclipsed altogether in 40 B.C., when a young man of half-Idumean—that is, half-Arab—descent was recognized with great ceremony by both Mark Antony and Octavian as their client-king in Israel. That young man was Herod the Great, a megalomaniacal Hasmonean descendant. He was completely lacking in loyalty to his forebears, but he still had to contend with the Hasmonean factions, each of which vied for Israel's throne. By 37 B.C. Herod had vanquished all the factions with the help of the Roman army. In the years it took to establish full military control, he had engaged in extensive slaughter throughout Galilee, the hotbed of resistance to his rule, including Emmaus and other towns mentioned in the New Testament. His rule was finally consolidated after an extensive siege of Jerusalem with an army of eleven infantry battalions and six hundred cavalry. Josephus describes the scene: "When the troops poured in, a scene of wholesale massacre ensued; for the Romans were infuriated by the length of the siege, and the Jews of Herod's army were determined to leave none of their opponents alive. Masses were butchered in the alleys, crowded together in the houses, and flying into the sanctuary" (*History of the Jewish War*, 1:342–346).

After his victory, to signify his authority to rule all of Israel in Caesar's name, the Romans gave Herod the title "King of the Jews."

Maintenance of Herod's position rested, on the one hand, upon continually currying Roman favor by funneling as much wealth to Rome as possible and, on the other hand, by resorting to unspeakable brutality to thwart his own people's every quest for freedom. Citing Josephus, the New Testament scholar Richard Horsley observes, "Herod, in fact, instituted what today would be called a police-state, complete with loyalty oaths, surveillance, informers, secret police, imprisonment, torture, and brutal retaliation against any serious dissent."

Herod exploited Israel on an unprecedented scale, using the proceeds of his extortionate tax policies both to underwrite a personal lifestyle of extraordinary luxury and to lavish so many gifts upon imperial figures that Josephus was moved to remark that "one can mention no suitable spot within his realm which [Herod] left destitute of some mark of his homage to Caesar." Herod was so intent on pleasing his overlords that he actually adopted the titles "Admirer of the Romans" and "Admirer of Caesar."

Herod's heartless slaughter of male infants that is narrated in Matthew 2:13–18 gives a sense of his willingness to kill in order to address even remote threats to his power. Indeed, Herod was so brutal that the Roman emperor Augustus is reported to have quipped, using a Greek pun, that it was better to be Herod's *hus* (pig) than his *hios* (son), because, as a Jew, Herod would not kill a pig.

The Significance of the Herodian Regime for the Ministry of Jesus

This environment of callous economic exploitation and homicidal repression of the people of Israel by Rome and its puppet, Herod, is the dangerously volatile setting into which Jesus was born. Its brutality and excesses were integral to the social fabric of his setting in life. The purpose of his ministry, in great measure, was to alleviate the suffering, hopelessness, and diminished life chances that Herod's reign had made so much worse for the people of Israel.

THIS HAS BEEN a brief survey of the epochal events in the history of Judaism. As we have seen, each had important political implications for Israel, and each left an indelible mark on Israel's life and faith. That all of these developments are reflected in the message and ministry of Jesus demonstrates how fundamental their influence was to the formation of his political awareness and attitudes. Yet there is an additional factor in Jesus' Jewish legacy that was critical to the development of his political consciousness: the teachings of the Hebrew scriptures themselves.

THE HEBREW BIBLE AND JUSTICE

The four Gospels show Jesus quoting the Hebrew scriptures often. Even taking into account that in their zeal to tell his story the Gospel writers may have ascribed biblical quotes to Jesus in addition to the ones he actually uttered, still the picture we have of him is of a man who is deeply familiar with the scriptures. His knowledge of the scriptures would have come in one of two ways, or both: through the oral tradition and memorization techniques by which much learning was typically imparted in late antiquity, or through his own ability to read.

John 7:15 implies that Jesus was literate, something that was uncommon in first-century Israel. The literal translation of John's Greek in that verse reads, "How does this man know *letters [grammata]* . . . ?'" And Luke's Gospel tells us that Jesus began his inaugural sermon reading aloud from the Book of Isaiah (Luke 4:16–17).

Whether he was literate or not, there is no doubt that as a religious man who was conversant with the scriptures, Jesus was familiar with the admonitions regarding justice that were so foundational to the biblical tradition. This is clear because Jesus' notions of justice and righteousness are fully consistent with those in the Bible.

What is the biblical notion of justice? The Hebrew Bible principally uses two terms to describe it: *mishpat* and *sadiqah.*

Mishpat is usually translated as "justice." Biblical justice is the establishment or restoration of fair, equitable, and harmonious relationships in society. The major implication of its meaning is that any member of the community has the same rights as any other, that everyone has the same inalienable right to abundance and wholeness and freedom from oppression. *Mishpat* also means "judgment" in the sense of balancing or working to resolve all conflicts—social, economic, and political—with the equal rights of all in mind.

Sadiqah is usually translated as "righteousness." Study of the uses of *sadiqah* and its related terms reveals that its focus is on behavior that fulfills the responsibilities of relationship, whether with God or with other persons. In other words, when people fulfill their relationship with God through obedience and observance of biblical ordinances *and*—sometimes this is overlooked in contemporary notions of righteousness—*with humanity*, too, then they are considered righteous. Or to put it another way, the basis of biblical justice is fulfillment of our responsibilities to and relationships with others as the ultimate fulfillment of our responsibility to God. In fact, the Book of Genesis declares that the reason God chose Abraham to be "the ancestor of a multitude of nations" (Genesis 17:4) was to bless "all the nations of the earth" with God's teachings of justice: "for I have chosen him that he may charge his children and his household after him to keep the way of the Lord by doing righteousness *(sadiqah)* and justice *(mishpat)*" (Genesis 18:18–19).

What is significant here is that both justice and righteousness are based on social relationships. Not on individual, personal piety or on individual conformity with ritual and liturgy, but on social interactions. In fact, in the Hebrew scriptures there is no word for "individual"; there is only the plural term for "people," that is, community. In other words, justice is the divinely ordained way of relating to one another in human society. For this reason, for any social or political endeavor to rightly claim to be consistent with the biblical tradition, it must have at its center justice for all people regardless of class, gender, color, or national origin.

However, it is important to acknowledge that, in practice, males in biblical Israel did not construe either *mishpat* or *sadiqah* to fully extend to the rights of women. In fact, this unequal treatment is actually sacralized by the Hebrew scriptures, whose pronouncements consistently treat women as second-class members of society. This is a terrible lapse that has caused untold misery for millennia, and does so today in ways too numerous to name. However, these patriarchal sensibilities do not reflect an inherent deficiency in the biblical ideals of justice themselves. The problem lies in the too often oppressive hearts of men. If these ideals were fully observed without distinction or exception, they would result in a much more just and harmonious world for all.

Gender biases notwithstanding, there are three areas of the Hebrew scriptures that were particularly important to the formation of Israel's notion of political, social, and economic justice: the Law Codes, the prophetic books, and the Psalms.

The Law Codes

The Law Codes consist of three different biblical passages: the Book of the Covenant (Exodus 20:22 to 23:33), which is the oldest of the codes, having originated while Israel was still a confederacy governed by council; the Deuteronomic Code (Deuteronomy 12 to 26), which was codified about 772 B.C.; and the Holiness Code (Leviticus 17 to 26), which originated sometime before or immediately after the conquest of Jerusalem by the Babylonians in 587 B.C.

All the Law Codes promote and legislate social justice and economic parity, and all are particularly concerned with the rights of the most vulnerable members of society: widows, orphans, strangers, and the poor in general. Protecting these members of society from economic exploitation was a distinct focus of the codes. The codes' stipulations include the following:

- Forbidding the charging of interest to poor borrowers (Exodus 22:25)
- Protecting the poor from exploitation by providing fair and just measures of weight and dry quantity (Deuteronomy 25:13–15), as well as measures of liquid quantity and physical length (Leviticus 19:35–36)
- Safeguarding the dignity of debtors by forbidding creditors to accost them at their homes (Deuteronomy 24:10–11)
- Protecting the earnings of hired servants by providing that wages be paid on the day they are earned (Deuteronomy 24:14–15)

- Specifically forbidding perversions of justice against the poor (Exodus 23:6)
- Prohibiting partiality and bribes in the courts because such actions inevitably inured to the benefit of the rich (Deuteronomy 1:17; Leviticus 19:15)
- Enhancing justice in the courts by increasing both the requirements for the valid testimony of witnesses and the penalty for false testimony (Deuteronomy 19:15–21)
- Instructing that truly needy persons be lent whatever they required, with any outstanding balance to be forgiven after seven years (Deuteronomy 15:7–11)
- Instituting the year of Jubilee, the end of a fifty-year cycle, when all lands were to be returned to the families of their original owners and all bondservants released (Leviticus 25:10)
- Sacralizing economic parity by allowing the poor to bring less expensive sacrifices to the Temple (Leviticus 12:8; 14:21–22)

These constitute the foundational laws of justice that governed Judaism and Jewish life in Jesus' time. Their insistence on justice was formative and foundational to the ethics and morality, the worldview and social consciousness upon which the ministry of Jesus was based.

The Prophetic Books

The pronouncements regarding justice in the prophetic books have been treated at length in our discussion of the major prophets. Suffice it to say here that the prophets' uncompromising pronouncements to those in power and authority about oppressive political, marginalizing social, and exploitative economic policies and practices served to embed in Judaism a forceful and enduring thirst for justice in all spheres of life. This is epitomized by Isaiah's prophetic pronouncement "Wash yourselves; make yourselves clean;/remove the evil of your doings/from before my eyes;/cease to do evil,/learn to do good;/seek justice,/rescue the oppressed,/defend the orphan,/plead for the widow" (Isaiah 1:16–17).

What is striking here is that, taken together, the Law Codes, the pronouncements of the prophets, even the edicts in Leviticus that make up the Holiness Code itself define holiness not in static doctrinal or liturgical terms, but in terms of actions: behaving with justice toward all others in obedience to God's laws. This is also expressed by Isaiah:

> *Is not this the fast that I choose:*
>> *to loose the bonds of injustice,*
>> *to undo the thongs of the yoke,*
> *to let the oppressed go free,*
>> *and to break every yoke?*
> *Is it not to share your bread with the hungry,*
>> *and bring the homeless poor into your house;*
> *when you see the naked, to cover them,*
>> *and not to hide yourself from your own kin?*
> *Then your light shall break forth like the dawn,*
>> *and your healing shall spring up steadily. (Isaiah 58:6–8)*

The Psalms

The Psalms were composed by an unknown number of writers in diverse settings and over at least five centuries, although they most probably originated during the monarchies of David and Solomon. Despite the span of time and the diversity of authorship, there is among them a good deal of emphasis on freedom and justice and deliverance from oppression. For instance, Psalm 10 likens economic exploitation to being attacked by a beast: "They sit in ambush in the villages;/in hiding places they murder the innocent./Their eyes stealthily watch for the helpless;/they lurk in secret like a lion in its covert;/they lurk that they may seize the poor;/they seize the poor and drag them off in their net./They stoop, they crouch,/and the helpless fall by their might" (Psalm 10:8–10).

Psalm 94 describes the consequences of oppression and exploitation as tantamount to murder: "They crush your people, O Lord,/and afflict your heritage./They kill the widow and the stranger,/they murder the orphan" (Psalm 94:5–6).

Some passages are cries for help: "Rise up, O Lord; O God, lift up your hand;/do not forget the oppressed . . . /Break the arm of the wicked and evildoers;/seek out their wickedness until you find none" (Psalm 10:12, 15).

Other passages describe how persons of means should treat their poorer neighbors: "It is well with those who deal generously and lend,/who conduct their affairs with justice . . . /They have distributed freely, they have given to the poor" (Psalm 112:5, 9).

Still other passages describe the ideal ruler. Psalm 72 begins with a prayer for such a leader: "Give the king your justice, O God,/and your righteousness to a king's son./May he judge your people with righteousness,/and your poor with justice . . . /May he defend the cause of the poor of the people,/give deliverance to the needy,/and crush the oppressor" (Psalm 72:1–2, 4).

The same psalm describes the reign of a just ruler: "For he delivers the needy when they call,/the poor and those who have no helper./He has pity on the weak and the needy,/and saves the lives of the needy./From oppression and violence he redeems their life;/and precious is their blood in his sight" (Psalm 72:12–14).

For all their hope for just rulers of Israel, the psalmists never lose sight that it is God "who executes justice for the oppressed;/who gives food to the hungry./The LORD sets the prisoners free;/the LORD opens the eyes of the blind./The Lord lifts up those who are bowed down;/the LORD loves the righteous" (Psalm 146:7–8).

There are many other passages in the Psalms that speak against oppression and oppressors and extol justice and those who practice it. Yet I believe that those passages are epitomized by one phrase, found in Psalm 99:4, which calls God simply "lover of justice."

The Significance of the Hebrew Scriptures for the Ministry of Jesus

The notion of the practice of justice as a divine imperative in Israel pervades the writings of the Law Codes, the prophetic books, and the Psalms, which were among the most influential and the most widely read and recited sections of the Bible for first-century Jews. As such, they had great influence on Jesus. This is reflected in Jesus' understanding of justice, which is unerringly consistent with the bedrock biblical notions of *mishpat* and *sadiqah*. In fact, in the Beatitudes alone Jesus quotes or directly refers to passages in the Law Codes, the prophetic books, and the Psalms. There can be no question of their influence upon his notions of justice and injustice, righteousness and unrighteousness—indeed, upon the very shape and thrust of his prophetic ministry.

IN THIS CHAPTER we have surveyed the historical trajectory of the Judaism to which Jesus was heir, as well as the political events and ideas of justice and liberation that undergirded and pervaded the Judaism of his day, and how all of these are reflected in Jesus' message and ministry. But before we consider the political strategies of Jesus, there is one more set of factors in the shaping factors of Jesus' politics to be considered, one that is perhaps the most important of all: the immediate crucible of events and conditions in which the politics of Jesus were forged.

✸

TWO

Birth of a Revolutionary: The Shaping of Jesus' Politics

1. POLITICAL FACTORS

ROMAN OCCUPATION

In the opening decade of the first century, the emperor Augustus declared his reign to be *Pax romana*, that is, a season of total peace in the Roman Empire. However, like all propagandists for injustice, Augustus neglected to note that the fruits of the "peace" he so ceremoniously proclaimed fell almost exclusively to the rich. Nor did he acknowledge that his "peace" was achieved and maintained by horrific political repression. The irony of Rome's claims of *Pax romana*, as scholar Klaus Wengst observes, is that the Roman Empire "produced terror and uncertainty and then offered itself as an active guardian of peace." It has been estimated that Augustus kept up to 100,000 legionnaires battle-ready at all times. Clearly, the Roman "peace" extolled by Augustus was no better than the false peace decried by the prophet Jeremiah: "They have treated the wound of my people carelessly,/saying, 'Peace, peace,'/when there is no peace" (Jeremiah 6:14).

For despite the declarations of Augustus to the contrary, in first-century Israel there was no real peace, and life for the Jewish subjects of the Roman Empire was hard and often dangerous. What the *Pax romana* must really have been like for those forced to live under it is expressed in an anti-Roman diatribe recounted by the historian Tacitus (c. A.D. 55–c. 120):

> [We] have sought in vain to escape [the Romans'] oppression by obedience and submissiveness. [They are] the plunderers of the world . . . If the enemy is rich, they are rapacious, if poor, they lust for dominion. Not East, not West has satiated them . . . They rob, butcher, plunder, and call it "empire"; *and where they make a desolation, they call it "peace" [my emphasis].*

Indeed, Josephus recounts that in Israel the so-called *Pax romana* was, in reality, a time of numerous violent uprisings against Roman rule. One account by Josephus is worthy of particular note. He reports that at around the time Jesus was born, the Roman military crucified some two thousand people in the Galilean city of Sepphoris as punishment for rebelling against Roman rule *(Antiquities of the Jews* 17:295).

Similar to the phenomenon of "lynchings" in the modern era, public crucifixions were intended to strike terror in the hearts of those who were lorded over. The Roman historian Quintilian (c. A.D. 35–c. 100) attests: "Whenever we crucify the guilty, the most crowded roads are chosen, where the most people can see and be moved by this fear. For penalties relate not so much to retribution as to their exemplary effect."

Although terrible enough, the several hours Jesus hung on the cross were atypically short. Most victims of crucifixion took much longer to die. Some hung immobilized for days before breathing their last. Josephus tells of one instance in which a victim lingered alive on the cross for two weeks.

There is no telling how long the crucified victims at Sepphoris lingered before breathing their last. However, we can be sure that their screams and agonized moans would have been a lasting source of fear and trauma for all who witnessed them, even for those who only heard descriptions of the horror. Some sense of the effect that the horror at Sepphoris would have had upon the collective psyche of the people of Israel—including the young Jesus—can be seen in the response of African Americans to the lynching of fourteen-year-old Emmett Till in 1955. Till's torture and murder induced terror and revulsion in the black community. The grisly images and gruesome descriptions of Till's mutilated body and the naked fear they raised remain emblazoned to this day in the memory of all who had the misfortune to be exposed to them.

The horrific victimization of Till, and their powerlessness in preventing or addressing it, only deepened the sense of dread in the twenty million African Americans living under the specter of Jim Crow and institutional racism. It is not hard to imagine that the Romans' crucifixion of two thousand men, women, and children would have struck the same deep fear and dread in the two and a half million subjugated inhabitants of first-century Israel. Yet, as if the mass "lynchings" at Sepphoris were not traumatic enough, the trauma was further compounded by the Romans' practice of refusing to allow the crucified dead to be removed from their impalement until their flesh had all but rotted away, thus assailing the senses of every person for miles around not only with the sight of death, but with its overwhelming stench as well.

The slaughter at Sepphoris holds two primary meanings for our understanding of Jesus. First, it occurred just a few years before Jesus' birth. Second, it occurred only a half-day's walk from Nazareth, the tiny village Jesus called home. Because of their proximity, it is probable that some residents of Nazareth were employed on the several major building projects taking place at Sepphoris, so the horror would have been powerfully present for them, and it would have lingered in their collective memory and compounded their fear and insecurity. There is little doubt that these factors, and the monstrousness of the slaughter at Sepphoris that would have become even more monstrous in its retelling, impacted the political consciousness of Jesus, and sensitized him to the horror of colonial oppression.

Roman oppression touched virtually every facet of life in Israel. Richard

Horsley gives a sense of the pervasive effects of the Roman occupation upon the Jewish people in general, and on Galilee, the home province of Jesus, in particular:

> The increased Roman military presence in areas like Galilee also brought with it demands for both . . . exactions of goods, and . . . "service to the state" . . . When it needed them, moreover, the army would simply take bread or wine or animals. In addition to seizing the peasants' draft animals for food, the soldiers might expropriate them for transport or other work. And the Romans could simply draft gangs of workers from the populace when needed.

Unfortunately, the Roman military's policy of seizing whatever it wanted also extended to the women of Israel. Rape has long been a strategic tool used by colonial powers to terrorize and demoralize occupied peoples, and it was used no less against Israel. That this was a significant reality in Israel is evidenced by the attempts of certain opponents of Jesus to discredit him after his death by charging that he was the product of rape by a Roman soldier named Pantera. Those opponents called Jesus "Yeshua ben Pantera," Hebrew for "Jesus, son of Pantera." What it is meaningful for our purposes is not the charge itself, but the fact that it was lodged, for such a charge would have been summarily dismissed as too far-fetched even to be considered unless the assault of Israelite women by Roman soldiers was a well-known phenomenon.

So hated were the Romans for their abuses and outrages that the Egyptian grave of the Roman general Pompey was desecrated more than a century and a half after his death by Jewish rebels still enraged at his invasion of Israel. Some sense of the terrible psycho-emotional toll taken on victims of despotic colonialism is provided by the Afro-Caribbean psychiatrist Frantz Fanon.

Fanon was in the employ of the French colonialist regime during its bloody war against Algerian freedom fighters in the 1950s. In his book *The Wretched of the Earth*, Fanon recounts that while treating imprisoned Algerian insurgents and villagers who had been brought to him for care, often after prolonged torture, he noticed patterns in their mental breakdowns. Eventually Fanon identified in his Algerian patients several primary "reactionary psychoses" to oppression, mental disorders that found expression in physical symptoms. These disorders include severe disruptions of women's menstruation cycles, hysterical lameness, and repeated masochistic episodes. He observed that these cases became more numerous as French repression intensified. After treating numerous traumatized subjects, Fanon came to the conclusion that the single most significant cause of these crippling reactionary psychoses was the brutal excesses of colonial domination.

The Significance of the Roman Occupation of Israel for the Ministry of Jesus

The pervasive presence of the Roman colonial domination of Israel is reflected in the Gospels. Luke begins his account of Jesus' birth by citing an edict issued by the emperor Augustus that all Israelites must return to their home villages to register in a census (Luke 2:1), apparently for reasons of taxation. In the midst of the spiritual loftiness of the Beatitudes, Jesus refers to Roman courts and prisons (Matthew 5:25), as well as to innocent passersby arbitrarily forced to do the bidding of Roman soldiers (Matthew 5:41; also see pages 171–72 in this book). Mark's account of soldiers compelling Simon of Cyrene to carry Jesus' cross to Calvary (Mark 15:21) is an example of this latter practice.

Moreover, the presence of the Roman military is treated as a commonplace in Jesus' healing of the centurion's servant in Matthew 8:5–13. Even a destructive demon that had occupied the *chora*, or country, is referred to in tongue-in-cheek fashion as "Legion," the official Roman term of reference for a military battalion, in Mark 5:9. In fact, so pervasive was the Roman military presence in first-century Israel that Mark's Gospel matter-of-factly uses no less than eight Latin military and economic terms, clearly expecting its readers to be familiar with them.

The contempt with which the Romans treated the people of Israel is most evident in the Gospels' recounting of the cruelty and contempt to which Jesus was subjected after his arrest. Jesus was stripped naked, humiliated, and flogged. The Fourth Gospel adds that he was beaten repeatedly by his Roman captors (John 19:3). The crucifixion account in the Gospel of Mark in particular portrays Rome's contempt and brutality toward its colonial subjects in all its horror:

> And they clothed him in a purple cloak; and after twisting some thorns into a crown, they put it on him. And they began saluting him, "Hail, King of the Jews!" They struck his head with a reed, spat upon him, and knelt down in homage to him. After mocking him, they stripped him of the purple cloak and put his own clothes on him. Then they led him out to crucify him. (Mark 15:17–20)

Finally, it is a measure of the pervasiveness of the harsh Roman colonial presence in Israel that all of the reactionary psychoses associated with colonial domination that Fanon identified also appear in the relatively few pages of the four New Testament Gospels. For example, the woman with the twelve-year issue of blood (Mark 5:25–35), the multiple accounts of lame and paralyzed persons (John 5:1–9; Mark 2:1–12), and the self-destructive Gerasene man (Mark 5:1–20) are all consistent with Fanon's description of reactionary psychoses in oppressed peoples. That these conditions appear in the New Testament without any indication that they are unique or isolated incidents is an indication of the depth of the trauma suffered by the people of Israel.

Therefore, more than any other factor, it was the Roman colonial occupation of Israel that created the setting for the formative years of Jesus. The suffering that the Romans visited on the Jewish people was so pervasive and so brutal that its influence on the political consciousness and social witness of Jesus was inescapable. For this reason it must not be forgotten that even while he is worshiped as the Son of God, until his last earthly breath Jesus was also an oppressed Roman colonial subject with all that meant.

HEROD THE PUPPET RULER

The legacy of Herod's ruthlessness was another important factor in the political setting of Jesus' ministry. As we noted in the last chapter, the cruel and tyrannical reign of Herod, Rome's puppet "King of the Jews," greatly compounded the suffering of the people of Jesus. Suffice it to say that in many ways Herod's murderous reign outdid the brutality of Rome, and all but choked the economic life out of Israel.

After his death in 4 B.C., Herod's legacy of terror and exploitation in the name of Rome continued under three of his sons, Archelaus, Antipas, and Philip, among whom his kingdom was divided. Of these three, the real heir to their father's legacy of decadence and cruelty was Antipas, whom Rome appointed ruler over Galilee, the home province of Jesus. It was Herod Antipas who was responsible for the beheading of John the Baptist (Mark 6:14–29) and who sought the death of Jesus as well (Luke 13:31; 23:6–12). The treachery and despotism of the Herodians loomed large in the world of Jesus and touched everyone around him for the entire span of his life.

THE PRIESTS

Another important factor in the political setting of Jesus was the aristocratic hereditary priestly class that was centered at the Temple at Jerusalem. This class consisted of the high priest and numerous elite priests, whose collective job it was to oversee the administration of the Jerusalem Temple, the central institution of Israel. Included in the priestly class were nonpriests such as the "elders" (gerousia), the heads of the richest families in Jerusalem whose wealth earned them full membership in the Sanhedrin, the ruling council of the Temple. Attached to the priestly aristocracy were Sadducees and Pharisees, the latter of whom were mostly nonpriestly "retainers" who served the priestly class.

The term "Sadducee" probably comes from a Greek rendering of the Hebrew word *Zadokim*, which signifies the descendants of the high priest Zadok. According to 1 Chronicles 6:3–8, Zadok was a descendant of Eleazar, who was Aaron's son and Moses' nephew. Until the Hasmoneans replaced the Zadokites in 143 B.C., only descendants of the Zadokite family were allowed to hold the office of high priest. In A.D. 34 Herod the Great removed the last Hasmonean high priest and returned the office to the Zadokites, but few ever held it again.

The Sadducees probably were not a religious sect or a political party as such, but rather were distinguished by their wealth and political and social influence. Though their prominence, like their name, seems to have come from their ties to the *Zadokim*, not all Sadducees were priests. However, virtually all were social and political conservatives who supported the status quo and maintained a mutually enriching relationship with their Roman overlords. In addition to being politically conservative, they were elitist in their belief that for religious piety to be legitimate it had to be under priestly control—which, of course, served to reinforce the priests' power.

Because of their social standing and financial wealth, the Sadducees apparently wielded significant influence over the hereditary priests. In fact, there seems to have been at least one Sadduceean high priest. The Sadducees' lack of belief in resurrection (although it was a widely held belief at the time), coupled with their concern for wealth, gives us the clear impression that their approach to religion was more materialistic than that of most first-century Jews.

The picture of the Pharisees drawn by the Gospels and other ancient sources is of a devout group of men whose main concern, in addition to scrupulously obeying scriptural laws and the nonscriptural "traditions of the fathers," was observing ritual purity, especially with regard to foods, tithing, and keeping the Sabbath. Generally then they had a much broader sense of religious piety than the Sadducees in that they advocated that the high ritual purity that previously had been associated only with the Temple should be extended to all aspects of daily life by regular ritual washings. Their approach to the Sabbath was not broader, however, but much narrower, even elitist. Their vehement insistence that all work cease on the

Sabbath, no matter how small or how necessary for health and well-being the work might be, posed few problems for the well heeled. But for peasants who had daily chores that could not go undone or for day laborers who did not eat if they did not work, in effect the Pharisees' Sabbath strictures valued ritual over actual human need.

The Pharisees' view that ritual purity should be practiced by everyone challenged the religious control of the Temple priesthood, but that was not the intent; the Pharisees were not political radicals. In fact, the Pharisees had little political power of their own. Despite their theological differences, politically the Pharisees were by Jesus' day firmly aligned with the hereditary priestly aristocracy.

Hereditary priests were a privileged aristocracy in the sense that as a class they claimed, and were accorded, favored social status based upon genealogy alone. Priests were considerably better off than all but a handful of Jews in Israel. Most priests resided in the Upper City of Jerusalem, its most well-to-do precinct. The Gospels depict the home of the high priest as large and luxurious, with a sizable courtyard, a large gatehouse, and a meeting room large enough to accommodate a gathering of the Sanhedrin's seventy-one members, including their servants and the Temple police (see John 18:12–18, for instance). Some sense of the wealth of the aristocratic priests is provided by Josephus, who also was of a priestly family. Josephus writes matter-of-factly of the lands his family owned outside Jerusalem, and reports priests amassing "a large amount of property from the tithes which they accepted as their due" (*The Life of Flavius Josephus*, 63).

As we saw in chapter 1, the fortunes of the highest echelons of the priests had been tied to the fortunes of the various political oppressors of their people since the institution of the high priesthood after the repatriation of the Jewish exiles by the Persians in 539 B.C. The priests' relationship with their Roman overlords in Jesus' day was no different; they maintained an accommodationist stance toward Rome to protect their own economic status. Their daily sacrifices to Caesar gave their allegiance a sort of religious imprimatur, despite Rome's harsh treatment of the priests' own people, and this endeared the priests to no one but the Romans. In return for the priests' cooperation, the Romans protected the Jerusalem

Temple, the primary source of the priests' wealth (in the form of tithes and offerings), and brutally disposed of anyone the priests identified as threatening their status and power. Jesus fell into this category.

The rift between the priests and the masses of the Jewish people was heightened by Rome's continuation of Herod's policy of undisguised control of the high priesthood. From his murder of the last Hasmonean-sponsored high priest in 34 B.C. onward, Herod appointed priests who offered not even the pretense of a legitimate claim to the position. Their primary qualification apparently was their willingness to do the bidding of Herod and Rome. Between 35 B.C. and his death in 4 B.C., Herod himself appointed seven high priests. One of them, Joseph ben Ellem, served only one day.

The long-standing dissatisfaction of the masses with the high priesthood was heightened by Herod's manipulations. In fact, the high priesthood was held in such contempt that when Herod died, rioters, emboldened by the news, demanded removal of the high priest Joazar, Herod's last appointee. The high priests' dependence upon Roman patronage to maintain their privileged status was made embarrassingly clear as Herod's successors continued his practice of appointing and deposing high priests. Apparently high priests were changed with such great frequency that John the Evangelist writes, with a tinge of sarcasm, as if the position was changed annually, "Caiaphas, who was high priest that year" (John 11:49; see also 18:13).

In addition, priests were widely perceived as avaricious and predatory. Dramatic accounts of the priests' greed and extravagance are found in the rabbinic writings. The aristocratic priests were said to entertain often, hiring expensive cooks for the festivities and drinking choice wine from crystal glasses. And there are accounts of more shameless extravagance. A female member of a high priest's family was said to have had the entire distance from her house to the Jerusalem Temple carpeted so she could comfortably walk there barefoot on the Day of Atonement, as was the custom. The widow of one priest is said to have cursed the scribes who negotiated her widow's allowance because she was granted only four hundred denarii a day for luxury items (a single denarius was roughly equal to one day's pay for the rank and file). There are numerous other accounts, of gold thread being used to tie the bundles at the Feast of Tabernacles, of dowries of a million gold denarii, and so on. Some of the accounts may be exaggerated, but the sheer number of them indicates that there was a basis in fact for the perception of priestly excess.

More serious than their reported greed was the priests' worsening of their people's political plight by using their religious legitimacy to defuse opposition to Roman repression. First-century Jews rallied against issues of particular concern on any number of occasions. For example, in A.D. 39 they protested the erection of ensigns in Jerusalem bearing the emperor's image. Yet there is never a mention of involvement of the high priest or any member of the priestly aristocracy in these protests, much less of their having led them. Indeed, as Richard Horsley observes, "the Jewish priestly aristocracy maintained a consistently cooperative relationship with the Roman [provincial] governments." According to New Testament scholar Sean Freyne, the average Jew in Israel "found himself in the rather strange position that those very people to whom he felt bound by ties of national and religious loyalty, the priestly aristocracy, were in fact his social oppressors."

The following lament preserved from the first century gives some sense of the priestly aristocracy's maltreatment of the people they were pledged to serve: "Woe unto me because of the house of Boethus . . . Hanin . . . Qathros . . . Ismail ben Phiabi . . . For they are High Priests and their sons are treasurers and their sons-in-law are Temple overseers and their servants beat the people with sticks."

Because of the priests' religious authority and the allegiance that authority elicited from their fellow Jews, it was the priests' role as agents of Roman interests that presented the major political problem for the people of Jesus. The Jews of Israel were caught between the proverbial rock of the priests' complicity with Roman domination and the hard place of their fear of incurring divine wrath by turning against the priesthood of their own faith.

The Significance of the Priests' Excesses for the Ministry of Jesus

That is why the Gospels portray the priests as the primary opponents of Jesus: because the priests' political quietism and their accommodation of Roman policies made them complicit in the Jews' subjugation. The crowning indignity was the priests' economic exploitation of their fellow Jews. Without question Jesus shared his people's sense of outrage.

The priests' hated role as agents of Rome is highlighted in John's Gospel, in which the high priest and chief priests inadvertently admit their betrayal of their people when they protest to Pilate, "We have no king but Caesar" (John 19:15 [RSV]). Because the sole focus of the priests' allegiance was supposed to be *malkuth shamayim*—recognition of no sovereign but God alone, their profession of loyalty to Caesar in both word and deed constituted the ultimate betrayal of their trust as priests of the God of Israel. But more than that, John's unflinching portrayal demonstrates the great degree to which the priestly class collectively had come to be perceived as an agent of the Roman Empire. In other words, opposition to the priests was tantamount to opposition to Rome. In this sense, Jesus' stance toward the priestly class was unquestionably political in nature.

2. ECONOMIC FACTORS

POVERTY

A. N. Sherwin-White observes that the world reflected in the Gospels "presents two classes, the very rich and the very poor." The "very rich" in Israel were a tiny upper class, no more than 5 percent of the population. It was comprised of Roman bureaucrats, aristocratic priests, a handful of rich landowners, and successful tax collectors. The rest of the people of Israel were poor, many to the point of destitution. The rabbinic writings tell of bands of homeless poor roaming the countryside, so desperate that when the poor tithe was distributed they sometimes stampeded like cattle. Matthew's Gospel tells of standing pools of unemployed village workers so desperate for a day's wage that they accepted work without even asking how much they would be paid (Matthew 20:1–16; note vv. 3–7). Poverty was so widespread that the Gospel of Luke portrays Mary as giving thanks to God that among the acts of salvation set in motion by the

Messiah she carried in her womb would be filling the hungry "with good things" (Luke 1:53). The sad observation by a second-century rabbi that "the daughters of Israel are comely, but poverty makes them repulsive" could easily have been written with the Israel of Jesus' day in mind.

Although in first-century Israel there was profound poverty and destitution, most of the poor were working poor. The great majority were peasants engaged in subsistence farming, which means that after they paid Roman taxes, there was barely enough for survival, and certainly no surplus for long-term planning, or even enough to meet emergencies. As biblical scholar John Dominic Crossan observes, "Peasants . . . were structured inferiors."

Most peasant farmers had land holdings of less than 6 acres, with, on average, only 1.5 acres available for cultivation, hardly enough to support a family. That is, if they were fortunate enough to have saved their farms from outright seizure by the Romans, or from dispossession for tax default, or from the machinations of the Herodians and their cronies who, it is estimated, owned one-half to two-thirds of the land in Galilee. To make ends meet, many farmers either had to hire themselves out for wages to supplement their meager crops, or go into debt, which was usually a worse alternative. Tenant farmers and sharecroppers often fared even worse, ending up in prison for defaulting on their debts or enslaved by their creditors.

The Significance of Poverty in Israel for the Ministry of Jesus

The presence of poverty in Israel pervades the Gospels and is reflected in narratives as diverse as Judas' complaint that the cost of the expensive perfume used to anoint Jesus' feet should have been "given to the poor" (John 12:4–5) and Luke's account of "a poor man named Lazarus, covered with sores, who longed to satisfy his hunger with what fell from the rich man's table" (Luke 16:19–31).

So deep and so debilitating was the effect of impoverishment on the psycho-emotional health of his people that Jesus found it necessary to explicitly affirm their worth with the validation "Blessed are you who are poor" (Luke 6:20). And when his disciples asked him how and what to pray for, he told them to keep the poverty and hunger of the people of Israel in view by praying: "Give us this day our daily bread" (Matthew 6:11). And to give the people hope in the face of their profound poverty, Jesus himself modeled the largesse that God's kingdom of justice promised on the occasions when he fed the thousands who had gathered to hear him share his vision of God's kingdom.

TAXATION

A major cause of poverty in first-century Israel was the Roman tax structure. That taxation was a significant issue in Israel is indicated by the Pharisees' use of it in their confrontation with Jesus in Matthew 22:17: "Is it lawful to pay taxes to Caesar or not?" (RSV). The Jewish scholar Salo Baron notes that

> even according to Caesar's most friendly decree, the Romans levied a tax as high as one-fourth of the crop . . . every other year . . . Especially after [Israel's] direct incorporation into the empire in 6 A.D. the multiple payments in kind and in personal services for the maintenance of Roman officials and soldiers, as well as such indirect payments as the numerous tolls and customs duties, must have made the life of a Palestinian farmer extremely arduous.

Typically, Roman provincial governors saw the territories to which they were assigned as cash cows to be milked in order to amass the greatest possible fortunes in the shortest possible time. So widespread was this practice that the Romans themselves joked about it. For example, it was punned about one provincial governor, Ventidius, that he "entered rich Syria poor and left poor Syria rich." During Jesus' lifetime, Israel fared no better under its imperial governors, especially Valerius Gratus (governed A.D. 15–26) and Pontius Pilate (governed A.D. 26–36), both of whom extracted every bit of tribute from the people of Israel that they could.

The impoverishing effect of secular taxation was compounded by the large amounts of religious taxation that the Jewish people rendered to the Jerusalem priestly hierarchy. Prior to the return from the Babylonian exile, no tithes or offerings were required of Jews for the support of the priests. Priests received small portions of the sacrifices offered by pilgrims, but that was all. But after the exile, the offerings from which the priests derived their income increased until they made up some twelve different classes of tithes and offerings. Although the peasantry did not always fulfill these obligations, any significant effort to do so could only have deepened their poverty. It has been estimated that the combination of secular and religious taxes consumed up to 40 percent of the peasants' subsistence. The scholar E. P. Sanders observes that "every year farmers had officials of their religion knocking on the door and asking for tithes." Because there were far too many priests to officiate simultaneously at Temple services (Josephus places the number at twenty thousand), the forty-eight weeks of the Jewish calendar were divided among the priestly families and organized into twenty-four "courses." Each priest officiated at the Temple only during his assigned course, that is, just two weeks per year. Still, each was the recipient of more wealth than the average Israelite could ever dream of.

Debt

Another factor contributing to the poverty in Israel was widespread indebtedness. Because with subsistence farming there is no surplus left after basic consumption, large numbers of peasants had to borrow funds from the wealthy in order to pay Roman taxes. Similar to the experiences of sharecroppers in America's southland, many farmers had no choice but to repeat this pattern of borrowing every year until their burden of debt became so great that they were no longer able to meet the payments and were forced into default.

The terrible consequences of debt default are reflected in Matthew 18:25–35, which describes two ways in which the lender could collect on a defaulted debt. The first was for the debtor himself to be sold into slavery. Some farmers with smaller defaults discharged them by making the painful choice of selling their eldest children (who commanded higher prices) into slavery so they themselves could stay to support the remaining family. Others committed suicide to avoid enslavement and the torture that often accompanied it. The practice of torturing enslaved debtors is reflected in Matthew 18:21–34, which, when correctly translated, matter-of-factly mentions that a lender seized his indebted worker and "delivered him to the torturers [*basanistais*] till he should pay all his debt."

In cases of extraordinary default, the lender could enslave the debtor's wife and children, then seize members of the extended family and all their possessions, down to the most distant relations. If the sale of those already seized still did not satisfy the debt, the lender could even enslave the debtor's neighbors. In at least one case a whole village was emptied in this way because everyone was either sold into slavery or escaped into the surrounding hills. Debt slavery was such a bitter issue in Israel that one of the first acts of the rebels in the Jewish War was to seize and burn the records of debts that were stored in the Temple.

The Significance of Taxes and Debt for the Ministry of Jesus

A significant indicator of the degree to which the effects of taxation and indebtedness pervaded the lives of the people of Israel is present in the words of Jesus himself. In Matthew's Gospel, Jesus clearly mentions debt default as if it were a reality with which everyone was familiar: he says of a slave who owes a large sum to a king, "as he could not pay, his lord ordered him to be sold, together with his wife and children and all his possessions" (Matthew 18:23–35). When asked by the disciples how to pray and what they should pray for, Jesus told them to ask, "[F]orgive us our debts" (Matthew 6:12). The Greek word signifying "debts" in Jesus' prayer is *opheleimata*, which does not occur often in the New Testament, but when it does appear in any of its forms, it refers to debt or other legal obligations, not "trespasses," as the King James Version translates it.

Furthermore, *aphiemi*, from which "forgive" is translated, also has "release" as a primary meaning, which would mean that Jesus' instruction to his disciples is that their prayer should be "release us [from] our debts."

In short, Jesus was deeply concerned about the spiral of financial indebtedness and dispossession that devastated so many in Israel. His concern to banish it from their lives is enshrined in his model prayer.

3. SOCIAL FACTORS

CRIME

The economic factors of pervasive poverty, hunger, dislocation, and dispossession that resulted from indebtedness and debt default, along with the debilitating psycho-emotional factors of abiding fear, insecurity, social alienation, and seething resentment of their colonial occupiers, took their toll upon the morale of the people of Israel, and the crime rate skyrocketed. But more significant than the rise in petty crime in Israel during this period was the increase in banditry, a social phenomenon in which groups of landless poor robbed and often killed those they encountered on rural roads and in vulnerable outlying settlements.

Banditry is a classic symptom of political and economic breakdown. Typically it occurs in rural areas in which a large portion of the populace is economically exploited and dispossessed. This situation certainly pertained in first-century Israel. In fact, banditry in first-century Israel was so widespread that Roman law counted it as a natural disaster, along with storms, earthquakes, fires, sickness, and natural death, and it was recognized as one of the most common causes of death (with old age and disease). The effects of banditry in Israel were so destructive that Josephus observes that bandits "were over-running much of the countryside and inflicting injuries on the inhabitants as much as a war would have done" (*History of the Jewish War* 1:304). However, recent anthropological studies have shown that often these "bandits" were not just thieves driven by purely economic considerations, but were what scholars have called "social" bandits.

Social bandits were outlaws with at least a partial political agenda. In every historical setting in which they occur, social bandits have always been a symptom of great political upheaval. In Israel many were rene-gades, insurgents, and nationalist guerrillas who rebelled against their ex-ploitation at the hands of both the Roman provincial government and wealthy Jewish landowners, many of whom were priests. There were oc-casions on which they attacked Romans, but most often they targeted rich Jewish landowners and others perceived as being complicit in the exploita-tion of their people. Their primary goal was economic: to seize booty; and they did so, much and often. But they also had a political goal: to disrupt commerce and discredit the ruling class by throwing the social order into disarray.

The Significance of Crime for the Ministry of Jesus

Social banditry in Israel is clearly in evidence in the Gospels. Instead of using *kleptais*, the usual word for "thief," a number of passages use the term *lestais*, which can describe a robber, but also can mean "insurgent" or "in-surrectionist." *Lestais* does seem to describe a conventional thief or robber in the parable of the good Samaritan (Luke 10:25–37). Yet Mark's use of *lestais* in 15:27 to describe the two men who were crucified with Jesus is re-vealing, for death by crucifixion was reserved by Rome for insurrectionists and rebels. It is also revealing that Barabbas is called *lestais* (Mark 15:7–15). In fact, Luke 23:19 explicitly describes Barabbas as "a man who had been put in prison for an insurrection that had taken place in the city."

The popular support Barabbas received at Jesus' trial is what would be expected for a known Jewish nationalist and insurrectionist against Rome. However, in the case of Barabbas there is a question of the likelihood that the Roman authorities would have freed a known insurrectionist, whether in actuality there was a custom of releasing a prisoner on the Passover or not. Indeed, there is no record outside the New Testament that such a practice ever existed. Perhaps Pilate released Barabbas to defuse an impending riot. Whatever Pilate's reason for releasing him, Mark's Gospel calls Barabbas a *lestais* and Luke refers to his role in an anti-Roman insur-rection. That social banditry is alluded to in the relatively few pages of the Gospels indicates that it was a significant phenomenon in the Israel of Jesus' day.

Whether it was social banditry or economically driven thievery, there is no question that crime permeated the life of first-century Israel. Jesus' assumption that the robbery on the road in the Good Samaritan parable was an experience to which his hearers could relate without further explanation reflects the pervasiveness of crime in the lives of his people.

PRIESTLY ELITISM

City versus Country

The historian Ramsay MacMullen has noted that in antiquity relations between city folk and country folk "[were] not friendly. The two worlds regard[ed] each other as, on the one side, clumsy, brutish, ignorant, uncivilized; on the other side, as baffling, extortionate, arrogant."

This attitude was reflected in Greek classical literature, in which rural dwellers were regularly referred to simply as *choritai*, "country folk," a dismissal that is used even today in urban locales to relegate people to inferior social status. In antiquity, the notion of the superiority of the sophisticated city dweller over the country dweller was even projected into the divine sphere. One of the fables attributed to Aesop relates that the simple-minded among the gods *(euetheis)* live in the countryside, while the superior gods live in the city.

This urban/rural schism was no less a fact of life in the Israel of Jesus' day. City dwellers, particularly Jerusalemites—and especially the Temple priests—counted their urban location and proximity to the Temple environs as factors that entitled them to superior social status over the country folk. The Gospel of John in particular reflects the elitism of city dwellers. John 7:15 portrays the Jerusalem priests as assuming, with haughty condescension, that the peasant Jesus must be illiterate. John also portrays the priests as assuming, with equal condescension, that the "crowd" of pilgrims listening to Jesus was necessarily ignorant of the Law, so much so that they dismissed them—the sheep of their own flocks—as "accursed" (John 7:49).

For their part, the country folk avoided the cities, usually venturing there only when necessary, for matters of commerce or imperial obligation (such as a census) or, in the case of Jerusalem, to participate in the various pilgrimages. Cities, particularly Jerusalem, were simply places in which the country dweller felt out of place. In Jerusalem were the hated Roman garrison, the condescending priests, the imperial courts of judgment, the brutal public executions. Also in Jerusalem were the unattainable urban luxuries that not only did nothing to strengthen the peasants' sense of self, but must have heightened their sense of the injustice of the social order. In addition, many of the absentee landlords who exploited the peasants and tenant farmers were rich Jerusalem priests. The matter-of-fact testimony by Josephus of his family's extensive land holdings, and of the extensive holdings of other priestly families as well, is just one indication of the priests' role as absentee landlords. Thus, for good reason, many rural dwellers regarded cities as hostile and discomfiting environs.

The Significance of City versus Country for the Ministry of Jesus

The picture of the peasant who seldom ventures into the city is also the picture of Jesus that emerges from the New Testament. The Gospels never portray Jesus as entering any city other than Jerusalem, not even the nearby Galilean city of Tiberias, and when he does go to Jerusalem it is only on special religious occasions. Indeed, Mark 1:45 tells us that at times Jesus purposely avoided *all* towns and cities. Further, even a cursory look at the Gospels reveals that Jesus was deeply ensconced in rural village culture. The metaphors he uses in his parables are almost exclusively agrarian, and they reflect almost exclusively the realities of village life, such as the planting of crops (Mark 4:1–9, 30–32), dawn-to-dusk field work (Matthew 20:1–16), and huts with mud-and-palm-thatched roofs (Mark 2:4).

Thus, in general the social setting of Jesus' ministry was characterized by a pronounced social and cultural divide between, on the one hand, city dwellers, particularly the Jerusalem priests, and, on the other, the country dwellers, who were the immediate compatriots of Jesus. This must have heightened Jesus' sense of alienation from the urbane Jerusalem priests and compounded his sense of the marginalization and exploitation of his people.

THE MARGINALIZATION OF GALILEANS

The country folk of Israel had ample reason to distrust and resent city folk, and especially the priestly aristocracy, whom many perceived as traitors. But the Galileans had even more reason for resentment.

It must be remembered that Jesus was not only an Israelite, he was also a Galilean who spent his life in the rural northern province of Galilee. Unlike Judea to the south, which proudly claimed Jerusalem as its social and economic center, Galilee was an agrarian province, with the exception of the hellenized cities of Sepphoris and Tiberias and a few lesser cities and large towns. All country folk experienced derision and condescension from urbanites, but Galileans were even more marginalized and more stigmatized.

First, Galileans had a distinctively accented pronunciation of Hebrew that caused them to slur their words in what was thought to be a "country" way. This accent sometimes resulted in mispronunciations that made Galileans objects of ridicule. For instance, it is recounted that a Galilean woman, intending to extend hospitality, meant to say, "Come, I will give you milk." But because of her Galilean accent her remark was heard as "Companion, butter devour you."

Further, the rabbinic writings report that because of their accents, Galileans were actually barred from leading community prayers outside of Galilee. The expression *Galili shota*—"Galilean fool!"—was common. It is reported that it was even hurled at the prominent Galilean rabbi Yose when, due to the imprecision of his Galilean syntax, he violated Jewish social conventions by inadvertently using too many words to inquire directions of a female stranger.

The Significance of the Marginalization of Galileans for the Ministry of Jesus

The distinctive and marginalizing Galilean pronunciation is reflected in the New Testament. For instance, Peter is identified as a confederate of Jesus by his Galilean *lalia* (accent) alone in Matthew 26:73. Another example is the name Lazarus, which occurs in the Gospels of Luke (16:19–31) and John (11:1–12:17). "Lazarus" is a slurred Galilean contraction of the proper name Eleazar. Inscriptional evidence reveals that Galilean pronunciation sometimes went so far as to shorten Eleazar to "Lazar," even "Laz."

Further, because Galilee was the most distant province from Jerusalem and, therefore, farthest from Temple control, Galileans were thought to be less diligent in their rendering of tithes and offerings to the priests. This perception caused much consternation among the priests, who responded quite bitterly. The Talmud reports the eminent rabbi Yochannon ben Zakkai as exclaiming, "Galilee, Galilee, you hate the Torah!"

AMMI HA-ARETZ ("PEOPLE OF THE LAND")

The priests responded to this seeming lack of diligence by branding the Galileans *ammi ha-aretz* (plural of, *am ha-aretz*). This pejorative Hebrew designation originally signified no more than its literal meaning of "people of the land," that is, those who derived their livelihoods from agricultural pursuits. The term is used to refer to the entire nation of Israel in Ezekiel 46:3 and 2 Kings 15:5. However, by the end of the Exile in 539 B.C., *am ha-aretz* had begun to have a distinctly negative connotation, as in Nehemiah 10:30, in which the returned exiles declared about those who had remained behind and apparently intermarried with Gentiles, "We will not give our daughters to the am-ha-aretz (*people of the land*) or take their daughters for our sons.".

By the first century the term had become fully negative, designating all Jews who did not abide by the prescriptions of the Law, especially statutes

regarding tithes and offerings. This meaning of the term is reflected by the
rhetorical question in the rabbinic writings, "Who is an *am ha-aretz*? . . . The
Sages said, 'Anyone who does not tithe his property properly.' "

The priests' suspicion of Galileans was not completely without cause.
In actuality, the Galileans were not always fully scrupulous in following
the tithing stipulations of the Law. But probably the main reason Galileans
sometimes overlooked the tithing prescriptions was that their often-
impoverished existence forced them to do so, not that they lacked respect
for the conventions of their faith. Given the economic realities that faced
them, many Galilean men (only males were subject to tithing requirements) must have had to choose between rendering tithes and feeding
their families. In the face of such a choice, nonobservance was the only viable option. But because tithes and offerings were the priests' chief source
of income, the inability or refusal of the Galileans to render the appropriate tithes significantly affected the priests' livelihoods, in that Galilee was
the richest agricultural region in Israel and tithes came primarily from
agriculture. Predictably, this caused the priests considerable dismay, which
eventually flared into outright hostility. Josephus informs us that by the
mid-first century the aristocratic priests had become so incensed at what
they perceived as the poor observance of tithing that they began sending
their servants directly to the threshing floors to collect the tithes *by force!*
(*Antiquities of the Jews* 20:181).

For these reasons, the term *am ha-aretz* came to be deeply derisive in
meaning; it implied the lowest character. To be called *am ha-aretz* was worse
than being called a thief, because a thief only cheated other people. But by
not properly rendering tithes, the *am ha-aretz* was believed to be stealing *from
God*: "Will anyone rob God? Yet you are robbing me! But you say, 'How are
we robbing you?' In your tithes and offerings! You are cursed with a curse,
for you are robbing me" (Malachi 3:8–9).

That is why the priests did not consider it possible for an *am ha-aretz* to
have good character or to be of sound intelligence. At times the priests
even seemed to devalue their very humanity with such homiletical hyperbole as "A man . . . should not marry the daughter of an *am ha-aretz*, be-

cause they are detestable and their wives vermin, and of their daughters it is said, 'Cursed be he who lies with any kind of beast.' " In this sense, *am ha-aretz* might best be understood as the Hebrew equivalent of "nigger."

The Significance of "People of the Land" for the Ministry of Jesus

There can be no question that Jesus was deeply troubled by the disrespect and even derision heaped upon the "people of the land." In several instances in the Gospels, he specifically addresses the spiritual and psychoemotional toll that the elitism and arrogance of the priests and city dwellers imposed upon his peasant compatriots, especially the beleaguered Galileans. With such affirming declarations as "Blessed are you who are poor, for yours is the kingdom of God" (Luke 6:20) and "You are already clean because of the word that I have spoken to you" (John 15:3), Jesus validated their worth and counterbalanced the priests' negative judgments. He tenderly told his rural compatriots to love themselves for who and what they were, rather than deny the distinctiveness of their class and culture in order to fit elitist conceptions: "You are the salt of the earth; but if salt has lost its taste, how can its saltiness be restored? It is no longer good for anything, but is thrown out and trampled under foot" (Matthew 5:13).

And the Gospels tell us that on several occasions Jesus gave the ultimate vindication to the peasants' struggles and suffering by offering words of assurance that left no uncertainty: "[T]he last shall be the first; and the first shall be the last" (Matthew 20:16; see also Matthew 19:30 and Mark 10:31).

THREE

How Jesus the Revolutionary Became Meek and Mild

A S WE HAVE SEEN, in his own time Jesus was a strongly political figure who had a deep commitment to the economic, political, and social well-being of his people. Yet in our time he has become meek, mild, and decidedly nonpolitical. How exactly did this remarkable transformation take place?

THE DILEMMA OF THE CROSS

When the apostle Paul wrote, in approximately A.D. 50, about the "stumbling block" of the cross (1 Corinthians 1:23), he was using the term literally, for the crucifixion of Jesus really was an obstacle to full faith in him for many in the first generations of Christians. The embarrassment of Jesus' execution as a criminal by the Romans, coupled with what appeared to be his powerlessness to resist Roman might, was difficult for many early followers to reconcile with their conception of him as the exalted savior of the world. Like the Roman soldiers in Luke's Gospel (23:36–37), many must have asked, If Jesus really was the savior of Israel, why couldn't he save himself? The answers provided by the Gospels and the letters of Paul were at least a generation away, so this question presented a profound challenge to the faith of the early believers.

Some of those early followers resolved their struggle by concluding that Jesus was not a being of flesh and blood at all. They came to believe that the Jesus upon whom their faith was built was a spirit only. They may have based this idea on misunderstandings of certain of Jesus' sayings, interpreting them to mean that he was a fully otherworldly figure, as with his assertion in John 16:28 that he "came from the Father," for instance. As to his bodily form, they argued that because Jesus was a spirit, his body was simply an illusion that *seemed* to have materiality, shape, and form. And, they continued, if Jesus only *seemed* to have had a material body, then he could not have been crucified—because there would have been no body to crucify! Instead, they reasoned that Jesus simply used his divine power to fool his executioners into believing that he had been crucified by making it *seem* so. This denial of the flesh-and-blood materiality of Jesus—and, by extension, denial of his bodily crucifixion—came to be called docetism (DOE-se-tism from the Greek word *dokein*, "to seem"), or the docetic heresy by the "orthodox" factions of the early Church.

Although this "docetic" denial of the materiality of Jesus gave comfort to those believers whose faith was challenged by the circumstances of his crucifixion, docetism itself held an implication that was deeply problematic: if the crucifixion of Jesus was only an illusion, then, by the same token, the salvation wrought by Jesus' cross must also be an illusion. Docetism denied what the apostle Paul articulated as the single most important tenet of his Christian belief: "I decided to know nothing . . . except Jesus Christ, and him crucified" (1 Corinthians 2:2). Also, it directly contradicted the unequivocal claim of John 1:14 that Jesus—called the "Logos," or the "Word," in this verse—"became flesh and lived among us." It is no wonder that docetism was vigorously rejected as heresy by Church authorities. The sharpness of the Church's rejection is reflected in the

Johannine letters: "By this you know the Spirit of God: every spirit that confesses that Jesus Christ has come in the flesh is from God" (1 John 4:2) and "Many deceivers have gone out into the world, those who do not confess that Jesus Christ has come in the flesh; any such person is the deceiver and the antichrist!" (2 John 7).

When the Letters of Paul and the four New Testament Gospels began to circulate in the early Church, those writings helped to ease the embarrassment and confusion caused by Jesus' execution. Jesus' prophecies of his own death in such passages as "I lay down my life for the sheep" (John 10:15), his prediction that he "must be killed and after three days rise again" (Mark 8:31), and Paul's teaching that "being found in human form, he humbled himself/and became obedient to the point of death—/even death on a cross" (Philippians 2:8) explained that Jesus' death was his own choice.

Since then, apparently few in Christendom have felt the need to explicitly deny the flesh-and-blood materiality of Jesus. Yet today Christianity is faced with a development that in its distorted presentation of Jesus' life and ministry rivals the grandest denials of the docetic heresy of old. It is a notion that, sadly, is unwittingly embraced by millions of Christians. In various ways it is articulated every Sunday, and to varying degrees it holds sway over every Christian denomination. It is not the heresy of denying the flesh-and-blood existence of Jesus in this world. *It is the heresy of refusing to acknowledge the importance of the political circumstances of Jesus' earthly life and their influence on his person and his ministry.*

THE NEW TESTAMENT clearly portrays Jesus, his family, and, with few exceptions, everyone he encountered throughout his life as impoverished and oppressed, exploited by the religious establishment, brutalized by their Roman colonizers. That this was his setting in life is undeniable. Yet from the picture of Jesus painted by the traditional, mainstream Church, we are supposed to believe that he was little if at all touched by the realities around him; that the direction of his message and ministry was not influenced by the deplorable conditions in which his people lived. Instead, we are told that his was only a narrowly spiritual, otherworldly message that, with few exceptions, was exclusively focused on citizenship in heaven. Moreover, we are to believe that Jesus had no interest in the economic and political issues of his day. In other words, this belief holds that although Jesus might have had empathy for the suffering of his people, he just did not want to get involved.

However, the belief that Jesus—or anyone else, for that matter, and particularly a person whose life was dedicated to the welfare of his people—could live for three decades in a social, economic, and political environment yet be untouched by and unconcerned with the realities of that environment is a fantastic assumption. It means that Jesus only *seemed* to be subject to or even to have noticed the political and economic realities that confronted him at every turn. In other words, we are to believe that Jesus only *seemed* to live in this world, that he only *seemed* to dwell in human society. In the final analysis, this belief, which I call "political docetism," is simply another, more modern form of the blasphemous docetic denial of Jesus as a man of flesh and blood living in the world.

POLITICAL DOCETISM: DENYING THE SIGNIFICANCE OF THE POLITICAL SETTING OF JESUS' LIFE

The mainstream Church today is, sadly, the foremost purveyor of political docetism. The political docetism of the Church takes several forms. The most widely held form asserts that Jesus was a spiritual leader with absolutely no interest in social and political issues, that his concern was not to challenge the harsh institutional immorality of the social order in which he was born, but only to change the morality of *individuals*. For this reason, this view argues, the realities of the social setting of Jesus hold no relevance for our understanding of him. According to this logic, if Jesus is concerned with change at all, it is only in the sense of seeking to change the behavior of *individuals*, not the social order or the body politic. In the final analysis, this view maintains that Jesus was executed not for political reasons but because his criticism of the *personal* behavior of members of the Jewish religious hierarchy led them to pressure Pontius Pilate into executing him—either in retribution for Jesus' public embarrassment of them, or for the blasphemy of declaring that it was he, not they, who would sit at the right hand of God.

Another example of political docetism is similar to the one described above, but different in the sense that it does concede that Jesus might have been concerned with the evils of the world. However, it holds that he identified those evils not with oppressive social and political structures but, again, simply with the personal behavior of individuals. Curiously, this view would have us believe that even Jesus' most stinging pronouncements against the social, economic, and political conditions of his day, including hunger, debt, and poverty—even those instances in the Sermon on the Mount in which he addresses such overtly civil and political measures as imprisonment and taxation at Roman hands—should be understood to be directed toward *individual* behavior. Disregarding all biblical pronouncements and historical facts to the contrary, this view concludes that if Jesus was crucified for political reasons, it was simply because his purely *non*political motives were misunderstood. Yet this view is undercut by one unassailable fact: that the charge for which he was executed was seeking to replace Caesar's sovereignty over Israel with the *malkuth shamayim,* the kingdom, or sovereignty, of God. This is evidenced by the inscription that was nailed to his cross: "Jesus of Nazareth, king of the Jews." By any measure, this goal constituted sedition, for which the only punishment was crucifixion. That is to say, Jesus was put to death by the Roman state for advocating—if not actually waging—social disruption and political revolution.

There is another factor that has fed into Christians' political docetism, namely a misunderstanding of the New Testament description of Jesus as the "Lamb of God." According to the Gospel of John, the title was first bestowed upon Jesus by John the Baptist. The Gospel tells us that when the Baptist saw Jesus approaching in the distance he exclaimed, "Here is the Lamb of God who takes away the sin of the world!" (John 1:29). Many have believed that this term compares the demeanor of Jesus to the gentleness and meekness of lambs going to slaughter. Yet given John's uncompromising preaching about the coming wrath of God, it seems more likely that he expected the Lamb of God to be a radical figure, perhaps one more in line with the triumphant Lamb in the Book of Revelation (17:14). Moreover, it just does not seem consistent that the fiery John the Baptist who so boldly challenged the prevailing political order that it beheaded him to still his tongue would describe someone he considered greater than himself as meek and timid. It simply is implausible that John would defer to Jesus and ask others to do the same if he considered Jesus that much less politically assertive than himself. Considering that the Gospel of John and the Book of Revelation both originated in the community founded by John the Gospel writer, then "tak[ing] away the sin of the world" most likely had a militant connotation, as with the conquering Lamb in the Book of Revelation: "[T]hey will make war on the Lamb and the Lamb will conquer them" (Revelation 17:14).

When all is considered, it is clear that the term "Lamb of God" does not signify a gentle lamb gone meekly to slaughter, but something uncompromising and much more bold. Nonetheless, this continuing misconstrual of the term has contributed to the docetic misreading of Jesus' politics as quiescent at best, nonexistent at worst.

The Consequences of a Nonpolitical Jesus

These politically docetic modes of thinking that deny to Jesus even a modicum of political consciousness might seem to be merely the product of a simple misunderstanding or innocent differences of theological opinion. However, they constitute a much more pernicious and destructive reality.

As we have seen, political docetism distorts and even denies important realities of the life of Jesus, which should be unacceptable enough for those who believe in him. But even worse, it denies to the victims of oppression and exploitation for whom Jesus felt such compassion and concern—

those Jesus called "the least of these"—the empowering example of his radical response to the social and political realities of his day. In this sense, the nonpolitical Jesus presented by mainstream Christianity ultimately serves the very forces he opposed by foisting upon oppressed peoples a model of Jesus that, tragically, is devoid of the power of Jesus' social witness. As a result, oppressive institutional structures are left essentially unchallenged by the considerable spiritual and material resources of the Church. In this historical moment, in which the dread specters of political repression, economic exploitation, self-righteous warmongering, racial and gender inequities, homicidal religious intolerance, and murderous xenophobia seem to raise their heads ever higher, the Church's continued political docetism can portend only greater dispossession and disaster for the masses of those Jesus came to serve and to save.

In short, preaching, teaching, and serving a nonpolitical Jesus constitutes an un-Christian abdication of responsibility to wage struggle against the demonic structures of oppression that militate against the justice of God.

That docetic biblical interpretations serve the forces of domination is not just coincidental. It is the consequence of two very crucial, yet very different, developments.

The Birth of the Nonpolitical Jesus

A major reason for the lack of popular awareness of Jesus' political radicality can be traced to the apostle Paul. Paul's ministry began a little more than a decade after the death of Jesus. Though he never met Jesus, Paul nonetheless became the most influential interpreter of Jesus' message and ministry. But Paul's view of the political realities of life was very different from Jesus' perspective.

Like Jesus, Paul was a Jew. But unlike Jesus, Paul was a Roman citizen with the benefits that such citizenship conferred (see Acts 16:37–39). In a time of terrible and widespread political insecurity, as a Roman citizen Paul always had available to him at least a modicum of the protection that was guaranteed by the Roman state. Whether Paul availed himself of that protection or not—his testimony of floggings at Roman hands makes it clear that sometimes he did not do so—he at least had the security of knowing that it was there for him if he chose to call upon it. In fact, the Book of Acts tells us that on at least one occasion Paul did save himself by declaring his citizenship to the authorities (Acts 22:25).

Paul's Roman citizenship was the result of his birth in Tarsus, an important trading hub and intellectual center in Cicilia (now Turkey). According to the ancient historian Strabo (63 B.C.–A.D. 24), Tarsus even surpassed Athens and Alexandria as a center of Greek culture and learning. It was at Tarsus that the celebrated meeting of Antony and Cleopatra took place.

Not only did inhabitants of Tarsus enjoy imperial protection, but they also were exempt from the economic pressures that weighed upon the people of Israel. In fact, under the Roman emperor Augustus, Tarsus received a variety of special privileges, of which exemption from imperial taxation was only one.

Paul seems to have spent a good deal of his early life in the Greco-Roman environment of Tarsus. From there he moved to Jerusalem, another major urban center, to study with an eminent rabbi, Gamaliel. In other words, Paul was a city person. The metaphors Jesus uses come from the country: sheep and weeds and sowers and tenant farmers. But Paul is obviously more comfortable with rhetorical clichés from Greek philosophy like "I do not do what I want, but I do the very thing I hate" (Romans 7:15), which paraphrases a saying of the Stoic philosopher Epictetus, and with Greek athletic conventions like "In a race the runners all compete, but only one receives the prize" (1 Corinthians 9:24). And when Paul does use imagery of a garden or an olive tree, it clearly is more academic than experiential: "So neither the one who plants nor the one who waters is anything, but only God who gives the growth. The one who plants and the one who waters have a common purpose, and each will receive wages according to the labor of each" (1 Corinthians 3:7–8).

So, as an urbanite, Paul did not grow up with the insecurity and fear that permeated the rural peasant culture in which Jesus spent his life. As we have seen, peasants in Jewish Palestine were typically vulnerable to raids by bandits and to arbitrary seizure of their property and produce by Roman soldiers, and women often were violated by them. Peasants were also subject to the pressure of multiple annual taxes that could amount to more than one-third of what in the vast majority of cases was no more than subsistence production to begin with. For that reason, hunger and economic ruin were always looming. It is estimated that the peasants of first-century Israel had an average daily caloric intake of a mere 1,400 calories, barely enough to sustain their strength and health. Their plight was so precarious that a twentieth-century description of peasant life in China might just as well apply to first-century Israel in its likening of the peasants' struggle for survival to "a man standing permanently up to the neck in water, so that even a ripple is sufficient to drown him."

This was the rural setting in which Jesus lived and delivered his message. Most of Paul's ministry, however, was in urban centers many miles or even an ocean away from the hardship that defined the lives and everyday existence of Jesus and every Jew Jesus knew. Although Paul's letters tell of numerous floggings and jailings, those same letters confirm that none of the punishments he suffered were because of his political status as a colonized Jew. In fact, had he not been a Roman citizen, his apostolic career might well have been cut far shorter by summary execution for any of his transgressions. Paul's travails were the result of his bold choice to preach a new religious doctrine that, because it lacked imperial approval or recognition, was considered disruptive to the social fabric, if not subversive.

Moreover, the Gospels relate that Jesus often took pains to keep his ministry secret, as in this instruction in Matthew 8:4 after performing a healing: "See that you say nothing to anyone." Yet Paul did not feel so constrained. Paul operated in the open, in synagogues, marketplaces, bazaars, and the like. Although his daring certainly arose from his searing sense of conviction, it cannot be overlooked that underlying it was the reality that, whether he chose to use them or not, on some level Paul always knew that he had access to the rights that Roman citizenship afforded him—rights that Jesus and his disciples never had. For Jesus was not a Roman citizen, not even a second-class citizen. He was a colonized subject of the Roman

Empire who was kept in line by sword and spear. Like his fellow Jews, he had no rights under Rome's occupation of his homeland, and no legal standing. As the Christian mystic Howard Thurman observed, "If a Roman soldier pushed Jesus into a ditch, he could not appeal to Caesar; he would be just another Jew in the ditch."

Yet despite the brutality visited upon his people by Roman rule, Paul never seems to acknowledge their suffering. In fact, some of the statements in Paul's letters seem like passive acceptance of the injustices of the Roman Empire, as in Romans 13: "Let every person be subject to the governing authorities; for there is no authority except from God, and those authorities that exist have been instituted by God. Therefore whoever resists authority resists what God has appointed, and those who resist will incur judgment. For rulers are not a terror to good conduct, but to bad" (Romans 13:1–3).

Some of his other statements actually seem to endorse injustice: "Were you a slave when called? Do not be concerned about it. Even if you can gain your freedom, make use of your present condition now more than ever" (1 Corinthians 7:21).

Although these sentiments raise questions about Paul's understanding of Jesus' teachings about justice, they must be understood in the context of his belief that at any moment Jesus would return to sweep steadfast believers into heaven; this is reflected in statements like "[T]he day of the Lord will come like a thief in the night" (1 Thessalonians 5:2).

This belief, known as apocalyptic (from the Greek word meaning "uncovering" or "revelation," signifying divine revelation of events to come), redirected the believer's gaze from the pain and injustice of the present reality to the expectation of deliverance into a just and pain-free new world that God would send down from heaven. Thus it wasn't political quietism (or what some commentators have mistakenly interpreted as a sort of biblical endorsement of political conservatism) that led Paul to preach that believers shouldn't worry about changing their present circumstances. It was his apocalyptic belief that because a new world of radical change would be instituted at any moment, believers need do nothing but "wait on the Lord."

That is why what appear in Paul's letters to be pro-slavery pronouncements or calls for uncritical acceptance of unjust government or tolerance, even advocacy, of class or gender oppression were in reality something quite different for Paul. In his letter to the Galatians, Paul unambiguously states his belief that through Jesus, God sanctioned a radically egalitarian social order: "There is no longer Jew or Greek, there is no longer slave or free, there is no longer male and female; for all of you are one in Christ Jesus" (Galatians 3:28).

Paul is clear that according to the witness of Jesus, no human being should ever unjustly dominate another. Indeed, he seems to even reject class distinctions.

So for Paul, it was not a question of *whether* social change should occur, but of *how*. For him, that social transformation would happen only by the direct intervention of God, not by human efforts. It was his sense of apocalyptic certainty that prompted Paul to counsel believers not to worry about the social and political circumstances of their lives. But even if they could change their circumstances, for Paul the coming of God's new world was so imminent that there was no need for their efforts.

Paul's apocalyptic worldview, then, was not only the basis of his theology, it was also his strategy for addressing injustice in the world: believers had only to hold fast to their faith and wait on the coming of the Lord in power, which Paul was certain would occur during his lifetime. Unfortunately, Paul's timetable was mistaken. Two thousand years later the *Parousia*, the Second Coming of Jesus that Paul expected, has not yet occurred, nor has the liberation of the world he believed it would establish yet come to pass.

The Church's misunderstanding of these aspects of Paul's thought and theology played an important role in the subsequent perception of a Jesus who is unconcerned with the political realities of his time. Yet there are several aspects of Paul's thought that really do dismiss the political dimension of Jesus' message, even taking into account Paul's apocalyptic expectation.

As we have seen, the plight of "the poor" was a primary concern for Jesus. However, it is not "the poor" who are the focus of Paul's concern, but "the sinners." Paul transformed Jesus' concern for collective social, economic, and political deliverance for his entire people into an obsession with the personal piety of individuals. Paul seems to have no room in his faith for thoughts of earthly freedom; it is heaven that holds his complete attention. For that reason, Jesus' central proclamation of the kingdom of God, which promises justice and deliverance on earth as in heaven, is all but nonexistent in Paul's writings. And when Paul does refer to it, he reduces it to a matter of personal piety, as in 1 Corinthians 6:9–10; where he warns that "neither the immoral, nor idolaters, nor adulterers, nor sexual perverts . . . will inherit the kingdom of God" (RSV).

Yet, as significant as Paul was for the misunderstanding of Jesus' message, there is another factor in that tragic process. The picture of the non-political Jesus who never challenged the horrors of empire and even tacitly accepted them, more than of any other cause, is the legacy of Christianity's encounter with the Roman emperor Constantine. For it was Constantine who officially transformed the faith founded upon the teachings of Jesus from the radical faith of the *oppressed* to the official religion of the *oppressor*.

POST-CONSTANTINIAN CHRISTIANITY

That Christianity began as the faith of the oppressed is a fact that cannot be stressed enough. Jesus, his disciples, and all who heard and followed him in his lifetime, with few exceptions, were poor, tyrannized subjects of the Roman Empire. The Book of Acts describes the Church as beginning with a gathering of peasants, mostly Galileans, who were possibly the most devalued of all first-century Jews, and whose fear of Roman brutality had been heightened by the torture and execution of their beloved leader (Acts 2:1–42). The sense of dread felt by those early followers was well founded, even prescient, because as bad as their treatment had been in the past, what the immediate future held for Christians was even worse. For generations after the death of Jesus, those professing faith in him were ruthlessly victimized by the Romans and often martyred for their faith.

The writings of Tacitus attest that the persecution, torture, and murder of Jesus' followers in the decades after his death were widespread. In a particularly gruesome passage, Tacitus recounts the first-century Roman emperor Nero's practice of using Christians as human torches to light the imperial gardens. The history of Christianity from the mid-first century through the early third century is filled with equally frightful accounts of persecution. The Book of Revelation recounts some of the tribulations of the early Christians at the hands of the Romans, such as beheading (20:4) and outright slaughter (6:9). In fact, Revelation opens by explicitly acknowledging, in 1:9, the Christians' shared subjugation: "I, John, your brother who share with you in Jesus the *oppression* . . ." (from the Greek *thlipsis*, "press down" [my translation]). Both the disciple Peter, apparently the earliest leader of nascent Christianity, and the apostle Paul appear to have been executed by Rome early in the sixth decade of the first century. Peter is said to have requested that he be crucified upside down because he felt himself unworthy to be executed in the same manner as his Lord. It is believed that Paul was beheaded, his years of unrelenting proselytizing having finally nullified his Roman citizenship.

Although in subsequent centuries this pattern of repression would slow and at times would even appear to have subsided, violent repression of Christians still periodically reared its head, sometimes with striking savagery. But on one fateful day in the early fourth century, all this would change.

ON OCTOBER 27, 312, the Roman general Constantine stood poised to face the much larger army of the general Maxentius to battle for the imperial throne of Rome. Lactantius (c. 240–320), an African Christian convert and a contemporary of Constantine, relates that as Constantine fitfully slept that night, the initial letters in the Greek spelling of "Christ," *chi* and *rho,* appeared to him in a dream, followed by the words *In hoc signo vinces,* "By this sign you will conquer." Taking this as an omen, Constantine adopted the initials as his battle standard.

The army of Constantine prevailed in the next day's decisive battle.

Joyously attributing his victory to the intervention of Jesus Christ, Constantine immediately announced his embrace of Christianity and reversed his predecessor Diocletian's edict of A.D. 303 that formally criminalized the practice of Christianity, and set in motion the most extensive of all Roman persecutions of Christians. With Constantine's action the repression and murder of followers of Christ that had been waged since the mid-first century now came to an end. This was a blessed development for Christians, because it finally afforded them the security of the official legitimacy and freedom from persecution their faith had long been denied. Yet, ironically, this development began a cycle of distortion of the Gospel of Jesus Christ that has never ended.

First, Constantine's action confused militarism and political domination with the cause of Christ. Indeed, it was Constantine who imported into Christianity his imperial title *pontifex maximus*, that is, "chief priest" of Roman civil religion. But now he was "chief priest" not only of the Roman pagans, but of Christians, too. That this self-declared "chief priest" of the Church was also *pontifex maximus* of Rome was a perversion of the very core of Jesus' gospel of liberation, for, like all empires, the Roman Empire was held together by repression, brutality, and violence.

This confusion of militarism and political domination with the cause of Christ continues throughout the subsequent history of the West. The Crusades, the Inquisition, the Holocaust, the genocidal "missionary" campaigns against the native peoples of the Americas, and the cruel enslavement of human beings in the "Christian" United States are only a few examples.

The problems caused by the Roman Empire's acceptance of the faith seem to mirror the questionable conversion of Constantine himself. First, he established the so-called *agentes in rebus* (Latin for "doers of things"), a group of fixers, informers, and enforcers who were the ancient equivalent of secret police. The historian A. N. Wilson calls Constantine's reign "the first totalitarian state in history." Worse, like the megalomaniacal Herod the Great, Constantine had members of his own family murdered. He ordered his wife Fausta and his firstborn, Crispus, who at one point had been his second in command, to be killed for reasons that remain unclear. His nephew Licinianus, who came to hold a rank similar to that of Crispus, was also murdered, apparently to remove him as a threat to Constantine's power. Finally, despite his pious claims and his fourteen years of leadership of the Church, Constantine never received Holy Communion. In fact, he was not baptized until a few hours before his death in 327 and ironically, Constantine's "Christian" vision was not his first vision. He had once claimed to have had a vision of the pagan god Apollo.

Thus the subsequent propaganda trumpeting the depth of Constantine's Christian faith and his devotion to the Church masked a man with unchecked imperial sensibilities who apparently used the faith to serve his own ends, and who guided that faith in the direction that suited his view of the world. The propaganda also ignored or glossed over Constantine's transgressions, his mean-spiritedness, his policies that dealt death in the name of life. In addition, it made the incredible claim that Jesus took sides in a murderous battle between contending generals willing to sacrifice the lives of countless others in order to gain glory and riches for themselves.

The legacy of Constantine's confusion of militarism with the Gospel of Jesus Christ lingers still. Even in the twenty-first century we see misguided heads of state trumpet their Christian faith, yet in the same breath order military invasions of other sovereign nations with the clear implication, if not the outright declaration, that their forays are divinely ordained. In the misguided tradition of Constantine, these leaders mistakenly and often disingenuously wrap themselves in the belief that their warmongering is blessed by God, just as Constantine believed of his own wars and atrocities.

Another serious consequence of Constantine's conversion to the Christian faith is that it introduced a hierarchical structure into Christianity—and fully legitimized it in the eyes of believers.

It is true that there was hierarchy in Christianity before Constantine. In First Corinthians, Paul notes, "God has appointed in the church first apostles, second prophets, third teachers . . ." (1 Corinthians 12:28). But the Church's hierarchy was a hierarchy of roles and functions, not of rank. In the Church's role-based hierarchy, no believer had a higher status than any other; all were God's children seeking grace. Indeed, the Letter of James says of class-based claims of privilege, "if you show partiality, you commit sin" (James 2:9). Paul expresses this as well in 1 Corinthians 12: "For just as the body is one and has many members, and all the members of the body, though many, are one body, so it is with Christ. For in the one Spirit we were all baptized into one body . . . Indeed, the body does not consist of one member but of many" (vv. 12–14).

When in Luke's Gospel John the Baptist asked for evidence that Jesus was the one for whom he had so faithfully waited, Jesus confirmed his messianic identity not with status claims, but by speaking in functional terms of earthly service and practical salvation: "Go and tell John . . . the blind receive their sight, the lame walk, the lepers are cleansed, the deaf hear, the dead are raised, and the poor have good news brought to them" (Luke 7:22).

But when Constantine converted to the faith, he also *converted the faith to Constantine* by introducing his own status hierarchy into it, for he didn't just become a believer, he became something unprecedented and ultimately heretical: he became *head* of the Church, its de facto emperor. In fact, the Church historian Eusebius of Caesaria (c. 260–c. 340) relates that Constantine called himself a "bishop ordained by God" and the "thirteenth disciple," meaning he believed he possessed a special status that transcended the need for consecration or even recognition by Church officials for its authenticity. Armed with his self-proclaimed preeminence in the faith, Constantine himself decided which leaders and theological opinions would hold sway in the Church. He accomplished this by conferring the legitimacy of his imperial office upon hand-picked clergy and Church leaders with selective invitations to participate in the exclusive doctrinal conferences and councils he convened.

To consolidate his hold on the Church, Constantine underwrote the annual expenses of clergy in North Africa whom he considered "servants of the lawful and most holy universal church," that is, those whose theology agreed with his own. To stifle opposition, he arranged for "persons of turbulent character," that is, those who disagreed with his theology, to be barred from Church proceedings. The result of these manipulations is that many of the dearest and most important doctrines of today's Christian Church are the direct result of Constantine's intrigue and machinations.

The ironic consequence of the financial support and favored rank that association with Constantine granted to Church leaders was the creation of an affluent, privileged ministerial class not unlike the privileged Jerusalem priestly class that Jesus died opposing. Thus the functional roles that once had *served* the Church were transformed into statuses that now *governed* it.

The legacy of Constantine's transformation of roles into privileged statuses can be seen today in many denominations and local churches in which pastors run their congregations like fiefdoms and denominational heads rule like emperors. Instead of considering fellow Christians "co-workers in Jesus Christ," as Paul did (Romans 16:3 [NAB]); or "friends," as Jesus came to call his disciples (John 15:15); or even sheep of the flocks they are called to serve, many pastors and denominational leaders relate to their congregants as if they are subjects who are expected to exalt the clergy simply because they are clergy, as well as provide them with the privileged lifestyles those clergy claim befits their exalted status. An example of these status claims is seen in the increasingly popular practice of ministers' having attendants, often called "armor bearers," to serve their every need, when in the testimony of the scriptures this was a privilege reserved for kings. One historic denomination states in its official polity that its elected bishops should be considered "first among believers." In a bizarre twist of the religion of Jesus, some churches now even feature VIP entrances!

The spectacle of ministers driving Rolls-Royces, living in multimillion-dollar homes, even owning private jet planes—bought with the dimes and dollars of their parishioners—and indulging in other excesses of luxury is the direct result of the un-Christian Constantinian transformation of the pastor's role of shepherd into a privileged status.

There are pastors and "evangelists" shamelessly living in mansions and estates with purchase prices in excess of $10 million. One traveling "faith healer"—many of whose "healings" have been shown to be dubious—is known to stay in the most extravagantly expensive hotel suites during his "crusades," some costing more than $10,000 *per night.* And this figure does not include the cost of the accommodations for his sizable entourage. This sounds more like Caesar traveling with his retinue than an evangelist on the road to spread the good news of Christ. Not to be overlooked is the spectacle of Christian religious leaders in some parts of the world sitting on raised thrones, extending their jeweled rings to be kissed, and actually being conveyed on litters carried on the shoulders of those whom they are supposed to serve.

Jesus defined Christian ministry with one unequivocal proclamation: "[T]he son of Man came not to *be* served, but *to* serve" (Matthew 20:28). There can be no question that these abuses of the people's trust bespeak a sense of entitlement and elitism that Jesus would never have sanctioned.

Jesus' rejection of great wealth and high worldly status in Luke 4:1–13 models the way all Christians should respond to them. Luke tells us that when Jesus was offered great riches and rank, he shunned them, refusing to exploit his God-given powers and gifts for self-gain. Most important, he refused to accept privileged treatment and exalted status. The unwillingness of Jesus, the head of our faith, to lay claim to exceptional treatment condemns every Christian leader who does claim or accept special status. To do so in the name of Jesus is no less than blasphemy.

The sad truth is that such excesses and even the use of nonbiblical titles like "Reverend," "Right Reverend," and "Father," which confer special statuses on their holders, are legacies of Constantine's heretical introduction of status hierarchy into the Church. Even what seems so small a thing as conferring upon a pastor's wife the title of "First Lady" is suspiciously reminiscent of the Constantinian status hierarchy. What is most ironic about the privileges bestowed upon minsters by unbiblical status hierarchies is that they replicate the privilege claims of the very status hierarchy—the Jerusalem Temple priesthood—that Jesus died opposing.

Constantine's actions seemed to broaden the appeal of Christianity by removing Rome's prohibitions against it and sponsoring doctrinal conformity. But in reality they served only to cheapen it. One Church historian offers this pointed observation of the state of the faith under Constantine: "Everybody sought membership in the church, and nearly everybody was received. Both good and bad, sincere seekers after God and hypocritical seekers after gain, rushed into communion. Ambitious, worldly, unscrupulous men sought office in the church for social and political influence. The moral tone of Christianity in power was far below that which had marked the same people under persecution."

Unfortunately, that is not all. Constantine's adoption of Christianity as the de facto religion of the Roman Empire had another result as well: it sped the Church's slide down the slippery slope of assimilation to the social mores and values of Greco-Roman culture. This was a disastrous development in that these values, such as social elitism, instructing slaves to honor their enslavers, and endorsing male domination of women, were in direct opposition to the gospel of freedom and equality taught by Jesus. In reality, though, the post-Constantinian Church only heightened the move toward assimilation that had begun long before. In fact, it is already evident in the New Testament letters known as 1 Timothy, 2 Timothy, and Titus.

These letters, which collectively are called the Pastoral Letters because of their focus on local church concerns, advocate the total subservience of women to men, at least in church matters (1 Timothy 2:9–15); treat class domination as desirable, even normative (1 Timothy 2:2); shamelessly declare that Christians who enslave other Christians should be considered "as worthy of all honor" (1 Timothy 6:1); and command slaves to "be submissive to their masters" and to "give [them] satisfaction in every respect" (Titus 2:9). All these values are diametrically opposed to the Gospel teachings of Jesus, but they are consistent with Greco-Roman thought. Sadly, they reflect the reshaping of the message of Jesus to fit Greco-Roman morality and social ethics, and not the other way around. How else can we explain the Church's millennia of acceptance, at times even its embrace, of slavery, the domination of women, the exploitation of the poor, overt materialism, and unchecked elitism?

Yet perhaps the worst consequence of Constantine's official embrace of Christianity was that by declaring the Roman Empire to be under God's guidance and sponsorship, it legitimized persecuting or even executing anyone who opposed the empire's oppressive policies—and even made doing so tantamount to a sacred duty. This offered the Church's imprimatur to every subsequent political regime throughout history, no matter how repressive it might be, as long as it declared itself to be Christian and characterized itself as acting in the name of Christ. In this way the radical, liberating faith of Jesus was perverted into a validating agency available to every deadly status quo seeking to silence the lion's roar of freedom. As biblical scholar Thomas D. Hanks observes, "[T]he post-Constantinian theological structures . . . all have this in common: they try to keep the lion in the cage."

Howard Thurman lamented that "too often the weight of the Christian movement has been on the side of the strong and powerful and against the weak and oppressed—*this, despite the gospel.*" Yet Thurman's observation is probably understated. For there is little question that the acceptance of the un-Christian ethics of political oppression, social domination, elitist privilege, and concretized hierarchy into the faith and theology of the Church has largely turned the message of Jesus into something so counter to what he lived and died for that surely he would stand against it were he walking the earth today.

IN A REAL SENSE, Jesus was the ultimate activist in that he dedicated his entire being to struggling to bring the world in line with the vision of love, liberation, and justice given to him by God. Yet his activism was born of his spirituality. Jesus defined spirituality holistically, as both *vertical* (love and service to God) and *horizontal* (love and service to humanity). In other words, for him true spirituality consisted of an active commitment to health, wholeness, and justice for all God's children as the highest expression of our love for God. Jesus articulated his holistic conception of spirituality in this way: "You shall love the Lord your God with all your heart, and with all your soul, and with all your mind . . ." and . . . *"You shall love your neighbor as yourself"* (Matthew 22:37–39).

In practical terms this means that when we who claim to know God become aware that any of God's children are caught in webs of oppression of mind, body, or spirit, it is our divine duty to struggle for the liberation and deliverance of our suffering neighbors in the same way that we would struggle for our own. In this sense, the only true evidence of one's love for

God—and the only true evidence of real spirituality—lies not in retreating to a private prayer closet, although it is important to go there to gather strength and guidance by communing with God undistracted. The only authentic evidence of spirituality is that we have personally sought and struggled for the health, wholeness, and freedom of others.

This is the spirituality of Jesus. By his own testimony, it is the manifestation of his anointing by the Spirit of the Lord. It is the basis of his message, his ministry, and the radical political legacy he has left us.

SUMMARY

The biblical tradition to which Jesus was heir is marked at every step by political issues: justice and injustice, domination and resistance, oppression and liberation. Indeed, the Exodus, the root event of biblical faith, was a liberation event that made the profound and lasting statement that the God of Israel is a champion of justice—that in conflicts between oppressed and oppressor, God takes the side of the oppressed, never the side of the oppressor. That is the basis of *mishpat*, the biblical concept of justice: that oppression and exploitation have no rightful place in God's plan for humanity. For that reason an important aspect of loving our neighbor as ourselves is struggling for the freedom of all.

Fueled by their faith in God's liberating love, throughout the millennia of biblical Israel's existence many men and women lived and died questing for justice. Their efforts and their devotion to *mishpat* are enshrined in biblical narratives spanning every stage of Israel's development. Century after century they held fast to *malkuth shamayim*, their unquestioned conviction that only God has the right to rule, even as their enemies defeated them, exploited them, starved them, broke them in body and in spirit and crushed them beneath the heavy heel of oppression.

It was into this landscape of hunger and poverty, turmoil and tumult that Jesus of Nazareth was born. Unfortunately, the hard truth of his setting in life has been softened by those who either misunderstood the realities of his origins or have sought to mask them for fear that the truth might somehow weaken their own political or ecclesiastical control. In such perennial Christmas favorites as "It Came upon a Midnight Clear" and "Silent Night," Jesus is portrayed as warmly ensconced in an uncomplicated setting of total and lasting "peace":

Silent night, holy night!
All is calm, all is bright . . .
Sleep in heavenly peace.
Sleep in heavenly peace.

The truth is that the harsh social, economic, and political factors of Jesus' life as a colonial subject of the Roman Empire helped to shape the holistic spirituality that undergirded his earthly message and ministry. In this sense, the ministry of Jesus paralleled God's self-revelation in the Exodus event: both God and Jesus intervened in history in response to the cry for liberation of the oppressed people of Israel. And like the God of the Exodus, Jesus not only responded to a particular system of political tyranny, he also asserted the justice of God as the basis for struggling to vanquish degrading social practices and oppressive political structures for all time to come. His repeated emphasis on the "kingdom of God," that is, the sole rulership of the God of justice; his unrelenting focus on freedom and liberation, on the right of all to have abundance in every sphere of inner life and outer life; and his ever present concern for the poor and unprotected together constitute a platform for liberation that far exceeds in its scope even the most ambitious secular political agenda.

LET US NOW turn our attention to the specifics of the radical guide for loving our neighbors as ourselves that is bequeathed to us by Matthew, Mark, Luke, and John: the politics of Jesus.

PART

TWO

❈

FOUR

Messiah and Tactician: The Political Strategies of Jesus

NOT EVERYONE SHARES the Christian belief in Jesus as the Son of God, the Savior of the world, the promised Messiah. Some do not even recognize him as a prophet. No matter what one believes, however, one fact is undeniable: Jesus was a leader. He was so great a leader that two thousand years after his death, at any given moment there are untold numbers of believers willing to suffer ostracism, imprisonment, torture, and even death for his namesake.

Jesus was not only a leader, he was a strategic leader. Careful examination of the Gospels reveals that he led according to well-considered strategies and tactics. He did not move aimlessly or in unplanned reaction to events and occurrences, but purposefully toward a clearly defined goal.

The goal of Jesus was realization of the kingdom of God. The kingdom (or sovereignty) of God was a new world order of transformed human relationships; it was social, economic, and political relationships in this world made holy.

This chapter will explore seven of Jesus' discourses and deeds as political strategies. The discussion of each strategy will contain a rereading of the New Testament passage or passages in which the strategy is found, to cleanse them of their post-Constantinian misinterpretations. In addition, each strategy will be illuminated by the use of contemporary examples and analogies.

Those looking for full-blown exegeses of the biblical passages that follow will be disappointed. Although I am a biblical scholar, my purpose in this chapter is not to plumb the depths of biblical scholarship, but to examine the strategic and tactical implications of these particular words and actions of Jesus.

STRATEGY ONE
Treat the People's Needs as Holy

"Pray then in this way:
    Our Father in heaven,
        hallowed be your name.
        Your kingdom come.
        Your will be done,
            on earth as it is in heaven.
        Give us this day our daily bread.
        And forgive us our debts,
            as we also have forgiven our debtors.
        And do not bring us to the time of trial,
            but rescue us from the evil one."

MATTHEW 6:9–13

"Father, hallowed be your name.
    Your kingdom come.
    Give us each day our daily bread.
    And forgive us our sins,
        for we ourselves forgive everyone indebted to us.
    And do not bring us to the time of trial."

LUKE 11:2–4

Despite all the pomp and circumstance permeating the Church to-day, the truth is that Jesus didn't found an institution, he started a movement. He ordained no bishops, pastors, deacons, or trustees. He issued no ecclesiastical decrees, wrote no complicated doctrines, established no churches, endorsed no religious hierarchies. Jesus simply taught the

men and women who heeded his call to put their love for God into practice by loving their neighbors as themselves. All Jesus had was a movement, plain and simple, and all who followed him in his lifetime were not
only his disciples, they were also partners in that movement.

Throughout history, movements have been propelled by the charisma
and commitment of their leaders, and by the high-flying enthusiasm or
burning resentments of their followers. Thus, movements usually proceed
more on the fuel of emotional fervor than on the strength of clearly articulated goals and ideals. Yet eventually the inevitable questions do arise:
What do we stand for? What is the purpose, the goal of our struggles? Unless it is a movement of rebels without a cause, these questions will be
asked.

The movement that Jesus led was no different in this sense, and the
questions raised by Jesus' disciples were no different, either. Thus, when his
disciples asked Jesus to teach them how to pray in Luke 11:1, this was the
meaning of their query: What is it that we stand for? What is our purpose
as we travel about, healing, teaching, being persecuted and sometimes
pursued?

There is little doubt that this was the underlying meaning of their
question. Certainly his disciples were not asking Jesus how to pray in the
literal sense, for prayer was an integral part of Jewish life. The thrice-daily
prayers enjoined in Daniel 6:10; the midafternoon prayer coinciding with
the afternoon Temple sacrifice; continual table blessings and recitation of
the Psalms—without question, Jews knew how to pray.

What the disciples needed to know, then, was not how to pray, but
what to pray for. What should be the focus of their spiritual ministrations?
What should they ask God to help them accomplish? But more than anything, by posing their question to Jesus, his disciples were asking what it
was that they had been chosen to help *him* accomplish. He'd explained
none of this when he called them from their homes and their everyday en-
deavors. He'd simply said, "Follow me," and they did. The power they felt
emanating from him, the courage, the spiritual energy—whatever it was,
at that time it was enough to cause them to uproot their lives and leave
their kin behind. But now the first blush of exuberance had passed. As they

listened to Jesus' ideas and his teachings in his Sermon on the Mount, they realized they had signed on to be part of something that not only was totally new in many ways, but seemed to put them outside the pale of their heretofore unquestioned religious traditions as well. If this thought had not hit them before, surely it hit them while they listened to their charismatic teacher explaining the familiar biblical commandments in new and challenging ways. Now it was time to know more about the movement they had given their lives to. So they said to Jesus, "Teach us."

Jesus did not answer them in the abstract, nor did he speak in parables. What he articulated for his disciples, simply and plainly, was a microcosm of the concerns and goals of the ministry that was becoming a movement before their very eyes.

The Gospels of Matthew and Luke give somewhat different versions of Jesus' response. This could mean that he uttered different versions of it on different occasions—which, in turn, might indicate that it was more likely an oft-repeated statement of the principles and concerns of Jesus' movement than a once-uttered prayer. In any case, the two versions contain the same elements:

1. Our Father (Father)
2. Hallow your name
3. Thy kingdom come, thy will be done
4. Provide daily bread
5. Forgive our debts
6. We have forgiven others
7. Keep us from temptation

The core meaning of both versions of the prayer is also the same: treat your neighbors and their needs as holy, that is, by striving to fulfill their needs as if serving God.

Jesus conveys his meaning by first telling his disciples to begin their entreaty to God not with "my father," but with "our father" or simply "father." Missing are instructions to pray for personal concerns; in no sense was this to be an individual prayer. Private, maybe, but never individual, never for one's own needs alone. In fact, there are no individual petitions anywhere in the Lord's Prayer; it is always "our" or "us" or "we." In this way Jesus makes certain to focus the disciples' gaze not on their personal circumstances, but on the plight of their people.

Next Jesus tells his disciples to pray, "Hallow your name," or "Sanctify your name" (*hagiastheto* in Greek). Because Roman state religion required that Caesar's name alone be hallowed (one of Caesar's Greek titles was actually *Soter*, or "Savior"), this was a radical call. But for every Jew, and certainly for Jesus and his disciples, God's name was already sanctified and holy. So why would Jesus tell his disciples to pray for God to become what God already is? What makes more sense is that Jesus was telling them to ask God, not to become holy, but to manifest God's holiness, as in "Our Father in heaven, *demonstrate* your holiness." In the Bible God's holiness is often coupled with God as judge, that is, vanquisher of injustice. For instance, Leviticus 22:32–33 specifically links the holiness of God's name with Israel's liberation: "You shall not profane my holy name, that I may be sanctified among the people of Israel: I am the Lord; I sanctify you, I who brought you out of the land of Egypt to be your God." This gives us a fuller flavor: "Our Father in heaven, demonstrate your holiness by manifesting your judgment." Or, to put it another way, "Our Father . . . we are ready for your judgment."

Judgment upon what? Upon Caesar's unjust kingdom. Jesus makes this clear by instructing his disciples to pray, "Your kingdom come, Your will be done." The manifestation of God's holiness, the arrival of God's kingdom, the enacting of God's will all mean the same in this context: that Caesar's kingdom must go; Caesar's will can no longer be allowed to rule. It is a spiritual law as well as plain common sense that no two kingdoms can exist in the same space and no two sets of will—that is, bodies of laws, edicts, and judgments—can rule simultaneously. As Jesus tells us elsewhere, no one can serve two masters.

So when Jesus told his disciples to pray, "Give us our daily bread," it was a prayer for the end of Caesar's kingdom, because by its very nature Caesar's kingdom would never let there be enough bread for everyone. Sufficient bread was the right of the "haves" alone; for the "have-nots" it remained a desperate daily hope. Similarly, when Jesus taught his disciples to pray, "Release us from our debts" (the Greek word here, *aphiemi*, means both "forgive" and "release"), it was also a prayer for the end of Caesar's kingdom, because Caesar's kingdom could not stand without the rapacious imperial system that forced its subjects into debt and dispossession in order to pay Rome the yearly monetary tribute that was its lifeblood.

And when Jesus told them to pray, "Lead us not into temptation [or "trial"]," that, too, was about empire. He was not teaching his disciples to ask God not to tempt them, because God is not a temptor, as we are reminded in James 1:13–14. Rather, Jesus was instructing his disciples to ask for strength to *resist* the temptation that, in the context of the rest of the prayer, could only be the temptation to serve Caesar instead of God—the temptation to give up their struggle and accept the empire as the object of worship it had made of itself, and to treat the rulers' needs as holy, instead of the people's.

On the level of teaching, the fact that these are the instructions Jesus offered as the most spiritually important makes it clear that the Lord's Prayer articulates the core principles of his ministry. On the level of strategy, the Lord's Prayer has other implications that are just as important.

First, the prayer is totally Jewish in the sense that its every phrase has a parallel in Jewish literature, as would be expected of a prayer taught by a Jew to other Jews. Yet Jesus uses no explicitly Jewish pronouncements in the prayer, like "God of Abraham, Isaac, and Jacob" or such. Nor does he use any explicitly self-referentially Christian phrase; nowhere to be found is "in my [Jesus'] name" or any sort of messianic mention. In this sense the prayer Jesus taught his disciples is a purposely *universal* prayer. This means that those whose needs the disciples are to treat as holy can never be limited to any one group. Jesus himself would model this by ministering to the needs of Samaritans, the age-old enemies of Jews, and by extending his healing hands even to the hated Roman military, as in his healing of the centurion's son in Matthew 8:5–13.

The Lord's Prayer raises another issue as well. Forgiving the debts of others means not only decrying the exploitative ways of commerce and empire, but also refusing to participate in them any longer. It is a declaration to once again honor the biblical commandment not to steal, cheat, hold others hostage to debt, or even charge interest for the necessities they might need to borrow. This held the important spiritual lesson that those who follow Jesus must clear their own consciences and transform their own practice so they can honestly declare that they themselves honor the dictates of God and not the ways of usurers.

This teaching on debt in particular might seem impractical in our complex world, but it has as much saliency today as it did in Jesus' time. Businesspersons can refuse to place profits before people. They can refuse to participate in unfair business dealings, refuse to pay substandard wages, refuse to force workers to labor without health-care or pension benefits, refuse to charge exorbitant interest rates and rental costs. For instance, Habitat for Humanity, a Christian organization that builds affordable housing for those in need, charges no interest on its mortgage loans. Its official Web site calls this "the economics of Jesus," which it describes as "people act[ing] in response to human need, giving what they have without seeking profit or interest." Similarly, lawyers can refuse to pursue unjust prosecutions, refuse to defend corporate wrongdoing, refuse to propose or impose laws and measures that are not in the best interests of the masses of God's children. In the final analysis, to pray "We have also forgiven others" means we have chosen to give others the same justice, the same freedom, the same measure of life unencumbered by the onerous weight of unjust policies that we seek to receive ourselves.

THE METHODOLOGY FOR serving the people contained in the Lord's Prayer is the methodology Jesus himself used. Indeed, this is how Jesus captured the allegiance of his disciples and the imagination of the people: he treated their needs as holy. It was not simply the power of his oratory that drew them to him; such an attraction could last only so long, and could never have survived the challenges and trials his followers eventually faced. Apparently, there was no halo above his head; nor are there reports of anything particularly striking about his appearance. Not even Paul, his unfailing advocate, made such claims about Jesus. Apparently, what drew people to Jesus and established his credibility was his selfless service to them. For the Lord's Prayer was not only a microcosm of his teachings, it was a codification of his actions. Let's take a closer look.

Our Father (who art in heaven). The egalitarian implications of this statement are unmistakable. Despite Jesus' own unique relationship to God, he preached that God was the Lord and Father of *everyone*. An early hymn to Jesus that Paul quotes in part in his letter to the church at Philippi pays tribute to the most striking evidence of Jesus' egalitarianism—his refusal to lord his singular relationship with God over others: "Christ Jesus, who, though he was in the form of God,/did not regard equality with God/as something to be exploited,/but emptied himself,/ taking the form of a slave" (Philippians 2:6–7).

As Paul's letter acknowledges, Jesus neither enriched himself nor exalted himself. Because he knew God as the Father of all humanity, Jesus ministered not only to poor Jews like himself, but to Samaritans, to the rich, even to Romans. In no uncertain terms Jesus declared his understanding of God as Father of all: "God makes his sun rise on the evil and on the good" (Matthew 5:45).

Your kingdom come, Your will be done. Jesus not only preached the primacy of the kingdom, or sole sovereignty, of God, he demonstrated it. This is reflected first by the very act of teaching that Caesar's kingdom must come to an end. This also was one of the reasons he publicly rejected the legitimacy of the Temple priesthood: because rather than working to establish God's kingdom of liberation and wholeness, in too many ways the priests were aligned with the interests of their Roman overlord, offering sacrifices on Caesar's behalf, even uttering "We have no king but Caesar" when their loyalty was questioned (John 19:15 [RSV]).

Jesus' total dedication to God as sovereign is also seen in his refusal to accept the kingship so enthusiastically conferred upon him by five thousand of his fellow Jews (John 6). The most poignant demonstration of Jesus' commitment to the sole kingship of God is his uncompromising rejection of the sovereignty of Caesar even as his own life hung in the balance. "You would have no power over me," he told Pontius Pilate, "unless it had been given you from above" (John 19:11).

The kingdom of which Jesus speaks, of course, is none other than the kingdom of God, the *malkuth shamayim*, the acknowledgment that only God is worthy of worship, and no other. No emperor, no king, no president—only God. It is this revolutionary proclamation that "Thy kingdom come" is meant to evoke.

Give us our daily bread, and release our debts. Bread was the main food staple in Israel. Seldom was there a meal without it. Indeed, in Hebrew the place-name Bethlehem means "house of bread"—that is, a place of sustenance and safety. On occasion after occasion, Jesus demonstrated his concern that the people have enough bread by feeding those who were hungry and by urging others to do the same. Here he also goes a step further: he gives particular attention to the crushing debt system that was a major cause of the people's lack of bread. In parable and pronouncement he denounced the injustice of economic indebtedness, even offering a clever and easily remembered slogan to remind his listeners that Caesar's callous economy is not the caring economy of God: "Render unto Caesar the things of Caesar, render unto God the things of God" (Mark 12:17).

THROUGHOUT HIS MINISTRY, Jesus treated the people and their needs as holy by healing their bodies, their souls, and their psyches. He even took pains to specifically preach to them that the poor and the hungry among them are blessed in God's sight and that they and their needs are holy before God. Moreover, he traveled incessantly to raise the people's consciousness that the present order sinned against the justice of God because it sinned against their well-being. Time and again he demonstrated through deed and through precept the better way of living that would be theirs when God's kingdom had come and Caesar's unjust kingdom had gone.

Most of all, Jesus reminded his people of what they too often seemed to forget, that the best way to serve God and to relate to one another was through love: "By this everyone will know that you are my disciples, if you have love for one another" (John 13:35). Not through self-righteous accusations and recriminations shall they be known, but by the love shown by one to another in concrete ways.

In short, Jesus was embraced by so many, even in the face of murderous imperial opposition, for the simple reason that he loved his neighbors as himself in both word and deed. Jesus' credibility was unquestioned among those who knew him best because every day he proved he was with them and one of them. He was not a self-designated leader, nor was he placed at the people's head by those in social or political control. Jesus was an authentic leader because he was organically tied to the people he served. He was recognized as their leader for one reason and one reason only: because he treated them and their needs as holy.

DIETRICH BONHOEFFER WAS a prominent pastor and theologian in his native Germany. In 1943 he was arrested for his part in a plot to end Germany's bid to rule the world by bringing about Adolph Hitler's demise. In a letter from the prison where he would meet his death in 1945, Bonhoeffer articulated what he understood as the responsibility of all Christians to treat the people and their needs as holy:

> We are not Christ, but if we want to be Christians, we must have some share in Christ's large-heartedness . . . by showing a real sympathy that springs . . . from the liberating and redeeming love of Christ for all who suffer. Mere waiting and looking on is not Christian behavior. The Christian is called to sympathy and action, not in the first place by his own sufferings, but by the sufferings of his brethren, for whose sake Christ suffered.

A touching and telling example of treating people's needs as holy by sharing in the "large-heartedness" of Jesus is given to us not by those with much, but by a group of women who had very little.

The Kireka slum on the outskirts of Kampala, Uganda, is home to thousands of deeply impoverished residents, including numerous refugees from the decades of long civil war in northern Uganda. Those fortunate enough to have a regular source of income in Kireka derive it almost exclusively from strip-mining rocks for construction purposes. The men mine large boulders and rocks, while the women in Kireka break the mined rocks into gravel with hand-held hammers, backbreaking labor that earns them a mere $1.20 per day. Yet when the women of Kireka heard of Hurricane Katrina's devastation of New Orleans and the Gulf Coast, in spite of their own poverty and slumlike living conditions they began a relief drive for Katrina's displaced victims. Dozens of women ultimately contributed over 1.6 million Ugandan shillings, or nine hundred dollars, of their hard-earned wages. This was an extraordinary gesture, especially given the fact that these same women had recently donated a portion of their earnings to the victims of the tsunami in Southeast Asia. What made this all the more extraordinary is that most of the women who contributed were infected with HIV.

Rose Busingye, the thirty-six-year-old Ugandan nurse who founded Meeting Point International, a relief organization in Kireka, explains that the Kireka women believe that "those who are suffering, they belong to us. They are our people. Their problems are our problems. Their children are like our children." Their motto is "One heart," which, Busingye explains, means "the heart of [humanity] has no race. It moves to another human being wherever there is suffering." There can hardly be a more articulate explication or a more dramatic demonstration of what it means to treat people's needs as holy. If, even in the midst of their own difficulties, those who have exceedingly little can treat other people's needs as holy, how much more must be required of those with wealth and worldly power?

THUS, by telling his disciples to bring the people's needs before God, Jesus taught them to treat the people's needs as holy, that is, with reverence and respect and special care. He made clear to them that using their strength, their gifts, their spiritual ministrations to make this a just world was the most important service they could render to God. He taught them to serve God by making sure that everyone has enough daily bread, that everyone is free from economic violence and exploitation, that everyone is delivered from the clutches of unjust kingdoms, principalities, and powers. In this way Jesus showed that the salvation that his followers must strive for is the salvation of all. In essence, what Jesus imparted to his disciples was that they must strive for true justice on earth, as in heaven, as their righteous service to God; that they must honor God by doing indiscriminate justice, by lifting up "the least of these" on the altar of God's justice and mercy; that they must set into motion a revolution of love and holistic spirituality that demonstrates love for God by treating the needs of even the least of God's children as holy.

This notion of treating the people and their needs as holy did not originate with Jesus, however. In chapter 1 we identified the Hebrew biblical concepts of *mishpat* ("justice") and *sadiqah* ("righteousness") as the ethical bases of Jesus' politics. Here we add another concept with the observation that the notion of treating the people's needs as holy reflects the Hebrew biblical concept of *hesed*.

Occurring some 240 times in the Hebrew Bible, *hesed* is one of the most important principles in Old Testament ethics. It has three basic meanings: love, strength, and steadfastness. The KJV translates *hesed* as "lovingkindness." More recent translations render it as "steadfast love." Both translations, particularly "steadfast love," imply an enduring perspective that grounds the treatment of others upon love, be they individuals or groups or different classes. "Love" as used in relation to *hesed* does not refer to simple sentiment, but to actions that are based upon caring responsibility for the well-being of others. For instance, in the Exodus liberation story, God offers *hesed* as a self-definition and, therefore, as the reason for divine intervention in the Hebrews' plight: "The LORD . . . /merciful and gracious,/ slow to anger,/and abounding in *hesed* (steadfast love) and faithfulness,/ keeping *hesed* for the thousandth generation" (Exodus 34:6–7). The Book of Hosea tells us that it is *hesed*, not doctrines or rituals, that is the true basis of religion: "For I desire *hesed* (steadfast love) and not sacrifice" (Hosea 6:6). Most important for our purposes, the political implications of *hesed* are reflected in its coupling with *mishpat* (justice) in Micah 6:8: "[A]nd what does the Lord require of you/but to do *mishpat* (justice), and to do *hesed* (practice steadfast love),/and to walk humbly with your God?" (my translation). Taken together, the biblical uses of *hesed* reveal that justice continually enacted and tempered by love must be the standard by which all actions toward others are judged.

What does it mean, then, to do *hesed*, that is, to treat the people and their needs as holy as a political strategy? In concrete terms, it means that every political decision must be based on what is best for the masses, on what their real needs are. The context must always be God's love and God's justice. In this strategy there is no room for self-serving. Every decision and policy must be justified by the people's actual needs and God's unfailing love for justice. And what is holy must not be profaned. Thus, in this sacred service there is no allegiance to Democrat or to Republican. Rather, our allegiance must be to making sure that every child has enough to eat, that old folks can live their last days with security and freedom from anxiety. Our allegiance must be to working to lower infant mortality rates, and to making the credit and financial systems more just so no one is crushed beneath the burden of debt. Our allegiance must be to crafting policies with our neighbors in mind, to listening and contemplating the people's challenges and needs with prayer and humility. This means that every politician, religious leader, and corporate official should begin his or her day with the following prayer or one like it: "Lord, give me the loving heart to see the people's needs and to feel their hurts, and the strength to serve them."

THE LORD'S PRAYER gives us the overarching perspective of the politics of Jesus' ministry. What he offered to those who would accept it was a prescription for changing the world. What follows are some of the more poignant examples of the tactics and strategies Jesus employed in his ongoing ministry to treat the people and their needs as holy.

STRATEGY TWO
Give a Voice to the Voiceless

Then they came to Jerusalem. And he entered the temple and
began to drive out those who were selling and those who were
buying in the temple, and he overturned the tables of the
money changers and the seats of those who sold doves; and he
would not allow anyone to carry anything through the temple.
He was teaching and saying, "Is it not written,
   'My house shall be called a house of prayer for all the nations'?
   But you have made it a den of robbers."
And when the chief priests and the scribes heard it, they kept
looking for a way to kill him; for they were afraid of him, because
the whole crowd was spellbound by his teaching.

MARK 11:15–19

As he came out of the temple, one of his disciples said to him,
"Look, Teacher, what large stones and what large buildings!"
Then Jesus asked him, "Do you see these great buildings? Not one
stone will be left here upon another; all will be thrown down."

MARK 13:1–2

This is not a temper tantrum. This action was planned. Jesus had
already shown he had trouble in mind when he cursed the fig
tree just before entering the Temple (Mark 11:12–14). No, this was no
spontaneous eruption of emotion. Apparently Jesus came to the Temple
prepared to confront the merchants, prepared to occupy the Temple, prepared to publicly denounce Temple activities, and he carried it all out

without a hitch. Jesus' protest was well planned, that much is clear. What is less clear is why he made it.

For centuries Christians have been taught that Jesus' dramatic demonstration at the Temple was a purely religious act. Either he was decrying its lack of spirituality, or he was protesting commercialization of its worship practices, or he was railing against rogue money changers for overcharging worshipers for the Jewish shekels they needed to make acceptable offerings, or he was critiquing the Temple's "legalistic," externally oriented worship in order to establish, or at least inspire, a "purer," more spiritual mode of worship. Though they vary in their details, all of these interpretations have this in common: each considers Jesus' action in the Temple to be purely religious. That is why all of them miss the point: Jesus was not committing a purely religious act by attacking the money changers and dove sellers, for the simple reason that the Jerusalem Temple was not a purely religious institution.

Even though the Temple was the religious center of Jewish life, it was also much more: it was the governing institution of Israel, the center of Israel's political life and power. It was at the Jerusalem Temple that the high priest held court and presided over the powerful Sanhedrin; it was at the Temple that the priestly aristocracy obediently represented Roman interests to their own people, at times even collecting taxes to place in Roman hands; it was at the Temple that priests issued pronouncements and decisions that affected the life of every Jew in Israel. But more than that, the Temple was the center of Israel's economy, its central bank and treasury, the depository of immense wealth. Indeed, so much of the activity of the Jerusalem Temple hinged upon buying and selling and various modes of exchange that it is no exaggeration to say that in a real sense the Temple was fundamentally an *economic* institution.

That is why what seems to have been simply a burst of outrage against wayward merchants was in reality much, much more: it was a very public attack aimed at Israel's center of power. In other words, it was an overtly *political* act. Mark's Gospel makes this clear. It tells us not only that Jesus attacked the money changers and dove sellers, but that he and his followers also seized the Temple grounds and temporarily halted commercial operations. Why? Because despite its veneer of holiness and religiosity, beneath its proclamations of justice and concern, the Temple did not treat the people and their needs as holy.

Mark's narrative leaves little doubt that this was the reason for Jesus' action. "Den of robbers," the scathing expression Jesus uses in his denunciation of the Temple merchants, comes directly from one of the most bitter attacks against the Temple in all the Bible: God's declaration of judgment upon the Temple in Jeremiah 7:1–15. In that passage, "the word that came to Jeremiah from the LORD" is a radical ultimatum: either Israel's upper class ends its rampant corruption, its oppression of the powerless poor, and its wholesale transgression of God's precepts, or the Temple will be destroyed. The Lord told Jeremiah: "I will do to the house that is called by my name, in which you trust, and to the place that I gave to you and to your ancestors, just what I did to Shiloh" (7:14).

Psalm 78 relates the fate of the holy site at Shiloh and the reason for it: "Yet they tested the Most High God,/and rebelled against him./They did not observe his decrees." For that reason, "[God] abandoned his dwelling at Shiloh,/the tent where he dwelt among mortals" (Psalm 78:56, 60).

When we look at the practices that went on at the Jerusalem Temple in Jesus' day, it is clear why Jesus was moved, like Jeremiah, to invoke God's judgment upon it. Its activities and the priests who administered them had become inextricably intertwined with systematic appropriation of the goods and resources of "the least of these" while hiding behind what Jeremiah calls "these deceptive words: 'This is the temple of the LORD, the temple of the LORD, the temple of the LORD' " (7:4).

As a class, the priestly aristocracy of Jesus' time were made wealthy by the people's Temple dues. Priests received a portion of every Temple sacrifice and offering. Given that in addition to normal Temple traffic the number of pilgrims on high holy days could swell into the tens, if not the hundreds, of thousands, this represented considerable wealth. As great as the priests' income was from their portion of the Temple sacrifices, however, they received even more from seven lucrative classes of prescribed offerings that were, in effect, taxes enacted solely for their benefit. These included a five-shekel payment for every firstborn child; the foreleg, cheeks, and stomach of every animal slaughtered; and even a portion of the proceeds from sheepshearing. These offerings were the priests' personal income. In addition to all of this, priests also profited from ad hoc offerings such as payment for a man's consecration or redemption after a sinful transgression. This could be as much as fifty shekels.

As a result, the income from the Temple dues virtually guaranteed the priestly class a privileged economic status beyond what most Jews could ever attain. It is true that the existence of a privileged class contradicted the biblical sensibility of egalitarianism, but alone it did not necessarily constitute abuse on the priests' part. After all, they could claim biblical warrant for their actions. What was sinful was that the priests' guaranteed wealth was not enough for them. Greed pushed them to engage in practices by which they enriched themselves even further by taking advantage of their status. Some priests became lenders to the same masses from whose tithes and offerings their wealth had come in the first place. Some were so mercenary that in the case of defaulted loans they actually seized their borrowers' farms and family homesteads, totally dispossessing those whom they were called by God to serve. In fact, the Jewish scholar Martin Goodman argues that this was the reason that the priests became lenders: "[T]he only logical reason to lend was . . . the hope of winning the peasants' land by foreclosing on it when the debt was not paid off as agreed."

The priests also profited from Temple concessions like money changing and the sale of necessities for sacrificial worship to pilgrims—like the sale of doves that was a focus of Jesus' attack in Mark 11. They also engaged in the ancient equivalent of crony capitalism by ensuring that members of Jerusalem's wealthiest families controlled Temple concessions and economic arrangements. They even developed the *prosbul* (Greek for "before the court"), a legal device that allowed them to circumvent the directive in Leviticus 25 to forgive all debts every seventh year, by depositing their debt certificates in the Temple treasury for the year's duration, then reclaiming the certificates when the year was over. This measure permitted the lenders to be in technical compliance with the biblical prescription while still keeping their borrowers indebted to them, thus effectively removing the indebted persons' only real protection against foreclosure and dispossession.

Even as they enriched themselves, the priestly aristocracy insisted upon full and timely tithes and offerings without concern for the effect this had on the ability of the working poor to provide for themselves and their families. The priests' insistence upon payment of tithes and offerings before all else too often resulted in worshipers' contributing more in Temple dues than they could really afford. And despite the priests' great wealth, there is little evidence that they tried to lighten the people's burdens by sharing their wealth with them.

There is an interesting account in the rabbinic writings that reflects the corruption in the Temple and the priests' awareness that Temple obligations represented a hardship for the Jewish poor. Simeon, son of Gamaliel, the rabbi the apostle Paul calls his teacher in Acts 5:34; 22:3, became concerned that the price of sacrificial doves was so unreasonably inflated that worshipers would be unable to afford them, which could result in supplicants' staying away from the Temple in shame and thus making no offerings at all. This would have had a chilling effect on Temple revenues and the priests' own income. As a result of Simeon's concern, the price of doves eventually was lowered by some 99 percent. That the cost could be dropped so drastically while the merchants still made a profit gives a sense of how disgracefully inflated the price of doves had become under Temple oversight.

In return for underwriting lives of luxury for the priests, the people got little. Despite all that they gained from them, the priests did not safeguard the people's interests as a shepherd is meant to protect a flock; they simply did not treat the people's needs as holy. Priests were oftentimes condescending and haughty to the masses, particularly the rural poor, as is so dramatically reflected in John 7:49, in which priests derisively remark about pilgrims observing Sukkoth, the Festival of Booths, "[T]his crowd, which does not know the law—they are accursed."

Moreover, priests seldom ventured out of the comfort of Jerusalem to minister to the people's needs. In the Gospels, priests appear outside the confines of Jerusalem only as interlocutors and enforcers of orthodoxy, never in pastoral roles. If the people did receive anything in return for all they gave to the Temple and the Temple priesthood, it was simply the hope that their compliance would stand them in good stead with God, as if underwriting the priests' highly privileged existence was a divine commandment.

Yet worse than reports of their greed was the priests' worsening of the political plight of the people of Israel by using the legitimacy of their religious station to defuse the people's opposition to the harsh Roman repression. Whether it was their intention or not, the priests' daily sacrifices to Rome gave their allegiance to Caesar a religious imprimatur of sorts. Priests argued that their cooperation with Rome was for the people's good, yet it was priests who benefited most. In return for the priests' cooperation, the Romans protected the Jerusalem Temple and its caretakers' wealth by brutally disposing of anyone the priests identified as threatening their status and power.

The Jewish people had long resented this treatment. In fact, similar outrage against the priests had smoldered for centuries. An early critique was issued by the eighth-century B.C. prophet Micah:

> Hear this, you leaders of the house of Jacob,
>   you rulers of the house of Israel,
>   who despise justice and distort all that is right;
>
> who build Zion with bloodshed,
>   and Jerusalem with wickedness.
>
> Her leaders judge for a bribe,
>   her priests teach for a price,
>   and her prophets tell fortunes for money.
>   Yet they lean upon the LORD and say,
>   "Is not the LORD among us?" . . .
>
> Therefore, because of you,
>   Zion will be plowed like a field,
>   Jerusalem will become a heap of rubble,
>   the temple hill a mound overgrown with thickets. (Micah 3:9–12 [NIV])

Josephus tells of several prophetic movements closer to the time of Jesus that were inspired at least in part by opposition to the priests. Two in particular seemed to have appeared not long after Jesus' death, during the time of Paul's ministry: those of Theudas and a man known to us now only as "the Egyptian," both of whom rejected the authority and legitimacy of the Jerusalem priestly aristocracy. In a sort of reverse Exodus, Theudas promised to lead his followers across the Jordan River out of Israel, away from Jerusalem rule. The unnamed "Egyptian" is said to have rallied thirty thousand followers with the promise of assuming leadership of Jerusalem. Both movements were crushed by the Romans.

Josephus also reports that a generation or so after the death of Jesus, a certain Yeshua ben Hananiah, "a simple peasant," walked the streets of Jerusalem pronouncing imminent judgment upon "Jerusalem and this holy house," apparently for its corruption and abuse of the people's trust. The priestly aristocracy was so threatened by Hananiah's critique, probably because they realized that it was also the masses' disgruntlement that he so publicly voiced, that they scourged him until his bones showed.

A further indication of the people's anger at the priests' economic practices is Josephus' report that one of the rebels' first acts at the outbreak of the Jewish War in A.D. 66 was to destroy the Temple debt archives: "They carried the fire to the place where the archives were reposited, and made haste to burn the contracts belonging to their creditors."

Josephus also tells us that during the sixth decade of the first century, a radical insurrectionist group of Jews called the Zealots undertook a campaign to purge Jerusalem of its aristocratic priests and wealthy elites. He reports that the Zealots "went so far as to commit murder . . . *starting with the most distinguished citizens.* They first seized and imprisoned Antipas, a man of royal descent and among the most powerful in the city so that *he was entrusted with the public treasury.* Next came Levias, one of the nobles, and Suphas son of Aregetes, both of royal [that is, priestly] blood, then the others of high reputation" (my emphasis).

Josephus issues what in the final analysis is a blanket assessment of the greed and exploitative practices of the priestly aristocracy: "[T]he high priest Ananias . . . was a great procurer of money . . . the other priests acted in like manner." The lament we cited in chapter 2 gives a sense of how abusive the priestly aristocracy was perceived to be: "Woe unto me because of the house of Boethus . . . Hanin . . . Qathros . . . Ismail ben Phiabi . . . For they are High Priests and their sons are treasurers and their sons-in-law are Temple overseers and their servants beat the people with sticks."

Matthew's account of Jesus' denunciation of the transgressions of the priestly aristocracy, personified by him as "scribes and Pharisees," gives us the most incisive Gospel picture of the priests' abuse and misdeeds:

> "The scribes and the Pharisees sit on Moses' seat; therefore, do whatever they teach you and follow it; but do not do as they do, for they do not practice what they teach. They tie up heavy burdens, hard to bear, and lay them on the shoulders of others; but they themselves are unwilling to lift a finger to move them . . . Woe to you, scribes and Pharisees, hypocrites! For you tithe mint, dill, and cummin, and have neglected the weightier matters of the law: justice and mercy and faith . . . Woe to you, scribes and Pharisees, hypocrites! For you are like whitewashed tombs, which on the outside look beautiful, but inside they are full of the bones of the dead and of all kinds of filth. So you also on the outside look righteous to others, but inside you are full of hypocrisy and lawlessness . . . You snakes, you brood of vipers! How can you escape being sentenced to hell?" (Matthew 23:2–4, 23, 27–28, 33)

In no uncertain terms Jesus condemns the priests' greater love of wealth than of holiness:

> "Woe to you, blind guides, who say, 'Whoever swears by the sanctuary is bound by nothing, but whoever swears by the gold of the sanctuary is bound by the oath.' You blind fools! For which is greater, the gold or the sanctuary that has made the gold sacred? And you say, 'Whoever swears by the altar is bound by nothing, but whoever swears by the gift that is on the altar is bound by the oath.'

How blind you are! For which is greater, the gift or the altar that makes the gift sacred?" (Matthew 23:16–19)

MARK TELLS US that Jesus returned to the Temple the day after his demonstration there, apparently still filled with outrage at the exploitation of his people. Mark then recounts that of all the areas of the Temple environs that Jesus could have chosen, he chose to station himself directly "opposite" the Temple treasury, watching "many rich people putting in large sums" (Mark 12:41). When a poor widow made her own meager contribution, Jesus took this as an opportunity to publicly denounce a system that made even those who had virtually nothing feel they had to contribute their last or risk being excluded from God's blessings, a system that was so focused on filling its own coffers and enriching those who administered it that in the name of God it would even leave widows destitute: "Truly I tell you, this poor widow . . . out of her poverty has put in everything she had, all she had to live on" (Mark 12:43–44).

By denouncing the Temple for its role in the impoverishment of the widow, Jesus shows it to be guilty of one of the worst sins in the Hebrew Bible, mistreatment of the needy widow—also one of the very sins Jeremiah said would result in the Temple's destruction (Jeremiah 7:6). It is not surprising that soon thereafter Jesus echoes Jeremiah's pronouncement that the Temple would be destroyed for failing to treat the people's needs as holy: "Do you see these great buildings? Not one stone will be left here upon another; all will be thrown down" (Mark 13:2).

When all the events surrounding Jesus' demonstration at the Temple in Mark chapters 11 to 13 are considered, it is evident that Jesus had destruction of the Temple in mind all the time. Just look at the chronology. Immediately before even entering the Temple he declared destruction upon a fig tree (Mark 11:12–14). It can be no coincidence that in a number of biblical texts destruction of a fig tree is symbolic of God's judgment for corruption and unfaithfulness.

In addition, when his disciples emerged from the Temple and noticed that the fig tree had died, Jesus responded by telling them that if they were truly serious about transforming their situation, they had the power to throw "this mountain" into the sea, if that was their choice. It is not coincidental that out of every image available to him Jesus used the phrase "this mountain." When his statement is considered in context, there is little question that he was referring to the same mountain that had been the focus of his activities for the last several intense days: Mount Zion, the mount upon which the Temple stood, the mount that was synonymous with the Temple itself.

This, then, was the meaning of Jesus' protest at the Temple: it was a repudiation of the Temple and those who ran it, repudiation of their abuse of the people's trust, their haughty dismissal of the people's worth, their turning the Temple of God into a profiteering enterprise, their exploitation of the people in the name of God and for the benefit of themselves and the Romans. It was a prophetic pronouncement to the priestly aristocracy that they must change or be judged by God.

This was the *meaning* of Jesus' very public display of outrage and indignation on the Temple grounds. But what was the *reason* for his action? What did he hope it would accomplish?

Jesus' action had several strategic purposes. The first was to discredit the notion that the Jerusalem Temple was the actual house of God, the place where God dwelled. Why would Jesus want to discredit the Temple as the house where God dwelled? First, because for Jesus it was a false notion. God had no earthly home to be claimed or controlled by one segment of humanity or another. On numerous occasions Jesus testified that the abode of the Father is in heaven; one comes into God's presence by a truthful disposition of spirit, not by visiting any particular earthly locale. Jesus proclaimed as much to the Samaritan woman at the well: "[T]he hour is coming when you will worship the Father neither on this mountain nor in Jerusalem . . . But the hour is coming, and is now here, when the true worshipers will worship the Father in spirit and truth" (John 4:21, 23).

As long as the people were deceived into believing that the Temple was God's inviolate dwelling place, it would be virtually impossible for them to critique or even question Temple practices. Similarly, because of their role as caretakers of the "house" of God, it appeared that the priests' right to lead and govern the people of Israel was divinely ordained and, therefore, not to be questioned. Thus, most Jews were unwilling to challenge the priests for fear of incurring God's wrath. The people of Israel would never be free of the control of the self-serving Temple hierarchy if those notions were left unchallenged.

Thus the people were in a catch-22 from which they did not know how to get free: they were taught to believe that if they did not support the Temple hierarchy, no matter its elitism and corruption and collusion with Israel's imperial overlords, they would incur God's wrath; yet if they made all the offerings asked of them, their already precarious economic circumstances would be rendered even more precarious. But even their harshest judgments of the authority of the priests were always haunted by the question: What if the priests really were the intercessors between God and the Jewish people?

What the people needed was to be freed from their awe of the Temple system so that they might be free from their paralyzing fear of offending God by rejecting the caretakers of God's supposed house. This is what Jesus saw when he surveyed the pilgrims and supplicants dutifully making their offerings. Jesus didn't want anyone else to be placed in the position of literally choosing between eating and paying Temple dues like the widow who gave her last penny. That is, he wanted no one else to be so deluded ideologically as to believe that supporting the Temple and its rich priesthood was more important than taking care of one's own needs. That's why Jesus staged his takeover of the Temple: to demystify its aura of holiness and to publicly reject the Jerusalem Temple as the house of God.

But Jesus' action had another purpose as well: to demonstrate to the masses that they had the right and the power to challenge those who lorded it over them. Jesus' dramatic protest at the Temple said, in effect, that the people's needs were at least as holy as the Temple rituals and the priests' pronouncements. He made evident for all that even the poorest of the poor had the right and the power to call the religious authorities to account.

Thus by his demonstration at the Temple Jesus intended both to demystify the power of the Temple authorities and to empower the people to resist those authorities. His choice to defy the priestly aristocracy in their home base and bring Temple commerce to a halt was intended to show their vulnerability, their lack of invincibility—in short, to bring their power into doubt. At the same time he brought into question whether they truly had God's backing.

That is why the priests "kept looking for a way to kill him," as Mark 11:18 reports: because Jesus was giving voice to the people's sentiments that the priests had previously suppressed by invoking the weight of their office. In effect, Jesus was letting the cat out of the bag. The people were "spellbound by his teaching" because he was giving voice to the feelings they had long held in silence. By implicitly invoking the Temple's destruction, then explicitly prophesying it, he brought the very mandate of the priesthood and the legitimacy of the Temple into question. He was helping the people to see that they were giving their loyalty and allegiance to a ruling order that did not obey its covenant with God to treat their needs as holy.

But most important, *Jesus' action gave a voice to the voiceless.* Publicly and powerfully he articulated the people's unspoken anger and resentment, not just to give vent to their feelings, but to empower them by giving them the inspiring thrill of hearing their own thoughts and sentiments spoken by someone just like them.

Jesus' giving a voice to the voiceless, his articulation of what people feared even to think, much less say—or if they did speak, they were not heard—had an immediate galvanizing effect. The Temple grounds were thirty-three square acres in size. How could Jesus have halted commerce on so large a scale, as Mark tells us, except that other pilgrims and worshipers were empowered and inspired to stand with him? Perhaps, just moments before Jesus' action, most could not have imagined publicly challenging even the most insignificant aspect of Temple practice. But one galvanizing act of courage later, one instance of hearing their own feelings spoken aloud with power and authority, one public evocation of God's call to purge injustice from Israel's seat of power, one act of defiance by a poor peasant like them who dared to take control, if only for a short while, and then walk away unbowed—and only when he chose to leave—and the people were empowered to stand up, too. All because Jesus gave a voice to the voiceless.

As a STRATEGY, Jesus' giving a voice to the voiceless through his demonstration at the Temple had several elements:

* confronting those in power at the seat of their power to discredit their authority   .
* symbolically occupying the seat of power to discredit the myth of its invincibility
* maintaining control of the site long enough to be perceived as an actual challenge to the authorities' power
* making all actions, gestures, and pronouncements dramatic enough to capture the people's imagination
* departing from the site unscathed, if possible, as an inspiring show of strength

The strategic goals of Jesus' demonstration at the Temple were:

* to highlight abuses
* to validate the people's complaints
* to invalidate the legitimacy of those in authority
* to empower the people by demystifying the authority's power

Possibly the best-known example of this strategy at work in contemporary times is the 1964 March on Washington, led by civil rights activists A. Philip Randolph, Roy Wilkins, Bayard Rustin, Ella Baker, Martin Luther King, Jr., and others. The purpose of the march, originally called the March for Jobs and Justice, was to protest the fact that white supremacy and bald-faced racism still reigned in America a full century after the signing of the Emancipation Proclamation. It was to be a gathering to demand that our nation live up to its creed of liberty and justice *for all*. But as its original name implies, at its inception the march was a protest, a collective statement of defiance and outrage against the racial and class injustice that was still legal in much of America, and that too often was continued as accepted social practice where it did not have the force of law. However, by the time the long-planned march took place, the federal government it sought to confront had become a virtual sponsor, or at least the government sought to give that impression.

Still, Martin Luther King, Jr., was determined that the outrage at the widespread injustice felt by African Americans and all Americans of goodwill would be given voice. Of course, this is not evident in the portion of King's address named for its famous refrain, "I Have a Dream," which is all most Americans have ever heard of what King said on that occasion. Most would be shocked to know that in actuality King's words were radical, defiant, even surprisingly threatening for such a setting. Just as Jesus indicted the Temple and its functionaries as a "den of robbers" that did not treat the people and their needs as holy, King chastised the American government for the same transgression. With the eyes of the world upon him he issued a scathing critique of America's betrayal of its own ideals:

[W]e've come here today to dramatize a shameful condition. In a sense we've come to our nation's capital to cash a check. When the architects of our republic wrote the magnificent words of the Constitution and the Declaration of Independence, they were signing a promissory note to which every American was to fall heir. This note was a promise that all . . . would be guaranteed the "unalienable Rights of Life, Liberty, and the pursuit of happiness." It is obvious today that America has defaulted on this promissory note insofar as her citizens of color are concerned. Instead of honoring this sacred obligation, America has given the Negro people a bad check, a check which has come back marked "insufficient funds" . . . And so we've come to cash this check, a check that will give us upon demand the riches of freedom and the security of justice. We have also come to this hallowed spot to remind America of the fierce urgency of Now . . . It would be fatal for the nation to overlook the urgency of the moment.

There were a number of speeches delivered that day, but it was King's address that galvanized the 250,000 in attendance in a way that Americans have seldom been moved before or since. His tone was strong and uncompromising. He did not call those in the seat of power a "den of robbers," but he did say that they had issued "a bad check" despite its being marked "In God We Trust." He indicted those who controlled America for having "defaulted" on the promises of the Declaration of Independence despite their claim that they held its precepts inviolate and dear. Lest the radical intentions of the March on Washington be downplayed or overlooked, he declared that the hundreds of thousands were gathered "to remind America of the fierce urgency of Now." He added an ominous warning that has seldom been quoted since: "It would be fatal for the nation to overlook the urgency of the moment."

It was with these uncompromising words that King threw down the gauntlet, inspiring and empowering Americans to fight for change. In the wake of the March on Washington and King's address, major civil rights legislation was enacted, and the last vestiges of legalized white supremacy were eventually dismantled. Activist groups and ordinary citizens were empowered to push for crucial measures like the civil rights and voting rights bills. Although two generations later America still has far to go, it is now a country more just and a good deal less dangerous for Americans of African descent. All of this has come to fruition because, like Jesus, Martin Luther King, Jr., and others of like conviction journeyed to the seat of America's power and in uncompromising terms gave an eloquent voice to those rendered voiceless by fear, intimidation, and a suffocating lack of belief in their own power. As the result of King's speaking the people's truth to power and the activism of the many he inspired, America was forced to begin to treat its citizens of color and their needs as holy. ·

The impact of the efforts of King and the other organizers of the march are still being felt. Not only have black Americans benefited from the courage of King and the many who stood tall in the temple of American power, but other groups have benefited, too: women, the aged, the physically handicapped, those of different sexual orientation. All this because Martin Luther King, Jr., A. Philip Randolph, Ella Baker, Roy Wilkins, and many others whose names are not known made their way to America's seat of power and gave powerful and uncompromising voice to the needs of those whose tongues had been long silenced.

Yet as domesticated as the March on Washington came to be, the very fact and audacity of it still sent a chill down the spine of the powers that be. *Life* magazine claimed that as the date of the march neared, the nation's capital was "suffering its worst case of jitters since the First Battle of Bull Run." On *Meet the Press*, television reporters voiced the widespread fear that "it would be impossible to bring more than a hundred thousand militant Negroes into Washington without incidents and possible rioting." The Pentagon had nineteen thousand troops at the ready on the outskirts of the District of Columbia, hospitals postponed elective surgery to be ready to accommodate riot casualties, the sale of alcoholic beverages was banned, and so many stores shuttered their doors that some 80 percent of all business revenue that day was lost, in spite of the huge influx of potential customers. In this sense, the March on Washington can be said to have occupied the temple of power and disallowed the conduct of commerce in it, just as Jesus did. Then, like Jesus and his followers, the marchers left the temple unscathed, but the memory and the power of their sacrifice and conviction remain and inspire to this day.

THERE IS ANOTHER example of giving a voice to the voiceless at the seat of power that in some ways is even closer to the radicality of Jesus' Temple protest than the March on Washington.

The treatment of Native Americans at the hands of the United States government is a sad and sordid tale of betrayal, lies, and indescribable pain. Wholesale murder, solemn treaties unilaterally discarded through government duplicity, land stolen, Indians' religions and customs forcibly outlawed in their own lands, children torn from parents and sent to boarding schools where they were systematically brutalized and often molested by pedophiles—the list of wrongs is painfully long. As a result, Native Americans have the highest rates of virtually every physical and mental health pathology in America. Without question they are the nation's most poverty-stricken and physically decimated population.

To seek redress for these historical wrongs and to compel the United States government to begin to honor its broken treaties by at least setting in motion the process to compensate Indians for the theft of their lands, in November 1972 a Native American organization, the American Indian Movement (AIM), led by Clyde Bellecourt, Dennis Banks, and Russell Means, set out from Los Angeles on what it called the Trail of Broken Treaties, a cross-country caravan that was to culminate at the Washington, DC, headquarters of the Bureau of Indian Affairs (BIA). As the government agency charged with oversight of Indian reservations, the BIA had mistreated, abused, and exploited Indians in such callous, inhumane ways and on a scale so great as to be almost unfathomable. Despite the depth of its members' pain and outrage, AIM's plan was to peacefully present to the head of the BIA "The Twenty Points," a list of reforms that would begin to make reservation life livable. Unfortunately, the BIA added insult to injury not only by refusing to meet with the group's representatives, but also by refusing to even consider AIM's demands.

When after pleas and much cajoling it became clear that the government agency charged with meeting the needs of Native Americans would not even listen to what those needs were, the several hundred outraged Indians in the caravan responded by taking control of the entire BIA headquarters and issuing a scathing critique of the BIA's generations-long mistreatment of their people. The resolute members of AIM maintained the takeover for seven days. Their action ended when the harried Nixon White House negotiated a settlement with AIM.

The American Indian Movement takeover of the Bureau of Indian Affairs headquarters in Washington was not as peaceful as the March on Washington. There was vandalism and some theft, but when the occupation was ended, AIM members left tired but unscathed. AIM's action empowered Indians around the country to challenge their collective plight and directly led to the 1973 siege at Wounded Knee, South Dakota, one of the most dramatic Indian efforts for self-determination since the Battle of the Little Big Horn in 1876.

There is an interesting side note to the Indians' action at the Bureau of Indian Affairs headquarters that gives a sense of the gratitude felt by the voiceless Indian masses for those among them who treated their needs as holy and gave voice to the truth of their plight. Because of his selfless, uncompromising activism, his having risked harm and death to treat his people's needs as holy, American Indian Movement leader Russell Means's Lakota people honored him with the name Oyate Wacinyapi, which means "works for the people."

THE USE OF the strategy of giving voice to the voiceless does not have to be so dramatic, however. It might involve as little as publicly asking a challenging question or making an outraged remark.

In 1950, Senator Joseph McCarthy of Wisconsin began a Senate inquiry into the presence of Communist Party members in the United States government. In short order McCarthy's investigation degenerated into a mean-spirited witch hunt that ruined the reputations, careers, and lives of numerous innocent American citizens. Many politicians and ordinary citizens were horrified by the ugliness of McCarthy's attacks, but were afraid to challenge or criticize his campaign for fear of bringing his wrathful gaze upon themselves.

On June 9, 1954, a blow was struck that signaled the beginning of the long-awaited end of McCarthy's vicious crusade. In yet another of his Senate subcommittee's hearings, McCarthy was arguing that G. David Schine, a young lawyer who had been drafted into the United States Army, should be excused from his military obligations to rejoin McCarthy's staff. With his argument apparently having little success with Joseph N. Welch, the lead Army counsel who opposed his request, McCarthy suddenly turned his ire on Frederick J. Fisher, Jr., a young lawyer at Welch's law firm who was not even involved in the Army proceedings, for his admitted short-lived membership in the Communist-affiliated Lawyers Guild while a young law student. Although Fisher had long since repudiated the socialist philosophy of the guild and was by then a dedicated Republican and was even secretary of the Young Republicans League, working closely with the son of the sitting Massachusetts governor, McCarthy still sought to get his pound of flesh by characterizing Fisher as a Communist.

Like many Americans, Welch had watched with disgust as McCarthy smeared reputations and destroyed careers. But now he'd had enough. Rising to his feet in the Senate chamber, he addressed McCarthy in a voice filled with outrage and sorrow: "Until this moment, Senator, I think I never really gauged your cruelty or your recklessness . . . You've done enough. Have you no sense of decency, sir? At long last, have you left no sense of decency?"

With this impassioned question, Welch gave voice to the outrage of countless Americans and confirmed for many others that no matter how noble his initial intentions might have been, Senator McCarthy did not treat the people's needs as holy, pursuing instead some personal agenda of his own.

That was all it took to discredit a powerful member of the United States Senate who essentially had held center stage in American politics. By giving a voice to the many who felt the same as he but for whatever reasons had been rendered voiceless, Welch broke the silence surrounding Senator McCarthy's witch hunts and emboldened others to do the same. In the aftermath of that hearing, McCarthy's popularity and power declined. His downfall was complete when the Senate censured him in December 1954 for behavior "contrary to senatorial traditions." Yet America's eventual freedom from the shadow of McCarthyism began the moment Joseph Welch gave voice to the thoughts and feelings of those rendered voiceless by fear, intimidation, and feelings of powerlessness.

GIVING A VOICE to the voiceless is a powerful strategy for political change. But Jesus' action in the Temple also demonstrates an important principle: that speaking truth to power and demystifying the might of those cloaked in the mystique of invulnerability is more than strategic. It is our sacred duty.

STRATEGY THREE
Expose the Workings of Oppression

"For the kingdom of heaven is like a householder who went out early in the morning to hire laborers for his vineyard. After agreeing with the laborers for a denarius a day, he sent them into his vineyard. And going out about the third hour he saw others standing idle in the marketplace; and to them he said, 'You go into the vineyard, too, and whatever is right I will give you.' So they went. Going out again about the sixth hour and the ninth hour, he did the same. And about the eleventh hour he went out and found others standing; and he said to them, 'Why do you stand here idle all day?' They said to him, 'Because no one has hired us.' He said to them, 'You go into the vineyard, too.' And when evening came, the owner of the vineyard said to his steward, 'Call the laborers and pay them their wages, beginning with the last, up to the first.' And when those hired about the eleventh hour came, each of them received a denarius. Now when the first came, they thought they would receive more; but each of them also received a denarius. And on receiving it they grumbled at the householder, saying, 'These last worked only one hour, and you have made them equal to us who have borne the burden of the day and the scorching heat.' But he replied to one of them, 'Friend, I am doing you no wrong; did you not agree with me for a denarius? Take what belongs to you and go; I choose to give to this last as I give to you. Am I not allowed to do what I choose with what belongs to me? Or is your eye evil because I am good?' So the last will be first, and the first last."

MATTHEW 20:1–16 (RSV)

M ost biblical commentators believe that with this parable Jesus sought to teach that God's grace is equally available to all, regardless of when or how one has come before God's throne. But when we look a bit closer, we see that this parable is not simply a story of divine benevolence; it is also fraught with the horrors of economic violence, depicting as it does an arbitrary and capricious landowner and humiliated, exploited workers desperate for work. But most significantly, our closer look reveals that the "householder" that is thought to represent God is not so benevolent as was previously thought, but rather is haughty (v. 4), insulting (v. 6), and dismissive (v. 14). Worst of all, he is exploitative, not only because the denarius a day he offers the workers is not a living wage, but because by even offering such an inadequate wage he knowingly exploits their desperation. After all, given the high unemployment reflected in verse 3, the workers would have no choice but to accept his terms, and he knew it. Therefore, when read on its own terms, it becomes clear that Matthew 20:1–16 is less about extolling the benevolence of God's grace than about decrying economic violence and exploitation.

In the traditional reading of this parable, the "householder" is God, the first workers called are the Jews, and those chosen thereafter are Christians. From this perspective, the message the parable appears to convey is that the benevolent God refuses to value those chosen first—the Jews—over those who come later. In this sense, it can be understood to be a statement about the universality of God's grace. That does seem to be the parable's meaning on one level. But when it is remembered that in the parable Jesus speaks of dispossessed peasants standing idle, exploited and humiliated, desperately seeking work, and that those to whom he told the parable, like his every audience, were poor peasants and dispossessed farmers, many of whom had themselves stood idle, exploited and humiliated, desperately hoping for work, it becomes clear that the details of the parable are not simply background, but in a very real way are crucial to its meaning. Indeed, in one sense these details are the point of the parable. I began to understand this one morning when the passage inexplicably brought to mind images from my own childhood.

When I was nine years old, my father, a self-employed brick mason, began taking me to work with him during my school vacations, not only in the summer, but in the spring and winter, too. Our workdays always began with a stop at a particular corner in a poor section of town. Although we never arrived later than 6:15 A.M., fifty or more men in dusty work clothes would already be there, greasy brown-bag lunches in hand. My father would call out, as would the drivers of the other trucks easing up to the curb, and an eager worker or two would scramble into our open truck bed to huddle against the morning chill as we sped down the highway. My father usually told the workers the wage he was willing to pay before we drove off, though sometimes he forgot until we'd arrived at the work site, which might be an hour and a half away; yet I don't remember any worker ever asking what he'd be paid at the day's end. Each apparently trusted, or at least hoped, to be treated fairly, but all seemed resigned to take whatever they could get. Apparently they were relieved just to get a day's work.

While reading the parable, I began to see the vacant, haunted eyes of those desperate men of my youth who wanted nothing more than a chance to earn enough for a day's groceries for their families. It became clear to me that this sense of desperation and resignation is what the workers in Jesus' parable must have also experienced. The difference is that my father never exploited or humiliated the few men who from time to time were in his employ. The same cannot be said of the householder in Jesus' parable.

The term rendered as "householder" in the Revised Standard Version is a translation of the Greek term *oikodespotes*. *Oikos* means "house." *Despotes* is the source of our word "master," or "despot." The parable tells us that in addition to any house or houses he might have possessed, this *oikodespotes* also owns vineyards so expansive that he must return repeatedly for laborers to work them. This describes a large estate rather than a simple farm. And because the estate produces a large crop, it might be considered a plantation. This would make the owner a "plantation master" or "planta-

tion owner," which is certainly a less benign term than "householder,"
but, as we shall see, it is also a more accurate one.

Jesus begins the parable by explaining that what he is about to say is an
analogy for the kingdom of heaven. He then goes on to detail the ways this
rich plantation owner interacts with desperate workers milling around the
marketplace. The owner sends the first round of workers into his vineyard
after agreeing to pay them each a denarius for their day's work. However,
this "agreement" is misleading. A denarius a day was apparently the going
wage for manual labor in Israel at that time, but it was not a *living* wage.
One denarius could barely feed one adult, much less a family. Any wage
that is not a living wage is unjust, no matter what the reason, and to be
forced to accept it is economic violence. Reasonable workers would never
agree to work for a wage that could hardly sustain them and their loved
ones, but they would *accept* it if left no other choice. The plantation owner
knew the workers' desperation and chose to exploit it. After all, the workers would not have been in the marketplace if they had had lands of their
own. They were so desperate that they would have accepted almost any
wage. This is reflected in the response of the other workers hired throughout the day who jumped at the plantation owner's offer without even asking what they'd be paid. They had no choice but to hope he would honor
his pledge to "pay what is right," which he apparently considered his decision alone. After all, he was rich and they were not.

That the plantation owner exploits the workers' desperation is bad
enough, but he adds insult to injury by asking those still hoping for work
why they are standing idle, as if they were unemployed by some choice of
their own, when he knows that almost certainly they are available for hire
because their own lands have been taken from them by one unjust means
or another. The not-so-veiled implication of his question is that they are
lazy; he doesn't even consider that they may have been victimized by rich
folks like him.

When it comes time for the workers to be paid, their hopes are disappointed, for the plantation owner's idea of what is "right" differs from
their own. Although the first group of workers has "borne the burden of

the day and the scorching heat," he insults their labor by paying them the same as others who have labored fewer hours, some far fewer. Some biblical commentators claim that the plantation owner's decision to pay all the workers the same is a positive egalitarian gesture. But one wonders how this could be so given that he makes no similar equalizing gesture with his own wealth and status. Many of these same commentators characterize the workers as resentful of their fellow toilers' good fortune, if it can be called that. But the workers do not protest his decision because their fellow workers—some of whom might be relatives and all of whom are neighbors—are compensated for their labor. The text says that they grumbled against the plantation owner, not each other. In other words, they were angry with the plantation owner because he did not do what was right, although he had pledged that he would.

If the actions of this plantation owner have not yet cast doubt upon the notion that he is a character representing God, what Jesus recounts next surely does. He tells us that rather than consider the validity of the workers' complaint, the plantation owner singles out their most vocal spokesman.

The first tip-off of the plantation owner's animus is that he addresses the worker he has singled out as *hetaire*, which, though usually translated as "friend," actually is not a term of affection. Rather, it is a distancing term, like "fella" or "buddy." It is the same term Jesus uses in Matthew 26:50 to greet Judas when Judas confronts him with Roman soldiers in tow. "Fella," the plantation owner says predictably, "I'm doing you no wrong," as if having the upper hand gives him the natural right to decide right and wrong. He then asks, "Didn't you agree with me to work for a denarius?" knowing full well that the desperate workers had no choice. If the plantation owner really wanted to do right, at that moment he would simply have paid his workers a living wage.

Then the plantation owner uses the strategy that managers and bosses still use today with great success: he makes an example of the spokesman by firing him. "Take your things and leave," he says. He then tells the worker why he is firing him: because he, the boss, does as he pleases. "Can't I do what I choose with what is mine?"

Then the final insult. He accuses the fired worker of jealousy, perhaps even evil intent, while declaring that he himself is "good." Apparently his self-definition justifies everything he does. Such a notion does bespeak a God complex, but its arrogance and callousness do not reflect the merciful, loving Father of Jesus. Biblical scholar Warren Carter puts it well: "[W]e should not assume that the householder is God . . . [C]lues such as his large accumulation of land and subsequent inconsistent behavior in not addressing the inequality of his own wealth suggest that that identification would be inappropriate." In fact, the plantation owner of Matthew 20 resembles nothing so much as one of today's arrogant and haughty corporate managers.

The parable ends with a class-reversal motif: "So the last will be first and the first last." When we see that a similar prediction of class reversal in Matthew 19:30 precedes the parable, the meaning becomes clear: Jesus is likening the kingdom of God to a greater reality that will correct economic injustice and economic exploitation. It is true that Jesus' prediction that one class ("the last") will take the place of another ("the first") does not seem to reflect the rejection of class hierarchies that he exhibits elsewhere. But critiquing class hierarchies per se is not Jesus' focus here; his immediate point is that God's kingdom will free the beleaguered workers from their exploitation and oppression. In effect Jesus is telling all who are exploited and oppressed that although this is the way things are now, it will not be so in the kingdom of God. Jesus' pithy reversal statement, while not an appeal to egalitarianism, explains God's justice in a way that workers would have been able to hear and understand in the heat of their anger, and that would give hope to those who had given up on having a better life.

And yes, Jesus' hearers certainly would have been angry by the parable's end. They would have angrily recognized the down-to-earth reality of exploitative wages and the arrogant, insulting demeanor of the plantation owner and his sense of entitlement to do as he chose. After all, they experienced it every day. But although they lived it, it is likely that until that moment many workers hadn't really understood all the dynamics of their plight, because in their scuffle to survive they had little opportunity to reflect upon the forces that tossed them to and fro. Lacking time and perspective to contemplate their predicament, more often than not they simply never identified the causes of the economic violence that engulfed them. Most had simply accepted their lot as the order of things, as if their plight was natural and God-ordained. This is how workers in peasant cultures throughout history have typically responded to oppressive circumstances. There is no reason to think that the response of the peasant workers in first-century Israel was different.

Jesus knew the beleaguered workers could never change their circumstances if they did not understand their own reality and the reasons for it. So he grasped their attention with a parable that highlighted the true injustice of their common situation. He painted in bold strokes the aspects of their plight they had not always focused on, if they ever had: the ruling elites' notion that their wealth gave them the right to play God, deciding "what is right" based on their own interests alone. He showed how the elites hid their role in the workers' pain and desperation by blaming them for their own plight. He made plain how the rich feigned ignorance of the cause of the masses' poverty and suffering when they knew that it was their own schemes and machinations that robbed the people of their ancestral homes and patrimonies. He brought to light how the rich anointed their own evil as good, and the workers' righteous discontent as evil. Jesus' process of deciphering, explaining, and laying bare the forces of economic violence that kept the people desperate and poor laid the groundwork for them to challenge those forces.

This strategy, then, treats the people's needs as holy by seeking to raise their consciousness of the forces that hold them hostage to poverty and oppression and want. It is an important tactic for those of us today who also seek to treat the people's needs as holy by freeing them from their economic shackles. We must be unrelenting in our efforts to lay bare for all to see the factors that today hold people hostage: the corporate cronyism, the unjust tax policies that benefit the haves and the have-mores beyond all others, the unjust social and economic barriers to upward mobility, and the arrogance and duplicity of the modern-day corporate plantation owners and the politicians in cohoots with them who define good and evil not by the tenets of the biblical faith they profess to believe, but by whatever serves their own selfish interests. Like Jesus, we must help workers understand what is their fair share of the fruits of their labor, how to get it, and what—and who—stands in the way. Although in this parable Jesus explains, in effect, that in the kingdom of God economic injustice will be vanquished, he was not suggesting that the victory will be accomplished by supernatural means. By highlighting in Matthew 20:13–16 the practice of those in control to isolate and punish spokespersons in order to intimidate workers and discourage them from actively opposing their mistreatment, Jesus demonstrates the need for workers to stand together in solidarity. Remember, in the parable the workers do not blame each other for the injustice of their treatment, they blame the plantation owner. Jesus tells his hearers that despite the plantation owner's machinations, ultimately justice prevailed. Those the plantation owner exploited—the last and the lowest—became the first. In this way the parable imparts a valuable lesson to laborers of all times and all circumstances: if together they steadfastly stand for justice by confronting the plantation owners of their own time with boldly prophetic sensibilities, ultimately they will experience the justice promised by the kingdom of God.

SINCE PRESIDENT RONALD REAGAN made union busting acceptable and perhaps even patriotic by destroying the Professional Air Traffic Controllers Organization (PATCO) in 1981, workers who stand up for their rights have been routinely demonized, while corporate managers have been lionized. As a result of the onslaught, the number of unionized wage and salaried workers in the United States has dwindled from 20 percent in 1983 to just 12.5 percent in 2004. Workers seeking better living standards are now blamed for corporations' poor financial performances, while the right of corporate heads to live in luxury is seldom questioned, despite the fact that many corporate executives receive salaries hundreds of times greater than that of the average wage earner. Indeed, corporate CEOs and high-flying investment bankers have become virtual cult heroes in America for increasing corporate profits not by better management, but by looting companies and destroying their workers' source of income and even the pensions many worked long and hard to earn. These latter-day captains of industry seem to live by the motto of Gordon Gekko in the movie *Wall Street*: "Greed is good."

In the history of America there have been many men and women, some known, some nameless, who have struggled to decipher and address the factors that undergird the oppression and exploitation of American workers and working poor. Walter Reuther and Cesar Chavez were two of them.

Walter Reuther is among the foremost figures who have treated American workers' needs as holy. His road to labor leadership began in earnest on May 26, 1937, with a self-sacrificial act. When he and some colleagues appeared at the gate of the Ford Motor Company's huge River Rouge plant to distribute leaflets calling the workers there to claim the full measure of their power and their rights with the slogan "Unionism, not Fordism," for their efforts they were beaten nearly to death by company goons. However, the beating seemed only to increase Reuther's fervor for justice for America's workers.

Having become president of a United Auto Workers (UAW) local at age twenty-nine, Reuther went on to become one of the union's most important strategists, directing sit-down strikes and various tactics to organize auto plant workers into unions. In 1946, he was elected national president of the UAW with the pledge to work for "a labor movement whose philosophy demands that it fight for the welfare of the public at large."

For the rest of his life, Reuther kept his pledge. Through his visionary leadership he helped workers to understand not only that they deserved better wages and better working conditions than corporate America had ever allowed them, but also that they had the power to demand them. Under his leadership, the UAW won more concessions than most workers had dared to imagine. A 1948 settlement with General Motors established the concept of an annual wage increase tied to a quarterly cost-of-living adjustment, which over the years has protected workers' purchasing power and significantly raised workers' living standards. His "We Live by the Year—We Should Be Paid by the Year" campaign for a guaranteed annual wage resulted in the Supplementary Unemployment Benefit, which requires that 95 percent of wages be replaced in the event of layoffs.

So many of the benefits that workers now take for granted are the result of Reuther's passionate leadership. Comprehensive health-care programs; tuition-refund programs; life insurance; profit sharing; severance pay; prepaid legal-service plans; bereavement pay; jury-duty pay; improvements in vacations, holidays, and rest breaks; healthy and safe working environments; and sound grievance procedures all added immeasurably to the well-being, safety, dignity, and self-respect of America's workers. Reuther even helped to establish one of the nation's earliest HMOs.

Consistent with one of his favorite sayings, "Progress with the community—not at the expense of the community," Reuther didn't limit his efforts to increasing the well-being of autoworkers. He called for a citizens' crusade against poverty, for federal housing and education aid, and for a national minimum wage for all workers. One of the few non–African Americans invited to speak at the March on Washington, Reuther was an active advocate for civil rights who worked closely with Martin Luther King, Jr., and even organized the Citizens Committee for Equal Opportunity, which was an early advocate of affirmative action.

Reuther's oft-expressed philosophy bespoke his dedication to treating the people's needs as holy: "There is no greater calling than to serve your fellow men. There is no greater contribution than to help the weak. There is no greater satisfaction than to have done it well."

BUT IN THE ANNALS of modern American struggles to attain justice for workers by laying bare the economic forces that controlled their lives there was a crucial labor movement much closer to the setting of Jesus' parable: a labor movement that served vineyard workers.

Until the first half of the twentieth century, the treatment of migrant workers in America was a sad and sordid tale. With no rights or legal protections, migrant workers were treated as beasts of burden, typically working "from can't see in the morning to can't see at night," as the saying goes, for virtual slave wages. Migrant workers were physically abused and maltreated, their children given little access to schools and education. They were denied adequate health care, denied decent housing, and routinely denied due process under the law. Despite the inhumanity of their treatment by the owners of the fields and vineyards in which they labored, few workers were willing to fight for better conditions. Some feared losing their jobs, others accepted their plight as their unalterable lot in life. With the exception of black sharecroppers in the rural South, there was no group of workers in America more aptly described by Jesus' term "the least of these" than America's migrant workers. It was in this setting that Cesar Chavez answered the call to treat the people's needs as holy by empowering them to free themselves from a system that treated them as less than human.

Cesar Chavez was born in 1927 on the outskirts of Yuma, Arizona. As the son of a prosperous merchant, he had a comfortable early life. In 1937, however, his father lost everything in a business deal gone bad. By 1938, Cesar, his parents, and his six siblings had joined the three hundred thousand itinerant migrant workers in California. From then on, in their seasonal treks to the crops in need of harvest, Cesar and his siblings attended sixty-five different schools; none of them graduated from high school. After a stint in the U.S. Navy during World War II, Chavez returned to the fields of California. Deeply disturbed by the California grape growers' treatment of workers, Chavez joined the labor movement. Picking apricots by day and organizing workers to vote in the evenings, Chavez registered more than two thousand workers in two months. Within a few years he was a full-time labor organizer for the local Community Service Organization (CSO). In 1962, he left the CSO to form the National Farm Workers Association (NFWA).

The NFWA, which became the United Farm Workers (UFW) in 1973, was a tireless fighter for the rights of migrant workers. As its president, Chavez led a number of successful marches, demonstrations, and worker strikes for a living wage and humane working conditions, including boycotts of California grapes and lettuce that gained nationwide support.

The greed and recalcitrance of the fruit growers were by far the main obstacles to fair wages and better living conditions for farmworkers, but they were not the only obstacles. Traveling from camp to camp to recruit members for the new union, Chavez initially found it very difficult to persuade migrant workers to fight for their rights. After generations of abuse and maltreatment, some had become resigned to their plight as inevitable, a part of the natural, unchanging order of things. Others, feeling powerless, feared losing their jobs if they protested their mistreatment. Like Jesus, Chavez had to help the workers understand the gross injustice of their situation and recognize that they had the same right to a decent quality of life as anyone else in America. Chavez accomplished this by explaining the unjust machinations, ploys, and divisive actions that employers used to keep them poor and downtrodden, and by describing the lives they could have under just and equitable conditions. But most important, through long and patient activism, he raised the consciousness of farmworkers so that together they had the power to claim those lives.

Under Chavez's leadership, unprecedented rights were achieved for migrant workers:

- the first collective bargaining agreement between farmworkers and growers in the United States
- the first farm contracts requiring rest periods, clean drinking water, hand-washing facilities, protective clothing against pesticide spraying, and outright banning of DDT and other dangerous pesticides
- contracts that replaced contractors or "jobbers" with union hiring halls, thus guaranteeing farmworkers' seniority rights and job security
- comprehensive union health benefits for farmworkers and their families
- the first union contracts regulating safety and sanitary conditions in farm labor camps, as well as banning discrimination against and sexual harassment of female workers
- abolition of the short-handled hoe that had crippled generations of farmworkers
- extension of state coverage for unemployment, disability and

worker's compensation benefits, and public assistance for farmworkers

Cesar Chavez never wavered from his quest to treat the people's needs
as holy, and he sacrificed his own well-being when necessary. During his
career as a leader and activist, he was beaten and jailed repeatedly. He also
went on extended fasts to bring attention to abuses and bad working conditions. One fast lasted for more than a month. Cesar Chavez's struggle to
treat the people's needs as holy continued until his death in 1993. "[F]ight-
ing for social justice," he said, ". . . is one of the profoundest ways in which
man can say yes to man's dignity." Or, as Jesus put it, to "love your neighbor as yourself."

IN THE PARABLE of the workers in the vineyard Jesus reflected his profound concern that workers and laborers be treated with fairness and justice. He also expressed his outrage at the economic violence with which
the wealthy enrich themselves at the expense of those who bear "the burden of the day and the scorching heat" of labor, be that heat literal or fig-
urative. He raised the people's consciousness of the forces that conspired
to exploit them and brought to their attention the solidarity through
which workers could change their condition. The parable of the workers
in the vineyard is a profound expression of Jesus' care that the real needs
of all who labor should be treated as holy.

STRATEGY FOUR
Call the Demon by Name

They came to the other side of the sea, to the country of the
Gerasenes. And when he had stepped out of the boat, immediately
a man out of the tombs with an unclean spirit met him. He lived
among the tombs; and no one could restrain him any more, even
with a chain; for he had often been restrained with shackles and
chains, but the chains he wrenched apart, and the shackles he
broke in pieces; and no one had the strength to subdue him.
Night and day among the tombs and on the mountains he was
always howling and bruising himself with stones. When he saw
Jesus from a distance, he ran and bowed down before him; and he
shouted at the top of his voice, "What have you to do with me,
Jesus, Son of the Most High God? I adjure you by God, do not
torment me." For Jesus had said to him, "Come out of the man,
you unclean spirit!" Then Jesus asked him, "What is your name?"
He replied, "My name is Legion; for we are many. He begged
him earnestly not to send them out of the country.

MARK 5:1–10

This passage is almost universally understood to be an account of
a healing—an exorcism—of a man gone wild with self-destruction. Mark tells us that the cause of the man's madness is possession by a
demon, an "unclean spirit." This understanding of Mark 5:1–13 is pretty
much self-evident, except for one small detail: the "unclean spirit" does
not ask Jesus not to send *him* out of the *man;* it asks Jesus "not to send *them*
out of the *country."*

Why is this significant? Because it informs us that the "man" in this account is not an individual man at all, but a *collective* man, a representative character meant to stand for the "country," or the people, of Israel. Similarly, the "unclean spirit" that has possessed the people and caused such self-destructive chaos among them is not an individual demon, but also a collective presence. Who or what was that collective demonic presence that had possessed the country? The demon identifies itself as "Legion; for we are many." At the time that Jesus lived, "legion" referred to none other than the Roman legions, the powerful and brutal Roman army, which, in fact, had occupied—was in possession of—Israel. Thus, what at first glance seems to be an account of an exorcism turns out actually to be a parable indicting the Roman military for its role in the upheaval that was devastating the social fabric of Israel.

Mark's veiled description of his country as having gone wild with self-destruction corresponds to the reality of his situation. In chapter 2 we saw that first-century Israel was indeed a country beset by an unclean spirit that expressed itself through a number of extreme social pathologies. Recall that the crime rate in Israel, particularly in the rural areas that were home to Jesus and virtually everyone he taught and ministered to, was so high that Josephus said it looked like the country had been ravaged by a war. The numerous matter-of-fact references in the Gospels to insanity, lameness, depression, abject dejection, bands of robbers, dispossessed farmers, enslaved debt defaulters, diseased beggars, disrupted menstrual cycles (which, as we have seen, are often the result of extreme social tensions and anxiety), and revolutionary upheavals depict a society that in many ways appeared to be coming apart at the seams.

Adding to the chaos was the fact that Israel's ruling class, principally the Jerusalem priestly aristocracy, participated in the dispossession and financial ruin of their own people by helping Israel's Roman overlords collect taxes set at onerous levels, this in addition to the taxes and dues extracted by the Temple hierarchy itself. These actions by the authorities triggered uprisings among the most desperate and bold, and caused widespread silent alienation among those unwilling to risk the torture and execution that awaited failed rebels. Furthermore, the priests' practice of tying their own welfare to maintaining the good graces of their people's oppressors—along with the historical phenomenon of attempts by priests and members of the Jewish upper class to assimilate into the culture of their people's oppressors—indicates anything but social stability.

Another factor corresponding to historical reality was, on the one hand, a pervasive feeling of powerlessness among the people to resist Roman might in any of its forms and, on the other hand, a tendency to blame themselves for the wretchedness of their lives as God's judgment for their moral failings.

Taken together, these factors indeed reflect a society in dire disruption and in the process of headlong self-destruction. So although on one level Mark 5:1–13 is an account of an exorcism, on another level it is a radical political parable in the guise of a healing story, a parable that tells the people of Jesus that it is not God's displeasure that has bedeviled them, but the misdeeds of those who lord it over them.

That is the reason Jesus tells this powerful parable: to free the people from the stultifying grip of self-blame by helping them identify the real causes of their problems. He reminds them that although ultimately they are responsible for their own lives and accomplishments, the wretchedness of their plight is not the result of irresponsibility or laziness or some inherent failing of their own. Rather, it is the result of exploitation and maltreatment by those who rule them. Jesus reminds the people that they have been abused, that they have been sinned against, that they have been victimized by those whom the fruits of their labor have so greatly enriched. He helps them to understand that circumstances are as they are not because there is something wrong with them, but because there is something wrong with those who oppress them.

Jesus does not soften his explanation with euphemisms or polite descriptions; he does not try to qualify his words or make them more palatable by "giving them balance" or by citing mistakes that the people have made. He wants his point to be fully clear. So he calls the Roman military presence in Israel exactly what it has proven to be to his people: a destructive, demonic, unclean presence. In other words, in perfect prophetic fashion, Jesus causes the demon to be known by its name. He speaks as a prophet should speak: boldly and on point, identifying the demon in no uncertain terms. He blames the people's plight not on the *victimized*, but on the *victimizer*, the Roman legions. He cuts through all excuses, obfuscation, and mealy-mouthed explanations to tell the people the unvarnished truth.

But it is not enough to help the people identify the source of their problems; they must also be helped to see that they have the power to solve their problems. So Jesus' parable illustrates that the people can break the demonic chains that bind them if they stop dissipating their power through self-defeating attitudes and behaviors. Mark buttresses Jesus' point by brilliantly demystifying the power of the Romans, ridiculing them as willing swine: "Send us into the swine; let us enter them" (Mark 5:12).

In *The Wretched of the Earth*, his book about the effects of the brutality of colonialism on subjugated people, the Caribbean psychiatrist Frantz Fanon relates the account of a young Algerian man who was self-hating and self-destructive. After extensive therapy, Fanon concluded that at the root of the young man's self-destructive behavior was torturous guilt at his inability to protect his people from the pain of their subjugation. What our Mark 5 passage and Fanon's account have in common is that they attribute their subjects' pathological behavior to the strain of living under the brutal military occupation of their respective homelands. When Mark's account is reread in this light, it becomes even clearer that it is the suffering of the people of Israel that the story describes.

WHAT JESUS' RESPONSE in Mark 5 tells us is that in our quest to treat the people's needs as holy we must be unfailingly prophetic. That is to say that we, too, must bring to light the true identity of the demons that cause the people's suffering. It is true that no one, whether rich or poor, strong or weak, should ever be absolved of responsibility for his or her own actions. And it is important that those in need be counseled to do as much as they can to help themselves. But it is more than important, it is our sacred prophetic duty, to identify and call by name the policies, governmental officials, corporate officers, events and developments, and greedy elites that are responsible for the impoverishment of the people. Calling the demon by name is an integral part of our vocation to treat the people's needs as holy. Thus, we must call by name every factor, condition, person, or persons that do not treat the people's needs as holy. We must call the demon by its name: evil.

We must call by name tax laws that favor the interests of the rich: evil.

We must call by name corporate boards and executives who underpay their workers while giving corporate executives annual salaries and bonuses so large that it would take the average worker centuries of labor to earn as much: evil.

We must call by name those who claim to hold the people's needs as holy, but instead betray them: evil.

We must call evil by name to remind the people that public officials are supposed to be *public servants*, and remind public servants that it is the welfare of the many that they are to serve, not the whims and wants of the privileged few.

We must call the demon by name in our churches, call by name ministers' crass materialism and their lack of prophetic engagement; must call by name their collusion with forces that exploit and oppress those whom they are supposed to serve.

We must call by name the perversion of Jesus' Gospel by prosperity preachers who blame the people for their sickness and poverty, instead of decrying the demonic mistreatment of the poor by those who hold only their own needs as holy.

We must call evil by name when pensions are squandered, when Americans are dispossessed of their livelihoods by greedy executives who export American jobs to regions in which they can better exploit workers' desperation.

We must call all the callous and uncaring practices and policies, the betrayals of trust, and the exploitation of weakness and despair what they really are: evil. Not just politics, not just benign neglect, not just thoughtlessness, not even gross selfishness, but *evil*. If anyone hurts others, limits

their life chances or denies them the fullest fruits of life for the sole purpose of enriching himself and those he counts as his own, by biblical definition this is *evil.*

UPSETTING THE STATUS QUO by boldly championing the people's needs
might cause some to recoil for fear of a backlash and further repression by
those in power. Yet calling the demon by name is an undeniable responsibility of those who seek to truly follow Jesus. The fact of a hungry child in
a land of plenty is evil. The fact of an elder facing the twilight of her years
without pension, health care, secure housing, and respectful treatment is
not just tragic, it is evil. If we are to follow Jesus we must call evil by its
rightful name.

ON AUGUST 29, 2005, one of the most powerful and destructive storms
ever to hit the United States struck the Gulf Coast. Hardest hit was the city
of New Orleans, most of which sat on land that was below sea level. When
the storm destroyed its system of protective levees, 80 percent of the city
found itself underwater. The city's sewage, clean water, and transportation
infrastructures were destroyed, along with some 200,000 homes in the
greater New Orleans area. Although hundreds of thousands of New Orleans residents fled as the storm approached, an estimated one hundred
thousand stayed behind, most because they were too poor or too sick to
leave, or had nowhere else to go. More than a thousand of these New Orleanians were killed and tens of thousands were rendered homeless by the
storm's destruction. By any measure, Hurricane Katrina was one of the
most catastrophic events to hit American soil. But what followed made a
terrible situation absolutely shameful.

    A horrified nation watched as those in New Orleans who had survived
the naked horror of Katrina's wrath were then forced to endure hunger,
thirst, decomposing corpses in their midst, exposure to withering heat,
and lack of even the most basic medical care while awaiting rescue by the
Federal Emergency Management Agency (FEMA). Incredibly, FEMA's help

did not arrive in New Orleans until days later. By then, oppressive conditions had become insufferable and absolutely inhuman. Most survivors had not had food or water since the levees broke. Untold numbers died from hunger, thirst, and lack of medical care. The photograph of a woman literally dying of thirst appeared on the cover of *Time* magazine. She died moments after the photograph was taken.

As the nation watched the unfolding of the ghastly scenario in New Orleans, rather than asking why so many Americans were left to endure so much for so long without even the most basic federal assistance, instead some influential journalists immediately demonized the hurricane's victims by blaming them for causing their own suffering.

After televised images made it clear that most of the storm's victims were poor, radio personality Rush Limbaugh grudgingly admitted the possibility that many of those stranded in the city were unable to flee the storm because they were too poor to own cars. Yet, incredibly, he still managed to play the "race card" and fault the underprivileged people of New Orleans for their own plight. "Well, why is that? Why can't they afford [cars]?" he asked. "What is it about New Orleans that doesn't pay? It's a sixty-seven percent black population. They have lots of black-run businesses. Why is this—they don't pay well enough down there?"

The Fox News Channel's Bill O'Reilly further demonized the impoverished among the hurricane victims as drug abusers: "Many, many, many of the poor in New Orleans . . . weren't going to leave no matter what you did. They were drug-addicted. They weren't going to get turned off from their source. They were thugs, whatever." Like Limbaugh, O'Reilly placed the blame for the horrendous treatment of the poor in New Orleans squarely on their own suffering backs: "[E]very American kid should be required to watch videotape of the poor in New Orleans and see how they suffered because they couldn't get out of town. And then, every teacher should tell the students, 'If you refuse to learn, if you refuse to work hard, if you become addicted, if you live a gangsta-life, you will be poor and powerless just like many of those in New Orleans."

Another Fox News commentator, Fred Barnes, took a different approach. Downplaying the hurricane victims' pain, he charged that they had, in effect, cheated other taxpayers by choosing to live in New Orleans in the first place: "They know they're going to flood. And when these things happen, they want the taxpayers all over the country to pay."

Predictably, some fundamentalist Christians hailed the storm as divine judgment on New Orleans for moral transgressions. The Web site of one fundamentalist church read, "Pray for more dead bodies floating on the . . . rancid waters of New Orleans."

Even Rev. Rick Warren, author of the hugely successful *The Purpose Driven Life*, though apparently well meaning, nonetheless seemed to place the responsibility upon the victims for alleviating their own plight, while attempting to blunt their ire against the government with such advice as "Play it down and pray it up."

In the meantime, Homeland Security chief Michael Chertoff and FEMA head Michael Brown, those who were primarily charged with rescuing the storm's survivors, tried to explain away their agencies' badly delayed response to the horrific conditions by attributing it to bureaucratic snafus and negligence on the part of state and local officials. Yet two days after Katrina hit land, as survivors in New Orleans were literally dying of thirst and lack of medical care, Chertoff announced that he was "extremely pleased with the response" of the government. Even as more stranded survivors perished from the government's neglect, President George W. Bush publicly praised FEMA chief Brown: "Brownie, you're doing a heck of a job." Bush even claimed that no one had anticipated the breach of the levees, despite years of public studies and reports as recent as one day prior to the hurricane's landing that the levees could not protect the city from a major storm, and despite, as well, urgent warnings by government meteorologists that Hurricane Katrina would be one of the worst storms this nation had ever seen.

In the news media, sensationalized reports were issued in print and on the air that made the hurricane victims look more like misfits and criminals than the law-abiding taxpayers that most were. Reporters claimed that the city was overwhelmed with roving armed gangs and large-scale shoot-outs. There were accounts of multiple rapes and numerous murders at the Convention Center and the Superdome, where tens of thousands of survivors were warehoused. These reports were later found to be false. In fact, after everyone was evacuated from the Convention Center and the Superdome, New Orleans Police Superintendent Edwin P. Compass admitted, "We have no official reports to document any murder. Not one official report of rape or sexual assault."

Unfortunately, the residue of these false portrayals of the hurricane victims lingered. Nor did the media balance their reports with the fact that some of those who attacked law enforcement authorities actually believed they were acting in self-defense. After being held at gunpoint for days without food or water, many in the crowds concluded they had been taken to the shelters to die.

To add insult to injury, the desperate efforts of thirsting, starving people to find food, water, medicine, and a change of clothing were called "looting," even though in the storm's aftermath most had not had food or water for days, many had lost their shoes in the swirling waters, and nearly all still wore the same filthy clothing they had worn for days.

In the midst of these accusations, however, other voices arose that observed that it was not coincidental that so many of those trapped in the flooded city were poor. They realized that it was not laziness or drug addiction that had trapped so many New Orleanians, but poverty. Many journalists began to refuse to demonize the victims and commenced to acknowledge the role of economic deprivation in the tragedy.

CNN's Paula Zahn pointedly asked FEMA director Michael Brown, "And finally tonight, sir, you said earlier today that part of the blame for the—what you think will be an enormous death toll in New Orleans—rests with the people who did not evacuate the city, who didn't heed the warnings. Is that fair, to blame the victims, many of whom tell us they had no way out, they had no cars of their own, and that public assistance wasn't provided to get them out early?"

Wil Haygood declared in the *Washington Post*, "To those who wonder why so many stayed behind when push came to water's mighty shove here, those who were trapped have a simple explanation: their nickels and dimes and dollar bills simply didn't add up to stage a quick evacuation."

Cynthia Tucker of the *Atlanta Journal-Constitution* wrote, "The aftermath of Hurricane Katrina—with its pathetic images of desperately poor people, mostly black people, stuck in New Orleans without food, water or adequate shelter after all the affluent people had fled—should come as no surprise. This is a natural consequence of a political and social culture that has decreed: You're poor? Why would anyone want to be poor? Tough luck. You're on your own."

Chris Lawrence of CNN described "babies three, four, five months old, living in these horrible conditions," and said: "These people are being forced to live as animals."

A number of elected officials spoke up as well. On ABC's *This Week*, Senator Barack Obama of Illinois said, "What's true in this country is what's true across the world, which is in the midst of natural disasters the poor and vulnerable end up getting hit the hardest." Obama then voiced his frustration. "I mean, it's puzzling," he said, "given [the president's] immediate response during 9/11, that he did not feel a greater sense of empathy towards the folks that were experiencing this enormous disaster."

Congressman John Lewis of Georgia wrote in *Newsweek*:

> It's so strange that when we have something like this happening, the president gets two ex-presidents—his father and Bill Clinton— to raise money. What they propose to do is good, and I appreciate all the work the private sector and the faith-based community are doing. But when we get ready to go to war, we don't go around soliciting resources with a bucket or an offering plate . . . By next year we'll have spent $400 billion to $500 billion in Afghanistan and Iraq. That money could be used to help rebuild the lives of people.

Some journalists in both the print and broadcast media bravely noted the difference in media portrayals of similar behavior in blacks and whites: when desperate blacks located much-needed supplies, they were said to have "looted" the goods; when desperate whites did the same, they were said to have "found" the goods. The rapper Kanye West used the platform of his fame to issue a similar indictment on a live September 3, 2005, fundraiser on NBC: "I hate the way they portray us in the media. If you see a black family it says they are looting. If you see a white family it says they are looking for food."

A physician from New York who was stranded in a hotel on Canal Street, one of the major retail areas in New Orleans, explained in an e-mail to his family, friends, and everyone else he could reach, "Most of it is not malicious looting. These are poor and desperate people with no housing and no medical care and no food or water trying to take care of themselves and their families."

David Corn, Washington editor of *The Nation* magazine, spoke to the accounts of looting plainly and passionately: "If I were stuck in New Orleans, waiting for help from a government that had failed me, and my family was without water, food or clothes, I'd grab what I could from where I could. I'd worry about payment later . . . Who would watch their kids go hungry rather than break a window at Winn-Dixie?"

Even several members of a group who are usually notorious for their narcissism and lack of social political involvement—young sports figures—came to the hurricane victims' defense. A number of NBA All-Stars, including Kobe Bryant, staged a fund-raising exhibition game. And Washington Wizards basketball star Etan Thomas publicly declared, "If I was down there, and starving for five days, after suffering that type of devastation, and I saw some armed troops coming down not with food or water or supplies but with guns drawn trying to enforce a curfew or whatever they were doing, I would have reacted the same way many of them reacted . . . I understand their frustration."

What is significant here is that courageous women and men of diverse backgrounds and professions stepped out of their own comfort zones to call the demon of callousness and uncaring and racial stereotyping by its real name. That is, they publicly disputed the fallacious assertions of those in power and declared the real causes of the continued suffering of so many. They exposed the mean-spiritedness, faulty logic, and outright duplicity of those who blamed the victims for their own pain. These men and women, journalists and politicians and social commentators and caring observers, upheld Jesus' call to speak up for the poor, to champion the cause of the poor. They used their resources to protect victims from being blamed for their own victimization. They identified the demon as lack of care for the poor and the purposeful, institutionally enforced impoverishment of America's most vulnerable. By raising their pens and their voices, they took the prophetic stance that Jesus calls all of us to take. Admittedly, many of them might not see their actions in that light, but that is not the important thing. What matters is that when it truly counted, these courageous voices of righteous indignation treated the people and their needs as holy.

THE COURAGE AND CONVICTION displayed in defense of the victims of Hurricane Katrina is one of the most recent instances of concerned Americans calling the demon by name. Another example of stepping outside one's own class and comfort zone to call the demon by name can be found almost two centuries ago.

America's turn toward industrialization in the early decades of the nineteenth century worsened the gap between rich and poor. Those benefiting most from the country's growing industrialization saw no reason to entertain questions about the source or the equity of their good fortune. Their first response, therefore, was to deny the existence of poor people. When that ploy didn't work the most prominent voices among the rich elite attributed the increasing poverty in America to the idleness and character failings of the poor themselves. This attitude toward the poor citizens of America, especially the urban poor, gained currency. It eventually became the widely accepted wisdom that the poor were poor as the result of their own depravity. But not every member of the economically privileged classes agreed with these notions or with the way the rich treated the poor. One who disagreed passionately was Mathew Carey.

Mathew Carey was a rich Philadelphia businessman who by all accounts was no social radical. Indeed, the historian Arthur M. Schlesinger, Jr., calls him a man of "conservative political views." Yet, unlike his conservative peers and contemporaries, Carey did not believe that poverty in America was the result of sloth or laziness or moral weakness on the part of the poor. He understood the cause to be the unwillingness of exploitative employers to pay workers a living wage. This so incensed Carey that in the late 1820s, at his own expense, he published a series of pamphlets challenging the industrialists' self-serving misportrayal of the poor and the reasons for their poverty. With such titles as *Appeal to the Wealthy of the Land* and *Letters on the Condition of the Poor*, the pamphlets cited statistics and the accounts of reliable reporters to describe a reality that the rich had tried to deny. He decried the near-starvation wages paid to the workers, arguing that "every principle of honour, justice, and generosity forbids the employer to take advantage of the distress and wretchedness of those he employs, and cut down their wages below the minimum necessary to procure a sufficiency."

He also skewered the "erroneous opinions" the rich held of the poor, including the notion that jobs were available to everyone who wanted to work; that the poor actually "may at all times support themselves comfortably" and therefore had no need for philanthropy or other aid; that their poverty was "chiefly, if not wholly" the result of "their idleness, their dissipation, and their extravagance"; and that any attempts to help to alleviate the plight of the poor were "pernicious, . . . [E]ncouraging the poor to depend on them, they foster their idleness and improvidence."

Carey's impassioned arguments apparently had little effect on the rich elites and industrialists to whom they were addressed. However, the challenges published by Carey and other advocates for the poor did bear fruit: they alerted those workers and small merchants whose circumstances were just a step or two above those of poor Americans to the reality that one day poverty could find them, too. So working people began to form coalitions to protect themselves against the wiles of the rapacious businessmen and industrialists. They formed groups like the Working-Men's Society in New England, which put the blame for the growth of the impoverished classes of America squarely where it belonged, on the "continued prevalence of irrational, anti-republican and unchristian opinions in relation to the worth and respectability of *manual labor*."

Mathew Carey was not poor. He was not a social zealot, nor did he stand to gain financially from an increase in the minimum wage. But he saw the plight of the people around him and was moved to treat their needs as holy. So he lifted his voice and called out the demon of their suffering, not by the false names and descriptions offered by elitist propaganda, but by its real name.

JESUS' TRIUMPH over the unclean spirit in Mark 5:1–13 teaches that, when properly used, the power of Jesus' Gospel can liberate societies from the grip of oppression and the multiple pathologies that oppression causes. Yet just a few verses later Mark tells us that the people were so frightened by such unaccustomed boldness that they rejected Jesus and sent him away. "They began to beg Jesus to leave," verse 17 tells us. In other words, they allowed their feelings of powerlessness to deny them the power of Jesus' prophetic witness. As a result, they remained in thrall to the whims and will of the Roman military and subject to the destructiveness of its unclean spirit.

We who profess to follow the politics of Jesus must not let fear or apathy have the last word. When we call the demon by name, some of us will be asked to take our message elsewhere or to soften the names we call out loud. We must not. We who profess to follow Jesus must continually ask God for the strength to call the demon by name, and then speak it.

STRATEGY FIVE
Save Your Anger for the Mistreatment of Others

And a leper came to him begging on his knees and said to him, "If you will, you can make me clean." Moved with anger, he stretched out his hand and said to him, "I do will; be clean." And immediately the leprosy left him, and he was made clean. And, snorting with anger, he sent him away at once, and said to him, "See that you say nothing to anyone; but go, show yourself to the priest, and offer for your cleansing what Moses commanded, as a testimony against them."

MARK 1:40–45 (MY TRANSLATION
FROM THE ORIGINAL GREEK TEXT)

For centuries Western biblical translators have softened the meaning of words and phrases they thought too challenging to the powers that be. For instance, the word "tyrant" occurs more than four hundred times in the Geneva Bible, an English translation published in 1560, yet the King James Version (KJV), published in 1611, does not use the word even once. Surely the English language had not changed that much in so short a time. Even taking into account the Geneva translators' professed antiroyalist sensibilities, the KJV's refusal to use "tyrant" even once seems to have more to do with King James's unwillingness to see in print a term that could cause Bible readers to cast a jaundiced eye on his own reign.

There are numerous other instances of translations that soften or completely change the meaning of biblical terms and phrases with political implications. By softening politically loaded biblical terms, phrases, and pronouncements, those in political control have sought to keep the gaze of the disprivileged masses focused upon personal morality, rather than upon the realization of the holistic justice of God that frees the oppressed and topples tyrants. One important example of this is the treatment of the Greek word *dikaiosune*, which most versions of the New Testament translate as "righteousness," a term that primarily connotes personal morality. Yet the association of "righteousness" with personal piety obscures *dikaiosune*'s powerful holistic—that is, social *and* spiritual—meaning of "justice." As we have seen, justice is not just pious personal practice; it involves the active, purposeful transformation of the entire social and political order by wresting a fair and equitable distribution of power and resources from those in authority and control.

When *dikaiosune* is translated with its holistic meaning of "justice," it can powerfully transform biblical meaning in ways that are more consistent with Jesus' meaning. At times the differences are profound and far-reaching. For instance, Matthew 6:33, "But seek first the kingdom of God and God's *justice* and all these things will be added to you as well," becomes a clarion call for believers to strive for the justice of God on earth as in heaven. Even the Beatitudes, which are almost universally understood as pertaining solely to personal ethical behavior, instead become instructions in social and political activism, as in Matthew 5:6: "Blessed are those who hunger and thirst for *justice*, for they shall be satisfied." And Jesus' response to John the Baptist's initial reluctance to baptize him becomes a statement of the meaning of Jesus' entire ministry: "Let it be so now; for it is proper for us in this way to fulfill all *justice*" (Matthew 3:15).

Another important example of this phenomenon concerns the rendering of the Greek word *thlipsis* as "tribulation." *Thlipsis* comes from *thlibo*, which, as has been mentioned, means "press or hold down"—that is, "oppress." Thus *thlipsis* should not be translated as "tribulation," which connotes a personal misfortune sometimes occurring by chance, but as "oppression," which is a political phenomenon, the intentional subjugation of less powerful segments of society by those with greater power, often by the most brutal means. When *thlipsis* is correctly translated as "oppression," its political meaning for Jesus can be fully seen. His instruction in John 16:33 for his disciples to continue in faith becomes both a social comment and an exhortation to persevere in their challenge to the current order: "In the world you have *oppression*; but be of good cheer, I have overcome the world." Similarly, the Book of Revelation becomes not just a collection of foretelling and predictions, but a powerful statement to Christians by John the Revelator about social solidarity and resistance in the face of political repression, as in "I, John, your brother, who share with you in Jesus the *oppression* and the kingdom and the patient endurance" (Revelation 1:9), and by Jesus himself, as in "I know your *oppression* and your poverty" (Revelation 2:9).

Not only did translators employ questionable renderings, but early scribes of the New Testament sometimes substituted other words for actual biblical terms and phrases that did not fit their own devotional expectations or political sensibilities. Such is the case with our Mark 1:40–45 text. Those familiar with the passage will notice major differences between my translation from the Greek text that began this discussion and the way the passage appears in the King James Version and most other translations of the Bible; this is because I have tried to correct the *misreadings* so the real meaning of the passage becomes clear.

First, in my translation, 1:41 does not read "moved with *compassion*" or the like, as found in most translations. Instead, it reads "moved with *anger*," from the Greek word *orgistheis* (filled with anger). This term *orgistheis* occurs in a number of authentic early Greek manuscripts of Mark's Gospel and, as we shall see, makes more sense in this context; yet English translations exclusively employ *splagxnistheis* (filled with compassion), the other term found in ancient manuscripts. Although strangely he upholds the traditional reading of the passage, Bruce Metzger, one of the world's foremost experts on the translation of ancient New Testament manuscripts, acknowledges that "it is easy to see why *orgistheis* would have prompted overscrupulous copyists to alter it to *splagxnistheis*." What Metzger refers to are the biblical scribes who were reluctant to see Jesus as subject to the all-too-human emotion of anger. Although the Gospels portray Jesus as an eating, drinking, flesh-and-blood social being, many Christians simply are reluctant to see him as fully human. Mark does not share this aversion,

however, because in several other passages he portrays Jesus as both angry
and indignant, as in Mark 3:5 and 10:14.

Apparently the meaning of the Greek word *embrimasamenos* in Mark 1:43
was also problematic for translators. The term originally described the
snorting of horses. When used to describe human actions and emotions, it
means "to snort with anger," which in turn means that the verse should
read, "snorting with anger." Instead of this correct reading, most translations offer watered-down phrases like "sternly charging him." Evidently
biblical translators have not been able to envision Jesus with any degree of
ire greater than "sternly charging" someone. Because scholars haven't acknowledged Jesus' anger in this instance, they have no idea what his anger
was in response to.

Their misunderstanding of Jesus' anger has had another consequence:
it caused translators to try to make sense of the passage by inserting words
that are not in the original text. The Greek phrase in Mark 1:44 that some
translations, such as the Revised Standard Version, for instance, render "as
a testimony [or proof] to the people" *(eis martyrion autois)* in actuality con-
tains no word that should be translated as "people." Also, the context of
the verse involves opposition, so it should be translated as "a testimony
against them"—against the priests—not "*to* them." In fact, this is the way
the RSV, the King James Version, and most other translations render the
same phrase in Mark 6:11: "And if any place will not receive you and they
refuse to hear you . . . shake the dust from your feet *as a testimony against
them.*" Clearly, the reason most translators have rendered the phrase differently in Mark 1:44 is that they have misunderstood Jesus' anger and the
opponents who caused it.

But why was Jesus angry? Certainly not because of any affront he
might have felt personally. If we know nothing else, we know that whatever anger Jesus displays in the Gospels is never because of his own mistreatment, but is his response to the oppression and mistreatment of
others. Unlike many of his people, particularly the religious authorities,
Jesus was not scandalized because a leper approached him. In fact, Mark
tells us that Jesus felt such empathy that he actually touched the man

(who may not have felt the touch of another for years), thus risking being ostracized himself by the Temple authorities as unclean. So how do we account for Jesus' anger? Surely Jesus was not angry at God for the man's condition. And surely he was not angry at the priests who had declared the man a leper according to their biblical mandate to protect their community from contagious disease. After all, weren't the priests just carrying out the dictates of God in Leviticus 13? These dictates instructed them to examine those with obvious skin disturbances to determine whether they should be declared "clean," and thus be allowed to again enjoy the full fruits of community life, or "unclean," and thus be excluded from the fellowship, companionship, and security of community life.

Leviticus 13 instructs priests in ways of keeping the contagion of leprosy from spreading, and among the ways is condemning those whom the priests determine to be lepers to "live alone in a habitation outside" the community (Leviticus 13:46). Although in Jesus' day men and women were regularly declared to be lepers, there was no clear definition of leprosy. Many skin conditions were identified as leprosy, although in reality some carried no contagion of any kind. Thus, the appearance of even a benign skin condition, like eczema or even psoriasis, could tear a life asunder. Although Leviticus 13 commands that those afflicted with leprosy are to physically live outside the village, nowhere does it counsel that they should be relegated to inferior social status, to living outside the love and care of village life. Indeed, "clean" and "unclean" were never meant to be judgments of character or of anyone's worthiness to be loved and considered and cared for. The concern of the scripture was hygienic and sacramental.

In practice, however, to be declared a leper was not only to be declared unclean; it meant that one was relegated to inferior social status, to be discriminated against, to be excluded, to be treated roughly and rudely. Lepers were required to wear torn clothes, have disheveled hair, and announce their presence by crying out "A leper is coming! A leper is coming!" Those afflicted with leprosy were not welcome in the homes of their neighbors because their presence rendered dwellings so unclean that all cooking, eating, and drinking utensils had to be destroyed, except those made of nonporous stone. Lepers were sometimes even driven away with sticks and rocks if they ventured too close to their neighbors.

But the same biblical prescription that banished those suspected of being lepers also included measures for lepers to be brought back into community life. They could be freed from their forced social exile if a priest examined them and found them to be clean. It may well be that the man confronting Jesus had been branded a leper, treated like a leper, when, in fact, he was not a leper. If so, added to the painful ostracism he had endured would have been the agony that his pleas to be reembraced as a healthy member of society were dismissed by those who could have helped him.

Indeed, Jesus' anger at the leprous man's plight makes the most sense if the man did ask the religious authorities to declare him clean, but their response to him was so lacking in justice and compassion that he was reduce to begging for relief. Indeed, that is what the scripture itself seems to be telling us, for the Greek term *ezebalen* in verse 43, which is usually translated as "sent him away," can also mean "sent him *back*," in which case the verse would read, "And snorting with anger, he sent him back." In fact, some scholars prefer this translation.

The picture that emerges from all these considerations is that Jesus was angry because this man was crying and begging on his knees as the result of his treatment at the hands of the priests.

It is true that lepers had a condition that set them apart, but for Jesus that was no reason for them to be treated as less than others. For they were not just lepers, they were human beings, mothers' sons and daughters, children of God. It was this systematic exclusion and crushing of the spirits of some of God's children by others of God's children, this violation of the fundamental freedom that permeates the Gospels, that fired the anger of Jesus and moved him to counsel this particular victim, and, by extension, all who are victimized by unjust power, to publicly repudiate the agents of injustice and the systems they administer. So when the man fell begging at Jesus' feet, the anger that welled up within Jesus was not anger at the leprous man, but at the authorities' refusal to treat his needs as holy.

But not only did the leper have to beg the religious authorities to be treated like a human being, he also had to give them an offering—that is, pay them—to be treated humanely again. That is what Jesus refers to when he says "offer for your cleansing what Moses commanded." Thus the system subjected the sick to a double oppression. Apparently, this Jesus could not abide.

Jesus' response shows us that there are things that we should be angry about, there are things we must say and do as a testimony against every action, system, policy, and institution that excludes any of God's children from the fullest fruits of life for any reason. That is to say, we must endeavor to love everyone, but we must also take sides. We cannot be against injustice if we do not take the side of justice. We must be angered by the mistreatment of any of God's children. When we see people hurt and excluded in the name of God, we should be angry. When we see Church leaders misleading and exploiting the faithful just like the religious leaders Jesus died opposing, we should get angry. When we see a tiny group of elites take most of the fruits of this nation's economic harvest for themselves, we should get angry. When we see corporate executives being paid in one year's salary what the average worker can never earn in a lifetime, we should get angry. When we see some Americans excluded like lepers from the best this nation has to offer because of their religion or their gender or their ethnicity or their class, we should get angry. But our anger, our outrage, our righteous indignation must remain focused on the perversion of policies and traditions meant for good into laws and practices that do harm and evil. Not on particular groups or personalities, but on unjust policies and practices.

But one thing more. Jesus told the healed man to "say nothing to anyone." Why the secrecy? It is my reading that, for one thing, Jesus wanted no one to have the opportunity to talk the man out of taking the public stand that Jesus instructed. But more important, perhaps, is the implication that Jesus didn't want the man to get caught up in talk without action. Jesus' instruction was to "go, show . . . , offer . . ." In other words, Jesus prescribed action, not talk.

It is important to *talk* about peace and justice and fairness and equity, but we must also *act* against the systems that stand in their way. We must move beyond conference after pious conference, meeting after prolonged meeting, beyond flowery pronouncements and empty talk, so we may again enter into systematic struggle to achieve the justice of God for all. We who claim to have biblical faith must remember, with all passion and faith, that, as Paul put it, "the kingdom of God does not consist in talk, but in power" (1 Corinthians 4:20 [RSV]). It is only through passionate *action* that we will manifest our authority to dismantle every oppressive and exclusionary principality and power that stands in the way of true community.

So what did Jesus do that was strategic? He took his focus off himself and placed it on the plight of the people. Despite the many times he was attacked, called the devil, his life threatened, his intentions questioned, Jesus never expressed anger except at the mistreatment of others. He did not even defend himself when soldiers struck him, as John's Gospel reports; he simply asked them why. Even when he railed at the religious authorities in Matthew 23, it was not because of their opposition to him, but because of their treatment of the people. Jesus saved his energy and his passion to fuel his service.

The example of Jesus tells us that we must be passionately and unwaveringly proactive in our struggle against practices, structures, systems, and attitudes of unjust entitlement that stand in the way of a fully inclusive and loving society. We must respond with passion and righteous anger to every barrier that excludes anyone from the fullest fruits of our nation's bounty. Jesus' example shows us that like his anger our own anger should propel us to go to the seat of unjust power, be it the temple, the church, the statehouse, or the White House, and give our collective testimony against today's priests of oppression that we the people are neither unclean nor unworthy, and therefore we will accept neither second-class status nor second-class treatment.

Jesus models for us that we must be outraged by social practices and policies that favor any of God's children over others. We must be outraged by systematic exclusions, all types of elitism, and every hierarchical structure that allows only the chosen few to fully enjoy the riches of community. And we must use that anger to move us to righteous action.

STRATEGY SIX
Take Blows Without Returning Them

"You have heard that it was said, 'An eye for an eye and a tooth for a tooth.' But I say to you, Do not resist an evildoer. But if anyone strikes you on the right cheek, turn the other also; and if anyone wants to sue you and take your coat, give your cloak as well; and if anyone forces you to go one mile, go also the second mile."

MATTHEW 5:38–41

This brief passage from Jesus' Sermon on the Mount is extraordinary for its ethical and moral content. Some Christians believe that in addition to giving instruction in personal ethics, it also expresses what they understand to be the essence of Jesus' political teaching. They believe that its political message is this: that those who follow Jesus should be stoically passive in the face of oppression. For them, "Do not resist an evildoer" says it all: the proper response to painful political realities is quietism, noninvolvement, and long-suffering.

But when we look at the context in which Jesus was speaking, we see that, contrary to popular opinion, Jesus was not counseling passivity. Those to whom Jesus was speaking were not people with social or political power, but those who lacked it. He was not speaking to the *abusers*, but to the *subjects* of abuse: "If anyone strikes *you* . . . wants to sue *you* . . . forces *you* to go one mile . . ." In other words, Jesus is not making a general statement, he is speaking specifically to those whose social, economic, and political standing make them walking targets of humiliation and abusive power. And what he is telling his poor and powerless hearers is how to exercise power even when they are overpowered.

Take his instruction "if anyone strikes you on the right cheek, turn the other also" (Matthew 5:39). A blow to another's right cheek implies a left-handed strike. Yet the left hand in Jesus' society was thought to be unclean; using it to initiate an action was taboo. For example, in Qumran, the Dead Sea Scrolls community, even a left-handed *gesture* carried a penalty of ten days of penance. And when in Matthew 25 Jesus describes the lot of those condemned by their refusal to help those in need, he places them at God's left hand.

Aversion to using the left hand was more custom than law in most of Israel. Still, most avoided using their left hand whenever possible. The only way one could be struck on the right cheek without the other using his left hand was with a backhand slap. Although it was a physical assault, a backhand slap typically was not an attempt to do harm; it was an insult. Thus by telling his hearers to turn the other cheek, Jesus, it appears, was simply telling them not to respond to insults, rather than telling them to submit to physical harm or destruction. But an insult of this type was more than a simple affront; it was a humiliating reminder of powerlessness and inferior status. Masters backhanded slaves, Romans backhanded Jews, husbands backhanded wives, parents backhanded children. Because of their powerlessness, the only prudent way those who were struck in this manner could respond was to acknowledge their inferior status with hung-head shame and silent humiliation. That is what Jesus seemed to advise.

But when we look more closely at the Gospel account we see that Jesus counseled not resignation and passivity, but a definite action: to offer the other cheek. Why? Because by taking an action, the powerless and the oppressed became more than victims; they became actors who asserted their humanity, their *somebodyness.* By turning the other cheek they took back their dignity and refused to be defined by those in power. Instead, they defined themselves, and their self-definition was this: that they were not inferior beings, and they would not perpetuate that fiction by hanging their heads. Rather, their voluntary submission to additional insult said "Strike me again if you like, insult me again, but I no longer care what you think of me. I now define myself."

Thus turning the other cheek made a bold statement of equality of humanity and self-worth. Even if those who were dominated were struck again, it was on their own terms; they had dictated the action. In the sense that the one striking and the one being struck were now both active participants in the act, they had become equals. In a word, turning the other cheek was an act of self-determination.

So, for Jesus, turning the other cheek was not passivity but a way for those who were the subjects of domination and abuse to take back their dignity and their power. When those who had been bullied and humiliated no longer acknowledged as important the thoughts of those who assailed them, the myth of the assailants' superiority was derailed and the whole edifice of their power was brought into question.

Walter Wink gives poignant testimony to the power of turning the other cheek. Wink, an American biblical scholar who was active in South Africa's struggle for freedom, tells of a black woman walking with her children on a South African street when a white man suddenly spat in her face. Instead of responding with anger, the woman turned to the scowling man and responded, "Thank you. And now for the children." His assertion of power thwarted, the offender hurried away without another word, confused and perhaps even shamed.

Jesus' instruction to "give him your cloak as well" makes a similar statement. Again Walter Wink helps us understand its true meaning. He explains that, typically, poor Jews in Israel owned only two garments, an outer garment (or "coat") and an undergarment. Poor people often pledged their outer garments as collateral for loans to pay taxes and other debts. This practice is reflected in Exodus 22:25–26: "If you lend money . . . to the poor among you, . . . tak[ing] your neighbor's cloak in pawn . . ." ("Coat" for Matthew corresponds to "cloak," or outer garment, in the Exodus passage. "Cloak" in Matthew's usage refers to an undergarment.)

Using an outer garment to secure a loan usually meant the borrower owned nothing else, for lenders much preferred land as collateral. So the scenario Jesus addressed in this instance is obviously that of a poor person being sued for default on a debt. Not just being sued, however, but sued for literally everything he owns but his undergarment. That makes Jesus' instruction, "give him your cloak as well," even more curious, because it meant going beyond the ruling of the court and giving up everything, including undergarments. Of course, Jesus was not counseling his listeners to engage in public nudity; he was using hyperbole and deliberately graphic exaggeration to make his point. In fact, he might have been alluding to the prophetic protest of Isaiah, who "walked naked and barefoot for three years" to publicly make his point (Isaiah 20:3). But an even closer look shows that with this statement Jesus was telling his listeners two very important things.

First he communicated that their plight was not just an unfortunate unfolding of the natural scheme of things; it was unjust and against the law of God. By Jesus' time, lending for interest to fellow Jews in need had become big business. Yet the Bible had unequivocal laws forbidding it. Exodus 22:25 is quite specific on the matter: "If you lend money to my people, to the poor among you, you shall not deal with them as a creditor; you shall not exact interest from them."

So the whole business of lending for profit was a transgression in the sight of God. That meant both the riches *and* the poverty that resulted from such a sinful practice. In other words, the people's poverty was not the result of laziness or incompetence; it was the result of the greed of others. To be poor while others are rich, and to have to pay to borrow what should be freely lent, if not freely given, is not the way of God's kingdom.

Jesus' second point was that his hearers should not passively comply with unjust practices. Rather than accept the unjust status quo, they should protest the injustice of forced impoverishment. That is what "give them your cloak as well" means. Telling those in power "Take it all, even my undergarments" is a public protest and a prophetic critique of a system that shows itself willing to strip people of all that they own in favor of those who have more than they. But "Take my cloak as well" is also an assertion of personal agency. It declares, "You cannot exercise your power by taking it from me because I have already exercised my power by giving it to you."

"[I]f anyone forces you to go one mile, go also the second mile" has given us the popular saying "Go the extra mile," which refers to doing more than one is asked as a gesture of industriousness, good will, or even love. But that is not the meaning of Jesus' statement. He is not telling his listeners to work hard to win over others. He is referring to *angareia*, a practice under Roman law that allowed a soldier to force a Jewish subject to carry the soldier's load for up to one mile. *Angareia* was yet another humiliating Roman practice from which no Jew was safe. It was the cause of bitter resentment. This is the law that is invoked upon Simon of Cyrene in Mark 15:21 to compel him to carry Jesus' cross to Golgotha. The practice was so frequently used—and abused—that Rome eventually passed special legislation to regulate it.

It is to the practice of *angareia* that Jesus referred when he said "if anyone forces you to go one mile, go also the second mile." But again, he was not telling his listeners to try to win a soldier's heart with kindness. He was telling them how to turn a humiliating experience into an assertion of their own power and humanity—that by *choosing* to bear a load for another mile they announced that they were not beasts of burden. They were engaging in an act of self-determination; they were doing what they themselves had decided. As a result, they proclaimed their humanity and reclaimed their dignity from what could have been pure public humiliation. This was particularly important for a man in that cultural milieu of intense honor and shame when he was confronted with *angareia* in the presence of his family.

So what Jesus taught in each of these instructions was how to assert one's power in the face of a more powerful opponent, and how his followers could fight evil without being transformed into the evil that confronted them. In other words, he taught how to resist without resorting to violence. As Wink points out, Jesus "articulates . . . a way by which evil can be opposed without being mirrored, the oppressor resisted without being emulated, and the enemy neutralized without being destroyed." What Jesus taught was passive resistance.

Wink offers a succinct and cogent description of passive resistance, which is also called nonviolence. He defines it as "a commitment to respect the sacredness of each person, whatever their class or role, while maintaining a resolute determination to overcome all forms of domination." Its goal is to attain justice in order to have true peace. It is the act of "keeping track of the other's humanity," as the scholar Cornel West puts it, while fighting their injustice.

That doesn't mean that one is not to resist injustice fiercely. Passive resistance is not passivity, nor is it cowardice. It is a deep commitment to changing the world around us without sacrificing any measure of our humanity. As such, it does not seek to avoid conflict or to shrink from the responsibility to take sides. After all, oppression and freedom, evil and justice will always be in conflict. Rather than avoid conflict, passive resistance actively *seeks* conflict and intensifies it in order to lay bare the workings of injustice.

One of the earliest recorded examples of nonviolent resistance is the Exodus account of the Hebrew midwives who refused to obey Pharaoh's command to kill Hebrew infants. The biblical Book of Daniel (chapters 3 and 6) also recounts disobedience to the ruler's edicts.

The strategy of nonviolent resistance was also used successfully in Israel during Jesus' lifetime. In A.D. 26, Pontius Pilate, shortly after he became procurator of Israel, ordered Roman ensigns to be flown in the Jerusalem Temple. This caused great consternation among Jews, who considered it blasphemous. For five days thousands prostrated themselves around Pilate's house in protest. Eventually Pilate tired of the demonstration and threatened to kill the protestors if they did not disperse. Rather than fleeing, however, the demonstrators bared their necks to the surrounding soldiers, pledging to die rather than accept Pilate's blasphemy. Realizing the depth of the people's resolve to resist him, Pilate could do no more than withdraw the offensive symbols.

In the twentieth century, the power of nonviolent resistance was successfully used again and again. A number of Asian and African countries freed themselves from the choking grasp of so-called Christian empires by means of nonviolent resistance, notably India and Ghana, which were among the first.

At midcentury, dictators in El Salvador and Guatemala were ousted by widespread nonviolent resistance.

With its campaign of passive resistance, the African National Congress brought down the brutal South African apartheid regime. Its cause was aided significantly by the highly publicized student protests that eventually persuaded 60 percent of all American colleges and universities to divest themselves of their South African investments, either in whole or in part.

The repressive Marcos regime was toppled in the Philippines by unrelenting but nonviolent popular pressure.

In the United States, the nonviolent civil rights struggle dismantled the last vestiges of legalized white supremacy through the use of economic boycotts, massive demonstrations, marches, sit-ins, and freedom rides. Relentless nonviolent confrontations with the United States government also helped to end the Vietnam War.

In Russia, tens of thousands of demonstrators prevented a coup against President Boris Yeltsin by the Soviet military, who opposed his much-needed governmental reforms, by surrounding the presidential residence to keep the military troops and armaments at bay.

These are paeans to the success of nonviolent resistance. But didn't Jesus say "Do not resist an evildoer"? How could Jesus be understood as teaching passive resistance or resistance of any kind if he specifically said "Do *not* resist"? One of the most lucid treatments of this question is provided by Walter Wink. He explains that *antistenai*, the term translated in Matthew 5:39 as "resist," in that case apparently means more than "resist." Often *antistenai* was used as a military term meaning "to set against" or "withstand," as in Ephesians 6:13: "Therefore take up the whole armor of God, so that you may be able to *withstand* on that evil day, and . . . stand firm." It is also the term used most often in the Septuagint, the ancient Greek translation of the Hebrew Old Testament, to denote military resistance. In addition, the first-century historian Josephus uses it almost exclusively to describe violent struggle.

In other words, rather than being rendered simply as "Do not resist an evildoer," Matthew 5:39 should more accurately be understood as meaning "Do not *violently* resist evil." Therefore, what Jesus taught his followers was that they should not resist evil by resorting to violence. In other words, they should not fight evil with evil, violence with violence; they should not diminish their own humanity by mimicking their oppressors' inhumanity. Telling his followers not to resist at all in the same context in which he prescribes resistance strategies makes no sense. Jesus' teaching of nonviolent resistance had a secondary purpose as well: to prevent the violent backlash and retaliation that surely would result from violent resistance.

So in this passage Jesus was not just teaching personal morality, he was telling his listeners how they could use their meager power to resist assaults on their humanity by those who lorded over them. Realizing that they did not have military might, Jesus was telling his hearers to use the power they did have.

How does nonviolent resistance work on a practical level? As Wink points out, the primary goal of nonviolent resistance is *conversion* of opponents to one's cause by appealing to their sense of decency and justice. Failing that, it hopes for *accommodation*, that is, that the opponents will agree to changes that will quiet the resisters' unrest. Failing both conversion and accommodation, the focus of nonviolent resistance becomes *coercion*, forcing the opponents to choose between changing their behavior and loss of prestige and power. "Coercion" as we use it here does not mean violent force. It means activities and actions that pressure opponents to change unjust practices and policies.

Thus, nonviolent or passive resistance has one purpose: to overcome injustice. It exposes the depth of the inequity by showing the lengths of self-sacrifice to which people will go to oppose it. Yet because the opponents of nonviolent resistance are not crushed or humiliated, the strategy offers a basis for reconciliation. Also, the willingness to take blows without giving them demonstrates that one will not be intimidated from the goal of justice or hamstrung by fear.

Below is Wink's summary of the actions and the elements of Jesus'

nonviolent teaching. In his summary one finds the principles and characteristics successfully used by Martin Luther King, Jr., Mahatma Gandhi,
and others:

- Seize the moral initiative
- Find a creative alternative to violence
- Assert your own humanity and dignity as a person
- Meet force with ridicule or humor
- Break the cycle of humiliation
- Refuse to submit to or to accept the inferior position
- Expose the injustice of the system
- Take control of the power dynamic
- Shame the oppressor into repentance
- Stand your ground
- Force those in power to make decisions for which they have not
  prepared
- Recognize your own power
- Be willing to suffer rather than retaliate
- Force the oppressor to see you in a new light
- Deprive the oppressor of a situation in which a show of force is
  necessary/effective
- Be willing to undergo the penalty for breaking unjust laws
- Die to fear of the old order and its rules
- Seek the oppressor's transformation

THE 1960s WERE not only turbulent; for many they were dangerous and
deadly as well. This was certainly the case for civil rights activists in the
Deep South. Many were murdered, many more beaten, tortured, and
maimed. More often than not, homicidal racists committed their evil
deeds with impunity; few were indicted for their crimes and only a handful were ever convicted. As a result, violence against those who sought to
gain full dignity and rights for all Americans went virtually unchecked.

Yet most civil rights workers did not respond to the attacks on their persons and their dignity with like violence. They did not fight back when attacked; they didn't even defend themselves. In the face of dangerous mobs they remained impassive. Many observers saw such passivity in the face of violence as folly, if not suicide, and loudly and often derisively said so. Yet the nonviolence of those civil rights workers was not passivity in the face of violent attack; it was a profound enactment of Jesus' strategy of passive resistance. The purpose of their passive resistance was to overcome injustice without repaying evil for evil.

Thus, Jesus' strategy of taking blows without returning them means self-sacrificial leadership. It means that one is willing to sacrifice in order to make this the world of wholeness and justice and love that the Gospels say it should be.

Not everyone is willing to make sacrifices to treat the people's needs as holy; that is understandable. But anyone who is not willing to endure some measure of sacrifice for the welfare of others is not qualified to be a leader.

Jesus said that the one who leads "must be servant of all." This means that a leader must be willing to bear the cross of self-sacrificial leadership in hopes of earning the reward bestowed by these precious words: "Come, you that are blessed by my Father, inherit the kingdom prepared for you from the foundation of the world" (Matthew 25:34). According to the politics of Jesus, those in positions of leadership, secular or religious, who are self-important and always seeking self-aggrandizement are not worthy to lead the people, because they do not treat the people's needs as holy.

STRATEGY SEVEN
Don't Just Explain the Alternative, Show It

After this Jesus went to the other side of the Sea of Galilee, which is the Sea of Tiberias. And a multitude followed him, because they saw the signs which he did on those who were diseased. Jesus went up on the mountain, and there sat down with his disciples. Now the Passover, the feast of the Jews, was at hand. Lifting up his eyes, then, and seeing that a multitude was coming to him, Jesus said to Philip, "How are we to buy bread, so that these people may eat?" This he said to test him, for he himself knew what he would do. Philip answered him, "Two hundred denarii would not buy enough bread for each of them to get a little." One of his disciples, Andrew, Simon Peter's brother, said to him, "There is a lad here who has five barley loaves and two fish; but what are they among so many?" Jesus said, "Make the people sit down." Now there was much grass in the place; so the men sat down, in number about five thousand. Jesus then took the loaves, and when he had given thanks, he distributed them to those who were seated; so also the fish, as much as they wanted. And when they had eaten their fill, he told his disciples, "Gather up the fragments left over, that nothing may be lost." So they gathered them up and filled twelve baskets with fragments from the five barley loaves, left by those who had eaten. When the people saw the sign which he had done, they said, "This is indeed the prophet who is to come into the world!" Perceiving then that they were about to come and take him by force to make him king, Jesus withdrew again to the mountain by himself.

JOHN 6:1–15 (RSV)

I n her song of thanksgiving for the Savior she carried in her womb, one of the things Mary gives thanks for is that God has "filled the hungry with good things" (Luke 1:53). And all of the Gospels portray Jesus as doing the same by filling the bellies of hungry crowds in miraculous ways. The passage above is the Gospel writer John's account of one of those feeding miracles.

John's details of this event differ from the accounts of the same occurrence in the other three Gospels. This could mean that John's recollection differed from the other Gospel writers', or perhaps that he was describing an entirely different event. His description might also be of the same event the others describe, but with details that for whatever reason they did not include. At any rate, the differences in John's report are minor. Except for one detail: John has told the story in such a way that it both challenges the policies of the religious authorities that contributed to the people's poverty and hunger, and demonstrates a radical alternative to those policies.

Our first hint of John's intention to make a political statement is in this small, often overlooked observation: that throngs of people went to Galilee to see and hear Jesus "as the feast of the Passover was drawing near." On the eve of the Passover pilgrims were supposed to be on their way to the city of Jerusalem, the home of the Temple and the seat of Jewish power. Yet John tells us that instead they journeyed to rural Galilee, the home region of Jesus. By any measure, this is a radical reversal of the intent and the practice of one of the most important festal days on the Jewish calendar, for it changed the site of the celebration of the first and greatest liberation event of Israel's faith—and the authority to preside over it—from the Temple and its priesthood to Jesus and wherever he happened to be.

This is our first clue, but it is not our last. John tells us further that rather than having to *give* a Passover offering at the Jerusalem Temple, as was traditional, the pilgrims who went to Galilee *received* an offering from Jesus. From these two small details we see that in the context of a feeding miracle John has managed to change the locus of power and legitimacy from the Temple and the religious authorities who run it to the sole person of Jesus. In John's retelling, the Passover, the great liberation event of the Exodus, is now presided over by the great liberator, Jesus.

Thus the passage redefines the locus of authority based on Jesus' modeling of generous, egalitarian relationships versus the religious authorities' elitist, exploitative worldview. The pilgrims are so grateful for what Jesus has brought about among them that they instantly reject the leadership and political primacy of both the religious hierarchy and Caesar's imperial order. Instead, they cleave to Jesus because his is the only way that truly treats their needs as holy.

But this is not simply another instance of Jesus being presented as replacing the important functions of the priests, a motif that occurs often in John's Gospel, as in "*I* am the good shepherd"; "*I* am the true vine"; "*I* am the bread of life," et cetera. Rather, it portrays Jesus as presenting a whole new way of doing things, as rearticulating humanity's relationship with God based not upon fear of divine displeasure, as taught by the religious authorities, but upon God's largesse and loving generosity. In this divine economy, the haves care for the have-nots, the rich for the poor; those who have bread share with those who have none; those in power are obligated to do their best to fulfill the needs of those entrusted to their care; those who profess to represent God concentrate on giving to the people rather than on getting what they can from them. After all, if the people's needs are holy, then fulfilling them is a holy act, a holy offering to God. But the emphasis on giving because God is a generous giver raises a question: Was the miracle of the feeding that it was a divine multiplication of matter, or was the miracle that of getting everyone to selflessly and completely share their own little supply with others who'd brought nothing, until everyone's hunger was sated?

The scripture is not absolutely clear. In either case, seeking to make sure the hungry are filled with good things is consistent with Jesus' view of how relationships are to be conducted in the kingdom of God. However, on the level of strategy the passage tells us much more.

As we saw in our consideration of Jesus' strategy of giving voice to the voiceless, in the decades before and after his ministry many leaders preached that radical changes were needed in the way the religious authorities governed Israel. To be sure, much of what they taught their followers was true. However, virtually all of it remained just that: teaching. But Jesus didn't just teach a different way, he demonstrated it, too. With his feeding of the hungry crowd in John 6 he put his teachings into *practice.* He didn't just tell, he showed, and showed without fanfare.

To demonstrate the difference between the old way and his way, Jesus asked Peter where bread might be bought to feed the crowd. John expressly tells us that Jesus' query was strategic: "This he said to test him, for he himself knew what he would do" (RSV). Peter responded with an answer from the old way of doing things, just as Jesus knew he would: we cannot afford to feed them. With this, Jesus demonstrated the falsity of that thinking. He showed that the difference between feeding the poor and hungry and not feeding them is simply one of choice. Needs can be met if a society and those who govern it see their responsibility as giving rather than taking.

By feeding the hungry crowd, Jesus gave the people the opportunity to experience what his new way meant in practice. He did not lobby or try to persuade them of the abstract or the speculative. Apparently, he did not define his divine mandate to the people, either. He simply showed them.

The effect of his demonstrating this new way of living was that in return the people gave him their complete and unreserved allegiance. Theirs was not the tentative acceptance of a still-untested principle, for now they knew what he offered. Because they had experienced Jesus' new way, the people could embrace it without reservation. Jesus made it clear that the kingdom of God is not a matter of talk, but of action. He did not lament their hunger or promise to do something about it, he simply fed them. Demonstrating the alternative gives people something to hold on to. It also gives credibility to a movement and its leaders in that it shows where a movement's true heart lies.

What did Jesus enact there on the shores of the Sea of Galilee that so moved the people that they were willing to give him their allegiance? He redefined their relationship to God and to each other as based on *gift* instead of *debt.*

Temple ideology, which in effect was not only religious but the prevalent political and economic ideology in Israel as well, was based on debt: indebtedness to God for divine favor and indebtedness to the religious authorities for their ritual intercession with God. These debts were to be paid with worship and reverence for God, deference to the religious authorities, and contributions of material goods and shekels for both.

Because indebtedness was seen as the divine model for humanity's relationship with God, it was also accepted as the pattern for human relationships. Debts were charged and debts were collected. Being in debt and holding others in debt became normative. Thus, not only were all Jews indebted to God and the Temple, but many in Israel also knew the anxiety and dispossession that were the results of financial indebtedness to their rich countrymen. But Jesus showed a new way: that the generosity of God was a gift freely given, not a debt to be paid. His way recalled God's clear and specific admonition: "If there is among you anyone in need, . . . do not be hard-hearted or tight-fisted toward your needy neighbor. You should rather open your hand, willingly lending enough to meet the need, whatever it may be" (Deuteronomy 15:7–8).

Thus, the way of God was to unreservedly give what was needed to those who needed it, as the truest expression of the Bible's call to love our neighbors as ourselves—and to give without strings of debt attached.

For Jesus, this is what it meant to love your neighbor as yourself: to give what the neighbor needs in the same way and for the same reason that God gives—simply because the neighbor needs it.

What Jesus modeled, then, was the kingdom of God in action. Actually, he was rearticulating and intensifying biblical ethics that had been a part of Jewish tradition for centuries, yet seemed to have been largely forgotten. If not forgotten, they were acknowledged little, if at all, and practiced less. These traditional ethics include the following:

- Forbidding charging interest to poor borrowers (Exodus 22:25)
- Instructing that truly needy persons be lent whatever they required, with any outstanding balance to be forgiven after seven years (Deuteronomy 15:7–11)

- Sacralizing economic parity by allowing the poor to bring less expensive sacrifices to the Temple (Leviticus 12:8; 14:21–22)

These ethics, among others, expressed care for poor people by protecting them from exploitation by those who held the resources they needed. Jesus' way goes further. It transforms lending, even by means of humane loans, into something even more humane: outright giving. Jesus explains his notion of gifting as the proper basis for human interactions in a number of passages in the Gospels, such as his instruction to the rich young man that if he is to be "perfect," he should sell all that he owns and give the proceeds to the needy poor (Matthew 19:21). Of course, gifting is not only in the form of money and material goods. For instance, the Good Samaritan did give money to the wounded stranger in the form of paying for what he crucially needed. But he also gave his time, his care, his presence, his advocacy, and his ongoing concern for the stranger's well-being.

In practical terms, then, Jesus' way—that is, Jesus' conception of God's kingdom—is a society based on love of others rather than self-centeredness and greed; an economy based on cooperation and consideration of others' needs rather than thoughtless competition; a government based on caring rather than cronyism; politics based on service rather than selfishness.

However, we must not miss John's intentional portrayal of this event's political radicality and strategic significance. First, the very fact of a gathering of this size held without the permission of the Roman colonizers was rife with political implications: it constituted sedition, a crime punishable by death on the cross. Then John makes sure to tell us that five thousand *men* had gathered to hear Jesus. Not five thousand people, but five thousand *andres*, "men"—the size of an army battalion. Then he tells us that these men who had knowingly committed sedition by coalescing around Jesus were so moved by the alternative way that Jesus taught and demonstrated that they sought to make him king. There had been a number of rebel leaders in Israel during the years of Roman occupation who had claimed kingship. All were killed, along with their followers, most after being horribly tortured. Every one of those five thousand men gathered in the desert at that moment proclaiming a new king would have known what was at stake. There was no more rebellious act they could have committed in the Roman Empire short of assassinating Caesar. And they knew it.

Therefore, on the level of strategy, it was what the people experienced of Jesus that moved them to accept his leadership and risk their lives by following him. It is no different today. The leaders who will excite the most enthusiastic following must first themselves live the lives that they call others to. Leaders must live what they advocate; they must live the alternative they proclaim. By living it, they model the new way and prove its worth.

The success of the early Christians is the greatest example of this truth. They lived a new way. In fact, before they were called Christians, apparently as a term of derision (see 1 Peter 4:16), that is how followers of the risen Christ referred to one another: as followers of the Way. This new Way was not just a bunch of slogans or selfish and self-congratulatory self-righteousness; it was not just different in its appearance, but different in its substance. Followers of the Way saw themselves as a new creation and they acted as such. They addressed each other as "brother" and "sister" and treated each other with the love and respect those terms elicit. They refused to engage in the selfishness and greed that had come to characterize so much of social and economic life. The Book of Acts describes life among the early Christians this way: "All who believed were together and had all things in common; they would sell their possessions and goods and distribute the proceeds to all, as any had need" (2:44–45). They held to strict rules of morality and, in many cases, to total chastity, even in the increasingly debauched environs of Rome. And they did not just mouth "Hallowed be your name" and "Let your kingdom come," they practiced those sentiments by refusing to bow to Caesar or acknowledge his claims to sovereignty. For generations, many held out against serving in the military, even if their refusal to kill meant they themselves would be killed.

In short, the followers of the risen Jesus did not just proclaim a new way, they lived it. It was this, the power of the testimony of their lives and the demonstrated strength of their convictions, that laid the basis for the faith of millions and modeled a new way of being human that has since transformed the world.

The rapid and extraordinary growth of the faith that arose in Jesus' name is the result of Jesus' earliest followers' living the alternative he taught, the result of their bearing witness to the truth of his teaching by living it.

Those followers did not just speak about love, they lived lovingly.

They did not just recite Jesus' admonitions to care for the poor and the needy, they carried them out.

They did not just proclaim their faith that Jesus rose from the grave, they demonstrated it by their willingness to die to establish the kingdom inaugurated by his ministry and death.

They did not just say "Thou shall not kill," they refused to kill even when by killing others they might save themselves.

They did not just proclaim "Thy kingdom come, thy will be done," they lived it, even when choosing God's sovereignty over Caesar's reign meant torture and certain death.

That does not mean that the choice of today's movements and their leaders to embody what they preach will make a noticeable difference in the world immediately, or even in the near term. Nor does it mean that those who make sacrifices will in their own lifetimes see the difference their sacrifices ultimately make. Sometimes the difference is subtle, its effects quietly taking root. Sometimes the effects are not seen for generations. But that should deter no one from living as they would have the rest of the world live, because history has taught us that convictions lived out with honesty and integrity will one day bear fruit.

An example of this is found in the life and witness of one of the least known of America's founding fathers.

From the day of his birth in February 1728, Robert Carter III was a charter member of America's colonial aristocracy. He lived next to George Washington and was the friend of Thomas Jefferson and Patrick Henry and other members of the Revolutionary-era elite, but he possessed one distinction: he was the richest of them all and held more slaves than Washington and Jefferson combined.

Carter enjoyed the perquisites and privileges great wealth afforded him. He raised his fifteen or more children in a large, distinguished mansion, Nominy Hall. He owned a textile factory, some twenty plantations that produced a wide range of cash crops, a commercial bakery that could produce one hundred pounds of bread at once, a one-fifth share of the Baltimore Iron Works, and nearly five hundred slaves.

Like Jefferson and Washington, Carter was first a Deist. Then in June 1777, while suffering from what he later described as "a Fever Heat" from a smallpox inoculation, Carter experienced what he called a "most gracious Illumination" of his spirit. That began for Carter a religious quest in which he read dozens of religious books and sought out preachers of every denomination. Historian Andrew Levy observes that Carter "sometimes journey[ed] alone on horseback for hundreds of miles in order to hear Methodist, Baptist, and Presbyterian preachers and exhorters proclaim the truth of the 'new birth.' " Carter later recalled that on July 12 of that year, in the midst of his quest, he confessed to his local church, "I . . . doubted, till very lately, of the Divinity of *Jesus Christ*—I thank Almighty God, that, that Doubt, is removed." A year later he wrote to Thomas Jefferson, "I do now disclaim it and do testify that Jesus Christ is the Son of God; that through him mankind can be saved only."

Unlike the conversions of many, however, Carter's conversion went beyond words and pious posturing. The slaveholder who never intervened in overseers' disciplining of his slaves now began to defend them openly. He scandalously requested the return of a slave's property based on the testimony of the slave alone: "I am informed that an Iron pott in the house of negroe George . . . was taken & carried to Your house, yesterday." Even more scandalously, not only did he worship with Baptists, who at that time were regarded as ignorant and illiterate and were subject to summary arrest, he also worshiped with integrated congregations.

As Carter watched the religious impulses of the slaves he had all his life dismissed as social inferiors—if not a lower form of human life—he observed that their experience of God was the same as his own. That realization, coupled with his own growing religiosity, convinced him of the equality of all humanity in the eyes of God—black as well as white. On September 5, 1791, Carter began to put into action what the signers of the Declaration of Independence only wrote about. He demonstrated his belief that "all men are created equal" by writing a straightforward document—a "Deed of Gift"—with which he freed every slave he owned, some five hundred, the largest number of enslaved human beings ever freed in America by anyone. Only the number freed by the Emancipation Proclamation surpasses it.

Carter not only arranged for his slaves' freedom, he made provision for their support during their transition to freedom, including giving them housing that had been built for whites and arranging for them to farm their own shares on his plantations. In a number of cases he evicted white tenants to accommodate the newly freed blacks and in one instance refused to rent one of his plantations to a well-to-do Episcopalian minister because, Carter explained, his "present wish" was "to accommodate the poor."

Carter's actions caused much consternation among his white contemporaries for setting what they feared was a dangerous precedent. He was ostracized, his liberationist intentions opposed at every turn. Some of his peers, including Thomas Jefferson and several other signers of the Declaration of Independence, objected to Carter's action as subversive to the colonies' social balance and racial relations, and a potential cause of a backlash by white workers against their new competitors for wage labor. So intent was an overseer at one of Carter's plantations to thwart Carter's plans that he actually produced forged documents that purported to void the Deed of Gift.

Because slaves represented wealth in America's plantation economy, Carter's emancipation of his slaves cost him much financially. Socially, it cost him much as well. To escape the controversy and the derision of his peers, Carter moved to Baltimore, where he died in 1804, virtually alone. Yet his courage and willingness to put into deeds the egalitarian, liberationist ethics of the faith that this nation's Founding Fathers only put into words, as Andrew Levy observes, "laid the primitive groundwork for an interracial republic, challenging in numerous small instances the notion that young America would fall apart if blacks and whites were free at the same time."

Robert Carter III showed what it really means to become a "new crea-

ture in Christ Jesus," in the words of the apostle Paul. He did not just proclaim the alternative, he demonstrated it through the witness of his own
life and the sacrifice of his livelihood. And our nation is far better for it.

IN MY VIEW, these are the basic strategies of the politics of Jesus. But this
list is not exhaustive. It is up to sincere followers of Jesus to uncover new
and creative ways to unleash the power of Jesus' politics for the justice of
God and the good of all.

PART

THREE

❈

FIVE

In Word or in Deed?
The Politics of Jesus and the
Politics of Politicians 1:

The Case of Ronald Reagan

BEGINNING WITH George Washington, American presidents have regularly invoked God's name and the Bible in their public statements. Washington, in his inaugural address, said, "It would be particularly improper to omit, in this official act, my fervent supplication to that Almighty Being, Who rules over the universe," even though Washington was not properly a Christian, but a Deist who believed in a natural religion based on human reason rather than on divine revelation. James Madison referred to the "Almighty Being whose power regulates the destiny of Nations." Even Thomas Jefferson, also considered a Deist, said it was a Supreme Being "who led our fathers, as Israel of old, from their native land and . . . who has covered our infancy with his providence and our riper years with his wisdom and power."

In the last century, Theodore Roosevelt remarked to supporters of his quest to secure the Republican presidential nomination, "We stand at Armageddon and we battle for the Lord!" Woodrow Wilson, who called himself a Christian even though he refused to sign antilynching legislation at a time when one black man, woman, or child was being lynched every other day, nonetheless declared, "America was born a Christian nation . . . to exemplify that devotion to the elements of righteousness which derived from the revelations of Holy Scripture." Franklin Delano Roosevelt, in his first inaugural address, promised to lead the United States to the uttermost extent of his abilities by "seeking divine guidance." In his second inaugural address, Roosevelt declared, "So we pray to Him for the vision to see our way clearly . . . to achievement of His will." President Bill Clinton, though not particularly known for religiosity, said at a Maryland church in 1994, "Our ministry is to do the work of God here on earth." Clinton also used the biblical term "New Covenant" as the rubric for his governmental policy programs.

Clearly, American politicians publicly expressing their faith is nothing new. What is new is a phenomenon seen in the presidencies of Ronald Reagan and George W. Bush that is unequaled in the history of the United States. It is not these presidents' professions of Christian faith that are remarkable; indeed, anything less would be not only surprising but also politically disastrous in this age when public declaration of biblical faith has become a virtual litmus test for political office. What is unique about presidents Reagan and Bush is the widespread public perception—and, in Bush's case, his own stated conviction—that God and their Christian faith guided not only their private life journeys, but their presidential policy decisions as well. In fact, Paul Kengor, a fellow at the Hoover Institution, a major conservative think tank, recently published two major studies of the faith journeys and spiritual lives of American presidents. The two volumes, which feature virtually identical book covers and titles, explore the religious faith of only two presidents. Their titles: *God and Ronald Reagan: A Spiritual Life* and *God and George W. Bush: A Spiritual Life.*

Reagan's belief that he was so guided was conveyed subtly. But his supporters have never been subtle. During and particularly after his White House tenure they have characterized his presidency as somehow guided by Divine Providence because of Reagan's Christian faith. Recent books such as *God and Ronald Reagan* and *Hand of Providence: The Strong and Quiet Faith of*

•

Ronald Reagan perpetuate this growing elevation of Reagan to the iconic status of God-guided occupier of the Oval Office.

On the other hand, Bush's claims to divine guidance have been shockingly explicit. This is an extraordinary development in the American presidency. Not even Abraham Lincoln, who often used biblical language in his addresses, claimed that his presidential decisions were divinely guided. In fact, Lincoln once warned, "Do not say that God is on our side. Let us hope that we are on God's side." Not even the famously born-again Christian Jimmy Carter or his supporters claimed certainty of divine guidance in his presidential duties.

It is true that Carter, like Bush, is reported to have said, "God wants me to run for president . . . American people want faith in their government." But the difference between Carter and Bush is that neither Jimmy Carter nor his supporters stated or even implied that his presidency or his politics were God guided. Although while in the White House he did speak of the importance of ethical and moral stands in politics, and he was not shy about discussing his faith, Carter did not trade on it. Nor did he pander to the forces of right-wing religion or formulate his policies and pronouncements according to their dictates. Although Jerry Falwell and his Moral Majority and Pat Robertson's Christian Coalition had already risen to national prominence, Carter refused to use his faith to court their considerable political clout. Unlike Bush, Carter has never cheapened his faith by using biblical language and catchphrases, or dramatic public professions of faith, to his own political advantage.

As the result of Carter's refusal to bow to the views of the religious right wing, its leaders have always treated Carter's presidency as having a much lesser pipeline to divine guidance than did the presidencies of Reagan or Bush. A measure of the difference in the right-wing religionists' judgment of Carter is that despite Carter's demonstrated Christian commitments, there is no volume entitled *God and Jimmy Carter* among the right-wing scholar Kengor's presidential hagiographies. A more telling measure is that despite the obvious depth of Carter's Christianity, the religious right zealously supported Ronald Reagan in his bid to unseat Carter.

Yet ironically, of the three presidents of professed evangelical faith,

Carter is the only one to have demonstrated his faith by actually engaging in nuts-and-bolts evangelism. While a state senator in Georgia, Carter volunteered for door-to-door "pioneer missions" in several American communities, including Springfield, Massachusetts, and the small town of Lock Haven, Pennsylvania. For numerous years prior to his presidency, Carter taught Sunday school and Bible study back home in Plains, Georgia, and he resumed those posts after leaving the White House. Indeed, the depth of Carter's personal Christian convictions has been demonstrated again and again by his self-sacrificial service to humanity, such as his post-presidential humanitarian missions throughout the world, and his engaging in manual labor to construct affordable housing for low-income Americans through Habitat for Humanity, an evangelical Christian organization. And a front-page March 2006 *New York Times* article cited Carter's pivotal role in eradicating a horrible disease that less than two decades ago annually afflicted millions of victims on the African continent alone: "[T]hanks to a relentless 20-year campaign led by former President Jimmy Carter," the article observed, "Guinea worm is poised to become the first disease since smallpox to be pushed into oblivion." Despite his lifelong dedication to evangelical Christianity, however, the American public's right-wing-influenced perception is that Carter's presidency was not in the same divinely guided league as the presidency of Reagan or Bush. Whether one accepts that opinion or not, what is clear is that neither Carter himself nor his supporters ever sought to give the impression that Carter's policies were divinely inspired or that his presidency was divinely led.

Seeking the guidance of God in all affairs, including public affairs, is a cornerstone of Christian faith. But claiming that one's actions and policies are directly guided by God—that is something different. By claiming the guidance of God in their political actions and decisions—strongly implied by Reagan and his boosters, openly stated by Bush and his own supporters—both presidents were doing more than making statements of faith. In effect, both were saying that *their* politics were synonymous with the politics of Jesus.

As responsible American citizens, people of faith, and simply persons of common sense, it is important that we ask if the politics of Reagan, the much revered and highly influential conservative icon, and the politics of Bush, who has been so highly lauded in religious circles, really are the politics of Jesus. If their claims are true, then we are right to infuse the legacy of Ronald Reagan with great religious honor, and perhaps even to equate a vote for George Bush with a boost for Christianity itself, as a number of ministers on the religious right have contended. More important, if the claims of the supporters of these presidents are true, then their presidential policies and official actions must be given unquestioned support as being divinely sanctioned. Conversely, if their policies and politics are *not* consistent with the politics of Jesus and the biblical tradition—that is, if they have not treated the American people and their needs as holy, regardless of class, race, or ethnicity—it is important that we know that, as well. In today's religiously charged political environment, there can be grave consequences when the name of Jesus is invoked in politics as if his teachings are being used as a guide when, in fact, they are not; there is a real danger that sincere Christians can be misled into supporting policies that militate not only against the teachings of Jesus, but also against their own security and material well-being.

Considering this question also has another important significance: it gives us a window into the counsel and pastoral guidance given to Reagan and Bush by the members of the clergy functioning as their religious guides and mentors. By their enthusiastic and steadfast support, these religious figures have indicated that, in their estimation, the politics of Ronald Reagan and George W. Bush are indeed synonymous with the politics of Jesus.

RONALD REAGAN, the fortieth president of the United States, died on June 5, 2004. In the days that followed he received almost unprecedented honors from every corner of the globe and every stratum of American society. But such honors were nothing new for Reagan. He had long been among the most popular of all United States presidents. A 2000 C-SPAN poll of historians and biographers ranked him number 11 on the list of presidential greatness. Another prominent poll cast him as number 7.

Many consider Reagan to be the key president of the twentieth century, after Franklin D. Roosevelt. So great is Ronald Reagan's influence that one political analyst observed, "[I]t's pretty hard not to conclude . . . that whether or not he was a great president, Ronald Reagan was a great man, in the sense that he changed the way people thought."

There are a number of factors that account for Reagan's popularity. On the personal side, he is praised for his moral character. It is said that he radiated an irrepressible optimism, great personal warmth, an unaffected sense of humility, and an amiability that seemed to be unacquainted with mean-spiritedness.

However much his personal character is extolled, Reagan is most praised for his performance as president. He is credited with hastening the demise of the Soviet Union, which he famously called an "evil empire." His challenge to Soviet President Mikhail Gorbachev before a wildly cheering West German throng at the Berlin Wall—"Mr. Gorbachev, tear down this wall!"—is enshrined in American memory as the exhortation that began Communist Moscow's fall.

On the domestic front, his economic policies—"Reaganomics"—were praised for lowering the raging inflation and soaring interest rates that then plagued the nation. He also spearheaded the 1986 overhaul of the federal tax code that eased many taxpayers' burdens and that many consider to have spawned an era of increased economic prosperity.

Reagan is also honored for restoring America's pride and waking the nation from what some called a spiritual malaise. Invoking the imagery of Matthew 5:14–16, he called America a "shining city on a hill" and imparted to Americans the sense that they were favored by God. Onlookers at his funeral procession were repeatedly heard to say, "He made us proud to be Americans again."

But what was most important for many was that Ronald Reagan was a man of strongly professed Christian faith. From the high perch of the presidency he publicly and unapologetically shared his beliefs in ways that warmed the hearts of fellow Christians. He was known to quote Bible verses in his speeches. A personal favorite was 2 Chronicles 7:14, which he quoted in his first inaugural address: "[I]f my people who are called by my name humble themselves, pray, seek my face, and turn from their wicked ways, then I will hear from heaven, and will forgive their sin and heal their land."

To critics of his Bible-based faith he responded, "I'm accused of being simplistic at times. But within that single Book are all the answers to all the problems that face us." While in office, Reagan met often with individual clergy and clergy groups, and made it a point to attend prayer breakfasts whenever he could. Moreover, by his own account, Reagan's religious beliefs influenced many of his policy positions, both foreign and domestic. He claimed that his determined opposition to the Soviet Union was inspired by his belief that its godless authoritarianism was against divine law. His advocacy for school prayer and his opposition to abortion rights are other examples of the meeting of his personal religious beliefs with public policy. Ronald Reagan's faith seemed deep and heartfelt, and it appears that he sincerely tried to let it guide his stewardship of the nation. President George W. Bush declared on the occasion of his death, "Ronald Reagan believed that God takes the side of justice and that America has a special calling to oppose tyranny and defend freedom." That seemed to be the feeling of most Americans.

Reagan characterized his presidency as "an opportunity to serve God." In a letter to one religious leader he wrote, "My own prayer is that I can perform . . . the duties of this position so as to serve God." He was careful not to publicly betray a belief that he was divinely guided. However, his thoughts were clear to those around him. Reagan's close friend Pastor Donn Moomaw shared his assessment of Reagan's thoughts upon becoming president: " 'This is God's plan.' . . . I think he really felt that." Frank van der Linden, an early Reagan biographer who felt that he was especially attuned to Reagan's spirituality, wrote that Reagan "felt 'called' to lead the nation . . . Reagan believes that he is ordained to fill" the role of president. Edmund Morris, Ronald Reagan's biographer, says Reagan believed he received divine counsel through "silent colloquies, usually at an open window."

Yet despite his professions of faith and his belief that he was divinely guided, the presidency of Ronald Reagan is marred by acts, pronouncements, and policies of astonishing callousness that can in no way be conceived as treating the people's needs as holy. Some were shockingly opposed to the Gospel of Jesus Christ that he loved so dearly.

Reagan is remembered as the great lover of freedom. On one occasion he said, "I think I basically stand for what the bulk of Americans stand for—dignity, freedom of the individual, the right to determine your own destiny." Yet his actions made a different statement. In reality, Reagan vehemently opposed full rights for certain segments of the American people. He was the first president since Dwight D. Eisenhower to oppose the equal rights amendment for women (ERA). He opposed the Civil Rights Act at the time of its passage and never repudiated his stand. He even publicly supported federal tax exemptions for educational institutions with avowed racist policies, like Bob Jones University in South Carolina.

It is tempting to conclude that these were isolated incidents or occasional lapses in otherwise sound moral judgment. However, they were not anomalies. In fact, Ronald Reagan committed the first in what became a clear pattern of heartless and un-Christian actions at the very outset of his march to the presidency. In a gesture so cruel that it is difficult to imagine any person of good will committing it—much less the devout Christian that Reagan claimed to be—Reagan opened his 1980 presidential campaign in Philadelphia, Mississippi, a city whose claim to fame—infamy is a better word—is the brutal 1964 Ku Klux Klan murders of three young civil rights workers who were there to support the local black population's efforts to exercise their constitutional right to vote. What made these murders even more heinous was that they were committed with the complicity of local law enforcement officials.

A basic Christian sense of love and justice should have moved Reagan to unequivocally speak out against the evil acts committed in Philadelphia, Mississippi, as he later would so forcefully speak against abuses in the Soviet Union. Yet he did not. Instead, he did the unthinkable: he added insult to injury by publicly declaring, "I believe in states' rights," invoking the euphemism long used by segregationists to justify their legacy of institutionalized racial violence. The grotesquely un-Christian symbolism of this gesture was unmistakable. The result was the legitimization—indeed, the valorization—of the evil of Jim Crow and its godless enforcers. Yet Reagan never did apologize, repent, seek forgiveness, or even acknowledge his sin.

Another aspect of presidential politics in which Reagan's policies militated against the teachings of Jesus has to do with the needy and most vulnerable of American society. As we have seen, concern for the poor and dispossessed is central to the Gospels. Admonitions to care for the poor permeate the Bible. Yet not only did Reagan ignore these admonitions to treat the needs of the poorest and most vulnerable Americans as holy, he seemed to declare war on them. He cut funds for the already underfunded community health centers in urban areas by a whopping 18 percent, thus denying 750,000 Americans access to health services, a move that increased human suffering immeasurably. As a result of his attack on disability assistance, 200,000 people, many of them severely disabled, became ineligible to receive their only source of income. A UPI dispatch on April 3, 1984, observed, "The Reagan Administration's budget includes welfare cuts for pregnant women and those who get aid under the program for the aged, the blind and the disabled, government officials said today." He cut federal housing assistance by two-thirds, and this resulted in the loss of some two hundred thousand much-needed affordable rental units in depressed urban areas, pushing many poor Americans into even worse substandard housing and triggering the biggest slide into homelessness since the Great Depression. He slashed the Comprehensive Employment and Training Act (CETA), which was the only source of important training assistance for great numbers of the chronically unemployed and working poor. Yet, even as he was cutting crucial aid to the poor, he was championing policies that benefited primarily the most affluent sectors of American society. As a result of those policies, the gap between the poor and the rich became wider under Ronald Reagan's presidency than at any time since the Great Depression.

His much-touted Reaganomics, which was based on what economists call supply-side economics, was really a rehashing of "trickle-down" theory, the elitist belief that the increased riches of the wealthiest Americans and the largest corporations that result from lower taxes will "trickle down" to less-well-off Americans in the form of more jobs. Reagan's budget director David Stockman admitted that Reagan's invocation of supply-side theory was simply a way to "sell 'trickle-down.'" Stockman conceded that Reagan "only had the foggiest idea of what supply-side was all about . . . no one close to him had any more idea." But many economists did: they contended that supply-side policy would result in very little trickling down of wealth to those in need of it. Those economists, including the Nobel Prize–winner James Tobin, argued that instead it would only make the rich richer.

Stockman also admitted that Reagan's claim that his 1981 Economic Recovery Tax Act was aimed at providing tax relief for the middle class was really a ploy to divert attention from the fact that by far his largest cuts went to the wealthiest Americans, whose tax rate was reduced by a whopping 60 percent. Reagan's tax policies were so friendly to big business that a survey of 250 of the nation's largest corporations found that from 1981 to 1983 more than half of them paid no taxes at all in at least one of those years.

By 1990 Reagan's 1981 tax act and the continuation of his trickle-down economic policies by his successor George H. W. Bush had resulted in a massive transfer of wealth from lower- and middle-income citizens to the wealthiest Americans and corporate elites. The poorest 20 percent of Americans saw their after-tax family incomes *drop* by 12 percent, while the wealthiest 1 percent of Americans saw their incomes *increase* by 136 percent! Wages for the average worker fell and the nation's home ownership rate declined. Indeed, there were more farm foreclosures in the Reagan years than at any time since the Depression.

But Reagan's most dramatic domestic spending cut was in funding for low-income housing subsidies. In his first year in office, Reagan cut public housing assistance funds in half. For several years he tried to kill federal housing assistance for the poor altogether. When told that his policies were causing a steep rise in homelessness, Reagan claimed that those living on the streets were there by choice. "People who are sleeping on the grates," he told *Good Morning America* on January 31, 1984, ". . . the homeless . . . are homeless, you might say, by choice."

All this occurred at a time when the Physicians Task Force on Hunger in America reported that some fifteen million Americans had an income of less than ten thousand dollars a year, and researchers at the Harvard School of Public Health found, in a 1984 study, that more than thirty thousand Americans had the stark choice of begging for food or starving. Yet apparently none of this had any meaning for the Reagan administration. Reagan's attorney general, Edwin Meese, publicly stated that he was not aware that there was any hunger in America. Reagan never publicly commented on Meese's incredible confession.

Reagan also showed his elitist politics by his handling of the 1981 strike by PATCO, the air traffic controllers' union. Instead of considering the merits of their wage and benefit demands, he summarily dismissed the twelve thousand striking air traffic controllers from federal employment. Reagan justified the suffering his action caused with the response, "A law is a law." This was a disingenuous reply, in that his role in the Iran-Contra arrangement—in which federal dollars were illegally funneled to right-wing South American guerrillas and death squads—proved his willingness to bend and even break federal laws if he felt there was a compelling reason to do so. Apparently Reagan did not consider attempting to keep twelve thousand American families from severe economic hardship a compelling enough reason to consider the air traffic controllers' concerns. Clearly, for Reagan the needs of these families were not holy.

Christian care for his neighbor, or even for the welfare of children, is nowhere in evidence in Reagan's PATCO action. Still, his treatment of the union was welcomed by big business. His dismissal of the union's concerns emboldened corporate managers across America to resist other unions' calls for fair wages and better working conditions, and it heightened anti-union sentiment in corporate boardrooms. Reagan intensified his onslaught against labor unions by appointing antilabor types to the National Labor Relations Board (NLRB), which had been instituted in 1935 with congressional approval by Franklin D. Roosevelt to protect labor, not to serve the interests of management. But labor's seat at the power-sharing table since the 1930s was effectively cancelled by Reagan. In the end, Reagan's policies legitimized corporate stonewalling and, against all biblical notions of justice, redefined as an honorable practice resisting the equitable sharing of corporate profits with workers.

So great was Reagan's disregard for the poor that when he was told that his draconian cuts in preschool funding would necessitate the reduction or even the removal of vegetables from the lunches of the program's children, Reagan tried to justify his action by reclassifying ketchup, an inexpensive condiment with little nutritional value, as a vegetable.

Yet at the same time Reagan was strengthening welfare for *corporations* by supporting economic policies that provided huge financial relief to big business in a number of forms, including tax loopholes, financial subsidies, and other considerations, he was demonizing *individuals* on welfare rolls. The typical welfare recipient was then and still is a white single mother, but Reagan didn't care; he focused his animus on black welfare recipients. Without the benefit of one supporting fact, he contrived false and inflammatory stories, such as the one about "strapping young bucks" buying T-bone steaks while struggling taxpayers had to make do with hamburger. His particular targets, however, were black female recipients, whom he called "welfare queens." Knowing it would inflame anger at this vulnerable constituency, he offered as truth the mean-spirited and completely false story of one "welfare queen" with eighty names, thirty addresses, and twelve Social Security cards, whom, Reagan said with false outrage, received over $150,000 in tax-free annual income.

But Reagan's attacks on African Americans were not limited to fictitious welfare queens. Despite his repeated declarations that racism was a "sin" and a "moral evil" that he saw as his "Christian responsibility" to oppose "with all [his] might," his actions made a different statement. He dismissed blacks' struggle for civil rights as just "making trouble" and derided the men and women who risked their lives to help America truly become the land of the free as "keeping alive the feeling that they're victims" for personal financial gain. In his first term, Reagan cut the budget of the U.S. Commission on Civil Rights and appointed anti-affirmative-action commissioners. "They turned the commission into a total mockery of what it was supposed to be," observed Ralph Neas, then executive director of the Leadership Conference on Civil Rights. Reagan even defended the "sincerity" of the neosegregationist Senator Jesse Helms when Helms tried to discredit the civil rights movement for honoring Martin Luther King, Jr., with a federal holiday—which Reagan also opposed—by questioning that martyred reformer's loyalty to his country.

In this way Reagan also made it acceptable, even noble, to turn back the clock on racial attitudes in America. So thick was the racist atmosphere in the Reagan White House that as Terrel Bell, Reagan's secretary of education, notes in his memoir, the utterance of racial slurs was commonplace among White House staffers, with routine references to "Martin Lucifer Coon" and "sand niggers." There seemed to be little hint of "love your neighbor as yourself" in Reagan's treatment of Americans of color. Jerry Brown, who succeeded Reagan as governor of California in 1975, said of Reagan, "He defined himself by those he opposed."

But what was probably Ronald Reagan's most egregious transgression of the Gospel of Jesus Christ was his ongoing support of the South African apartheid regime, one of the most oppressive regimes on the face of the earth.

In the tradition of Constantine's Rome, South Africa's apartheid regime wrapped itself in the mantle of professed Christianity, while its brutal un-Christian practices crushed the lives of its millions of indigenous people. Black South Africans were forced from fertile lands into fetid townships. Cruel migratory-labor laws split apart families for eleven months at a time. Systematic education for black children was gutted. Due process for black defendants was virtually nonexistent. Torture and government-sanctioned violence and murder against black South Africans were rampant. All this to ensure that twenty-eight million black South Africans were completely denied the human rights white South Africans enjoyed, such as the right to vote, the right to assemble peacefully, and the right to express one's interests and opinions openly and freely. In short, South Africa was the world's only constitutionally enshrined racial supremacist dictatorship. It maintained control of its black population by unspeakable cruelty and violence. Yet despite the fact that he professed to treasure human rights for all, Ronald Reagan supported that racist regime without reserve. Despite apartheid's institutionalized murder and torture, despite its devastation of families—though he claimed to champion strengthening families—Reagan supported the apartheid regime of South Africa without a meaningful word of criticism.

As Americans became more aware of the horrors of the apartheid regime, many raised their voices against it, clamoring for American corporations to discontinue doing business with South Africa, and for the United States government to take a positive step for justice by imposing sanctions designed to force real social reforms. Ronald Reagan responded to these pleas by crafting a new policy of nonopposition to apartheid that gutted the previous policy of confronting it. This new policy was cynically called "constructive engagement." In actuality, the measure contained not one meaningful antiapartheid provision. Seething with outrage, Archbishop Desmond Tutu, the South African Nobel Peace Prize laureate, declared that constructive engagement was "an abomination" and pronounced Reagan's attitude toward South Africa as "immoral, evil, and totally un-Christian."

In the meantime, innocent black South Africans continued to be jailed, tortured, and murdered by the thousands. But Reagan firmly maintained his support of the South African government's tyranny. In 1985 he took a further step: despite the apartheid regime's having shown no meaningful movement toward changing its repressive policies, he declared that it was now a "reformist administration" and, incredibly, argued that it had already "eliminated the segregation that we once had in our country"—the segregation whose horrors he had ignored in Philadelphia, Mississippi.

By 1986 Congress had finally had enough of the South African bloodbath. With the Comprehensive Anti-Apartheid Act of 1986 it officially enacted limited sanctions against South Africa. But apparently even limited sanctions were too much for Reagan. He unceremoniously vetoed the bill. Congress overrode the veto, but Reagan held fast and refused to enforce the sanctions in any meaningful way.

Still determined to support the apartheid regime, in October 1987 Reagan submitted a required follow-up report to Congress on the 1986 act that argued against calls from across the world for the United States to put greater pressure on the increasingly barbaric South African authorities.

The report concluded that additional sanctions "would not be helpful." The report was so supportive that the South African prime minister declared with glee that Reagan "and his administration have an understanding" of what he termed "the reality of South Africa."

Reagan's stance toward the brutal apartheid regime of South Africa never changed. He left office unapologetic for the suffering and death caused by his support for a regime that by every measure was an abomination in the sight of God and flew in the face of every precept of the Gospel of Jesus Christ.

ONE CARTOONIST SATIRIZED the vicious deeds hidden beneath Reagan's popular appeal in an assemblage of four broadly smiling and enthusiastically gesticulating Americans, each captioned with one of the following: "Reagan supported apartheid, but he was always personable"; "He crushed workers' rights, but he was someone you could sit down and have a beer with"; "He tripled the national debt, but he had such charisma"; "He backed death squads throughout South America, but he always looked for the best in everyone."

The old adage that much truth is told in jest could not be more true than in this instance. Despite his affability, Ronald Reagan consciously chose to assist tyranny and ignore brutality in South Africa and South America just as he had in Philadelphia, Mississippi. In his domestic policies he dismissed the plight of the least fortunate and demonized the most vulnerable, in effect blaming the victims of his policies for their own victimization, while he rewarded purveyors of economic injustice and exploitation with laws and edicts that greatly enriched them. His mean-spirited policies and racist, inflammatory fabrications were the cause of inestimable pain and suffering for millions. In the final analysis, the presidency of Ronald Reagan revived the fiction that one could be honorable and a racist, too. In his presidential policies and his politics, Ronald Reagan showed no *hesed*— steadfast love—except to a select circle: rich persons in America, mostly of European descent, and those elsewhere in the world who were useful to his dominationist vision of the world. He ignored the interests of the poor and the powerless and demonstrated little interest in vouchsafing justice for them.

Yet in spite of his pattern of cruel and un-Christian transgressions, Reagan is revered as a man of great Christian faith. Ironically, it seems that most Christians in America not only overlook Reagan's unjust, un-Christian actions, but honor him. But by any fair measure, the actions of President Ronald Reagan are summarily condemned both in practice and in precept by the love-based politics of Jesus.

SIX

In Word or in Deed? The Politics of Jesus and the Politics of Politicians 2:

The Case of George W. Bush

"I believe God wants me to run for President."
GEORGE W. BUSH
AUSTIN, TEXAS, JANUARY 1999

GEORGE W. BUSH

President George W. Bush has been more vocal about his faith than Ronald Reagan was. Bush's openness about his beliefs has made him a favorite of conservative Christians throughout America. He is celebrated as an avid Bible reader and a devout born-again Christian whose belief in God guides his every decision, whether public or private. No other president has hosted so many Bible studies and prayer meetings. Nor has any president's religious life been as open and accessible as that of George W. Bush. He has discoursed on the Bible and knelt in prayer with other world leaders. At a White House meeting in December 2002, Bush declared to the prime minister of Turkey, Recep Tayyip Erdogan, "You believe in the Almighty, and I believe in the Almighty. That's why we'll be great partners."

George W. Bush believes even more ardently that his presidency is divinely sanctioned than Ronald Reagan believed his own was. In the early days of his campaign for the Oval Office, Bush repeatedly asserted, "I believe God wants me to run for president . . . God wants me to do it." That was also the assessment of a number of religious leaders. James Robison, a nationally known pastor and confidant of Ronald Reagan, said of Bush, "He just wants God to use him." After Bush met with a group of ministers in April 1999, a San Antonio pastor remarked, "[I]t was obvious that this man's heart gravitated toward the things of the Lord."

Despite his claim to be divinely called to the presidency of the United States, on a number of occasions Bush has disavowed any thought of receiving direct guidance from God. In his 2004 State of the Union address, Bush stated, "We do not claim to know all the ways of Providence."

A written statement from the White House in June 2004 sought to discredit charges that Bush had earlier claimed that God called him to invade Iraq: "The President actually said, 'Going into this period, I was praying for strength to do the Lord's will . . . [But] I'm surely not going to justify war based on God.' " Reporter Bob Woodward reports a similar response from Bush: "I'm surely not going to justify war based on God . . . In my case I pray that I be as good a messenger as possible."

If Bush himself disavows believing that his presidency is ordained and guided by God, White House officials and major Republican spokesmen do not. They have worked hard to give the impression that God placed Bush in the White House to do God's will. A month after the terrorist attack on the World Trade Center, Tim Goeglein, Bush's deputy director of the Office of Public Liaison, told *World Magazine*, a conservative Christian publication, "I think President Bush is God's man at this hour, and I say that with a great sense of humility." Still, he said it.

General William "Jerry" Boykin, Bush's deputy undersecretary of defense for intelligence, publicly declared that Bush was chosen by God to lead the global fight against Satan. In October 2003 he told one gathering, "Why is this man in the White House? The majority of Americans did not vote for him . . . He's in the White House because God put him there for a time such as this."

Keynote speakers during the Republican National Convention in 2004 repeatedly implied subtly but clearly that God is behind Bush's presidency by repeatedly thanking God for making Bush president. Former mayor of New York City Rudolph Giuliani repeatedly proclaimed, "Thank God George Bush is our president." Governor George Pataki of New York was even less subtle: "He is one of those men God and fate somehow lead to the fore in times of challenge."

Not only is Bush's presidency lauded as God-ordained, he himself is praised as a man of high personal moral rectitude. In *The Faith of George W. Bush*, Stephen Mansfield portrays Bush as a man of uncompromising honesty. As an example of Bush's honesty, Mansfield relates that while taping a radio speech to be aired when he visited Oklahoma a few days later, Bush refused to say "Today I'm in Oklahoma," because during the taping he actually was in Washington, DC, and to declare otherwise would be deceitful. In another anecdote, Mansfield relates that Bush's honesty caused him to refuse to take credit for signing legislation that enacted a multibillion-dollar conservation project in the Florida Everglades because the bill was approved prior to his presidency, although it would have been a considerable feather in his political cap. Mansfield reports that when he was asked about it, Bush simply explained, "It's legislation that was passed before my time."

Apparently Bush's devotion to his beliefs has set the tone for the entire White House. On his first day in office he called for a national day of prayer. Staffers report that he opens every cabinet meeting with prayer and a reading from the Christian devotional classic *My Utmost for His Highest*. Presidential speechwriter David Frum described the moral tone of the Bush White House as so pious that when he emphatically answered a query in a cabinet meeting with "I'm *damn* sure," he felt the temperature plummet until he expressed his certainty in a more acceptable manner.

Moreover, Bush has surrounded himself with others of strong Christian faith. Karen Hughes, former counselor to the president and now undersecretary of state for public diplomacy, has been a Presbyterian elder. Secretary of State Condoleezza Rice is the daughter of a Presbyterian minister. Chief of staff Andrew Card is the husband of a Methodist minister.

And Secretary of Commerce Don Evans has been a close compatriot of Bush since both regularly participated in weekly Bible study in Texas during Bush's pre-governor days. John Ashcroft, the attorney general in Bush's first term of office, professes a very strong faith and has publicly stated that he believes his ascension to attorney general was God-ordained (a curious notion, in that his appointment came on the heels of his defeat by a dead man in the Missouri race for the United States Senate; his opponent, Mel Carnahan, died weeks before the election was held).

Rarely has a president propounded religion's role in government as fervently and consistently as George W. Bush. Bush not only has publicly expressed his beliefs but has attempted to integrate his faith with policy at the most practical level by proposing that a number of governmental functions with regard to poverty and social uplift be replaced by faith-based initiatives offered by faith-based institutions. As one administration official put it, "[W]e do understand that the political vision we serve is fueled by faith." That is, George Bush's faith.

Rev. James Robison explained what he sees as the significance for America of the born-again conversion of George Bush: "The undeniable change in George W. Bush is revealed in his total commitment to help his country preserve freedom's blessing, to feel compassion for those who suffer, his love for God, his faith, and his desire for peace around the world."

Yet despite his much-vaunted Christian belief, George W. Bush has exhibited a pattern of behavior that is even harder to reconcile with faith in the Gospel of Jesus Christ than the troubling presidential behavior of Ronald Reagan. Indeed, in many ways it seems to epitomize the unjust brand of governance that was so detested by the biblical prophets and opposed by Jesus Christ himself.

In a personal letter to Bush, Rev. Bob Jones III told him that liberals despise him "because they despise your Christ." However, this seems to hold little in common with reality. The truth is that if Bush is despised, it is not because he worships Christ, but because he uses the name of Christ to legitimate unjust policies that cause immeasurable pain and dislocation to the very ones Christ enjoined his followers to care for.

"Compassionate conservatism," a concept created by longtime Bush advisor Marvin Olasky, was a cornerstone of Bush's campaign for the presidency. The political right in America, particularly Republicans, had long been accused of supporting policies that favored the rich and ignored poorer Americans. Bush used the catchphrase "compassionate conservatism" to signal a new direction for his party. The term evoked biblical images of mercy and carried both an implication and a promise. The implication was that Bush cared for those whose social or economic circumstances warranted empathy and support. The promise was that he would act out of that care and champion compassionate policies.

Despite his claims of compassion, however, the Bush presidency has shown virtually no concern for the poor and even less compassion. Instead, the Bush administration has consistently enacted policies that benefit the rich at the expense of the poorest and most vulnerable members of American society. Conservative political commentator Andrew Sullivan lamented that Bush "could have cut tax rates across the board and removed tax loopholes for wealthy corporations. Instead, he cut taxes substantively only for the very rich [and] clotted the tax code with even more corporate giveaways."

Rich Cizik, vice president for governmental relations for the National Association of Evangelicals and a vocal supporter of Bush, cautions, "One must be careful not to assume that because Bush is a man of faith that he uses religious faith to fill in the moral gaps in our economic system."

Cizik's statement is telling, for it is precisely with regard to issues of economic life and sustenance for rank-and-file Americans that Bush should be guided by biblical ethics. It is when formulating the policies that will affect lives in the most fundamental ways that faith and compassion are most important. This is when the most basic and the most pressing question posed by the politics of Jesus must be asked: Is this policy good news for the poor or not?

Bush loudly proclaims the role of his faith with regard to other issues, like abortion and gay marriage, neither of which so directly affects the welfare of as many Americans as issues of economic sustenance. He even made the expansive gesture of flying to Washington solely to sign a congressional bill with which lawmakers hoped to intervene in the tragic Terry

Schiavo end-of-life case. But when it comes to the most basic issue of the quality of people's lives—their day-to-day sustenance—it seems that for Bush the teachings of Jesus are nowhere in view.

If Bush's faith is truly a biblical faith, how can his economic policies *not* be informed by that faith? What the observation of Bush ally Cizik divulges—albeit inadvertently, apparently—is that Bush *selectively* uses the moral ethics of his religious faith, and only when it fits his agenda.

Take the centerpiece of Bush's economic program, tax cuts. Bush and his congressional supporters claimed that this measure would bring much-needed income tax relief and greater after-tax income to all Americans, particularly the middle class, and would make a positive difference for America's working poor. However, in practice it was so skewed toward the interests of the rich that it is almost a textbook example of economic injustice.

According to Citizens for Tax Justice (CTJ), if Bush's 2001 budget had been enacted as he proposed it, some 45 percent of the tax cuts he sought would have gone to the richest 1 percent of the population, that is, those making over $373,000 a year, and a full 53 percent of the tax cuts would have gone to the wealthiest 5 percent, those making $147,000 or more annually. Even worse, 27 percent of taxpayers would have received no tax cut at all. The bottom 60 percent of taxpayers, with an average income of $21,400, would have averaged yearly tax savings of just $260, or $5 per week. Yet the richest 0.5 percent of taxpayers would have expected to realize a gain from lowered taxes that averaged $46,000 a year, or $885 per week—some 177 times the income gain of most Americans.

The tax cut of 2003 is no less unjust. First, in 2003, 31 percent of American taxpayers received no benefits at all from the Bush tax plan, and 49 percent of all taxpayers received $100 or less in reductions, for an average tax cut of only $19. From 2003 to 2006, the bottom 60 percent of American taxpayers will average an annual tax cut of just $80, while during the same four-year period the wealthiest 1 percent of Americans will receive an average annual tax cut of $20,160. By 2006, those receiving $100 or less will increase to 88 percent of all taxpayers, for an average tax cut of only $4.

Moreover, the Bush tax cut increased the child tax credit for the wealthiest Americans from $600 to $1000, while those earning less than $26,625—those for whom the increase would make a real difference—received no increase at all.

One of Bush's proposed tax cuts in particular illustrates his dedication to making the rich richer, despite Jesus' command to the contrary: his plan to eliminate the estate tax. Bush presented this provision as a merciful measure to save family farms from being lost when heirs were unable to pay estate taxes. In reality, there never was a crisis to address and, therefore, there was no honest justification for gutting the estate tax. Under existing laws farm couples could already pass farms worth up to $4.1 million tax-free to their heirs, as long as the heirs continued to farm the property for ten years. Thus, 96 percent or more of all farms were already effectively exempt from estate taxes, and therefore exempt from the drastic measures Bush claimed they were vulnerable to, such as tax seizure. In other words, President Bush knew that the impending loss of family farms that he claimed as the reason for his repeal of the estate tax *would never happen.* In fact, when pressed for the truth, the American Farm Bureau, an ardent supporter of the estate tax repeal, eventually confessed that they could not identify even one farm that was lost because of estate taxes. The unassailable fact is that Bush's repeal of the estate tax benefits no one but the wealthiest Americans. Fewer than three thousand, or about 1.9 percent of all estates in the entire country—only 1.9 percent!—would realize any benefit from repeal of the estate tax, and every one of those estates is valued in excess of $5 million.

Bush tried to hide his transgression by disingenuously dubbing the existing tax on large estates a "death tax" to imply that the estate tax was a grotesquely unfair measure. But it was not "death" that was taxed; it was seven-figure inheritances. Sadly, in this case, too, Bush has cynically lied to the poor in order to benefit the rich.

Referring to *New York Times* columnist Daniel Altman's comment that Bush's proposals, if fully adopted, "could eliminate taxes on investment income and wealth for all Americans," economist Paul Krugman observes, "Mr. Bush hasn't yet gotten all he wants, but he has taken a large step toward a system in which only labor income is taxed"—that is, wages of working men and women, while wealth in forms much more typically owned by the rich would not be taxed at all.

One commentator put the measure in perspective: "If a working person has to pay taxes on every dollar he or she earns by the sweat of his or her brow, why shouldn't others have to pay taxes on every dollar they simply inherit? Why do people who work for a living get the shaft, while those who inherit their wealth pay no taxes?"

It is estimated that Bush's tax reductions will cost Americans some $50 billion a year for most of the next decade. Ironically, the reductions will not be paid for by those who will benefit most, but by cuts in the services that are relied upon by those who will benefit least. Bush has enacted new eligibility requirements that make it harder for low-income families to obtain a range of government benefits, including Medicaid, housing assistance, the school lunch program, preschool programs, and a range of educational programs. As a result of his policies, 36,000 senior citizens have been dropped from meal programs; 532,000 citizens have been removed from home-heating-assistance rolls; 33,000 children have been cut off from child care and 50,000 from after-school programs; and 8,000 homeless children have been dropped from education programs. But that is not all. While cutting taxes for the rich, Bush also

- tried to eliminate overtime pay for 8 million workers.
- refused to extend unemployment benefits for those forced from the workforce by the economic recession.
- proposed cuts of 29 percent in already-scheduled highway construction and maintenance, costing workers 140,000 highway construction jobs in 2002 alone.
- revoked previously approved federal grants for safety and health training programs in 2001, and in his 2003 budget proposed cutting enforcement of workplace safety and health standards for workers.
- stripped 170,000 government workers who were reassigned to the new Office of Homeland Security of all civil service and col-

lective bargaining rights and protections to which they had previously been entitled.

- appointed as his first attorney general John Ashcroft, who, although also a born-again Christian, while a U.S. senator from Missouri consistently voted against crucial worker safety and health measures, Social Security, Medicare, the patients' bill of rights, raising the minimum wage, and maintaining prevailing wage guarantees. Ashcroft even voted against protection of overtime and the forty-hour workweek.

As a result of this onslaught against the poor, the number of Americans without health insurance has increased more than 10 percent since Bush took office. In 2000, the year Bush was elected, 39.8 million Americans had no health insurance. By the end of 2002, Bush's second year in office, the number had risen to 43.6 million—more than 15 percent of the American population. The number of those living below the poverty line of $17,960—for a family of four!—has increased by 3 million, also an increase of about 10 percent. That means that now 33 million Americans, including 13 million children, are at risk of hunger every day. Nearly 8.5 million Americans are forced to regularly skip meals or have too little to eat, sometimes having to go a whole day without eating.

So, on the one hand, the Bush tax cuts hit working Americans with a double whammy: (1) the $3.5 trillion cost of the tax cuts represents money that is not available for crucial social needs such as improving education, health care, and Social Security and Medicare; and (2) the vast majority of Americans have received little or nothing in return for their sacrifice. On the other hand, the number of affluent Americans who paid no federal income taxes at all more than doubled between 2000 and 2002. Surveying the disastrous effects of Bush's policies on rank-and-file Americans, Dr. George Akerlof, recipient of the 2001 Nobel Prize for Economics, called Bush's policies "the worst in two hundred years."

Symptomatic of Bush's lack of care for the poor is his treatment of the federal/state Children's Health Insurance Program (CHIP) in Texas. According to the *Austin Chronicle*, while Bush was governor Texas had the highest number of uninsured children per capita in the nation. To remedy this health crisis, the Texas House of Representatives wanted to provide medical coverage to children in families earning up to 200 percent of the federal poverty level (which would be about $33,000 for a family of four). But Bush fought to limit coverage to children of families with incomes below $25,000, knowing full well that his plan would leave out nearly half of the five hundred thousand needy children that would have been covered by the higher threshold. Shamefully, at the same time he was fighting to limit medical coverage for Texas children, Bush was fighting even harder to give a $2 billion tax cut to the richest families in Texas and to provide a $45 million tax break to the Texas oil-and-gas industry. He explained, "These are tough times for the oil and gas industry."

When CHIP legislation was passed over his opposition, Bush dragged his feet implementing it. According to *Time* magazine: "Bush took his time to start up CHIP . . . When CHIP finally did start . . . a total of five years had passed since the legislature first attempted to cover many of the same youngsters. The delay freed Texas from having to spend billions of dollars in matching state grants, leaving enough money for Bush to pass $1 billion in tax relief in the 1997 [Texas] legislative session."

When Bush left Texas for Washington, the number of uninsured children in his state was 1.5 million, by far the highest in the nation.

This emphasis on treating the interests of the rich as more worthy than the desperate health needs of children prefigured the callous policies of Bush's presidency. It is impossible to know the extent of the suffering and death among poor Texas children that Bush's opposition to more comprehensive health care for them caused. What is clear is that it is an unconscionable and egregious transgression of the Gospel of Jesus Christ.

At the Fifty-third Annual Prayer Breakfast at the start of his second term in office, Bush told the gathered ministers and dignitaries that for him prayer is a reminder to hear "the cry of the poor and less fortunate." Yet the proposed budget he sent to Congress just days later made it clear that it was a cry that he himself had not heard or had simply ignored. One well-known economist sadly observed of Bush's 2005 budget proposal that it "really does take the food from the mouths of babes" and "really does shower largesse on millionaires even as it punishes the needy."

The overall thrust of the 2005 budget, like that of previous Bush budgets, is again to favor the interests of the rich over the needs of poor and struggling Americans. The budget would make it more difficult for low-income working families with children to receive food stamps, and would remove some three hundred thousand low-income Americans from the rolls of food stamp recipients altogether. It would also deny child-care assistance to about three hundred thousand children of low-income working families. Bush's budget called for eliminating the Community Services Block Grant, a $637 million program that helps to support the community-action agencies that for thirty-five years have provided housing, nutrition, education, and employment services to low-income people as part of the fight against poverty. No matter what Bush's rhetoric, these are not pro-family measures.

President Bush's 2005 budget, if every measure in it was passed,

- would cut the Low-Income Energy Assistance Program, which helps people pay their heating bills, 8.4 percent at a time when the steep rise of oil prices made the aid this program offered to struggling Americans even more crucial.
- would cut funds for training nurses, dentists, and other health professionals a whopping 64 percent. In addition, a program that trains doctors at children's hospitals would be cut 33 percent.
- would eliminate a block grant that provides $131 million for preventive health services previously mandated by federal law to address "urgent health problems" identified on a state-by-state basis.
- would cut by 6.5 percent a Public Health Service program for chronic-disease prevention and health promotion. The program supports efforts to prevent and control obesity, which many health professionals, including federal health officials, say has reached epidemic levels in America.
- would eliminate a $9 million program for the treatment of people with traumatic brain injuries.

- would cut $60 million from Medicaid, a measure that Lawrence
  A. McAndrews, president of the National Association of Children's Hospitals, said would force many children's hospitals, for
  which Medicaid provides more than 40 percent of their revenues, to reduce or even eliminate services. "[T]he care of all
  children, not just those on Medicaid, would be affected by the
  reduction of services," lamented McAndrews in a February 2005
  statement.

- would eliminate or substantially reduce forty-eight programs in
  the Department of Education for a net reduction of 1 percent in
  that agency's funding at a time when public education needs
  more, not less, support to remain viable. The programs targeted
  include Upward Bound, Gear Up, and Talent Search, all of which
  help students from disadvantaged backgrounds prepare for college. Also targeted is vocational education, which primarily
  serves poor and lower-income students and is an essential
  stepping-stone for them to achieve the American dream.

While Bush's 2005 budget called for cutting these crucial programs for
low-income families, it sought to give high-income families even more tax
breaks. It proposed to proceed with the phaseout of two little-known tax
provisions that place a limit on the tax deductions and exemptions that
can be claimed by America's richest households. More than half of the
benefits from this measure would go to people with annual incomes of $1
million or more, for an annual average tax cut for them of more than
$19,000. A full *97 percent* of the benefits of this tax cut would go to those
with yearly incomes of $200,000 or more.

The savage cuts the 2005 Bush budget sought in education, health care,
veterans' benefits, and environmental protection programs would have
saved only about $66 billion per year. By simply rolling back Bush's pro-
posal for more tax cuts on capital gains and on dividends for those in high-
income brackets, the government would save more than $120 billion per
year—almost twice the amount to be gained from Bush's cuts in programs benefiting the neediest Americans. The effect of such a rollback on

most of America's families would be negligible, and in many cases would be more than offset by preservation of many of the social services that families rely on. Still, Bush refuses even to consider the slightest change in windfalls he has chosen to give the rich.

Bush's tax cuts have reduced tax revenue to a share of the economy not seen since 1959. This means that the government has fewer funds available for crucial social and health programs because they have been spent on tax breaks for the rich and on its growing military excursions. It is difficult to understand this as biblical logic.

Bush's tax cuts have had other consequences, some of them deadly.

One particularly tragic example is that despite a 2001 FEMA report that ranked the destruction of New Orleans by a hurricane as one of the three most likely catastrophic disasters facing this country, Bush, in part to fund the tax cuts, between 2001 and 2005 cut federal funding for strengthening the city's protective levees by 12 percent. As a result, when Hurricane Katrina hit, federal budget cuts had all but halted major work on the levees for the first time in thirty-seven years. Moreover, Bush's budget for 2006 calls for cutting a record $71.2 million from the Army Corps of Engineers, which is charged with strengthening New Orleans's flood defenses. The extraordinary devastation and loss of life that ensued is a direct result of the collapse of those levees.

SOME OBSERVERS ASCRIBE malicious intentions to Bush's economic policies, given those policies' one-sidedness against the interests of poor and vulnerable Americans. Others see Bush policy initiatives as sincere, if unsuccessful, attempts to address the problems of the U.S. economy. Rev. James Robison is thoroughly convinced of the righteousness of Bush's intentions. He contends that "as a result of [Bush's] faith commitment, the well-being of others became the priority directing his life and future." In 2000, Bush confessed to Rev. Jim Wallis of the Call to Renewal clergy group, "I don't understand how poor people think . . . but [I'd] like to." Yet in that same year Bush himself described his allegiance as not to all others, as Robison characterized it, but specifically to the upper class. In a speech at a New York fund-raiser in 2000, a smiling Bush declared, "This is an impressive crowd. The haves and the have-mores. Some call you the elite. I call you my base."

To be sure, these statements represent conflicting views about the breadth, if not the depth, of Bush's concern for the well-being of others, especially the needy and the vulnerable. What can be stated without fear of contradiction, however, is that in their totality, the economic policies of George W. Bush and his congressional supporters have disproportionately benefited the rich while disproportionately harming the poorest and the most vulnerable in American society. In this sense, those policies stand in direct opposition to the most basic biblical admonitions about the care of the needy. His policies are virtually bereft of *mishpat* (justice), *sadiqah* (righteousness), and *hesed* (steadfast love) for the hungry and the hurting. By the most basic measure of the Gospel of Jesus Christ, Bush's domestic policies are patently un-Christian. Because Bush has turned his back on the poor and refused to treat their needs as holy, his politics stand in harsh opposition to the politics of Jesus.

Like Ronald Reagan, Bush made a pilgrimage to the segregationist Bob Jones University. And his virtual abandonment of the survivors of Hurricane Katrina, most of whom were poor and black, does bring his racial attitudes into question, as do his opposition to affirmative action and his apparent insensitivity to the needs of the urban poor, who are disproportionately black. But Bush's initiatives seem to be driven not by race but by class, as indicated by his gleeful admission that America's wealthy elites are his "base." Yet his one-sided allegiance to the upper class of America does not stop at domestic policies that exploit the country's poor. Dangerously, it also extends to an idolatrous ideology of world supremacy.

IN SEPTEMBER 2002, through the office of then–national security advisor Condoleezza Rice, the Bush administration released a congressionally mandated document, the National Security Strategy (NSS) of the United States. The report, which has come to be known as the Bush doctrine, begins with the incredible assertion that there is "a single sustainable model for national success"—America—that is "right and true for every person, in every society."

The notion that any one social or political model is true "for every person, in every society" is absurd, given the plethora of cultural, religious, and historical differences in the world. Moreover, the assumption that anyone can unilaterally decide that they have the right to impose their views and way of life on others is extremely dangerous.

As George Soros explains in his book *The Bubble of American Democracy*, "The supremacist ideology of the Bush Administration . . . postulates that because we are stronger than others, we must know better and we must have right on our side."

The Bush doctrine, Soros goes on,

> is built on two pillars: First, the United States will do everything in its power to maintain its unquestioned military supremacy and, second, the United States arrogates the right to preemptive action. Taken together, these two pillars support two classes of sovereignty: the sovereignty of the United States, which takes precedence over international treaties and obligations, and the sovereignty of all other states . . . [There is a] contradiction between the Bush administration's concept of freedom and democracy . . . When President Bush says, as he does frequently, that "freedom" will prevail, in fact he means that America will prevail.

Jim Winkler, general secretary of the United Methodist General Board of Church and Society, called the National Security Strategy "a dark vision of eternal war." In the April 2003 issue of *The Christian Century*, Robert N. Bellah, the respected scholar of civil religion, called the National Security Strategy "the most explicit blueprint in history for American world domination . . . nothing if not a description of empire."

Indeed, the National Security Strategy is an unmistakable rationale for achieving national supremacy, a clear-cut strategy for expanding and maintaining an empire. Behind its high-flying rhetoric is the language of force and coercion, the unvarying lingua franca of domination. The NSS touts America's "unparalleled military and great economic and political influence." It makes the high-minded statement, "These values of freedom are right and true for every person, in every society," then claims for the United States the sole right to define freedom.

The truth is that the Bush doctrine flies in the face of the Judeo-Christian tradition of respect for the humanity and integrity of others. Indeed, more than sixty chapters of the Bible reflect a negative view of empire. The rhetoric of empire certainly is not consistent with the politics of Jesus, who scolded his disciples, "[T]he Gentiles lord it over one another, but it is not to be so with you." This doctrine represents the very kind of dominationist sentiment that Jesus so adamantly stood against. In fact, it is little different from the ideology of the Roman Empire that crushed the people of Israel underfoot and ultimately executed Jesus in its quest to subjugate the whole world. In this sense, the NSS articulates the oppressive imperial rhetoric of Caesar, not the liberating Gospel of Christ. It represents an idolatrous ideology—yes, idolatrous—in that it replaces God's love for all humanity with its own judgment that some of God's children (that is, Americans, and not all Americans, either) are more worthy of the fruit of the tree of life than others. Moreover, because Bush's supremacist ideology ultimately values might over right, it is directly counter to every biblical notion of justice and righteousness. It literally savages the universal love ethic of Jesus Christ.

When observers realized the imperial implications of the NSS, predictably, Bush denied it. He told a gathering of armed forces veterans, "We have no territorial ambitions, we don't seek an empire." In response to a German reporter's assertion that some Europeans see resonances of the Roman Empire in the Bush administration's foreign policies, then–national security advisor Condoleezza Rice similarly replied, "I wouldn't accept the comparison to the Roman Empire, of course, because the United States has no imperial ambitions."

Yet few have taken those denials seriously, even within Bush's own administration. Ron Suskind of the *New York Times* reports that soon after America's invasion of Iraq a senior advisor to Bush admonished him, "We're an empire now, and when we act, we create our own reality . . .

We're history's actors . . . and you, all of you, will be left to just study what we do."

In May 2003, Bush insider William Kristol, former chief of staff to Dan Quayle and editor of the influential conservative periodical *The Weekly Standard,* admitted the push toward empire to Fox News: "If people want to say we're an imperial power, fine."

Even religious figures have jumped on Bush's imperial bandwagon. In a statement reminiscent of the fourth-century Christian Eusebius of Caesarea's fawning declaration that the Roman emperor Constantine was *theostephes,* "crowned by God," Pat Robertson gushed of Bush, "God's blessing is on him. It's the blessing of heaven on the emperor."

Empires are built on violence and greed and gross disrespect for the rights, even the humanity, of everyone but those sanctioned by the empire. As conservative columnist George F. Will candidly admits, "Empire is about domination." The very notion of empire violates the politics of Jesus in the most fundamental ways. By definition it entails war and greed, theft and deception. It is inescapably a culture of death masquerading as a culture of life. It is a handful of leaders making an idol of their own culture and their own desires. An empire is a nation playing God.

That Christians can speak without shame and revulsion of our nation as an empire is a legacy of Emperor Constantine's assumption of the de facto headship of the Church to add to his rulership of the Roman Empire. The resultant fiction that Constantine was an emperor whose actions were guided by God has legitimized the depravities of empire for almost two millennia. This fiction finds a corollary in American Christians' celebration of a head of state with imperial ambitions who trumpets his faith while doing the exact opposite of what that faith demands.

We must remember that Jesus was the victim of empire, not its proponent. In his most fundamental teaching on prayer, the Lord's Prayer, he instructed his disciples to pray for Caesar's empire to be superseded and replaced. Jesus himself consistently stood against the empire by openly challenging the religious establishment, whose calculated political quietism served to perpetuate the Romans' rule. Even when facing torture and death he refused to acknowledge the power of empire as legitimate.

The lesson of Jesus' example is that imperial sensibilities of any kind are incompatible with the Gospel and the politics of Jesus. To put it simply, one cannot be a follower of Jesus and an advocate of empire, too.

An appropriate response to empire by people of sound faith—a response that Jesus would undoubtedly applaud—ironically is provided by the lower-ranked priests of the Temple at Jerusalem. A generation after Jesus' execution, those priests took the unprecedented action of refusing to further engage in the long-standing symbolic practice of offering sacrifices to God for the well-being of Caesar and the Roman Empire. Those courageous clerics understood what all followers of Jesus must: that the role of people of biblical faith is to oppose empire, not to support it.

That is why the supremacist ideology of the Bush doctrine is idolatrous: because it is the ideology of empire—and empires worship their own might rather than the righteousness of God. It is also un-Christian because it exhibits a real lack of love and respect for everyone outside Bush's select circle of caring. And it points to another pattern of practice that in Christian terms—indeed, in terms of simple moral decency—is even more troubling. That is George Bush's apparent lack of respect for human life.

IN HIS BOOK *A Charge to Keep*, George W. Bush writes, "All of us have worth. We're all made in the image of God. We're all equal in God's eyes." Elsewhere in the book he writes that his faith "teaches that life is a gift from our Creator." These sentiments are reflected in his opposition to abortion. As an outspoken opponent of abortion, he makes it clear that he cares for the unborn. It is for the lives of the *already* born that Bush seems to lack compassion. In fact, he has exhibited a startling indifference to the suffering of others.

In his six years as governor of Texas, George W. Bush signed 154 death warrants. In the entire history of the United States of America, no governor of any state has sent more persons to their deaths. Even when presented with evidence of possible innocence, George W. Bush refused to reconsider those executions. Despite the complexity of death penalty cases, Bush spent on average only fifteen minutes each considering the cases of those whose lives hung in the balance, even in the face of overwhelming evidence that the system that sought their death was seriously defective. In fact, a two-hundred-page October 2000 report on the death penalty in Texas issued by the lawyers of the Texas Defender Service detailed "a thoroughly flawed system" marred by "racial bias, incompetent counsel, and misconduct committed by police officers and prosecutors."

Those whose executions Bush refused to reconsider included inmates who were hopelessly mentally ill or profoundly retarded, and even those convicted on the basis of evidence found to be questionable or downright false. Not only did Bush refuse to show even a shred of mercy in these cases, he actually advocated measures that would result in more deaths. He opposed a bill that would have granted profoundly mentally retarded convicts life in prison without parole instead of execution. This despite the fact that one such inmate thought he was sentenced to die because he couldn't read. The man desperately tried to learn, thinking that would save him. Another repeatedly asked his lawyer what he should wear to his own funeral, thinking he would be alive to attend it. Bush's only stated reason for opposing this bill was this: "I like that law the way it is now." In 1999, he even vetoed a bill that would have required Texas counties to set up systems for ensuring that indigent defendants had proper legal representation.

Despite there being serious doubts about the guilt of a number of condemned prisoners, only once did Bush block an execution, and that was only a temporary measure. In fact, he actually bragged about how hard it is to escape the Texas death chamber, gloating that convicted killers get only one chance to make an appeal—"one bite of the apple," as he jokingly put it—even if evidence turned up after the trial that could change the verdict.

Not only did he show no reluctance to put other human beings to death, he was observed smirking over pending executions. Conservative journalist Tucker Carlson, normally a Bush supporter, reports that after Bush rejected born-again death row inmate Karla Faye Tucker's plea for her life to be spared, in Carlson's presence Bush mocked the condemned woman. "Please don't kill me," Bush whimpered, his lips pursed in parody. Bush's heart was not softened even by Ms. Tucker's credible claim that she'd experienced the same faith conversion that Bush professed.

As governor, Bush was correct in refusing to factor Tucker's conversion into his legal decision. At a news conference at that time he rightly concluded that "judgments about the heart and soul are best left to a higher authority." But laughing at the impending death of a fellow human being is difficult to reconcile with Bush's faith claims.

Carlson was horrified by Bush's hard-heartedness. He relates that when Bush saw the shock on his face, Bush immediately changed from his smirk—"smirk" is Carlson's description—to a more appropriate expression. Carlson also reported that Bush used profanity during the interview.

Is this an anomaly? One wishes it were. The whole nation witnessed Bush's chilling smirk when he defended his record number of executions during the presidential debates of 2000. "Guess what?" the Texas governor said with that trademark smirk. "The three men who murdered James Byrd, guess what's going to happen to them? They're going to be put to death," he remarked, even as he spurned the Byrd family's pleas for him to back hate-crime legislation in Texas.

It is true that the men who murdered Byrd simply because of his race committed a heinous crime, and they were rightfully convicted by a jury of their peers. Yet to a Christian they are still God's children, still worthy of compassion despite their sins. This is basic to the teachings of Jesus Christ. However, that was not George Bush's response. His was to smirk and to show no evidence of caring in any way about the impending deaths of those his faith tells him to at least attempt to love.

BUSH'S LACK OF respect for human life was made even more painfully clear in an incident that was strangely underreported by the national news media. Because of the terrible death, destruction, and untold human misery that war portends, one would expect sadness and somberness in the commander in chief on the eve of his declaring a war. But those who met with Bush in the hours before he declared war on Iraq, including several lawmakers, instead described him as "cocky and relaxed," even "in high spirits." More incredibly, in the moments before he was to appear on national television to announce that the war had begun, Bush was caught on camera pumping his fist as though he were at a sporting event, and declaring, "Feels good." Journalist Paul Waldman called Bush's response "a glimpse of the president's vulgar callousness."

A year later, as some six hundred Americans lay dead and many times that number lay grievously wounded, Bush showed even more clearly his lack of respect for human life. While families mourned their dead and horribly maimed young, Bush did the unbelievable: he performed a spoof of his claims of the existence of WMDs that had been the basis for his declaration of war upon Iraq, at the March 2004 annual dinner of the Radio and Television Correspondents' Association. Displaying photographs of himself searching behind curtains and looking under furniture for Iraq's phantom weapons of mass destruction, Bush joked, "Those weapons of mass destruction have got to be somewhere," and "Nope, no weapons over there . . . Maybe under here?"

Moreover, Bush has so little respect for human life that despite the admonition of his Lord and Savior to love one another, Bush openly and gratuitously speaks of killing other human beings, even on national television in the hearing of children. What is worse, when he talks of killing he does not speak only of nameless, faceless armed forces; he talks of killing individuals whom he calls by name. After the invasion of Iraq, Bush boasted that Saddam Hussein and his top lieutenants would be hunted and killed. Not captured, or neutralized, or stopped. Killed. The same with Osama bin Laden. "We will kill him," he said of bin Laden. "Bring him back dead or alive."

In a particularly macabre move, but one sadly consistent with his lack of respect for life, Bush actually gloated over the killing of Saddam's sons and allowed their mutilated bodies to be put on display so the grisly images would be shown around the world. It is hard to understand this as the behavior of a true follower of Jesus Christ.

. . .

MR. BUSH'S LACK OF CONCERN for human suffering was again evident
when he visited hurricane-ravaged New Orleans in September 2005. *New
York Times* columnist Bob Herbert wrote of that visit with barely concealed
outrage: "Instead of urgently focusing on the people who were stranded,
hungry, sick and dying, he engaged in small talk, reminiscing at one point
about the days when he used to party in New Orleans, and mentioning
that Trent Lott had lost one of his houses but that it would be replaced
with 'a fantastic house—and I'm looking forward to sitting on the
porch.' "

It is tempting to conclude that President Bush has been misunderstood
or that his opponents have misportrayed him. After all, the prospect of a
commander in chief who exhibits little respect for human life is chilling.
Yet Bush's lack of empathy for the suffering of those outside his designated
circle apparently is deeply rooted. No less than Bush's own mother, Barbara Bush, has publicly exhibited the same callousness.

In September 2005, while touring the Houston Astrodome, into which
thousands of displaced victims of Hurricane Katrina were jammed, Mrs.
Bush remarked, "What I'm hearing, which is kind of scary, is they all want
to stay in Houston . . . And so many of the people in the arena here, you
know, were underprivileged anyway, so this is working very well for
them."

These were not private comments taken out of context. Mrs. Bush
spoke them publicly, on camera, in the midst of the traumatized, suffering thousands, most of whom had lost everything and had no idea how
they would rebuild their shattered lives. Although apparently she meant
well, her comments cannot be dismissed as the errant observations of
some woefully misinformed person; Mrs. Bush is a former first lady of the
United States who undoubtedly was formally briefed about the extent of
the hurricane victims' suffering. It was not that she did not know about
the horror those people faced. Her comments indicate that because they
were "underprivileged"—that is, because they were not "have-mores"—
she simply could not identify with them as human beings who could feel

pain the same as she. It is almost as if their being "underprivileged" meant that they were a different order of humanity. The callousness toward the suffering of the survivors of the New Orleans horror betrayed by Mrs. Bush suggests that her son's apparent lack of respect for the suffering of those outside his select circle of caring is frighteningly real.

Bush's lack of respect for human life and the contempt he and his cohorts hold for average Americans is reflected in their attitude toward the military. Bush himself and everyone close to him who so fervently pushed for the Iraq war successfully maneuvered to avoid serving their country when called to do so in the Vietnam War. Though they now make support for their war effort a litmus test of patriotism, none but Bush even bothered to join the military. Vice President Dick Cheney, of those in Bush's circle probably the most openly contemptuous of average Americans, declared without a hint of apology that he had more important things to do than defend his country: "I had other priorities in the 60s than military service." He must have had other priorities, because he received not one, but *five* military deferments. And when the Selective Service extended the draft to married men without children, Dick and Lynne Cheney's first child was born exactly nine months and two days after the rule change. One is reminded of the condescension of the steel magnate Andrew W. Mellon, who, after paying a less-well-off young man to take his son James's place in the military, told James that "a man may be a patriot without risking his own life or sacrificing his health. There are plenty of lives less valuable."

Assistant secretary of defense Paul Wolfowitz, former chairman of the Defense Policy Board, and Bush's White House chief of staff Karl Rove also sought and received deferments. As for our commander in chief, he himself sought the special treatment he believes is the due of rich elites like himself. He mysteriously received a much-coveted appointment to the Texas Air National Guard despite the hundreds on the waiting list ahead of him. General Colin Powell, now Bush's ex–secretary of state, shared his thoughts on the rich using their wealth to avoid military service in his 1995 autobiography, *My American Journey*: "I am angry that so many of the sons of the powerful and well placed . . . managed to wangle slots in the reserves and National Guard units. Of the many tragedies of Vietnam, this raw class discrimination strikes me as most damaging to the ideal that all Americans are created equal and owe equal allegiance to their country."

Yet despite his privileged appointment, Bush still walked away from his National Guard weekend-warrior duties nearly two years before his six-year obligation was up. Despite Bush's denials of going AWOL, not one Guardsman of the more than six hundred who were in Bush's unit during that period remembered seeing him at any time in his last two years of service. Nor could anyone in the Alabama National Guard attest that he served the remainder of his Texas duty there, as Bush contended, despite a $3,500 reward offered by a group of veterans for any verifiable shred of evidence. To this day, that reward remains uncollected. Texas political commentator Glenn W. Smith puts Bush's dereliction of duty into perspective: "I believe that the George W. Bush who occupies the White House today, and pursues those selfish and dangerous policies, is very much the same man who believed in the Vietnam War . . . so long as he and his privileged brethren could hide from danger while others risked their lives."

THE ATTITUDE OF BUSH and his peers that their own lives are more important than the lives of others is the same elitist sense of privilege that Jesus passionately opposed in his own day. At least in this instance, their attitude is closer to that of Jesus' opponents than to Jesus' Gospel. Those who think like this may well love their neighbors as themselves, but only if their neighbors belong to the same socioeconomic class as themselves.

A more recent and more telling example of Bush's lack of respect for human life actually involves a group of Christian ministers.

Even before his second term began, Bush made it clear that one of the foremost goals of his remaining White House years was the privatization of the Social Security system, an arrangement that, not surprisingly, would result in a windfall of commission revenue for investment firms, corporate money managers, banks, and insurance companies. Although Social Security is in need of an eventual overhaul, most economists agree that without any adjustment it can last another four decades or so. With slight adjustments, it can remain viable for much longer. Still, Bush postured as if the Social Security system was in imminent crisis. When polls showed that his message was not faring well with the American people, he took another approach. In January 2005, Bush convened a group of African American ministers to enlist them in his privatization scheme. This is the pitch he made to the assembled clergy: "African American males die sooner than other males do, which means the system is inherently unfair to a certain group of people."

Yet this statement is not just misleading, it is false, as Bush and his actuarial advisors surely were aware. Actuarial tables attest that an African American male who lives to age sixty-five can expect to live and collect benefits for another 14.6 years, still short of the figure for white males of 16.6 years, but not by much, particularly when measured by the relatively small amount of benefits that white males' additional life span affords them. But when it is factored in that the average income of African American males is far less than that of whites, African American males actually receive a higher percentage of their income in benefits than do their white counterparts.

Furthermore, Social Security is also a disability program. Study after study has shown that health care received by African Americans is inferior to that of whites, so as a result they are more likely to draw on Social Security disability benefits than are white males.

What this all means is that Bush's argument—that black Americans should support the privatization of Social Security for the reason that, as it now stands, African Americans do not get their fair share of benefits because they die earlier than whites—is a brazen untruth. Amazingly, there is no indication that any of the assembled black ministers raised a word of challenge or outrage at Bush's reasoning.

It is shameful that Bush would so dishonestly exploit black people's shorter life expectancies to further his own agenda. What is more shameful still is that neither as the president nor as a Christian did he decry the fact of black people's shorter life spans—even though it was black people to whom he was speaking. Nor did he suggest that black Americans' inferior health care or any other cause of their shortened life spans should be addressed. Indeed, he expressed no dismay at these sad realities at all. What his ploy did express was a glaring lack of respect for the lives of a huge number of Americans. Representative Charles B. Rangel of New York said of Bush's statement, "It is one of the cruelest things that I have ever read, and I regret that it comes from the office of the president."

"It is puzzling to me that we are even having this debate about whether Social Security is good or not for African Americans," said an incredulous Senator Barack Obama. "I frankly found the statement that the president made somewhat offensive . . . The notion that we would cynically use those disparities as a rationale for dismantling Social Security as opposed to talking about how are we going to close the health-disparities gap that exists, and make sure that African American life expectancy is as long as the rest of this nation . . . is stunning to me."

Rich Cizik of the National Association of Evangelicals put the president's approach to Social Security in perspective: "I don't think when Bush approaches the issue of Social Security reform he's exercising his religious belief system."

There is little question that the only reason Bush raised the issue of African Americans' lower life expectancies at all—he never raised it before the Social Security argument nor has he raised it since—was to serve his own spurious ends and the ends of the elites whose interests are his primary concern. If he has shown no concern that black Americans face premature death relative to white Americans, if he has shown no concern that the preponderance of his economic policies adversely affects the quality of their lives, it is highly unlikely that he actually cares if blacks receive their fair share of Social Security benefits. And is it merely another striking coincidence that privatization of Social Security would be a great windfall for America's rich corporate elites?

THE ANECDOTE by Bush speech writer Frum cited above about the chill he received in a Cabinet meeting when he used the word "damn" in the sense of "absolutely"—as in *damn* sure—does appear to bespeak a high moral tone in the Bush White House. Although Frum did not take the Lord's name in vain, his use of the mildly profane term still was viewed as unacceptable. But one wonders if Bush's pious disdain for profanity is sincere or just hype to burnish his carefully crafted image as a devoutly pious Christian.

Sitting on the dais at a September 2000 campaign stop in Naperville, Illinois, Bush spotted Adam Clymer, a longtime political reporter for the *New York Times*. Unaware that his microphone was on, Bush remarked to Vice President Dick Cheney, "There's Adam Clymer—major asshole—from the *New York Times*." Fortunately, the noise level of the crowd was so high that most of those in the assembled crowd, which included many children, were spared from hearing Bush's profanity. It was, however, caught on tape by news crews. When confronted with Bush's public profanity, his campaign had no comment.

In fact, despite claims of Bush's great personal piety and rectitude, White House aides have divulged that Bush himself is given to profanity-laced tirades and obscene gestures. He is reported to have made an obscene gesture at reporters setting up for photographs in the East Room of the White House for the August 2005 signing of the Central American Free Trade Association (CAFTA) trade bill.

In addition, a June 2004 news report, citing unnamed White House aides, relates that Bush routinely uses profanity and angrily calls aides insulting, profane names when he is frustrated or perceives someone as disloyal.

Observers like Stephen Mansfield have made much of what they put forward as Bush's great honesty and personal integrity. Without offering examples of the characteristics he extols, John DiIulio, former head of the White House Office for Faith-Based and Community Initiatives, wrote after ending his White House tenure, "In my view, President Bush is a highly admirable person of enormous personal decency. He is a godly man and a moral leader." David Frum also looked back at his time with Bush and, again without illustration, described him as a man who exhibits "decency, honesty, rectitude, courage, and tenacity."

If Bush is honest in his personal life and relationships and responds with truthfulness regarding details and facts in situations like those narrated by Mansfield, that indeed is admirable and important for a man of biblical faith. After all, Jesus enjoined unwavering truthfulness upon his followers when he said, "Let your word be 'Yes, Yes' or 'No, No'" (Matthew 5:37). There is little reason to doubt Bush's conduct in situations of the type that Mansfield shared. It must be noted, however, that the particular acts of honesty Mansfield cites contain no real cost or sacrifice, for there was little at stake. What is of importance is not demonstrations of honesty that have little import for or impact upon anyone other than Bush himself.

What is of utmost significance is the honesty with which a president governs. Is he truthful to those whom he leads and whose interests he is pledged to serve with the justice that the Bible commands? Is he honest under pressure, when honesty has a real cost? Does he tell the people the truth and accept their judgment, or does he shade truth or utter outright untruths when falsehood serves him better? These are profound questions, for if a leader is not honest, he cannot be just. Unjust and untruthful leaders are condemned again and again in the Bible.

These questions are important because, while George Bush might be a truthful and honest and trustworthy man with regard to personal piety and personal relationships, when the record of his presidency is surveyed, unfortunately a pattern of untruths, deceptions, and thinly veiled injustices becomes clear. For instance, a closer look at Mansfield's anecdote about Bush's unwillingness to take credit for legislation in which he had no part reveals that it is contradicted by the facts again and again. For example, Bush claims to have supported a patients' bill of rights as Texas governor. Yet this is a lie. In reality, he vigorously opposed the measure. When the bill moved forward despite his active opposition, he reluctantly let it become law without his signature, but at no point did he support it. Another example is in the show Bush made in 2002 of pledging $15 billion to fight AIDS. In reality, most of the funds had already been earmarked for AIDS programs when Bush took office. What's more, he had tried to siphon off the AIDS funds for use elsewhere. Bush even took credit for providing low-income heating assistance when, again, he was releasing funds that he had tried to cut.

Although deceptions such as these might seem minor and could be dismissed as mere politics, they indicate much more serious problems with honesty. No less than Ron Reagan Jr. has ruefully observed, "Politicians will stretch the truth . . . But George W. Bush and his administration have taken 'normal' mendacity to a startling new level . . . and ultimately have come to embody dishonesty itself." One syndicated journalist decried what he called "a dangerous national disease, and that's the Bush administration's culture of deceit . . . its relentless, almost pathological, undermining of the truth."

PROBABLY THE MOST embattled area of truth in George W. Bush's administration has to do with the circumstances of his declaration of war against the sovereign state of Iraq. The major reasons Bush gave for his incursion were his claim of a significant link between Iraq and the terrorist organization al-Qaeda and the contention that Iraq possessed a stockpile of weapons of mass destruction (WMDs) that it was poised to use against the United States.

In his 2003 State of the Union address Bush asserted, "Our intelligence sources tell us that [Saddam Hussein] has attempted to purchase high-strength aluminum tubes suitable for nuclear weapons production." But Bush knew this was not true. Three weeks earlier, Nobel Peace Prize laureate Mohamed El Baradei, head of the International Atomic Energy Agency, had already informed Bush that the tubes were "consistent with" manufacturing requirements for ordinary, conventional artillery and "not directly suitable" for nuclear armaments. In fact, an Italian lawmaker, Senator Massimo Brutti, told journalists that Italian secret services warned the United States in January 2003 that a dossier claiming an Iraq-Niger uranium deal were false: "At about the same time as the State of the Union address, they [Italy's SISMI secret services] said that the dossier didn't correspond to the truth."

Yet in a May 2003 interview on Polish television Bush claimed, "We found the weapons of mass destruction. We found biological laboratories. And we'll find more weapons as time goes on. But for those who say we haven't found the banned manufacturing devices or banned weapons, they're wrong. We found them."

This simply is untrue, and Bush knew it. The sad reality is that to this day no evidence has ever been found to support any of Bush's claims. Even before Bush went to war, the chief UN weapons inspector, Hans Blix, pointedly and emphatically informed Bush that he had uncovered no evidence whatsoever of WMDs and doubted they existed. David Kay, the Bush administration's own chief weapons inspector in Iraq, also repeatedly warned Bush that no weapons of mass destruction would be found. The administration's response to Kay, a former Marine, was to attempt to discredit his patriotism.

Indeed, the Bush administration has done all it can to mislead America about the war. In his first three State of the Union addresses, Bush did not mention Osama bin Laden once, yet he spoke of Saddam Hussein, Iraq, or "regime change" a total of ninety-nine times. Congressman Henry A. Waxman of California estimates that between 2002 and January 2004 top Bush administration officials made a minimum of 237 false or misleading statements about Iraq. The net result was the impression that Iraq was an actual terrorist threat to the United States. In reality, as early as September 21, 2001—just ten days after the 9/11 attacks—Bush was apprised during the "President's Daily Brief," a thirty- to forty-five-minute early-morning national security briefing, both that the U.S. intelligence community had no evidence linking the Iraqi regime of Saddam Hussein to the attacks and that there was no credible evidence that Iraq had any collaborative ties with al-Qaeda whatsoever.

In July 2004, after an exhaustive two-year investigation, the National Commission on Terrorist Attacks upon the United States (the 9/11 Commission) confirmed what had become obvious: there was no indication that Iraq played any role in the events of September 11, 2001, or in any other terrorist activities against the United States. In other words, each of Bush's pretenses for war was shown to be false. (Apparently, that is why from the start he had so furiously attempted to derail the commission's formation. Failing that, he allocated just $3 million for the entire investigation. By way of comparison, $4 million was allocated for a study of gambling—*in 1996.*)

The Bush decision to attack Iraq was based on such dishonesty and was so counter to United States interests that career diplomat John B. Kiesling, political counselor to the U.S. Embassy in Athens, Greece, resigned from the Foreign Service in protest. In his letter of resignation he charged, "We have not seen such systematic distortion of intelligence, such systematic manipulation of American opinion, since the war in Vietnam . . . We spread disproportionate terror and confusion in the public mind, arbitrarily linking the unrelated problems of terrorism and Iraq. The result, and perhaps the motive, is to justify a vast misallocation of shrinking public wealth to the military."

Thus, all of the claims Bush used to prod the nation to war were untrue, and apparently he knew it. At this writing, more than twenty-five hundred American lives and the lives of tens of thousands of Iraqi civilians have needlessly been lost. The Iraqi war costs Americans $4 billion every month, $133 million a day. Billions of dollars have been spent on the war that could have been used to restore the funds the president cut from social programs and services desperately needed by so many American citizens. Given these realities a simple sense of decency would cause most to at least take stock of their priorities. Not Bush. He claims that his declaration of war was God-sanctioned. Journalist Bob Woodward reports that Bush expressly attributed his decision to invade Iraq to God's guidance.

Bush's father, President George H. W. Bush, had waged a successful military campaign against Iraq in the early 1990s. Yet when Woodward asked if George W. Bush had consulted the former president before embarking on his own war with Iraq, incredibly Bush indicated that he had not availed himself of his own father's hard-won experience. "There's a higher father that I appealed to," Bush replied piously. *Haaretz,* a major Israeli newspaper, reports that while meeting with Palestinian Prime Minister Mahmoud Abbas, George W. Bush actually claimed to be the recipient of audible divine guidance. "God told me to strike at al Qaida," he said, according to *Haaretz,* "and I struck them, and then he instructed me to strike at Saddam, which I did."

Apparently these statements are not flukes. In September 2002, *Time* magazine correspondent Michael Duffy wrote of Bush and the 9/11 attacks, "Privately, Bush even talked of being chosen by the grace of God to lead at that moment."

Despite Bush's claims, any notion that he acted under divine guidance in any way is finally discredited by his pattern of deception and half-truths. If Bush truly believed that he was working at the behest of God he would have reveled in that truth, not dirtied it with lies. The sad reality is that George W. Bush has committed the terrible sin of misleading his countrymen—many to their deaths—to serve his own questionable ends. What are those ends? Or, put another way, Who or what stood to benefit most from a war with Iraq? The American soldiers? The millions of Iraqis caught in the middle of violence and chaos? The American people, who are paying hundreds of billions of dollars for the war, but have gotten nothing in return but the greatest sense of insecurity that America has known in more than half a century? It is none of these. Those who have gained most from the war are a handful of multinational corporations, specifically oil-related corporations and building contractors. It is an ugly fact that many of those close to President Bush and Vice President Cheney stand to make billions of dollars as the direct result of the Iraqi war.

Without question, the biggest beneficiary of the war on Iraq is Halliburton, the corporate behemoth that Dick Cheney headed until accepting his party's nomination for the vice presidency in 1999. On March 25, 2003, Halliburton received an open-ended, $7 billion no-bid contract to rebuild the same Iraqi oil fields that the vice president had so relentlessly prodded the president to destroy. Cheney claims that the $36,086,635 Halliburton paid him in 2000 and the $27 million it paid him in the preceding four years had nothing to do with its receiving the $7 billion contract in a process that didn't allow competing bids. But in a June 2004 article, the *Washington Post* reported that an Army Corps of Engineers e-mail confirms that Halliburton's multibillion dollar contract "had been 'coordinated' with the office of Vice President Cheney."

Moreover, Cheney himself still personally profits from the war. In September 2003 he declared, "I have no financial interest in Halliburton of any kind and haven't had now for over three years." Yet even as he spoke, Cheney was receiving some $165,000 in deferred compensation yearly, and he did so through 2005. Not to mention the 433,333 Halliburton stock options he still holds. Admittedly, when compared to his $60 million salary windfall, the three-quarters of a million dollars Cheney has received from Halliburton while serving as vice president is small potatoes for him. Yet according to the Congressional Research Service, this compensation clearly constitutes a financial interest in Halliburton. Add to it his $20 million retirement package (not including stock options), and a very disturbing picture arises: the vice president of the United States apparently has a standing loyalty to, and a substantial ongoing financial interest in, the one firm that stands to profit far more than any other in a war that he fought tooth and nail to drag his country into. In other words, Vice President Dick Cheney profits from the war every day it drags on, and from every deployed soldier's suffering and sacrifice. One wonders why this apparent violation of the public trust is not being investigated in a manner even approaching the Congress's $44 million obsession with the Whitewater inquiry, which was about a real estate deal that had actually lost its principals $44,000.

Yet even as Halliburton's executives and shareholders benefited from the Bush administration's unprecedented largesse and special breaks, the firm maneuvered to avoid paying federal income taxes by incorporating in numerous tax haven countries, from the remote island of Vanuatu to Bermuda. Incredibly, by its own admission, in 2002 Halliburton paid federal taxes of only $15 million on its *billions* of dollars of income.

Halliburton is not the only politically well-connected firm to profit handsomely from Bush's war with Iraq. Bechtel Corporation, one of the world's largest construction companies, counts among its paid directors George P. Shultz, who was secretary of state under Ronald Reagan and secretary of the treasury under Richard M. Nixon, and is a former president of Bechtel. Just six months after the invasion of Iraq, Bechtel received more than $1 billion in contracts for infrastructure work in Iraq, including a no-bid contract worth up to $680 million over six months. What all these corporations have in common is that the welfare of "the least of these" is nowhere in their sight.

The tale gets more sordid. In May 2003, Bush signed an executive order that gives oil companies—and only oil companies—*complete immunity* against lawsuits and contractual disputes arising from discrimination, labor law abuses, environmental disasters, even human rights violations! The major recipient of this executive order is Halliburton. This unprecedented action literally declares that Halliburton and other oil companies are no longer bound by American law in Iraq, and therefore can exploit the suffering of that nation with impunity. "In terms of legal liability, it is a blank check for corporate anarchy, potentially robbing Iraqis of both their rights and their resources," says Tom Devine, legal director of the Government Accountability Project.

When faced with naked greed and profiteering by some American corporations in World War II, President Franklin D. Roosevelt denounced them for maneuvering to "make profits for themselves at the expense of their neighbors—profits in terms of money or in terms of political or social preferment." One wonders at the irony that President George W. Bush's declaration of war on Iraq has given his corporate cohorts the exclusive opportunity to do what Roosevelt tried to guard against: to greedily garner profits for themselves at the expense of their neighbors. Neighbors they are supposed to love as themselves.

ALTHOUGH ITS RAMIFICATIONS pale in comparison to the Iraq war controversy, there is another example of Bush's deceit of the very people he was sworn to serve that is notable for the contempt it shows for truthful governance.

The energy giant Enron Corporation filed for bankruptcy on December 2, 2001. The company had reported a third-quarter loss of $638 million in October, then in November made the stunning admission that it had inflated its profits by $600 million over five years. Enron's stock lost $26 billion in market value in just seven weeks, a figure that would mushroom to almost $80 billion in the course of a year. In the aftermath of Enron's bankruptcy filing, it became clear that the fall of the energy giant was caused by greed, dishonesty, and fraud of scandalous proportions. Top Enron executives had looted the company of tens of millions of dollars, not only leaving thousands of its rank-and-file workers unemployed, but leaving them without much-needed medical benefits as well. Worse, workers' hard-earned pensions evaporated before their eyes because the firm had refused to let them sell the Enron stock that comprised their entire retirement portfolios even as the company itself teetered and crashed. In fact, Enron chairman and CEO Kenneth Lay even advised employees to buy more stock while he and other executives had already dumped almost $1 billion worth of their own shares.

The Enron debacle had wide-ranging economic and political implications, and devastating effects on the lives of hundreds of thousands of employees and stockholders. Sadly, many stockholders were employees whose entire pensions were invested in Enron stock. Thus the unfortunate workers at Enron were hit with a double whammy: they not only lost their jobs, but they lost their pensions, too.

And not only Enron employees were affected. Tens of thousands of individual and fund investors lost their entire investment. While Enron's executives were profiting from their corruption, 571 mutual funds lost almost $1 billion. One New York City municipal employee pension fund lost $109 million. A Florida state employee pension fund lost a whopping $385 million.

Yet as Enron was nearing its collapse, some 500 of its executives received $54.6 million in bonuses. In the year preceding the bankruptcy, $745 million in cash and stock awards were disbursed to 144 company executives. Enron chairman and CEO Kenneth Lay alone received $150 million as the company slid toward insolvency. In contrast, not one severance check to Enron's rank-and-file employees after the debacle exceeded $13,500.

This was a classic tale of terrible suffering, dreams destroyed, once-secure futures now rendered frightfully anxious and devoid of hope. Righteous indignation would be expected to rise in the breasts of those with even the smallest sense of decency. Certainly the self-described standard bearer of "compassionate conservatism" would be expected to raise his voice in outrage. Yet George W. Bush had little to say. In fact, at first he said nothing critical of Enron at all, even after it was clear that the firm had betrayed the American people on a breathtaking scale. Bush left it to Secretary of the Treasury Paul O'Neill to articulate the administration's position. Ignoring the criminal actions that caused Enron's collapse—indeed, seeming to imply that they were simply mistaken business choices—O'Neill said simply, "Companies come and go." He then chalked it all up to the everyday workings of capitalism: "Part of the genius of capitalism is people get to make good decisions or bad decisions, and they get to pay the consequences or enjoy the fruits of their decisions." The problem is that it was thousands of innocent Americans having no say in Enron's decisions who paid the consequences. One wonders how a cabinet-level spokesman for a president who is the self-described apostle of "compassionate conservatism" could speak with such dispassion of so great a tragedy without even one mention of the terrible suffering of Enron's many victims. Bush himself finally spoke on January 22, 2002—some six weeks after Enron's collapse and after congressional hearings had made it clear that the issue was not going away—belatedly claiming he was "outraged."

The reason for Bush's reluctance to speak against Enron becomes clear with one important fact: that Bush had a close association with Enron chairman and CEO Kenneth Lay that stretched at least as far back as the 1992 Republican National Convention, according to the reportage of the *Houston Chronicle*. Or even back to 1989, as Lay himself told the *Dallas Morning News* in 2001. In fact, in a 1997 letter to Lay, Bush calls him one of his "old friends." Apparently, what Bush sought to hide by keeping silent about Lay and the Enron mess was a sordid tale of cronyism.

Lay was a former business associate of Bush who had supported him in every one of his campaigns for public office. When Bush ran for governor of Texas in 1994, Lay and his wife donated $47,500 to Bush's campaign, while contributing $12,500 to that of his opponent Ann Richards, the incumbent governor. In fact, in 1994 Enron's political action committee and Enron executives—including Lay—collectively gave $146,500 to Bush, as against $19,500 to Richards. Total donations from Lay and his wife include $122,500 for George W. Bush's gubernatorial runs, $100,000 for his presidential inauguration, and $250,000 for the presidential library of Bush's father, George H. W. Bush. Enron and its executives gave George W. Bush a total of $736,680 for his two gubernatorial campaigns, his first presidential campaign, his election-recount fund, and his first inaugural gala.

Lay even lent Bush a corporate jet during his campaign for the White House. So close was Lay's association with Bush that Bush called him "Kenny Boy," and Lay was Bush's personal luncheon guest on Bush's first full day in the White House. To this day, Enron under Lay's leadership ranks as the top contributor to Bush's political career. And Bush has counted no less than seventeen former Enron executives or consultants in top-level positions in his administration, including his chief economic advisor, Larry Lindsey.

But rather than honestly admitting the close ties of his administration to the fallen corporate giant—and his close personal ties to Lay—Bush lied. He told the American people that he hardly knew Lay and hadn't spoken to him in months. Although it might have been technically correct that he had not spoken directly to Lay recently, Bush's statement still was untrue, because his assertion intentionally gave the false impression that he had only a passing acquaintance with Lay. He did not tell the American people that Lay was his personal luncheon guest on his first day in office, or that he'd had a relationship with him for at least a decade. He didn't describe him as a friend, or even a business associate. Bush never set the record straight, nor did he ever express the righteous indignation over the lives torn asunder by rank corporate greed that one would expect from a man who so publicly promised compassion for those in need. The words of the prophet render their judgment on all involved in the Enron travesty: "Woe to him who builds his house by unrighteousness,/and his upper rooms by injustice;/who makes his neighbors work for nothing,/ and does not give them their wages" (Jeremiah 22:13).

.   .   .

FINALLY, an old proverb holds that a person's character is reflected in the company he keeps. If that saying is true, then Bush's disdain for the needs—at times even the humanity—of those outside his elite circle of caring is chillingly confirmed by his choice of Richard B. Cheney as his second in command. Dick Cheney's voting record while a congressman from Wyoming is a frightening study in contempt for workers, struggling single mothers, children, students, even the elderly. Evidence of even a modicum of compassion for the vulnerable and needy in American society is virtually nonexistent in Cheney's record. The following is just a sampling of his positions.

While a congressman, Dick Cheney

- voted against the 1984 Hunger Relief Act, which expanded eligibility for the federal food stamp program.
- cast *ten separate votes* against funding nutrition programs for children, including one vote in 1983 opposing a move to protect food programs for women and infants from budget cuts, a position so callous that he was joined by *just fifteen* of his 435 House colleagues.
- voted in 1983 to limit Social Security cost-of-living adjustments for retired Americans living on fixed incomes, and in 1998 voted against limiting out-of-pocket expenses for Medicare recipients—most of whom, again, were seniors. His votes were so consistently counter to the interests of senior citizens that a Cox News Service headline declared, "Senior Groups Call Cheney's Voting Record a Disaster."
- voted in 1982 against providing mortgage assistance for low-income home buyers.
- repeatedly voted against maintaining funding for Head Start programs.
- opposed college student aid programs contained in the Higher Education Act.

- repeatedly voted against programs designed to provide assistance to displaced workers.
- voted in 1985 against legislation requiring factory owners to notify employees before closing plants.
- during the recession in the early 1980s, voted to block extension of unemployment benefits and provisions that would provide health insurance for the unemployed and their families.
- voted against the Equal Rights Amendment in 1983.
- voted to support Ronald Reagan's veto of the Civil Rights Restoration Act of 1987.
- voted against measures that would help local school districts offset the cost of desegregating public schools.
- voted against hate crime legislation in 1988.
- as a strident supporter of apartheid in South Africa, actually voted against sanctioning South Africa's regime for its racially repressive policies. He was also a vocal opponent of Nelson Mandela's release from prison.

Cheney has been quick to accuse his political opponents of being out of touch with the "values of America." Yet on numerous occasions his congressional votes were so extreme that out of the 435 members of the House of Representatives

- he was *one of only nine* who in 1988 opposed granting time off for federal employees to care for sick family members.
- he was *one of only eight* who in 1987 voted against renewing the Older Americans Act, a program providing nutritional and other support services for the elderly. If Cheney's opposition had been successful, it would have effectively shut down the entire program.
- he was *one of only four* to vote against the Undetectable Firearms Act of 1988, legislation written to prohibit the production and importation of weapons that would not be detected by metal detectors, including plastic guns.

Now, one could argue that the fact of Cheney's congressional votes being so counter to the vast majority of his colleagues' indicates courage to stand for his principles. What is troubling is not his willingness to stand for his principles. What is troubling is the mean-spiritedness of the principles that he stands for.

Cheney's positions while in the White House, both as Ronald Reagan's aide and as vice president to George W. Bush, have shown no discernible difference from his congressional votes. One of his first acts as vice president was to convene secret meetings of the heads of America's top oil corporations to help formulate the very governmental policies that would regulate them. America's oil companies have since gone on to post record earnings. Yet when questions of conflict of interest arose, Cheney not only refused to divulge the decisions made at those meetings, but even what was discussed, even the names of the attendees. In the last five years Cheney has gone to extraordinary lengths to keep that information not only from the American people he is sworn to serve, but even from the United States Congress!

In addition, Cheney was a major player in the Bush administration's deceptions that fueled America's declaration of war on Iraq. Again and again he publicly repeated the fictions that Iraq was behind the 9/11 acts of terrorism and that Iraq possessed megatons of weapons of mass destruction. He capped his assertions by claiming that there would be no significant resistance to the American occupation of Iraq; indeed, he claimed that the Iraqi people would actually honor American troops as heroes. In a widely distributed Associated Press interview on November 28, 2005, Lawrence Wilkerson, chief of staff to former Secretary of State Colin Powell, contended that Cheney knew all the while that American troops would be greeted with fierce and deadly resistance rather than with flowers. "[O]therwise," said Wilkerson, "I have to declare him a moron, an idiot or a nefarious bastard."

Moreover, Cheney has rejected domestic and international policies such as the Geneva Accord, not to mention moral decency, by doggedly advocating the use of torture for prisoners held in America's "war on terror." In a November 18, 2005, interview with Britain's ITV news, Admiral

Stansfield Turner, a former director of the CIA, condemned Cheney as a "vice president for torture." Said Turner, "He [Cheney] advocates torture . . . I just don't understand how a man in that position can take such a stance."

Judged by the damning evidence of his congressional voting record and his political actions and policy positions since, Dick Cheney has been a mean-spirited, destructive, extremist right-wing presence on the American political landscape for decades. It is difficult to imagine a political record less compassionate and less Christian. Elmer Andersen, the former governor of Minnesota and a fellow Republican, put Cheney's politics in perspective: "I am more fearful for the state of this nation than I have ever been—because this country is in the hands of an evil man: Dick Cheney."

Yet President Bush expressed his endorsement of Cheney's hateful politics and his shameful refusal to treat the people's needs as holy by *twice* choosing him as his running mate, his de facto chief advisor, and the man entrusted to continue Bush's legacy if his term as president were to end prematurely. One can only conclude that George Bush's political views are the same as those of Dick Cheney. Unfortunately for America, indeed for the world, the politics of neither official are in any way consistent with the politics of Jesus.

❁

SEVEN

Reagan, Bush,
the Politics of Jesus, and
the Politics of the Church

ORE APPALLING than the betrayal of the politics of Jesus by
these professed Christian political leaders of America is the
fact that their respective onslaughts on the poor and vulnerable were never challenged by the major religious voices of this country—
the televangelists and pastors to whom both Ronald Reagan and George
W. Bush have lent such willing ears. Indeed, the religious figures in question actually aligned themselves with them. This has been particularly so
in Bush's case. How could these ministers of the Gospel actively support
political deeds that in so many ways have been counter to the teachings of
the Gospel and the entire ethical tradition of the Bible? There can be only
one answer: because they do not practice the politics of Jesus. They practice the politics of Baal.

Remember the prophets of Baal (1 Kings 18) in chapter 1 who aligned
themselves with the despotic King Ahab? Despite the terrible effects of
Ahab's exploitative, repressive policies on their own people, those prophets

never challenged Ahab's actions or took him to task. Instead they supported him, made excuses for his sins, and pronounced his transgressions holy. Yet their support for Ahab was not predicated on their belief in his *sadiqah*, his righteousness, for he was not righteous. Rather, it was based upon their own self-interest. It was in the false prophets' interest to maintain the status quo that gave them privileged status. It was in their interest to ignore Ahab's mistreatment of the poor, because their silence enabled them to stay close to the seat of earthly power. Most important, it was in their interest to support the king, because in return for their loyalty he recognized those false prophets as the true—that is, the politically correct— prophets of God, with the all the rank, riches, power, and deference that came with that exalted status.

Sadly, many Christian leaders supported Reagan in his wrongdoing and continue to support Bush in his transgressions just as the prophets of Baal supported Ahab. Not all religious leaders have done so, however. Some of the so-called liberal religious leaders have spoken up, and some so-called conservatives have, too. For instance, in the summer of 2002, forty evangelical leaders wrote Bush calling for an "evenhanded U.S. policy" toward Israel and Palestine. They rejected "the way some have distorted biblical passages as their rationale for uncritical support" for Israel as a danger to world peace. In December 2002, as war with Iraq began to seem more and more imminent, an interdenominational group of 125 bishops, nuns, clergy, and laypersons signed a full-page ad in the *New York Times* that read, in part, "President Bush: Jesus changed your heart. Now let Him change your mind."

Some religious leaders were even more pointed in the counsel they offered. After visiting Iraq in January 2003, Roman Catholic Bishop Thomas Gumbleton of Detroit remarked, "The Bush administration's war on Iraq violates every value we hold as people of faith and conscience." The National Council of Churches and the leaders of United Methodism, Bush's own denomination, went even further: they respectfully tried to personally present their biblical views to him about the impending Iraq war. Yet they were turned away because, unlike the prophets of Baal, they were unwilling to say what the president wanted to hear. Despite their failure to stop Bush's march to war, these religious figures discharged their prophetic duty: they spoke truth to power, even if those in power refused to listen.

In contrast, those in the Church who had Bush's ear offered few words of challenge or critique to him, except with regard to their own particular issues of interest, such as same-sex marriage. They used every resource and every effort to be heard on that issue and another issue of great concern, violation of the rights of the unborn. They raised their voices to their highest pitch while decrying these issues, yet, shockingly, they never decried violation of the rights of the *already* born, like Reagan's racist behavior or Bush's lack of respect for human life, and the shameful abuse of the poor by them both. These presidents flagrantly violated the teachings of Jesus Christ in the name of Jesus Christ, yet to this day the Christian leaders who were closest to Reagan and Bush—those on the religious right—have said virtually nothing against their unjust policies. They had ample opportunity to confront both presidents; they were invited to interact with both often enough. Indeed, in a 2005 interview, Rev. Jerry Falwell bragged that the Council for National Policy (CNP), which he cofounded with Tim LaHaye, the conservative minister and coauthor of the best-selling *Left Behind* novels, is made up of "four or five hundred of the biggest conservative guns in the country." Falwell went on, "Ronald Reagan, both George Bushes . . . you name it. There's nobody who hasn't been here." Referring to the Arlington Group, the CNP's select inner circle, Falwell boasted, "We often call the White House and Karl Rove while we are meeting. Everyone takes our calls."

But rather than use their intimate access to the corridors of power to hold Reagan and Bush to the high standards and responsibilities laid upon them by the Gospel of Jesus Christ, instead these religious leaders have reduced the demands of holiness from doing just and righteous deeds to voicing religious slogans and pious rhetoric. In other words, as long as Reagan and Bush called themselves "men of faith," quoted scripture, and kept certain religious leaders close, these handpicked ministers chose to be silent about the betrayal of the Gospel by both Reagan and Bush and their wholesale violations of the politics of Jesus.

But why didn't these supposed men of God speak up and set our heads of state straight? Why didn't they condemn the presidents' un-Christian policies and show themselves willing to rise up in prophetic indignation if their counsel was ignored?

It is true that these religious leaders may have been seduced by earthly power and its benefits, like the prophets of Baal. However, their abdication of their duty to the Gospel of Jesus Christ cannot be fully explained by the allure of proximity to the seat of worldly power. The truth is that these religious leaders have endorsed unjust presidential policies because those policies agree with their own views of the world.

Some supported Reagan's supremacist racial politics because they themselves held the same racial attitudes as he. They supported his opposition to civil rights for all Americans because, like him, they were opposed to, or at least were ambivalent about, granting the fullest fruits of citizenship to every segment of American society, regardless of class, gender, or ethnicity.

They supported Bush's elitist assault on the homeless, the unemployed, the least economically secure, and the most socially vulnerable because they themselves identified with or aspired to upper-class wealth. They didn't care to struggle to establish God's kingdom of justice on earth as in heaven. They didn't want to change a politically and economically unjust pie—they just wanted a bigger slice of it. They were more concerned with staging huge (and extremely profitable) conferences, building luxurious churches, and garnering the trappings of wealth than with lifting up the poor. And the allure of the millions of dollars promised by Bush's faith-based initiatives may have been a factor as well.

The old-time prophets of Baal should have spoken truth to power, and today's Christian leaders should do the same. They should have confronted both Reagan and Bush and recited the words of the prophet Isaiah in their hearing: "Thus saith the LORD: . . . /Is this not the fast that I choose:/to loose the bonds of injustice,/to undo the thongs of the yoke,/ to let the oppressed go free,/and to break every yoke?/Is it not to share your bread with the hungry,/and bring the homeless poor into your house;/when you see the naked, cover him . . . ?" (Isaiah 56:1; 58:6–7).

As supposed shepherds following the model of Jesus they should have declared to our political leaders, "Woe to you . . . hypocrites! for you . . . have neglected . . . justice and mercy" (Matthew 23:23). If they were branded as "troublemakers" for their truthfulness and turned away as the prophets of God were also turned away by Ahab, the religious leaders who had these presidents' ears should have paraphrased Elijah's outraged response to Ahab: "We have not troubled America, but you have . . . because you have forsaken the commandments of the LORD and followed the Baals" (see 1 Kings 18:18). Instead, they stand indicted by Jesus' warning: "Beware of false prophets, who come to you in sheep's clothing but inwardly are ravenous wolves" (Matthew 7:15).

If they truly were servants of the radical Gospel of Jesus Christ, that's what they would have done. But the religious leaders so close to Ronald Reagan and George W. Bush chose not to. They have chosen to forget that Jesus was more concerned with the needs of the poor than with the desires of the rich; that he enjoined his followers to value all God's children in equal measure; that he exhorted them to be merciful and kind and honest and just. They have chosen to forget that Jesus said to those who grant unjust favors to members of their own social circle or economic class or race or ethnicity: "[I]f you love those who love you, what reward do you have?" (Matthew 5:46). They have chosen to forget. That is why, despite all their pious claims, the ministers and pastors who have elected to cozy up to those in power rather than confront them do not practice the politics of Jesus. Their politics are the politics of Baal.

A telling example of the wrongheadedness of the politics and biblical understanding of these ministers and pastors is seen in the difference in their treatment of the transgressions of President William Jefferson Clinton and the transgressions of President George W. Bush.

Bill Clinton committed an immoral and deeply offensive act by engaging in sexual activity in the Oval Office with a twenty-five-year-old White House intern, a woman young enough to be his child, and then lying about it. One can understand that shame and fear of humiliation in the eyes of the world caused Clinton to lie. But his actions were still wrong. The American people, particularly the Church, responded with justified disgust and denunciation. The Congress even voted to impeach Clinton for his lie.

As immoral as Clinton's act was, it was a transgression against himself, his family, and the young woman and her family. Although many Americans were offended and sorely disappointed by Clinton's action, in actuality the greatest harm was to these two families, with no material harm to anyone else.

However, George Bush's untruths about his reasons for embroiling the United States in a spiraling war with Iraq have cost unfathomable human suffering—thousands of lives lost, with even more lives made hellish by catastrophic injury and loss of homes and possessions. Yet the same religious leaders who so vociferously denounced Clinton for his lapses in personal morality have uttered not a word about the death and destruction caused by the much greater sin of George W. Bush. Why? He represented their personal interests, to be sure. But more than that, Bush's crimes against humanity have escaped sustained public religious scrutiny because great numbers of mainstream Church leaders, especially those on the religious right, nowadays have reduced Jesus' gospel of justice and liberation to a narrow doctrine of personal piety that focuses solely on individual sins, while ignoring the much more deadly sin of gross social injustice.

The prophet Isaiah admonished us, "seek justice,/rescue the oppressed" (Isaiah 1:17). This is a clear call for radical change in the destructive and self-seeking political structures that dominate the world today. Yet despite an overwhelming number of clear biblical pronouncements to the contrary, too many Christian leaders persist in reducing everything to the personal and the individual. The trenchant admonition of the sixth chapter of the Letter to the Ephesians is reversed in their practice. Ephesians announces, "We wrestle not against flesh and blood"—that is, individuals—"but against principalities, against powers, against the rulers . . . in high places" (6:12 [KJV]). But today's religious leaders act as if the scripture says the opposite: Our struggle is *not* against principalities and powers and rulers in high places.

Sadly, many of these clergy have replaced God's call to establish justice in the world with narrow, hyperspiritualized calls for Christians to spend their time "praising" God. Their notion of praising God is not the substantive holistic praise modeled by Jesus that seeks to establish God's kingdom of health and wholeness and justice on earth as in heaven. Their idea of praise is not the praise that is offered by consistently acting with justice and love in the world. It is not the praise made manifest by the actual work of our limbs; it is praise offered only with our lips, our liturgies, our Sunday worship.

This form of praise does not ask, "What would Jesus have us do?" but simply "What would Jesus have us sing and shout?" The focus of too much of today's religiosity is not on actions, just on words. This narrow, one-dimensional form of praise is epitomized by the popular but tragically mistaken assertion that is heard in so many churches today: "Hallelujah is the highest form of praise!" In fact, a popular book by a well-known minister and teacher lists numerous forms of praise, yet praising God by striving to make this a just world is not one of them. But how can the praise of our lips be more important than praise offered by the works of our hands?

WHEN THE RELIGIOUS LEADERS of America saw the injustice coming from the White House, they should have addressed it by taking the prophetic stance Jesus enjoined upon us. They should have reminded our heads of state that our God is a God of justice, a friend to the poor, a lover of peace, a demander of truth, a hater of exploitation and elitism and bullying of the vulnerable. They should have reminded them that those who truly follow Jesus bring good news to the needy, release to those unjustly imprisoned, and liberation to those held fast by ungodly bonds of any kind. They should have reminded the political leaders of our nation that when they bring intentional lies and bad news to those who are poor and needy and vulnerable and weak, by their own actions they declare themselves to be enemies of the Good News of Jesus Christ.

If the religious leaders who had access to President Ronald Reagan and President George W. Bush had confronted them with the truth of Jesus' gospel of justice, would Reagan have persisted in his wrong? Would he have continually turned his back on the poor? Would he have opposed the

Equal Rights Amendment, the Civil Rights Amendment? Would he have persisted in his dastardly racial politics, in his support of the brutal apartheid regime? Would he have legitimized the racism of Bob Jones University or implicitly endorsed the horror of Philadelphia, Mississippi? Would he have so callously ignored the welfare of "the least of these" and further enriched the already rich at the expense of the suffering poor? Would he have told false stories to inflame anger against the most vulnerable Americans? Would he have devalued the children of the needy so deeply that he was willing to feed them ketchup in lieu of vegetables?

Would Bush have unleashed his own onslaught on the poor? Would he have pushed a world supremacist agenda that valorizes the imperialistic wiles of Caesar rather than the freedom and justice offered by Christ? Would Bush continue to show so little regard for human life outside his narrow circle of caring? Would he still have started an unjust, unprovoked war that has sent innocent young men and women to horrible deaths based on intentional untruths? Would he have built so profound a pattern of lies and prevarications and betrayals of those he was pledged to serve?

We do not know, because apparently the religious leaders that were close to Reagan and are so close to Bush never confronted them. But one thing is sure: these leaders did not proclaim the politics of Jesus to them. If they had, neither president would have been able to present his injustices to the world as the hand of God's justice. But because these religious leaders have not proclaimed the politics of Jesus, they have become like the false prophets so roundly condemned by the prophet Ezekiel for calling unjust authorities virtuous and telling the world that God is on their side: "Its prophets have smeared whitewash on their behalf, seeing false visions and divining lies for them, saying, 'Thus says the Lord GOD,' when the LORD has not spoken" (Ezekiel 22:28).

EIGHT

✵

The Politics of Jesus:
Conservative or Liberal?

I N HIS FINE LITTLE BOOK *In the Name of Jesus*, the late Christian mystic
Henri Nouwen declares: "Words like 'right wing,' 'reactionaries,' 'conservative,' 'liberal,' and 'left-wing' seem more like political battles for
power than spiritual searches for the truth."

Sadly, this is an accurate description of the Church in America today.
In print, in pulpits, on television, and even on the silver screen, Christians
use "conservative" and "liberal" either to support their own positions or
to dismiss others'. Seldom is either designation used in an informed way.
In fact, these terms, especially "conservative," are so often bandied about
in Jesus' name that the confusion surrounding them has obscured and distorted for most Americans the true meaning of his politics.

For instance, some confuse *moral* conservatism with *political* conservatism. But the two certainly are not the same, though many politicians
and Church leaders would have us think they are. Others hold the mistaken belief that moral or fiscal *liberality*—that is, *looseness*—is the same as

political *liberalism.* This, too, is wrong. Still, not only have we divided the Church along this ill-informed conservative/liberal fault line, but, worse, we have come to associate whatever understanding we have of these terms with particular political parties.

This chapter will attempt to clarify the true meanings of these hot-button terms. It will also seek to answer a question that is playing such a divisive role in the Church today: Which political practices and policy decisions seem closest to the politics of Jesus, those called "conservative" or those characterized as "liberal"?

IN THE SERMON on the Mount, Jesus asks, "Why do you see the speck in your neighbor's eye, but do not notice the log in your own eye?" (Matthew 7:3). This question could be posed to every political faction on the horizon. In American politics there has always been name calling, accusations, and angry recriminations. Yet the charges and denunciations between conservatives and liberals today have escalated to a fever pitch. The two camps have engaged in an ongoing public discourse of venomous, hateful, even homicidal claims and charges—often in the name of Jesus—that in its scope is paralleled in America only by the mean-spiritedness and paranoia of the Salem witch hunts of the seventeenth century and the McCarthy witch hunts of the 1950s.

Although both factions bear considerable blame in this contentious exchange, it seems that religious conservatives have been the major malefactors. In part this may be because conservative politicians have amassed a much more effective network of communications. In his book *What Liberal Media?* Eric Alterman has shown that despite conservatives' charges that most communications media in America are controlled by liberals, the truth is that the vast majority are run by conservatives. No less than William Kristol, one of the top conservative strategists in America, acknowledged as much. "I admit it," said Kristol. "The liberal media were never that powerful, and the whole thing was often used as an excuse by conservatives for conservative failures."

In addition, conservatives control most political think tanks in America, and their think tanks are America's best endowed by far. In fact, these right-wing foundations have been so successful that when one of the largest, the John M. Olin Foundation, funder of such major conservative think tanks as the Federalist Society, the Heritage Foundation, and the American Enterprise Institute, ceased operations at the end of 2005, it caused little anxiety among conservatives, despite the Olin Foundation's having disbursed some $400 million to conservative causes since 1973. But the most significant factor by far in the mischaracterization of liberalism is the constantly repeated charge by conservative commentators that liberals and political liberalism are to blame for virtually all that is wrong with America. In fact, in 1990, then Republican House Whip Newt Gingrich hired professional pollsters to produce what political commentator Bruce J. Miller calls "a lexicon of demonization." Gingrich circulated the results of the poll in a memo entitled "Language: A Key Mechanism of Control." The memo instructed conservative politicians to describe liberals as often as possible using pejorative words and phrases, including sick, pathetic, traitors, anti-flag, anti-family, anti-child, anti-jobs, corrupt, selfish, cheat, steal, criminal rights, permissive attitudes, pessimistic, and radical.

Ann Coulter, a darling of the right, has made a cottage industry of demonizing liberalism. In newspapers, magazines, and three bestselling books, she makes such statements as these: "Liberals hate America"; "Liberals seek to destroy sexual differentiation in order to destroy morality"; "Liberals . . . promote immoral destructive behavior . . . they embrace criminals . . . Every pernicious idea that comes down the pike is embraced by liberals . . . Liberals hate society." With unclear logic she concludes, "Even Islamic terrorists don't hate America like liberals do."

Apparently, conservative television commentator Sean Hannity is so intent on issuing his own broadsides against liberalism that he wants Americans to know that he equates it with wickedness without even having to open his 2004 book, *Deliver Us from Evil: Defeating Terrorism, Despotism, and Liberalism.* Journalist Michael Savage shows eagerness for his own ideas to be similarly signaled by the title of his book, *Liberalism Is a Mental Disorder.*

But not only do conservatives paint the political philosophy of liberalism as the product of insanity, they actually characterize it as the creation of the devil. Rev. Jerry Falwell, founder of the Moral Majority, is widely reported to have declared, "[W]e're fighting against liberalism . . . we are fighting against all the systems of Satan . . . our battle is with Satan himself."

Rev. Bob Jones III, president of the conservative Bob Jones University (which, coincidentally, still embraced racial segregation as an official institutional policy as late as 2000), likened liberals to Christ-haters in the letter to President George W. Bush that was cited above: "You owe the liberals nothing. They despise you because they despise your Christ."

Tony Perkins, president of the Family Research Council, equates liberalism with "anti-Christian dogma." On his group's Web site during the 2005 senatorial dispute over confirmation of several of President Bush's lower-court judicial nominees, Perkins charged liberals and liberalism with trying to destroy Christianity in America by "quietly working under the veil of the judiciary, like thieves in the night, to rob us of our Christian heritage and our religious freedoms."

Coulter makes the blanket charge, "Liberals hate all religions except Islam." Then, to ensure that it is clear that she considers liberals completely godless, she puts it more succinctly: "Liberals hate religion," as in *all* religions.

Coulter finally seems to summarize the conservative view. Despite the fact that many of those who have made the greatest social contributions to America have been political liberals, including Theodore Roosevelt, Jane Addams, Franklin D. Roosevelt, Susan B. Anthony, Dorothy Day, Martin Luther King, Jr., and even Abraham Lincoln, Coulter still declares that "there is only one thing wrong with liberals: they're no good."

Not only are today's conservatives uncivil in their rhetoric, but they seem to ignore some of Jesus' most important pronouncements, such as "Love your enemies." By this Jesus did not mean to give enemies free rein to wreak harm and havoc. He was referring to the disposition of one's heart, to the importance of "keeping track of the other's humanity," as the scholar and cultural critic Cornel West puts it, even while decrying the other's actions. Yet it seems that conservative politicians overlook this central teaching of Jesus. Seldom in the public sphere does one hear conservatives speak of love. More often they talk about hate and the destruction of others.

For instance, conservative antiabortion activist Randall Terry has declared to fellow antiabortionists, "I want you to let a wave of hatred wash over you. Yes, hatred is good." Even President George W. Bush used the language of hate as he whipped up support for his invasion of Iraq: "I hate Saddam. He tried to kill my daddy."

But not only is conservatives' antiliberal rhetoric hateful and insulting, it sometimes borders on the murderous. A popular bumper-sticker slogan credited to Michael Gunn, a Mississippi legislator, asks, "If guns are outlawed, how can we shoot the liberals?" A bumper sticker displayed by Florida antiabortion activist John Burt seems to advocate vigilante slayings of proponents of legalized abortion. "Execute murderers and abortionists," it exhorts. At a Washington conference staged by the Judeo-Christian Council for Constitutional Restoration in April 2005 and entitled "Confronting the Judicial War on Faith," Edwin Vieira, a prominent conservative lawyer, seemed to threaten "liberal judges" with death. Vieira said that his own "bottom line" for judges who do not share his conservative agenda is that of the murderous Joseph Stalin. "[Stalin] had a slogan," Vieira said, "and it worked very well for him whenever he ran into difficulty: 'no man, no problem.' " So threatening was the conservatives' tone against the federal judiciary, particularly Supreme Court Justice Anthony Kennedy, that Dana Milbank of the *Washington Post* suggested in print at the conference's end that Kennedy might consider getting "a few more bodyguards."

Talk of hatred and killing seems to have invaded even some conservative church pulpits. When discussing those they consider America's political enemies, some of the nation's most prominent conservative religious figures publicly advocate subjecting them to violence and death. Rev. Jerry Falwell called not for reconciliation or peacemaking with Middle Eastern terrorists, but for their murder. "Kill them all," he said. "Blow them away in the name of the Lord."

When speaking of Middle Eastern terrorists, Ann Coulter sounds like a terrorist herself. "We should invade their countries," she says, "kill their leaders, and convert them to Christianity."

As much as Ann Coulter hates terrorists, she does not stop with them. She expresses similar hatred for all whose political opinions differ from her own. Rather than condemning the monstrous crime of Timothy McVeigh, who murdered scores of innocents in Oklahoma City, including preschool-aged children, instead Coulter has said, "My only regret with Timothy McVeigh is he did not go to the *New York Times* building," that is, to kill more innocent persons there. To date she has neither retracted this venomous statement nor apologized to McVeigh's victims or their families. This from a woman who calls herself a follower of Jesus.

Ironically, as dramatic and vivid as these condemnations are, upon a closer look it becomes clear that they have nothing to do with true liberalism. Although conservatives' characterizations of liberalism are treated as accepted wisdom nowadays, they are really *mis*characterizations, attempts to portray liberals as perverse, extremist, and un-American. But what these critics must remember is that conservatism has its own crazies and extremists, including some of the most dangerous and hateful groups in America. Neo-Nazis, homicidal antiabortionists, and murderous anti-Semitic racists like the Knights of the Ku Klux Klan all count themselves as conservatives in good standing. In fact, the creed of the hate-mongering Ku Klux Klan reads like a pious, God-fearing Christian confession: "We, the Order of the Knights of the Ku Klux Klan, reverentially acknowledge the majesty and supremacy of Almighty God and recognize His goodness and providence through Jesus Christ our Lord."

Clearly there is enough extremism to go around. But a spirit of sobriety tells us that just as at its base true conservatism is not about hateful rhetoric and murderous behavior, neither is true liberalism about permissiveness or moral laxity. Indeed, moral permissiveness, moral looseness, and irreligiosity are no more representative of true American political liberalism than cross burnings and slave-owning churchgoers are representative of true political conservatism.

Still, in the last few decades conservative politicians and power seekers have attached all kinds of baggage to liberalism. Today liberalism is so saddled with exaggerations, caricatures, and stereotypes that what it has meant for this country seems to have been forgotten. The true nature of conservatism is not much clearer. So what is conservatism, and why do conservatives attack liberalism with such fury?

CONSERVATISM

The first thing to keep in mind is that conservatism and liberalism are not cultural formations, moral identities, or even religious categories. They are political philosophies. What this means is that they are differing approaches to how society should be organized, how wealth and services should be used and distributed to the people, and how the freedoms that make up our lives should be practiced and protected. In other words, liberalism and conservatism are different definitions of what is right and just in practice, and what is not.

It is important to note that political conservatism is not the same as moral conservatism. Some conservative politicians have worked hard to confuse the two, apparently to gain the political support of the religious right. So far this strategy has worked well for conservative politicians—so well that they have managed to virtually equate their own political agenda with Christianity itself. But there is a vast difference between the morality of Christianity and the politicality of conservative politicians.

Moral conservatism is about morality and ethics. It is concerned primarily with personal piety as expressed through biblically endorsed moral and ethical conduct, particularly with regard to family and sexual relations, though it includes all other social interactions as well. To be sure, Christianity is—and should be—*morally* conservative. That is, Christians should cleave to the morals and ethics set down in the Bible and the best of the Christian moral tradition as articulated by Jesus, particularly in his moral discourse in the Sermon on the Mount. This is moral conservatism. But it is not the same as *political* conservatism.

As students of the New Testament know, Jesus' moral conservatism called for sincerely and wholeheartedly reclaiming the morality and ethical teachings of the Old Testament. In the Sermon on the Mount, he even intensified some Old Testament strictures, such as those regarding adultery and divorce.

Yet despite Jesus' *moral* conservatism, by no stretch of the imagination was he a *political* conservative. His goal was not to maintain or *conserve* the unjust distribution of wealth and power in Israel in which a few—mostly members of the religious establishment—lived lives of wealth and privilege while the masses struggled to survive. Jesus was not about *conserving* the status quo, he was about *changing* it. Indeed, transforming the unjust social and political order under which his people suffered was of such paramount concern for Jesus that, as we saw in chapter 4, he specifically taught his disciples to pray for a new, just political order: "Pray like this:/*Thy* kingdom come./*Thy* will be done,/on earth as it is in heaven" (Matthew 6:9–10 [RSV]).

However, despite its unquestionable importance for Jesus, greater equality of wealth and opportunity for the common people has never been conservatism's concern. The sad truth is that despite the positive role moral conservatism plays in the preservation of traditional social and religious values, a major defining feature of *political* conservatism in every society in every historical era has been its unerring dedication to maintaining and conserving wealth, power, and authority in the hands of those who already possess it—that is, the rich elites who dominate their societies. When the political landscape in our nation is surveyed, it becomes tragically clear that this is also the case with American political conservatives today, for seldom have they advocated an idea whose primary purpose was to help common people. For all its pious self-presentation, political conservatism in this country has historically been one of the greatest obstacles to the social and economic well-being of ordinary Americans. An examination of politics in America reveals that the primary concern of conservatism today is what it has always been: to serve the haves. The definition of conservatism in *The HarperCollins Dictionary of American Government and Politics* clearly reflects this: "Conservatives are most often found among those who have, or have the potential to have, wealth and property."

At the most basic level, then, political conservatism is about maintaining the status quo, preserving the political and social order as it already exists, no matter how few ordinary citizens' interests are served by that social order and no matter how unjust it might be. In a nutshell, the purpose of political conservatism is to preserve the balance of wealth and power as it already stands.

Therefore, as a political doctrine, conservatism is the ideological means by which rich elites justify the privileged existence they enjoy at the expense of their poorer countrymen. An oft-cited observation by John Kenneth Galbraith, former U.S. ambassador and the most widely read economist of the twentieth century, puts it this way: "The modern conservative is engaged in one of man's oldest exercises in moral philosophy; that is, the search for a superior moral justification for selfishness."

Jesus reminds us that a tree is known by the fruit it bears. Nowhere is this more true than with regard to the fruits of political conservatism. Take Medicare, for example.

When Medicare was proposed in the mid-1960s by President Lyndon B. Johnson, conservatives vociferously opposed it. Future president George H. W. Bush, then a congressman from Texas, was so opposed that he predicted that if Congress adopted Medicare, America's entire health-care system would collapse. Despite Medicare's obvious benefits for poor and middle-class Americans, Bush's future boss, Ronald Reagan, went so far as to attack it as "the advance of socialism." Apparently, if it had been left to conservatives, the poor and elderly Americans most in need of health care would have had no access to it. One would hope to find that the lack of concern for the needs of the poor and vulnerable that conservatives have shown in the case of Medicare is an exception. Unfortunately, it is closer to the rule.

THE HISTORICAL ROOTS OF POLITICAL CONSERVATISM

Conservatives have existed in every society in which there have been significant disparities in wealth. In Jesus' day it was little different. Indeed, his response to the conservatives of his own setting in life is at the heart of the politics of Jesus.

As we have seen, the conservatives of Jesus' day were the hereditary Jerusalem priestly aristocracy and the rich Jerusalem elites, which included the Sadducees, who were almost exclusively men of wealth, and the Pharisees, who were influential retainers aligned with the aristocratic priests. The Gospels tell us that Jesus opposed the conservative machinations used by these elites to protect their privileged existence. He was outraged by their selfish participation in the repression and exploitation of their own people. He rejected the misleading, self-serving pronouncements they made as if they were speaking for God when too often they were just spewing self-serving rhetoric. Jesus firmly stood against their commitment to a social order that enriched a few over the just-as-deserving many. From this he never wavered, nor did he ever retract one word.

That is how Jesus responded to the conservatives of his day. With unfaltering fervor he opposed their maintenance of a class-based social order that violated the law of God by perpetuating extreme disparities of wealth. Just as Jesus' commitment to the well-being of the poor never wavered, conservatism's basic dedication to the interests of rich elites has remained consistent as well, although the details have differed throughout history from society to society.

Conservatism in America

The roots of conservative politics in America can be traced to the eighteenth-century British Tory party, the political elitists who aligned themselves with British royal authority and imperial interests. The Tory party in America—later called Whigs—is remembered for the same reason: they also aligned with the British aristocracy, in their case by opposing the Declaration of Independence and the Revolutionary War because they believed that maintaining the status quo best served their own political and material interests.

After America won its independence, the memory of England's abuse remained so bitter for the former colonists that initially some of the signers of the Constitution of the new nation, including Thomas Jefferson, refused to endorse it until a Bill of Rights was added that would guard against the rise of an aristocracy in America like the one they had just freed themselves from. The primary purpose of the Bill of Rights was to ensure that in the new republic the common people and free laborers would enjoy the same protections as the rich.

Even with the Bill of Rights in place, however, during the succeeding decades the men of wealth in the young republic still managed to do exactly what the Founding Fathers had tried to guard against: they evolved an American aristocracy, a rich elite class made up of slaveholders and captains of commerce who too often succeeded in making their own narrow interests the primary concern of the government. An example of the single-minded commitment of this wealthy class to maintaining its wealth and privilege during America's early years is dramatically reflected in their response to the newly elected President Andrew Jackson.

By all accounts, Andrew Jackson was a populist who never forgot his South Carolina backwoods roots. He was also a staunch defender of slavery who became famous for his skill at slaughtering Native Americans. But neither Jackson nor most of his peers saw any contradiction in this because in Jackson's time, as in most of this nation's history, the principles of populism and democracy were applied only to white men. His blind spots notwithstanding, soon after assuming the presidency, Jackson set out to limit the ability of the rich elites and landed gentry to continue to "bend the acts of government to their own selfish purposes . . . to make the rich richer and the potent more powerful." The response of the "rich and potent" upper class to Jackson's populism was to launch a full-scale assault, not just on his policies—that would have been too revealing of their true motives—but primarily on his character instead. Andrew Jackson was the first president to be elected by a decisive popular mandate rather than by the electoral college, yet that meant nothing to his conservative opponents, who contrived to destroy his presidency by attacking him on every possible front.

What raised the conservatives' ire was what they considered to be Jackson's blasphemous decision as holder of the highest office in the land to align himself with the interests of the common people rather than join the rich in exploiting them. So with the fury they reserved for those who dared to challenge their economic supremacy, the wealthy elites, represented by the conservative Whig party, derided Jackson's casual manners and lack of social affectations as "ignorant." They called his mother a "Common Prostitute," claimed that Jackson was the issue of her marriage to a "Mullato Man" (an unthinkable sin in that day), and claimed that Jackson was not lawfully married to his wife, Rachel (their marriage had taken place under dubious circumstances). In a curious prefiguring of contemporary conservatives' practice of publicly demonizing those who refuse to go along with their agendas, Jackson's opponents published the notorious "Coffin Handbill," which listed some eighteen murders Jackson was alleged to have committed. To punctuate his supposed crimes, the name of each of the eighteen alleged victims was accompanied on the handbill by the image of a coffin. Although as a young duelist Jackson had killed at least one opponent—a lawyer named Charles Dickinson, for impugning the dignity of Rachel—most of the charges on the Coffin Handbill were unsubstantiated. Still, so widely was Jackson smeared in this way that one Jackson contemporary, Harriet Martineau, claimed that when a schoolboy in faraway England was asked who killed the biblical figure of Abel, the boy answered, "General Jackson, ma'am."

Parenthetically, the "Coffin Handbill" and the unsubstantiated murder accusations bring to mind *The Clinton Chronicles*, the video promoted by Rev. Jerry Falwell that charged President Bill Clinton with personally participating in some fifty-odd murders. The video also claimed that Clinton personally stole millions in public funds and was a major drug dealer to boot. Falwell himself gloated on CNN's *Crossfire* in May 1994, "I have on hours of videotapes produced the comments, testimonies, the view of Arkansas people who are saying these things."

These charges were found to be contrived and groundless, and the video has since been discredited as an absurd exercise in character assassination. Falwell now disavows any personal role in the video's production or distribution, despite his own gleeful televised statements and the unchallenged documentation of his involvement in the affair that was reported in the *Washington Post* on May 21, 1994. But Pat Matrisciana, founder of the conservative Citizens for Honest Government and the video's actual producer, acknowledged Falwell's role: "He [Falwell] did some infomercials . . . and sold lots and lots of videos. He became our largest distributor." Matrisciana also admitted that Falwell asked him to include statements in the video that both knew to be false.

AFTER JACKSON'S PRESIDENCY, conservatism's historical commitment to preserving the riches and power of elites was continued in the mid-nineteenth century principally by rich slaveholders, plantation aristocracy, and a budding class of industrialists. The depth of the slavers' and plantation owners' obsession with preserving the status quo is seen in their willingness to split the nation and cause the deaths of millions of fellow Americans in a devastating civil war, rather than willingly give up any measure of their unjust privilege.

When the Civil War ended, the sacrifices of soldiers on both sides who had been pawns in that war went mostly unrewarded. Many returned to ruined, overgrown farms. Others straggled into the nation's cities looking for work. Historian Howard Zinn observes of the latter,

> The cities to which the soldiers returned were death traps of typhus, tuberculosis, hunger, and fire. In New York, 100,000 people lived in the cellars of the slums; 12,000 women worked in houses of prostitution to keep from starving; the garbage, lying 2 feet deep in the streets, was alive with rats. In Philadelphia, while the rich got

fresh water from the Schuylkill River, everyone else drank from the Delaware, into which 13 million gallons of sewage were dumped every day.

By the latter part of the nineteenth century, working conditions at the hands of industrialists, Reconstructionists, and other exploiters of human misery were just as barbaric as the living conditions. Female laundry workers in Troy, New York, labored long hours daily in 100-degree temperatures for thirty-five to fifty cents per day. Railroad brakemen fared considerably better, but still most received no more than $1.75 for a twelve-hour day doing work that was considerably more dangerous than most. Zinn reports that in 1889 alone, "22,000 railroad workers were killed or injured," according to Interstate Commerce Commission records.

Periodic national financial crises wiped out small businesses and threw untold numbers of workers into homelessness and starvation, yet the rich elites continued to prosper. The Morgans, Astors, Vanderbilts, and Rockefellers, among others, became richer than ever. These capitalists became so rapacious and the plight of working Americans so deplorable that on July 4, 1876, the Workingmen's Party of Illinois issued a Centennial Declaration of Independence. It declared in part:

The present system has enabled capitalists to make laws in their own interests to the injury and oppression of the workers.

It has made the name of Democracy, for which our forefathers fought and died, a mockery and a shadow, by giving to [those with wealth and] property an unproportionate amount of representation and control over Legislation . . .

It has allowed the capitalists, as a class, to appropriate annually ⅞ of the entire production of the country . . .

It has therefore prevented mankind from fulfilling their natural destinies on earth—crushed out ambition, prevented marriages or caused false and unnatural ones—has shortened human life, destroyed morals and fostered crime, corrupted judges, ministers, and statesmen, shattered confidence, love and honor

> among men, and made life a selfish, merciless struggle for exis-
> tence instead of a noble and generous struggle for perfection, in
> which equal advantages should be given to all, and human lives
> relieved from an unnatural and degrading competition for
> bread . . .

The very next year, workers' unrest exploded into crippling strikes. Particularly hard hit were railroads, which were among the nation's largest employers. The railway owners used the clout their wealth provided to push state governments to send the National Guard to break the strikes. When National Guard troops were unable to halt the unrest, federal troops were moved in. By the time the railroad strikes of 1877 had ended, one hundred people had been slain, virtually all of them workers, and a thousand had been jailed.

Big business prevailed in this instance, just as it has in so many historical cases, simply because the government held fast to the strategy that served conservatives so well: it pretended neutrality and fairness while constantly serving the interests of the rich. What kept the wheels of this unjust system in motion were graft and cronyism. J. P. Morgan, Jay Gould, and others of the rich big-business elite paid government officials millions of dollars in bribes, and as a result were able to make millions more at the public's expense. What sustained this system, even when its illegality no longer could be hidden, was a mutually enriching alliance between America's politicians and America's rich upper crust (who were often one and the same). Legislators had long been enlisted to do the bidding of big business, but at the end of the nineteenth century there was another branch of government that even more effectively and more shamelessly served the interests of the rich: the Supreme Court of the United States of America.

The original purpose of the Fourteenth Amendment to the Constitution of the United States was to protect the legal rights of the nation's beleaguered citizens of African American descent, who were victimized daily in numerous nefarious ways with no legal recourse. The amendment declared, "nor shall any State deprive any person of life, liberty, or property, without due process of law." But rather than utilizing the amendment's provisions to protect blacks, at the urging of the nation's corporate elites the Court used it to protect big business instead. When state governments, increasingly concerned about corporations' price gouging and often rapacious policies, finally began passing statutes to regulate unbridled corporate profiteering, the Supreme Court was enlisted to counter the trend by accepting the argument that under the law corporations were "persons" whose "prosperity"—their immense wealth—should also be protected under the due process clause.

In 1886 alone, the Court used this ruling to strike down some 230 separate state laws regulating corporations. In fact, the Court was so zealously engaged in protecting the interests of big business that it seems to have forgotten about America's vulnerable black citizens altogether. Between 1890 and 1910, of the 307 Fourteenth Amendment cases heard by the Supreme Court, only 19 dealt with the rights of blacks. The Court's overarching concern for the interests of the rich elites was in effect summarized by Supreme Court Justice David J. Brewer in an 1893 speech to the New York State Bar Association: "It is the unvarying law that the wealth of the community will be in the hands of the few . . . and hence it always has been and until human nature is remodeled always will be true, that the wealth of a nation is in the hands of a few, while the many subsist upon the proceeds of their daily toil."

This sense of radical entitlement was the prism through which conservative jurists interpreted the United States Constitution. It is little wonder that rich businessmen's greed and unchecked privilege have resulted in some of the most shameful episodes in America's labor history. A particularly tragic example is the Ludlow Massacre.

In September 1913, eleven thousand coal miners went on strike protesting unsafe working conditions and virtual serfdom near the town of Ludlow in southern Colorado. After the mine owners evicted them from their company-owned shacks in retribution, the miners set up tent colonies to house their hungry, ill-clad families, even as they sought to negotiate with the owners for decent wages and humane living conditions. But the mine operators never even tried to negotiate in good faith. Their only concern was forcing the laborers back into the mines without making a single concession. To break the strike, the Colorado Fuel & Iron Corporation, which was owned by the Rockefeller family, hired goons from the notorious Baldwin-Felts Detective Agency who proceeded to attack the miners with rifles and Gatling guns. When the resolute miners still refused to give in, at the behest of the rich business operators, Governor Teller Ammons dispatched the National Guard to break the strikers' will. On April 20, 1914, two companies of the Colorado National Guard stationed themselves in the hills above the largest of the strikers' tent colonies, which housed a thousand people, and without warning or provocation, rained machine-gun fire on the defenseless workers and their families. Then the Guardsmen descended upon the camp, setting ablaze everything in their path. An account from that time recounts the horror:

> From the blazing tents rushed the women and children, only to be beaten back into the fire by the rain of bullets from the militia. The men rushed to the assistance of their families; and as they did so, they were dropped as the whirring messengers of death sped surely to the mark. [One leader of the strike] fell victim to the mine guards' fiendishness, being first clubbed, then shot in the back while he was their prisoner. Fifty-two bullets riddled his body . . . Fifty-five women and children perished in the fire of the Ludlow tent colony. Relief parties carrying the Red Cross flag were driven back by the gunmen, and for twenty-four hours the bodies lay crisping in the ashes.

The tragic account ends with the prophetic observation "Peace can never be built on the foundation of Greed and Oppression."

The exploitative fruit of conservative politics in early twentieth-century America was in abundant evidence in the misery visited not only upon miners, but also upon meatpackers, migrant laborers, and factory workers. The captains of industry treated the nation as their personal feeding trough and its workers as their serfs. The rich industrialists so devalued the humanity of laborers that Frederick Taylor, the inventor of the assembly line, which increased productivity but turned human beings into easily expendable cogs in the wheels of industry, explained with misplaced pride, "In our scheme, we do not ask the initiative of our men. We do not want any initiative. All we want of them is to obey orders we give them, do what we say, and do it quick." To the workers themselves he said, "[We] have you for your strength and mechanical ability, and we have other men for thinking."

The politics of naked greed and bald exploitation that masqueraded as patriotism and righteous public service outraged the nation's more liberal politicians. President Teddy Roosevelt declared the need for a "square deal" for rank-and-file Americans: "[W]hen I say I am for the square deal, I mean not merely that I stand for fair play under the present rules of the game, but that I stand for having those rules changed so as to work for a more substantial equality of opportunity and of reward for equally good service."

Although President Franklin D. Roosevelt was himself a charter member of America's rich elite, his disenchantment with the greed and hypocrisy of many members of his own class moved him, in close collaboration with his labor commissioner, Frances Perkins, to craft the set of programs he collectively called the New Deal to protect average Americans.

Roosevelt's New Deal instituted the most powerful protections ever seen in the United States against the greed of the rich elites and the concentration of power in their hands. The many crucial safeguards included the Federal Emergency Relief Administration, which provided federal funds to relieve the suffering of unemployed Americans during the Great Depression; the National Labor Relations Act, which for the first time protected trade unionists from retribution by their employers; the Fair Employment Act, which struck a significant blow against segregationist practices by prohibiting all employers doing business with federal agencies from "discriminat[ing] against persons of any race, color, creed, or nationality in matters of employment"; the Fair Employment Practices Commission (FEPC), which was empowered to investigate and take steps to eliminate acts of discrimination; and, of course, the Social Security Act.

A grateful America embraced Roosevelt's humane measures wholeheartedly, while, predictably, conservatives opposed them tooth and nail. Fortunately, the conservatives' opposition had little effect. In fact, with the victory of Roosevelt's liberalism, by the end of the 1940s political conservatism in America was decidedly on the wane. Roosevelt's Democratic Party held almost two-thirds of the Senate seats. By the end of the decade observers like the historian Louis Hartz and the literary critic Lionel Trilling were claiming liberalism as the sole intellectual tradition in America, which was simply another way of declaring that conservatism as a political force in America was dormant, if not dead.

After several years of relative quiescence, the demagoguery and "Redbaiting" of Joe McCarthy and Richard Nixon in the 1950s began a resurgence of political conservatism that has culminated in its powerful position on today's political scene. Most conservative commentators, however, trace the roots of America's awakened conservatism to the 1953 publication of Russell Kirk's *The Conservative Mind.* Observes Lee Edwards, a fellow at the Heritage Foundation, a major conservative think tank, "With one book, Russell Kirk made conservatism intellectually acceptable in America . . . Kirk gave the conservative movement its name." The accuracy of Edwards' observation is evinced by the paucity of public uses of the term "conservative" before Kirk's study. For instance, when William F. Buckley published *God and Man at Yale* in 1951, he called himself an "individualist." When Barry M. Goldwater was elected to the Senate a year later, his preferred terms of self-reference were "progressive Republican" and "Jeffersonian Republican."

The most significant contribution of Kirk's work, however, was that it energized conservatism by giving it the historical and philosophical heft and reflective self-understanding it had lacked. More important, it offered a coherent rationale for the values underpinning conservatism's worldview. That political conservatives from old-guard William F. Buckley to neoconservative William Kristol embrace *The Conservative Mind* gives a sense of its influence on America's conservatives.

According to Kirk, political conservatism is based on six tenets. They can be summarized as follows:

- Divine intent, as well as personal conscience, rules society.
- Tradition fills life with variety and mystery, while most "radical systems" are characterized by "a narrowing uniformity" and "egalitarianism."
- To be civilized, society needs "orders and classes," although "[u]ltimately, equality in the judgment of God, and equality before courts of law, are recognized by conservatives."
- Property and freedom are closely linked, but economic "leveling" is undesirable.
- Humanity's "anarchic impulse" and "the innovator's lust for power" must be controlled by "[c]ustom, convention, and old prescription."
- Social change must happen slowly and gradually.

One would expect that most Americans share these beliefs, if taken in their most benign forms. Most would agree that there is a divine intent that governs society, that tradition is important to the conduct of healthy lives in a healthy society, that abrupt and sudden drastic change can be disruptive and even destructive both to society and to individual lives, and so on. Yet when we look at the actions and extremist policies that have often resulted from these beliefs, we find that some of the basic tenets of political conservatism are not only problematic, but actually are opposed to the politics of Jesus.

"Orders and Classes"

The conservative notion that civilized society requires "orders and classes" directly contradicts the politics of Jesus and the biblical tradition. What conservatism overlooks is that one of the principal features of the kingdom of God that Jesus preached is that it is to sweep away all forms of elitism and gross class disparity. Indeed, the class differences that made some rich and some poor, some free and some slaves, some secure and some held fast by fear and insecurity, in Jesus' vision were to be replaced by abundant life for all, with no lording it over another.

It is the promise of removing class barriers that underpins Jesus' "good news to the poor," for the most welcome news to "the poor" as a class is that they no longer must be poor. And if "the poor" as a class no longer exists—that is, if goods and resources are distributed in the just and equitable fashion that the Bible intends—then neither would there be a "rich" class. In fact, with the admonition "Woe to you who are rich," Jesus rejects the legitimacy of a "rich" class altogether. In other words, Jesus' declaration of "good news to the poor" proclaims God's rejection of the extreme disparities in wealth and power upon which the class distinctions of "poor" and "rich" are based.

This is not to say that Jesus declared "class warfare," in the sense of one class opposed to another, because he never opposed people, only wrongheaded principles, sinful practices, and selfish, self-serving ideologies. If he can be understood to have declared "war" in any sense, it was war against the continued existence of classes at all. This is also how the apostle Paul understood the meaning of Jesus' ministry, as standing against all forms of class distinction and differentiation: "There is no longer Jew nor Greek, there is no longer slave nor free, there is no longer male and female; for all of you are one in Christ Jesus" (Galatians 3:28).

Another factor that conservatism overlooks is the great extent to which the disparity between rich and poor in America is the result of shameless exploitation of workers, unfair manipulation of markets, appeals to racial exclusivity, the "old boy" network of clandestine reciprocal relationships, preferential governmental policies, and corporate cronyism. Conservatism's blind eye to such arrangements allows conservatives like jurist Robert Bork to say, with no sense of nuance or irony, "In America, 'the rich' are overwhelmingly people—entrepreneurs, small businessmen, corporate executives, doctors, lawyers, etc.—who have gained their higher incomes through intelligence, imagination, and hard work." Bork and those who think like him ignore the many fortunes built and handed down by robber barons, exploiters of unskilled—even unpaid—labor, and successful purveyors of illegal schemes and corrupt business arrangements.

Conservatism's belief in the necessity of orders and classes is reminiscent of the institutionalization of classes and orders in the Roman Empire. This is a troubling thought, because the desire to perpetuate the wealth and privilege of its upper crust was what drove Rome to invade and brutally subjugate virtually the entire known world, and torture to death those who opposed it—like Jesus.

But membership in Rome's political and economic upper class did not come cheaply. Those in the senatorial stratum, the tiny class whose power was second only to the might of the emperor, had to possess wealth and property worth *250,000 times* a laborer's daily wage. Acceptance as a member of the *equites* class, which in power and privilege was next in the imperial hierarchy, required a net worth of *100,000 to 125,000 times* the going daily wage.

The Roman upper class's exorbitant wealth as compared to the incomes of the laboring rank and file brings to mind the huge economic divide between America's upper class and its working class. A telling example is the gap between the compensation of chief executive officers and that of workers in America's largest corporations. For the last fifteen years or so, the average salary of a CEO of a major corporation has ranged from 85 times to 419 times the average worker's salary. In the last five years the differential has hovered at the 300-to-1 level. In 2004, the average CEO was paid $9.84 million in total annual compensation as compared to the average worker's $33,176. Or to put it in the terms used by Rome, the average CEO's salary was 109,333 times the average worker's daily wage. Keep in mind that this is not net worth, which is usually a significant multiple of income; it is only one year's salary. In other words, the actual difference in the wealth of the privileged classes of America and America's workers is even greater than it was in imperial Rome. To look at it from another angle, it means that the average worker would have to work *three hundred years* to make what the average CEO makes in one year. This is a travesty by any measure. No wonder Jesus warned, "[W]oe to you who are rich,/for you have received your consolation" (Luke 6:24). Jesus taught that all God's children should live together in love and fellowship. A society built on the maintenance of social and economic classes stands in the way of the development of Jesus' beloved community. We must never forget that, in large measure, it was against grave disparities in wealth that Jesus struggled and strove and preached and proclaimed God's judgment. Jesus did not say, "Blessed are the peace*keepers*." He did not bless those who strove to maintain society as it was. He taught, "Blessed are the peace*makers*," the ones who actively strive to make the kind of world in which true peace for all is a reality. When there are classes dedicated to maintaining their privileged status over other classes, true peace cannot reign.

GRADUAL CHANGE

Conservatism's insistence on gradual change seems innocent enough. Gradualism can be a good thing, as it can enable society to accommodate new developments and implement them in stages that are less disruptive than an abrupt shift. Yet some changes in society need to be rapid, if not immediate, as in cases of gross social injustice. It is a sad fact, however, that the notion of gradual change has too often been used by conservatives as a strategy to *hamper* change, or to halt it completely. Just look at the historical record.

When the American revolutionists talked of independence, the Tory conservatives argued that they should move gradually. But what the Tories really meant was that America should remain a British colony. This despite the groundswell for freedom represented by the ninety other "declarations" issued throughout the colonies by 1776. In other words, it was the political conservatives who in 1776 opposed America's war of freedom. Even after our nation gained its independence, indeed, well into the 1790s, Federalist conservatives—those who supported states' rights over federal oversight and jurisdiction (sound familiar?)—continued to consider the Declaration of Independence suspect because it contained phrases like "Liberty," "inalienable Rights," and "all men are created equal."

And when President Abraham Lincoln pressed for the abolition of slavery, the few conservatives even willing to entertain the notion counseled gradualism. But their actions showed that what many of them really meant was that the commercial enslavement of other human beings should remain the law of the land.

And when President Lyndon Johnson forged ahead to secure the passage of the voting rights and civil rights bills that would finally give full legal rights to all Americans regardless of color, creed, or class nearly two hundred years after "We hold these truths to be self-evident" was written, conservatives counseled him to proceed slowly. But what they really meant was not to proceed at all.

And when the civil rights movement stood poised to finally tear down the walls of legally enforced white-skin-color privilege, conservatives—at least those who did not violently and openly oppose full rights for blacks—again counseled gradualism. But what they really meant was that the vicious system of Jim Crow segregation and black peonage should continue to be the law of the land. Indeed, one of the most eloquent indictments of conservatives' insistence on gradually changing social injustices was offered by Dr. Martin Luther King, Jr., in his "Letter from a Birmingham Jail."

Despite the searing injustice faced daily by black citizens in America's South, many of those who claimed to support King's efforts charged that the social change he sought was too rapid. A letter from one "supporter" cautioned, "[I]t is possible that you are in too great of a religious hurry . . . The teaching of Christ takes time to come to earth." Even the evangelist Billy Graham urged "his good personal friend" Martin Luther King to "put the brakes on." To these critics King responded:

> [T]ime is neutral. It can be used either destructively or constructively. I am coming to feel that the people of ill will have used time much more effectively than the people of good will. We must come

to see that human progress . . . comes through the tireless efforts and persistent work of [people] willing to be co-workers with God, and *without this hard work time itself becomes an ally of the forces of social stagnation . . . [T]he time is always ripe to do right.* (my emphasis)

In his historic "I Have a Dream" address, King was even more direct, decrying "the tranquilizing drug of gradualism." Although many conservatives claim to honor King's legacy, it is doubtful that King would agree.

Even though conservatives preach the gospel of addressing injustices, suffering, and insecurity gradually, the Gospel of Jesus does not. Nowhere does Jesus advocate chipping away at wrongs little by little. Nowhere is he hesitant; the people's needs cannot be treated as holy gradually, step by step, drop by drop. With fervor and immediacy, Jesus preached the advent of a new, just, healthy social order.

Take his healings, for instance. He did not gradually heal suffering bodies, nor did he advocate the gradual healing of his own suffering society. Jesus' healings were immediate. Eyesight restored, dead limbs reanimated, leprosy put to flight—these were immediate, with no hesitation. Likewise, when Jesus told his disciples to pray for the replacement of Caesar's unjust kingdom with God's kingdom of justice, he told them to pray with immediacy, the immediacy born of his desire to see the suffering that Caesar visited upon his people come to an end. Even Jesus' prophecies—that is, what he predicted was to come as the result of what had already been done—all had an air of immediacy.

Yet here is the paradox: despite conservatives' avowed embrace of gradualism, despite their claimed dedication to gradual change as a fundamental constituent of their social vision, their actions say something different: *that they only insist upon gradual change when the change threatens their own interests.* For when it comes to policies that serve their own agendas, conservatives have no problem pushing for rapid, revolutionary change. In fact, that is what the Republican conservatives of the 104th Congress called their Contract for America: a "revolution." Newt Gingrich, then Speaker of the House and the chief architect of the Contract, proudly announced, "We are the new revolutionaries," a sentiment echoed again and again by Gingrich's fellow conservatives.

What all this indicates is that for conservatives, gradualism is not a matter of principle or a religious precept, but a matter of self-interest. Conservatives counsel gradualism only when its purpose is to dramatically slow—or stop altogether—social or political changes that challenge their ascendancy. However, the politics of Jesus enjoin us to work immediately for justice whenever we encounter injustice. That is why conservatism's emphasis on gradualism is fundamentally in conflict with the politics of Jesus.

DIVINE INTENT

Polls show that most Americans hold in common with conservatives the belief in a Supreme Being who rules the earth. Indeed, this is the most basic belief of the Judeo-Christian tradition: that God is sovereign over all creation. This basic belief becomes problematic, oppressive, even deadly, however, when those at the pinnacle of wealth and power claim with absolute certainty that they know—and are acting under the direct guidance of—the mind of God.

Some of the most extreme manifestations in this nation of the dangerous conviction that one's own beliefs are the beliefs of God are seen in the bombings of abortion clinics and the murders of abortion providers by conservative Christian fanatics. But they are also seen in the way political and religious conservatives vigorously and often angrily attempt to force their views and interests on everyone as if their interests, by definition, are God's interests. This is not faith; it is arrogance. Abraham Lincoln, in his second inaugural address, acknowledged that neither he as president nor anyone else could speak for God. "The almighty has his own purposes," he famously said. Indeed, Jesus was unashamed to admit that even he did not have complete knowledge of the mind of God: "But about that day and hour no one knows, neither the angels of heaven, nor the Son, but only the Father" (Matthew 24:36).

But conservative politicians seem to think they know better. By invoking the name of God over their policies and practices, they purposely give the distinct impression, if they do not state it outright, that their thoughts, their actions, even their opinions fulfill God's fondest intentions. Exemplifying this attitude, Antonin Scalia, who is widely considered the most conservative jurist on the current Supreme Court, stated in the journal *First Things* that government "derives its moral authority from God. Government is the 'minister of God' with powers to 'revenge,' to 'execute wrath,' including even wrath by the sword . . ."

At times, however, conservatives' certainty of being the instrument of divine intent has been tinged with cynicism. We have already seen how President George W. Bush justified his declaration of war against Iraq by claiming, "God told me to attack Iraq, so I did." Another case in point is the tragedy of Terri Schiavo.

Terri Schiavo was the severely brain-damaged woman whose husband, Michael, sought to have her feeding tube removed—which would make her death imminent—after her doctors deemed it medically certain that she would never emerge from the coma in which she had lain for fourteen years. Michael Schiavo claimed he was honoring his wife's wish to die rather than live by artificial means. The Schiavo case came to public attention when Terri's parents sought legal assistance to keep her feeding tube inserted.

Many Americans were rightly alarmed by both the legal and the moral issues surrounding Terri Schiavo's plight, not to mention the human suffering it involved. A number of political and religious figures took principled public positions against Michael Schiavo's battle to remove the feeding tube, based on their sincere conviction that it was the divine intent that Ms. Schiavo's life should not be terminated by human decision. But some public figures, all of whom identified themselves as conservatives, reacted with exaggerated displays of righteous indignation that seemed more designed to establish their political bona fides as America's moral conscience than to express sincere concern for a fellow human being.

For example, Tom DeLay, then majority leader in the House of Representatives, who has expressed his belief that he is on a mission to bring a "biblical worldview" to American politics (although he has been censured for ethics violations by his congressional colleagues on three different occasions), seemed to declare that God gave him a brain-damaged patient to help him with that mission. "[O]ne thing that God has brought to us," he said, "is Terri Schiavo, to help elevate the visibility of what is going on in America." (DeLay was indicted soon thereafter on charges of money laundering, conspiracy to commit money laundering, and conspiracy to funnel campaign contributions illegally, though the third charge was dropped.)

When the Supreme Court reluctantly declined to overturn lower-court rulings in the Schiavo case, congressional conservatives, with great fanfare and displays of religious fervor, passed what they called Terri's Law to revoke Michael Schiavo's right to disconnect his wife's life-sustaining equipment. President George W. Bush added to the grandstanding with the expansive gesture of interrupting his vacation to return to the White House for the sole purpose of signing the bill, when delivery of documents to his Texas ranch, which was the standard procedure, would have produced the same result.

The Supreme Court rejected the legality of the bill. Doctors removed the feeding tube, and Terri Schiavo died thirteen days later, on March 31, 2005. Conservatives reacted with a sense of self-righteous certainty so overblown that they actually threatened vengeance against the judges in the case. "The time will come for the men responsible for this to answer for their behavior," DeLay said. Pat Robertson told his nationwide Christian Broadcasting Network television audience that "liberal judges" were more dangerous than the World Trade Center suicide bombers. John Cornyn, a senator from Texas, dared to suggest that a recent spate of murders of judges had been caused by the judges themselves, who, he said, "are making political decisions, yet are unaccountable to the public"— ironically, a charge that Cornyn and other conservatives had rejected when the Supreme Court actually did make a political decision: its selection of George W. Bush as president.

As a result of the conservatives' demagoguery, George W. Greer, the circuit court judge in the Schiavo case, was forced to travel with armed bodyguards. Then suddenly the raised voices around Terri Schiavo fell silent. Whereas conservative politicians' righteous pronouncements and grand legislative maneuvers for Ms. Schiavo had dominated the media, now they were nowhere to be found. Why? Because polls taken in the midst of the controversy showed that conservatives' public demonstrations of righteous outrage were not profiting them. In fact, the polls indicated that most Americans rejected their grandstanding. So the politicians dropped the Terri Schiavo case as quickly as they had pounced upon it.

USA Today columnist DeWayne Wickham observed, "The real villains in this matter are the pandering people who for reasons of self-interest—and self-aggrandizement—have prolonged for much too long the suffering of all those who really love [Terri]."

President Bush's grand actions had already caused some observers to wonder if the immense attention given to the Schiavo case was a function of politics rather than of convictions. Their doubts about his sincerity were heightened when it came to public attention that in 1999, as governor of Texas, Bush had signed the Advance Directives Act, a measure that allows a patient's surrogate to make the same life-ending decision on the patient's behalf that Michael Schiavo had made—the very right that the president now made a public show of opposing.

If these conservative politicians had indeed acted out of deep religious convictions, if they truly believed that they were serving divine intent, they would have persisted in their efforts to save Terri Schiavo no matter what the pollsters reported. That they did not persevere brings the integrity of their convictions into serious question, and provides us with an enduring example of the cynicism and manipulation that accompanies the invocation of divine intent as justification for one's own political actions.

SO FAR WE HAVE EXAMINED some of the ways the basic tenets of political conservatism violate the politics of Jesus. Although not a tenet, there is another aspect of conservatism that transgresses Jesus' politics just as seriously.

Treatment of the Poor

A consequence of the Terri Schiavo tragedy that conservatives surely did not intend is that it raised a burning question: If conservative lawmakers are willing to expend so much energy and outrage in saving one person from starvation, why can't they muster comparable energy and outrage to feed the many Americans who face hunger and starvation every day? This brings us to the most unfortunate of conservatives' wrongheaded notions: the notion that the poor and needy are somehow to blame for their own plight, or that it is their natural lot in life.

As we have seen, conservatism views the existence of class differences as necessary for a civilized society. Unfortunately, conservatives' support for the maintenance of class differences when so many economic disparities are the result of injustice has served to mute their sense of outrage over the predicament of less fortunate Americans. Jesus' anger over the plight of the poor is nowhere to be found in conservative discourse. This explains, at least in part, how presidents Reagan and Bush, who considered themselves staunch Christians, could treat the poor of America so shamefully and still believe themselves righteous.

Ironically, despite their very public professions of Christian faith, conservatives seem to owe their ideas and attitudes toward poverty more to the ideas of Herbert Spencer, the British philosopher, than to Jesus and the Bible.

Although he lived and wrote in England, Herbert Spencer had great influence on American political thought in the last decades of the nineteenth century. A measure of his enduring influence is that his notion of the "survival of the fittest" remains an important part of our social lexicon (the phrase was coined by Spencer, not Charles Darwin).

Spencer argued that the pressures of impoverishment and constant struggling for subsistence were actually a positive thing that, in the end, would have a positive result: it would lead to human advancement, for the crucible of poverty would allow only the best from each generation to survive. Those with the most skill, intelligence, ingenuity, and tenacity would rise, while those of lesser talent, smarts, and character would fall by the wayside. In other words, only humanity's strongest and "fittest" would survive. But in order to allow this superior caste to evolve naturally, Spencer reasoned, it was important that the poor be given no assistance at all. No matter how harsh their plight, no matter how many pressures and conditions were beyond their control, they should be allowed to rise or fall on their own. Charity was allowed in Spencer's scheme, because he thought that performing charitable acts might further enhance the moral character of the fittest who had already risen. Besides, charity was only a temporary intervention that would have no effect on the ultimate evolutionary outcome. But government aid to the poor in any sustained form would only slow the evolutionary process. So for Spencer, public welfare laws were strictly to be prohibited, as were public education and the regulation of housing conditions, no matter how squalid those conditions. There were to be absolutely no measures to promote equality of any kind, even equality of opportunity for social and economic advancement. For Spencer, it was equality that was the enemy of humanity, rather than inequality.

Spencer's thought had "an electrifying effect" in America in the 1880s and 1890s. Spencer's ideas and policy perspectives were embraced by a number of American politicians, and his thought became an integral part of American social philosophy. Not only does his notion of "survival of the fittest" continue in our social and political consciousness, his attitude toward poverty does as well, principally in conservatism's view of poverty. For instance, echoes of Spencer can be clearly heard in conservative Pennsylvania Senator Rick Sanctorum's statement in opposition to increased funding for child care for the poor: "Making people struggle a bit is not necessarily the worst thing."

When conservatives pursue "benign neglect" of the poor as a social policy, they reflect Spencer, not Jesus. When they weaken or dismantle programs designed to help the poor, such as welfare, Medicare, Medicaid, housing aid, feeding programs, and so on, they reflect Spencer, not Jesus. When they demonize the poor and blame the vulnerable and needy for their own victimization, they reflect Herbert Spencer, not Jesus Christ. Spencer stood the teaching of Jesus on its head. In Spencerian thought, Jesus' teaching "To whom much is given, much is required" became "To whom much has been given, *nothing* is required."

The influence of Spencerian social thought is always present in conservative social policies, to one degree or another. It is clearly reflected in the disdain for the poor that permeated the policies of Ronald Reagan and permeates those of George W. Bush and congressional conservatives. It appeared in another form in the administration of President Richard M. Nixon, one that is so transparent it would be laughable if it were not so tragic.

In 1970, President Nixon charged an interagency committee with what at the time appeared to be an admirable task: lowering the number of Americans living in poverty. However, Nixon's committee succeeded in turning the admirable into the unconscionable. Instead of recommending new policies to strengthen the federal government's inadequate efforts to alleviate poverty, the committee urged the devious strategy of *lowering the official poverty line* so there would be fewer Americans who fell below it. In other words, the number of poor Americans and their desperation would remain the same, but now fewer of them would be counted.

Outraged critics charged Nixon with trying to "end poverty with the stroke of a pen." Ultimately, public indignation caused the proposal to be scrapped. But Nixon's committee refused to be outdone. Eventually it came up with an even more disingenuous proposal: that the federal government stop using the word "poverty" altogether! In a *New York Times* interview a government source explained, "Poverty is a value-laden, highly politicized word and that's not the kind of word we like. We would like a less value-laden concept like income distribution or mean or median or some other word devoid of emotional complications."

Yet that is the point. Poverty *is* value-laden and politically charged. Human suffering and abject need *should* evoke deep emotion in those who claim to be followers of Jesus. The values Jesus taught command those who claim to heed his call to make the alleviation of poverty in this and in every country a passionate part of their political agenda. Yet incredibly, in a 1990 paper the conservative Heritage Foundation continued Nixon's attempt to deflect attention—and much-needed relief—from America's poor by charging the U.S. Census Bureau with conducting a "disinformation campaign" designed to give the impression that "the living standards of America's 'poor' are far lower than in reality they are."

Can one imagine Jesus or any of the biblical prophets ever speaking about the poor without compassion and love, anger and outrage, much less complaining that they are not as poor as we thought? Yet many of America's conservative politicians have done this without shame or remorse. It brings to mind the question posed in the First Letter of John: "How does God's love abide in anyone who has the world's goods and sees a brother or sister in need and yet refuses to help?" (1 John 3:17).

Journalist Mona Charen typifies conservatives' Spencerian attitude toward poverty in America. When discussing public welfare programs, Charen cites statistics like the following:

> Only 2.6 percent of those age sixteen or above who work full time are poor, according to the Bureau of the Census. But 23.6 percent of those who do not work are poor. For African Americans, the number in poverty who do not work is 44.7 percent. It is constantly urged that the reason people don't work is that jobs are unavailable, yet according to a Census Bureau survey, only 4.1 percent of the idle list inability to find work as the reason for their joblessness.

Charen apparently does not care that according to any credible estimate, real poverty and its continued causes far exceed official estimates. Nor does she seem to care that most observers admit that the official poverty line of $19,157 for a family of four is well below the point at which families actually experience the onerous effects of poverty. The truth is that few American families can sustain a decent standard of living even with half again that amount of annual income.

Moreover, if, as Charen claims, only 4.1 percent of America's poor cite lack of jobs as the reason for their impoverishment, this still does not mean that the rest are poor because they are *unwilling* to work. There are many other reasons for poverty in the United States that conservatives apparently overlook, such as temporary or chronic illness of the worker or a dependent family member (particularly if the family has no health insurance), artificial barriers to upward mobility based on race or gender or class, or joblessness of such long duration that workers no longer consider themselves a viable part of America's workforce. There are many other reasons that are totally out of poor people's hands, like lack of transportation, or lack of child-care assistance for working mothers (which some conservatives, like Vice President Cheney, have consistently voted to limit or stop altogether). Also conveniently overlooked by conservatives like Charen is the deleterious effect of generation after generation of inequities and exploitation of rank-and-file Americans by the rich ruling elites. Conservatives ignore the fact that for centuries it was illegal for millions of Americans, particularly African Americans, to accumulate wealth or to receive formal education or vocational training. They forget that for millions more struggling Americans, insurmountable artificial barriers were raised, usually by conservatives, to thwart any hope of upward economic mobility, and that often conservatives raised the barriers while proclaiming the name of Jesus, but following the dictates of Herbert Spencer.

Rather than acknowledge the many reasons for poverty that are out of poor people's control, conservatives tend to blame the victims for their plight. Here again their practice is counter to the politics of Jesus. No matter how downtrodden or degraded a person was, Jesus never condemned the person; he reached out to heal the circumstance or lift the person out of it. Nor did Jesus ever blame victims for their own abuse and exploitation. Instead, he blamed their victimizers, as in his Mark 5 indictment of "Legion"—signifying the Roman military occupiers of Israel—as the cause of the young man's self-destructive impulses, rather than any misdeed on the part of the young man himself. In this Jesus echoed the biblical prophets, who consistently blamed the powerful for the poverty of the people and exhorted their societies to compel those of wealth and power to redress injustice. Indeed, in the Sermon on the Mount, rather than blaming poor people for their poverty, Jesus pronounced them "blessed," not only in order to counter the devaluation of their worth by the rich elites, but also to remind the downtrodden and the needy that their poverty was not of their own doing, and neither was it their natural lot in life.

In fact, the Gospels tell us that it was the rich, not the poor, who were the subject of Jesus' condemnation. "Woe to you who are rich," Jesus said. "Woe to you who are full now."

His parable of the rich man and Lazarus (Luke 16:19–31) was absolutely uncompromising against those who amassed wealth while others were mired in material need. However, many Christian religious leaders in America today ignore the clear pronouncements of Jesus and identify not with the poor but with the interests of the rich. One reason for their troubling lapse is that many of those religious leaders have become rich themselves. By serving America's richest citizens they are also looking after their own interests. When Jesus declared, "Your heart is where your treasure is," he could well have spoken it directly to today's pulpit aristocracy.

The evidence is damning. There are individual ministries today that gross $100 million or more, affording those at the head of those ministries (which, in an odd twist, usually bear the names of the preachers themselves!) lifestyles of wealth, splendor, and privilege that most of their parishioners can only imagine. Nor do those preachers hide or downplay their wealth as in years past. Today they blatantly display it.

One well-known televangelist held her wedding extravaganza at a palatial five-star Wall Street hotel. The festivities were filmed for broadcast on a Christian television network with two commentators grandly reporting every step and subtlety of the celebration as if it was the coronation of European royalty, not the joining into "one flesh" of servants of God: the thousands of white orchids adorning the hall, the eighty-member bridal party, the bride's 7.76 carat diamond ring.

The televangelist Pat Robertson is reported to have had a clandestine arrangement with Mobutu Sese Seko, the late dictator of the Congo (then Zaire), that allowed Robertson to leave Zaire with planeloads of diamonds after flying into the country "humanitarian" supplies of much lesser value. Moreover, Robertson appeared on Zairian television to praise

Mobutu, who for decades had been reviled by humanitarian organizations worldwide for imprisoning, torturing, and killing thousands of his countrymen, including his infamous February 16, 1992, order for his troops to shoot down Sunday churchgoers holding a demonstration for political reform. Over two hundred were killed. Robertson also denounced the United States government for deposing the Liberian dictator Charles Taylor, whom he extolled as a "Christian, Baptist president" despite Taylor's butchery of thousands of his countrymen. One can only wonder if the televangelist's lucrative, exclusive gold-mining deal with Taylor's government had anything to do with his public defense of the murderous Taylor.

The Web site of a televangelist couple appealed for donations so both husband and wife could have their own Cessna Citation X jets, valued at $20 million apiece. (There was no need to raise money for airport fees, however; they already own a private airfield.) The Web site explained, "When God tells Kenneth to travel to South Africa and hold a three-day Victory Campaign, he won't have to wait to make commercial travel arrangements. He can just climb aboard his Citation X and go!"

A St. Louis televangelist is paid a whopping $900,000 in salary by the board of the ministry that bears her name. This in addition to the $10 million housing compound it has provided for her.

A foundation started by an Atlanta area pastor paid him more than $3 million in salary and benefits in the course of four years—almost half of the foundation's $6.17 million in total disbursements, apparently in violation of federal law—including a $350,000 Bentley sedan. His response: "We're not just a bumbling bunch of preachers who can't talk and all we're doing is baptizing babies. I deal with the White House . . . You've got to put me on a different scale."

The wealth of those religious leaders and others like them comes from the hard-earned wages of ordinary workers, yet it is exceedingly difficult to find ministers who actively oppose the exploitation of their rank-and-file benefactors at the hands of the elites. Like the opponents of the apostle Paul in 2 Corinthians, they seem to follow "a different gospel," one that does not include these verses: "No slave can serve two masters . . . You cannot serve God and wealth" (Luke 16:13). Nor do they seem to take seriously Jesus' admonition "It is easier for a camel to fit through the eye of a needle than for a rich man to enter the kingdom of heaven."

Whether one agrees with his theology or not, a notable exception to this ministerial greed and obsession with conspicuous consumption is the Reverend Rick Warren, the author of *The Purpose-Driven Life*, the bestselling nonfiction book in American history. Despite having sold some twenty million books worldwide for a vast personal fortune, Warren continues to live in the same modestly comfortable home that he lived in before his windfall. Although his wealth is from his book and not from the dimes and dollars of his parishioners, Warren still gets around in a Ford Expedition rather than a Rolls-Royce or a chauffeured limousine. And he has paid back every penny in salary that his church paid him over twenty-four years as its pastor; he serves now without financial compensation. The sincere concern modeled by ministers like Rick Warren not to pervert the Gospel of Jesus Christ with greed and self-aggrandizement should be the rule rather than the exception. The prophet asks: "Should not shepherds feed the sheep? You eat the fat, you clothe yourselves with the wool, you slaughter the fatlings; but you do not feed the sheep" (Ezekiel 34:2).

WHEN THE BASIC TENETS and worldview of political conservatism are closely considered, it becomes evident that conservatism's belief in the necessity of economic classes, its insistence on changing social conditions gradually, its anemic concern for the plight of America's poor and underprivileged, and its desire to maintain the status quo even when it is rife with injustice set it firmly outside the politics of Jesus.

LIBERALISM

Political attacks and purposeful distortion have conspired to muddy the real meaning of political liberalism in America. Political liberalism today is dismissed as a godless mix of immorality, irreligiosity, and irresponsibility that is in love with bloated government and huge, inefficient bureaucracies. The derogative tag "tax-and-spend liberal" is a favorite conservative catchphrase. What is obscured by this skewed rhetoric, however, is that liberalism is the bedrock of our nation. No less than President George Washington declared, "As mankind become more liberal, they will be more apt to allow that all those who conduct themselves as worthy members of the community are equally entitled to the protections of the civil government. I hope ever to see America among the foremost nations in examples of justice and liberality."

What is significant about Washington's hopeful vision is that it is synonymous with the core vision of American political liberalism: equal status under the law for all, and governmental protection of the poor from the rich, the weak from the strong. Liberalism embodies a commitment to the rights of all people—not just the privileged few.

But as important as liberalism is to democracy, for the last fifty years its meaning for America has been systematically distorted. From Joe McCarthy's attacks on liberals as privileged "striped pants," through Richard Nixon's false depiction of a "liberal elite," through Ronald Reagan's disingenuous characterization of "tax-and-spend liberals," through George H. W. Bush's successful misportrayal of liberals as tree huggers and coddlers of criminals, through the masterful half-truths and outright misrepresentations of today's conservatives and neocons, liberalism has come to be characterized as something un-American and un-Christian. Liberals are stereotyped as unpatriotic, immoral, elitist spendthrifts, and enemies of everything pure and good. Rather than being extolled for its commitment to each American's having the right to life and that more abundantly, liberalism—with its insistence that government protect those whom Jesus called "the least of these"—is now misportrayed by conservatives as advocating the erosion of individual freedoms. To this charge the historian Arthur M. Schlesinger, Jr., a former top aide to President John F. Kennedy, gave bold reply:

The individual freedoms destroyed by the increase in national authority have been in the main the freedom to deny black Americans their elementary rights as citizens, the freedom to work little children in mills and immigrants in sweatshops, the freedom to pay starvation wages and enforce barbarous working hours and permit squalid working conditions, the freedom to loot national resources and pollute the environment—all freedoms that, one supposes, a civilized country can readily do without.

As the economist Robert Kuttner puts it, "Liberals and conservatives agree, in principle, about the value of liberty. But where liberals differ is their insistence that liberty requires greater equality than our society now generates."

The commitment of liberalism is not just a sentiment; it is a dedication to justice that is enacted through hard-won public policies that take seriously Jesus' call to care for our neighbors and "the least of these" among them. In fact, many of the rights that Americans now take for granted would not be ours to enjoy if not for the faith, commitment, and struggles of political liberals and liberalism.

At its most basic, then, liberalism believes in freedom, independence, and the rights of the individual. It seeks to ensure real opportunities for unfettered upward mobility and decent standards of living *for* everyone, regardless of class, creed, or color, while expecting *from* everyone basic levels of responsibility for their own lives. But liberalism does not stop there. Liberalism also believes that when those rights and opportunities are threatened, the government of the people must take a stand to protect them. Liberalism believes that the poor, the disenfranchised, and the pow-er*less* must be shielded from exploitation and domination by the power*ful*. *The Harper Dictionary of Modern Thought* captures it well: "Liberalism in its most characteristic contemporary expression emphasizes the importance of conscience and justice in politics, advocates the rights of racial and religious minorities, and supports civil liberties and the right of the ordinary individual to be more effectively consulted in decisions which directly affect him."

It was liberalism that produced *The Grapes of Wrath*, John Steinbeck's epic novel that exposed the terrible exploitation and suffering of Midwestern farmers and led to radical reforms that were more in line with the biblical ethic of care for the poor. It was liberalism that produced *The Jungle*, Upton Sinclair's passionate exposé of the barbaric treatment of workers in the meatpacking industry, which brought to public awareness the unholy alliance between corporate elites and political conservatives, and inspired outraged Americans to finally demand the legislative protections for workers that liberals had long advocated.

If not for liberalism, we would not have Social Security, Medicare and Medicaid, unemployment compensation, the right to form labor unions, student loans, child labor laws, the minimum wage, workplace safety regulations, oversight to ensure the purity of our food and drugs, civil rights legislation, or the environmental protection movement—to name just a few of its achievements. Other progressive liberal initiatives that raise the quality of life for everyday people, not just for the privileged few, include:

- guaranteed bank deposits
- the protection of investors by the Securities and Exchange Commission
- the Federal Reserve Bank
- the Food and Drug Administration
- the National Park Service
- the Forest Service
- the National School Lunch Program
- food stamps for needy and low-income families
- the Women, Infants, and Children (WIC) program, which provides nutritional support for low-income pregnant and nursing mothers and their infants through age five
- the Voting Rights Act
- equal rights for women
- earned income tax credits for workers

These and other liberal governmental policies and programs have so greatly enhanced the quality of life for Americans that today most cannot imagine life without them. But in addition to their benefits for everyday

Americans, what these liberal policies have in common is that all of them were actively opposed by conservatives; if conservatives had prevailed, none of these programs would have seen the light of day. As one commentator observed with more than a tinge of irony, if not for liberalism, Secretary of State Condoleezza Rice might now be scrubbing floors not her own and Supreme Court Justice Clarence Thomas would either be picking cotton or would have been lynched for marrying a white woman—and not a high-tech lynching, either.

What liberalism is *not* is a cultural description. Liberalism doesn't belong to any particular political party as such. It is not headquartered in Hollywood or New York City or Washington, DC. It exists wherever Americans stand up for the rights and well-being of all Americans. Nor does it refer to individual personal morality as such. Like conservatism, liberalism focuses on social morality. But unlike conservatism, liberalism has as its goal making the best fruits of life available for all, not just for the privileged few. In biblical terms, what underlies liberalism is what Jesus likened to the greatest of all commandments: loving your neighbor as yourself. If there is a liberal bias, that is it. On C-SPAN's *Journalists' Roundtable* in 1993 the noted journalist Helen Thomas put it this way: "A liberal bias? I don't know what a liberal bias is. Do you mean we care about the poor, the sick, the maimed? Do we care whether people are being shot every day on the streets of America? If that's liberal, so be it."

The History of Liberalism

The roots of Western political liberalism reside in seventeenth- and eighteenth-century Europe. As philosophers and historians can attest, liberalism represents one of the shining achievements of the Western world. Its origins are found in the works of thinkers like John Locke, David Hume, Jeremy Bentham, John Stuart Mill, and Immanuel Kant—a veritable pantheon of the most honored minds in the Western political philosophical tradition. Each of these thinkers lived in a deeply elitist and hierarchical society in which privilege and wealth were hereditary, and aristocracy was the order of the day. Against the rich conservatives and landed aristocrats of their time who sought to preserve their dominance and privilege, in various ways these thinkers laid the groundwork for fuller equality under the law for all.

Liberalism in America

Even scholars critical of liberalism admit that it is the liberal tradition that fueled the American Revolution. Because of the egalitarian sensibilities the revolutionaries espoused (with regard to white males, at least), it is not an exaggeration to say that the Declaration of Independence is a liberal document, nor is it an exaggeration to say that the American Revolution itself was a liberal movement. The Declaration's seminal pronouncement, "We hold these truths to be self-evident, that all men . . . are endowed by their Creator with certain inalienable Rights . . . Life, Liberty and the pursuit of Happiness," is nothing less than a microcosm of the liberal creed. In a real sense, *it was liberalism that gave birth to American democracy.*

Thus, the United States of America was conceived as a liberal democracy. However, the nation's implementation of its liberalism was seriously flawed, in that initially—and to varying degrees for almost two centuries thereafter—the full range of privileges and benefits promised by liberal democracy were reserved for white men only. Still, even with its flaws, the generosity of heart at the core of the liberal impulse, both religious and political, shaped our country from its very founding. It informed the development of religious freedom, democratic institutions and elections, and the necessary separation of church and state. It advocated equal protection under the law, freedom of speech and of the press, and liberal education. It was liberal activists who led the charge for abolition, spearheaded the union movement, worked for women's suffrage, and sponsored the civil rights movement of the 1950s and 1960s. Jane Addams, Fannie Lou Hamer, Martin Luther King, Jr., Dorothy Day, Paul Wellstone, and Walter Rauschenbusch (author of the 1907 liberal religious classic *Christianity and the Social Crisis*), all were great Americans whose greatness hinged on their selfless commitment to and personal sacrifice for the liberal creed.

Liberalism and the Shape of Government

Desire for a small central government is usually associated with political conservatism. Thomas Jefferson was the earliest major political figure to insist that America's central government be kept small. However, Jefferson's insistence on limited government was not fueled by conservatism, but by liberal sensibilities: he wanted to protect rank-and-file Americans from ruling-class abuse. Jefferson was so committed to the protection of Americans' personal freedoms that he would not endorse the new Constitution until a bill of rights was added to ensure that the freedom and well-being of the common people and laborers would not be trampled by a large governmental bureaucracy in the same way the British Empire had trampled the rights of colonial America.

With the advent of the presidency of Andrew Jackson, two decades after Jefferson's term ended, the focus of liberalism began to shift away from a commitment to small government. Jackson was less concerned about the size of government than about the degree of influence that the rich and powerful had upon it. Jackson wrote:

It is to be regretted that the rich and powerful too often bend the acts of government to their selfish purposes . . . [E]very man is entitled to protection by law; but when the laws undertake to add to these natural and just advantages artificial distinctions, to grant titles, gratuities, and exclusive privileges, to make the rich richer and the potent more powerful, the humble members of society—the farmers, mechanics, laborers—who have neither the time nor the means of securing like favors to themselves, have a right to complain of the injustice of their government.

Thus Andrew Jackson's liberalism inspired him to strengthen the government for the same reason that Jefferson's liberalism moved him to keep it small: to protect the "humble members of society" from the wiles and exploitation of the rich and powerful.

The irony is that conservatives in America initially supported a large, interventionist government, beginning with Alexander Hamilton's advocacy for a working partnership between the interests of the business and financial sectors of America and a sizable federal government that would further those interests (an arrangement that treated the interests of workers as of secondary importance at best). But when faced with Jackson's campaign to turn the government from favoring the interests of the rich and powerful to serving the interests of those the rich had long exploited, suddenly conservatives favored a smaller, noninterventionist government. Why? Because a smaller government would have fewer resources with which to regulate and restrain big business's rapacious treatment of workers.

So, contrary to conservatives' rhetoric today, they did not always advocate a smaller federal government. They embraced it only when the forces of liberalism began to subject their unchallenged profiteering to much-needed governmental constraint and oversight. In other words, conservatives were staunch advocates of larger government as long as government catered to the interests of the rich, but when the federal government was no longer their ally in profit making, rich conservatives wanted its power to be reined in. Theirs was a selfish and self-serving response that had little to do with principle and much to do with profits. As the former U.S. senator George McGovern explains in *The Essential America*: "If there is any one overall defining difference between liberalism and conservatism throughout our history, it has been the effort of liberals to utilize the powers of government to serve the well-being of rank-and-file Americans, as compared to the conservative preference . . . for maintaining the stability and prosperity of the business and commercial interests of the nation."

In the decades following Andrew Jackson's presidency, efforts to free government from the considerable influence wielded by rich businessmen became less and less successful. A tax code favoring the wealthy, free grants of government land to railroads, shameful abuse of workers' rights, banks risking depositors' funds as they pleased, unconscionable corporate greed at every turn—all occurred with virtually no governmental regulation or challenge as the result of the machinations of the "rich and potent" whose influence Jackson had tried so hard to rein in. The suffering this unchecked greed caused average Americans is incalculable. American industry grew rapidly in the wake of the industrial revolution that followed the Civil War. With industrial expansion came business consolidations and mergers that concentrated wealth in fewer and fewer hands, until by 1890 an aristocracy of just 1 percent of American families held more than half of America's riches. (Every contemporary measure of American wealth attests that an aristocracy of this type still exists in America today.) The richer the elites became, the more they sought to influence and control the workings of American government, and the more successful they were at it. Big business was born.

The first serious challenge to corporate elites' domination of the federal government began with the emergence of the People's Party—better known as the Populist movement—in 1892. As historian Milton Viorst observes, with the Populists on voting ballots, "For the first time since the Jackson era, the major parties offered the voters clear-cut alternatives on basic economic and political questions."

The Populists reasoned that just as government had served the interests of the rich elites, it could be turned to serve the needs of ordinary Americans to combat the injustice and corruption of big business and protect working people from it. The spirit of the party is expressed in the historic "Cross of Gold" speech by William Jennings Bryan, the 1896 Populist Party (and Democratic Party) nominee for president: "[I]n this land of the free . . . [w]hat we need is an Andrew Jackson to stand, as Jackson stood, against the encroachments of organized wealth."

The twentieth-century heir to the liberalism of the Populists was the Progressive Party, led by Theodore Roosevelt. The Progressives sought to give the common citizenry a greater voice in government by pushing for voting policies that included initiative, referendum, and recall balloting; direct primaries that allowed voters, rather than party elites alone, to select political party nominees; the direct election of U.S. senators by voters; and women's right to vote. The Progressives also defeated staunch conservative opposition to the graduated income tax, thus forcing the rich to begin to assume their fair share of responsibility for the cost of maintaining the nation's infrastructure. The fact that these measures are taken for granted today is testimony to the tenacity and commitment of the liberals of the Progressive Party.

Moreover, the Progressives were crucial to the passage—also against fierce conservative opposition—of the Pure Food and Drug Act, which protects Americans from careless and unscrupulous producers of pharmaceuticals and foodstuffs. And they played a major role in the movement to protect the natural environment from big business's unregulated practices of destructive strip-mining and poisoning of the nation's waterways.

The liberalism of the Progressives also recognized that it was the lack of legal protection for workers' rights that allowed the monied interests to callously exploit rank-and-file Americans. They realized that totally unregulated markets led not to freedom for the average American but to the tyranny of the rich. For that reason, Progressives insisted on a federal government that was dedicated to the rights and well-being of all Americans—not just the privileged few; a government that would intervene to ensure that life for the average American would be more equitable and just. Indeed, no less a political figure than Abraham Lincoln had earlier acknowledged, "Government should do for people what they cannot do for themselves." And in a parable Jesus asks, "Who then is the faithful and wise manager, whom the master puts in charge of his servants to give them their food allowance?" (Luke 12:42, my translation from the Greek text).

As the Progressive Party presidential candidate in 1912, Theodore Roosevelt described his vision of the role of government in a San Francisco campaign address:

The only way in which our people . . . can protect the working man in his conditions of work and life, the only way in which the people can prevent children working in industry or secure women an eight-hour day in industry, or secure compensation for men killed or crippled in industry, is by extending, instead of limiting, the power of government ... There was once a time in history when the limitation of governmental power meant increasing liberty for the people. *In the present day the limitation of governmental power, of governmental action, means the enslavement of the people by the great corporations* who can only be held in check through the extension of governmental power. [my emphasis]

Democrat Woodrow Wilson, Roosevelt's opponent in the election, was also a political liberal who believed that it was government's role to protect the poor and the vulnerable. Responding to charges that a larger role for government betrayed the vision of Jefferson, Wilson asserted, "[I]f Thomas Jefferson were living in our day, he would see what we see ... [that w]ithout the watchful interference, the resolute interference of the government, there can be no fair play."

For trying to employ these principles in his presidency, Wilson is to be commended. Yet the truth of the matter is that his belief in "watchful interference" did not extend to his conservative views on race and racism. As noted earlier, he refused to sign an antilynching bill at a time when one African American man, woman, or child was being burned, hanged, shot, or beaten to death every other day. Wilson chose not to love those particular neighbors as himself, or to hold their right to life, liberty, and the pursuit of happiness as holy. The lesson to be learned is this: one must just as diligently practice "watchful interference" against one's personal illiberalism as against society's. That is true liberalism.

THE GREAT DEPRESSION was a time of suffering and dislocation the likes of which America had not seen since the Civil War. The collapse of the stock market in 1929 was the culmination of a string of national economic catastrophes that actually began with the collapse of the unregulated agricultural sector in 1921. The Depression was characterized by record numbers of foreclosures and bankruptcies, vast unemployment, and pervasive poverty. Between 1929 and 1933, the gross national product shrank by half.

Steel plants operated at just 12 percent of capacity. Thirteen million workers were unemployed, roughly one-third of the workforce. Some two million men were reduced to wandering the land looking for any kind of work they could find, with most finding none.

The suffering of the masses was compounded by rapacious preying on workers by big business. The rank and file had no protection from unhealthy, sometimes even inhumane working conditions and no safety net to sustain them while they were out of work. In this time of such terrible suffering, it was political liberalism that again came forward to rescue the American people from the depredations of the rich, in the form of Franklin D. Roosevelt's New Deal, a well-thought-out package of crucial federal regulations and measures with a mandate to protect working people, relieve the masses' pain, and rebuild the nation's economy.

In 1938, Herbert H. Lehman, the former governor of New York, looked back at the impact of the New Deal and its reforms:

> The New Deal was a revolution, peaceably accomplished. Part of this revolution consisted of the establishment of the responsibility of government for the basic economic welfare of Americans not only as farmers, laborers, and businessmen, but as individuals. The Social Security system—which provided a program of old age and unemployment insurance, and for the support of the blind, the needy, and of mothers with dependent children—was a revolution all in itself. I am convinced that liberalism saved America in the 1930s.

Disturbingly, as important as the New Deal protections for the rights of workers and America's poor were to rank-and-file Americans, conservatives still searched for ways to counter them. The 1940 Republican presidential candidate, Wendell Wilkie, the head of a utility company, began calling the New Deal "big government." Wilkie actually charged that Roosevelt's New Deal was worse for America than corporate tyranny. Wilkie's claims were rejected by most Americans and he lost to Roosevelt by five million votes, but a new strategy had been born with which pro-corporate apologists could deflect attention from the effects of their policies on average Americans: they would denounce "big government" as causing the suffering that was actually caused by the greed of big business.

After Roosevelt's era, another high-water mark in liberalism's quest to make life more just and fair and equitable for all Americans was reached with the presidency of his former protégé Lyndon Baines Johnson.

In his 1964 State of the Union address Johnson declared unconditional war against poverty in the United States. But not only did Johnson declare war on poverty, he set out to eradicate it. Johnson's goal was to create what he called the Great Society, in which every American, not just the privileged few, would have equal access to all the good things America had to offer. He used his considerable political acumen and his vast store of political capital—and his storied ability to twist political arms—to make his vision a reality by introducing a broad slate of social programs designed to reduce the class barriers caused by the extreme disparities of wealth in America. The impact of Johnson's antipoverty programs was so great that it was felt even on Indian reservations, which historically have benefited exceedingly little from social initiatives. Noted Indian activist Russell Means called Johnson's programs "the best thing ever to hit Indian reservations." The innovative programs and policies Johnson introduced include the following:

- Medicare (1965) and Medicaid (1966), the systems of national health insurance for the elderly and the needy
- Operation Head Start (1965), designed to provide school-readiness education for disadvantaged children
- Operation Follow Through (1967), designed to keep Head Start students from losing their early gains
- Upward Bound (1965), designed to prepare bright, financially disadvantaged youths for college
- Higher Education Act (1965), to provide scholarships, low-interest loans, and expanded work-study assistance for undergraduates
- Open Admissions programs, which allow college admission to any high-school graduate and provide remedial assistance to those in need of it

- Neighborhood Youth Corps (1965), to provide basic educational and job-readiness skills for underprivileged youth
- Job Corps (1964), a residential program to provide basic life, education, and job-readiness skills for inner-city youth
- Concentrated Employment Program (1967), which gave block grants to support community groups' efforts to address unemployment
- Work Incentive Program (1967), which trains and places welfare recipients
- Civil Rights Act of 1964, the most comprehensive civil rights legislation ever passed, which made illegal all discrimination based on race, religion, gender, and national origin
- Civil Rights Act of 1968, which extended the provision of the 1964 Civil Rights Act to the advertising, financing, sale, or rental of public and private housing
- Affirmative Action and the Equal Employment Opportunity Commission, to enforce the provisions of the Civil Rights Acts

Despite the success of Johnson's program initiatives in easing much of the immediate suffering of America's poor and vulnerable, our nation has seen no liberal initiatives of this scope since. In spite of his social vision, Johnson's presidency was derailed by serious missteps with the Vietnam War. The election of Richard M. Nixon to the White House in 1968 after Johnson declined to stand for reelection signaled the advent of the conservative turn in which America now finds itself. The sad reality is that today this nation is faced with the most far-reaching—and most successful—effort that has ever been mounted to turn the clock back to the days when rich elites and big business held America fully hostage. Just as conservatism lay in disarray in the mid-twentieth century, liberalism is in disarray at the beginning of the twenty-first century. The rising rate of poverty in the United States as the rich get richer is sad evidence that this is America's lot today.

THE MEANING OF LIBERALISM

There are a number of significant texts and studies that explore the history and philosophical underpinnings of liberalism. However, what may well be the most succinct and heartfelt presentation of the practical meaning of liberalism is found not in an academic text or a learned treatise, but in a series of political speeches.

In his address to the Seventy-seventh Congress on January 6, 1941, as war was waged against the forces of fascism and totalitarianism on four continents, President Franklin Delano Roosevelt articulated the Four Freedoms that he believed were the inalienable rights of every member of human society: freedom of speech, freedom of religion, freedom from want, and freedom from fear. On January 11, 1944, Roosevelt went further. In his eleventh State of the Union address, Roosevelt not only reaffirmed the Four Freedoms, he expanded on their economic implications, in what he initially termed an "economic Bill of Rights," but which came to be known as the Second Bill of Rights.

For Roosevelt, these rights were constitutional entitlements for every American, regardless of class, creed, or ethnicity. Thus, in his Second Bill of Rights, not only did Roosevelt share his vision for America but he offered, in effect, a timeless summary of what American liberalism stands for. As all of America listened, Roosevelt declared that in addition to freedom of speech, freedom of religion, freedom from want, and freedom from fear, every American, irrespective of class, creed, or color, is entitled to the following rights:

- The right to a useful and remunerative job in the industries or shops or farms or mines of the nation
- The right to earn enough to provide adequate food and clothing and recreation
- The right of every farmer to raise and sell his products at a return that will give him and his family a decent living

- The right of every businessman [the term then in use], large or small, to trade in an atmosphere of freedom from unfair competition and domination by monopolies at home or abroad
- The right of every family to a decent home
- The right to adequate medical care and the opportunity to achieve and enjoy good health
- The right to adequate protection from the economic fears of old age, sickness, accidents, and unemployment
- The right to a good education

What underlies Roosevelt's Second Bill of Rights is the same principle that underlies all liberalism: justice for all, regardless of class or economic station. Indeed, that is the goal of liberalism: full freedom, justice, and equality for every American. Freedom from want of the basic necessities of life. Freedom from exploitation. Freedom from undue disparities of wealth. Freedom from unfair barriers to social mobility and economic well-being. Freedom from the domination of rich elites.

There is also another important implication of the Second Bill of Rights: it cannot be implemented by "less government." Its protections must be maintained by a government dedicated to safeguarding Americans' rights and interests, and to giving assistance to those who stand in need of it. That is why, whether it is their intention or not, conservatives who advocate smaller government are, in effect, advocating less protection for those Americans who need it.

In addition, Roosevelt's Second Bill of Rights demonstrated a point that seems to have been lost on today's conservatives: that national security is about much more than war abroad. The greatest national security is security at home. That is how Roosevelt summed up his address: "All these rights spell security."

A Tale of Two Texans

Finally, the difference between liberals and conservatives can be seen in the dramatic differences between two well-known Texans.

Lyndon Baines Johnson was born in central Texas. His father, Sam

Johnson—respectfully called "Mr. Sam" by his neighbors and constituents—was a member of the Texas House of Representatives. Although Sam Johnson came from a family of such social prominence that
a Texas town—Johnson City—was named after it, Sam Johnson was himself a confirmed populist who identified not with the monied interests but
with the common men and women of Texas. He was a well-known champion of the laboring masses. Lyndon's political worldview and class sensibilities were shaped by both Sam Johnson's populism, and his financial
struggles and eventual bankruptcy. Lyndon's social perspective was also
shaped by his own experiences with his poorer neighbors and the impoverished Mexican Americans he taught and befriended as a public school
teacher.

George W. Bush is not a Texan by birth, but it is Texas that he claims as
home, and rightfully so. Although beyond junior high school he was educated in northern prep schools and universities, it was to Texas that he
returned. His various turns of career, including oil-drilling ventures and
part ownership of the Texas Rangers baseball team, all took place in Texas.
He married and started his family in Texas, began his political career in
Texas, and ultimately became the state's chief executive.

The political family that shaped George Bush was very different from
Johnson's, however. Bush's grandfather, the patrician Prescott Bush, a
successful investment banker, was a U.S. senator from Connecticut.
George W. Bush's father, George H. W. Bush, was also a successful businessman, and even more successful as a politician than his father, Prescott.
Before George H. W. Bush was Ronald Reagan's vice president, and eventually the nation's forty-first president, he had also been a congressman
from Texas and the director of the Central Intelligence Agency.

The differences in the politics, social background, and class interests
that the Johnson and Bush clans bequeathed to their sons could hardly
have been greater. They are possibly best seen in this one fact: in 1965,
when President Lyndon B. Johnson proposed the Medicare program that
would give millions of elderly Americans relief and succor, a congressman
from Texas—George H. W. Bush—was among those who vehemently opposed it.

As Texas politicians, both Lyndon B. Johnson and George W. Bush were familiar with the needs of their constituents. Both knew of the many Texans made wealthy by the state's booming oil-and-gas industry, and both were aware of the huge numbers of those who languished on the bottom rungs of the Texas economy. Both also knew the national statistics: the high levels of poverty and unemployment; the millions of men, women, and children without health insurance; the millions more without an adequate safety net in old age. Yet their responses to those needs as president are very different.

On a scale rivaled only by Franklin D. Roosevelt's New Deal, Johnson's Great Society mounted a broad-scale fight against poverty; its agenda included making education and health care more widely available, strengthening and beautifying crumbling urban infrastructure, addressing rising crime and delinquency, and making the right to vote a reality for all Americans.

In addition, by creatively utilizing the courts, the regulatory agencies, and executive orders, Johnson expanded the numbers of those eligible for existing programs, including the Food Stamp Program; he increased Social Security benefits and indexed them to inflation; and he reduced the yearlong eligibility waiting period for those in need of Aid to Families with Dependent Children (AFDC).

Unfortunately for all Americans except the rich, George W. Bush is no Lyndon B. Johnson. Not only has he proposed virtually no substantive policies to help those in need, even the middle-class Americans who are losing economic ground, he has labored to gut or altogether do away with the programs that do make a difference for the needy, programs and policies that year after year liberals crafted and struggled to enact into law over conservatives' myriad and well-organized campaigns to stonewall them.

It is true that Johnson was not known to be a particularly religious person. He had a reputation as a profane man who cussed and swore and who sometimes met with subordinates while seated on the Oval Office toilet with his pants around his ankles. During his time in Congress he voted against virtually every civil rights bill, including legislation aimed at ending the poll tax, and ending segregation in the armed forces; he even voted against antilynching legislation. (After an eventual change of heart, he reportedly said of his commitment as president to achieve full rights for all African American citizens that he would "out-nigger" every politician in America.) The conflict in Vietnam became a full-fledged war under his watch; he gradually increased the number of troops there from sixteen thousand when he assumed the presidency to over half a million when he left it. Along the way he was as untruthful about the Vietnam War as George W. Bush has been about the war in Iraq, maybe more so. Just as Bush based his invasion of Iraq on false claims that Iraq was behind the 9/11 attacks, Johnson predicated his ongoing war against North Vietnam upon fabricated claims that a U.S. Navy vessel had been bombed in the Gulf of Tonkin. Indeed, the term "credibility gap" was coined to describe the difference between the truth and Johnson's stream of misleading presidential statements. Moreover, Johnson's adroitness at political corruption and underhandedness is legendary. There is no question that he stole the 1948 Texas senatorial race from Coke Robert Stevenson, nor that Mexican pistoleros with guns drawn were dispatched to forcibly keep Stevenson from inspecting questionable ballots, nor that while in Congress Johnson escaped indictment for corruption, and possibly bribery, only because President Franklin D. Roosevelt intervened on his behalf.

At no point did Johnson ever claim any great familiarity with Jesus. Yet despite his tendency toward political corruption and dishonesty and his outward irreligiosity, Lyndon B. Johnson somehow transcended those limitations in a way that seemed to heed Jesus' call by using his presidency to treat the needs of "the least of these" as holy, without religious rhetoric or fanfare, and without pandering to any religious lobby. Despite all his missteps and dissembling with regard to the Vietnam War he inherited, when it came to domestic policy, Lyndon B. Johnson ultimately obeyed Jesus in the way that truly matters: through his social and political actions. It is ironic that a man otherwise so morally flawed would show such care for America's poor and vulnerable that he seems to have crafted his social policies according to the words of Jesus: "[J]ust as you have done it to the least of these, my brothers [and sisters], you have also done it to me."

President George W. Bush, on the other hand, has made some of the grandest religious gestures of any sitting president, yet he has spent his time in office in constant, though unadmitted, opposition to Jesus' command to treat the people's needs as holy. At times Bush has actually seemed to be on a crusade to violate in every conceivable way Jesus' command to care for the poor, the needy, and the vulnerable. Rather than heeding the call of the one he so publicly calls his Lord and Savior, Bush has instead dedicated his presidency to serving the avarice of the rich that Jesus taught his followers to stand against when he said, "Be on your guard against all kinds of greed" (Luke 12:15). Sadly, President George W. Bush has unquestionably earned the denunciation that Jesus issues in Matthew 25:45: "[J]ust as you did not do it to . . . the least of these, you did not do it to me."

Two Sons of Privilege

It can be said that it is unfair to compare the social visions of presidents with such widely divergent economic and social origins as Johnson and Bush. Yet even when compared to a president with a similarly privileged and politically well-connected family, Bush fares no better.

Like Bush, Franklin Delano Roosevelt was born into great wealth and an enormously well-connected family. Like Bush, he was never at the mercy of an employer who could terminate his job and destroy his livelihood, never felt taken advantage of or humiliated by a boss, never went home stooped with pain or exhaustion from a hard day of physical labor. Yet this did not stop Roosevelt from caring for average Americans. Indeed, his presidential policies proved to be extraordinarily empathetic to both the abject poor and the working poor of America. Like Lyndon B. Johnson, Roosevelt made some shameful decisions, including forcing Americans of Japanese descent to live in detention camps during World War II— whether they were U.S. citizens or not. And like Johnson, Roosevelt made no great pronouncements about his faith. Yet it is almost as if Roosevelt constantly had before him Jesus' admonition, "From everyone to whom much has been given, much will be required."

That is why when Roosevelt did appeal to the religious community, it was not to make grandstanding religious statements but to ask for support in his quest to fulfill the people's most pressing needs. A letter to the Reverend Amos A. F. Whitehurst of Kingfisher, Oklahoma, dated September 24, 1935, is representative:

Dear Reverend and Sir:

Your high calling brings you into intimate daily contact not only with your own parishioners, but with people generally in your community. I am sure you see the problems of your people with wise and sympathetic understanding.

Because of the grave responsibilities of my office, I am turning to representative Clergymen for counsel and advice,—feeling confident that no group can give more accurate or unbiased views.

I am particularly anxious that the new Social Security Legislation just enacted, for which we have worked so long, providing for old age pensions, aid for crippled children, and unemployment insurance, shall be carried out in keeping with the high purposes with which this law was enacted. It is also vitally important that the Works Program shall be administered to provide employment at useful work, and that our unemployed as well as the nation as a whole may derive the greatest possible benefits.

I shall deem it a favor if you will write to me about conditions in your community. Tell me where you feel our government can better serve your people.

May I have your counsel and your help? I am leaving on a short vacation but will be back in Washington in a few weeks, and I will deeply appreciate your writing to me.

Very sincerely yours,
Franklin D. Roosevelt

What a grave contrast to George W. Bush! Despite his many pronouncements of faith, Bush has shown no serious interest in truth, justice, or the plight of the suffering. Indeed, he seems almost to go out of his way to craft policies that are counter to the politics of Jesus. Instead of good news to the poor, Bush's policies are bad news. Instead of peace, he seems dedicated to war. Instead of compassion for the needy, he brings them added pain and insecurity.

SOME CONCLUSIONS WITH REGARD TO
LIBERALISM AND CONSERVATISM

In this chapter we have identified the various ways in which some of the most basic tenets and practices of political conservatism contradict the politics of Jesus. We have stressed the constructive elements of liberalism because what is positive about liberalism has been greatly obscured in modern political discourse. However, despite the significant ways that political liberalism is consistent with the politics of Jesus, it must be recognized that liberalism also has substantial areas of inconsistency with Jesus' teachings.

One shortcoming of liberalism is that its stress on human freedom and human liberation can lead to self-indulgence. Some liberals confuse freedom *from* with freedom *to*. That is, they sometimes confuse freedom from oppression with freedom from personal moral restraints and watchfulness.

Another of liberalism's shortcomings is that, despite the nobility of its social concerns, in too many quarters it has lost its spiritual center. Its emphasis on freedom from religious compulsion has made liberals reluctant to share their personal religious testimony or to articulate their moral and ethical positions in religious terms. Without a religious or spiritual referent, in many cases liberal discourse has become self-referential, stressing liberal ideas rather than the spirituality that inspired them.

Worse is liberalism's tendency to define itself in terms of the conservative policies and principles it opposes. Too much time and effort are spent criticizing and attacking conservative ideas, some of which are deserving of greater respect and more thoughtful consideration. In addition, liberalism's stress on social justice and *collective* piety can take its focus off the importance of *personal* piety. As a consequence, liberalism too often lacks the transformational power of personal religious witness and spirituality that is conservative religion's stock in trade.

Conservative religiosity is much more effective with regard to its personal transformational power. Its willingness to use religious language in public discourse and to focus on everyday personal piety keeps it in touch with its religious roots. Its emphasis on personal morality, when not extreme or narrowly oppressive, can lend an important measure of predictability of behavior to the social fabric of America. Even its tendency to be wary of social innovation can serve society well, if applied in a thoughtful and considered fashion and not taken too far, though too often that is the case. And though its sense of certainty can be oppressive and even deadly when taken to extremes, it can also offer succor and security to those most in need of it, while allaying anxiety and doubt about one's worth in the household of God.

However, conservative religiosity is too often reactionary; it is too willing to portray as religious in nature political and policy stances that in the final analysis are not at all well grounded in the biblical witness. Conservatives' religiosity also has too often given way to a self-righteousness that has led them to reject and to demonize everyone who disagrees with them, and even to go so far as to deride members of their own faith who hold differing views, labeling them as "irreligious," as "unsaved," as people who "don't know Jesus." In some cases, mainstream conservatives have even portrayed Christians who disagree with them as confederates of Satan!

And conservatism's exclusive focus on personal piety contributes to what often manifests as a lack of attention to social justice and relieving the plight of the poor. This has allowed conservatives to forget too easily Jesus' admonition to care for "the least of these," and to identify with the rich instead. One of the ways their political identification with the wealthy is expressed theologically is in their preaching of a "prosperity gospel." This is a distortion of the Gospel of Jesus Christ because it gives no thought to addressing the social and institutional factors that produce the extremes of wealth and poverty in America. Instead the prosperity gospel promises to bring wealth to its adherents if they have "faith" and "sow a seed," that is, make a substantial financial donation to "the kingdom," when too often "kingdom" means the coffers of the preachers' own churches and personal "ministries."

To point out conservatism's endemic slant toward the interests of the rich is not to say that religious conservatives do not care about the plight of the poor at all. Indeed, with regard to the needy in the developing world and particularly after disasters at home and abroad, religious conservatives have sometimes been more effective than liberals. Conservatives have opened hospitals and schools and run major ongoing relief operations like Feed the Children and Samaritan's Purse, both of which have worked for decades to bring food, clothing, and a decent quality of life to tens of thousands of children in America and in numerous foreign lands.

Liberals, on the other hand, have too frequently tended to focus on changing laws and governmental policies by banning overtly oppressive practices in poor countries in order to achieve more equitable distribution of wealth. Although giving foreign aid is consistent with the politics of Jesus, at times liberals may place too much faith in dispensing government aid, which in reality may do little to help the poor in corrupt or poorly governed countries. Changed laws can make little difference if there is not enough enthusiasm to enforce them, and although aid can be greatly helpful in stable, well-governed countries, in less stable countries it can get caught in bureaucratic bottlenecks or diverted into the pockets of corrupt officials. In no way, however, am I minimizing the important work of such liberal-leaning organizations as Doctors Without Borders, the Carter Center, and the Bill & Melinda Gates Foundation, which are doing some of the most important work to help the poor people of the world. My observations summarize what seem to be more general modes of approach.

Some sense of the difference in approach can be seen in the immediate aftermath of the terrible destruction of America's Gulf Coast by Hurricane Katrina in 2005. People of good will from all points on the political spectrum rallied to save victims of the catastrophic disaster, many at great personal cost and sacrifice, some even at dire personal risk, seeking to fill the gap left by the federal government's shamefully tardy and woefully inadequate response to the storm victims' suffering. Many liberal religious and secular groups were immediately on the scene with much-needed supplies and assistance, including perennial liberal gadfly Michael Moore, who made a huge contribution of time, money, and organizational appeals to help those in need. Still, a major response of liberals was to work tirelessly to force the government to use its power and resources to fulfill its responsibility to alleviate the people's pain. On the other hand, conservatives showed little interest in pressing the government to fulfill its responsibilities to the hurricane victims, but conservative religious organizations were a major presence in relief efforts. Both responses are crucial, but conservatives' efforts have sometimes tended to be more hands-on, and thus at times have yielded more immediate results in disaster situations.

But what is problematic with conservatives' humanitarian relief efforts is that they are often so closely tied to evangelism that the aid they offer becomes a means of disseminating not only food, and not only Bibles, but also the conservative political ideology that seeks for every knee to bow to conservatives' imperial worldview. In this sense, conservative humanitarian efforts can be understood to have an underlying agenda that the politics of Jesus would never condone.

NEITHER LIBERALISM
NOR CONSERVATISM . . .
BUT SOMETHING MORE

It is essential to keep in mind that ultimately the liberal-versus-conservative debate is not about Democrats versus Republicans. Historically, there have been those who subscribe to the worst of conservatism and the worst of liberalism in both political parties.

Through most of the nineteenth and twentieth centuries both Democratic and Republican conservatives allowed business interests to hold sway over the national agenda with few challenges or restraints. Tax codes favoring the rich, lack of concern for labor conditions and the rights of workers, free land granted to railroads, a virtually unregulated hand for banks and large corporations to conduct business and set prices and rates however it suited them—Democrats and Republicans alike have turned a blind eye to these excesses and abuses.

In addition, there were conservatives in both parties who opposed con-

stitutionally guaranteeing blacks the right to vote and who shamefully invoked "states' rights" to prevent the federal government from putting a
stop to the lynching of black Americans and the violent intimidation of
black voters. And there have been liberals and conservatives in both parties who pushed "political correctness" of one sort or another to sometimes absurd extremes.

Most important, in today's divisive political climate, one must remember that not all conservatives are Republicans and not all liberals are Democrats. In fact, it was a group of Democrats, famously called Dixiecrats
because most hailed from the South, who were the most stalwart twentieth-
century advocates of white supremacy and the staunchest opponents of
equal rights for all Americans under the law. These included Theodore G.
Bilbo, James O. Eastland, Strom Thurmond, and George Wallace, all Democrats (though Thurmond switched from the Democratic to the Republican
Party in 1964). Democratic senator Ernest "Fritz" Hollings, another staunch
supporter of racial segregation, referred to African diplomats—most of
whom were better educated and more culturally refined than he—as "potentates down from Africa [who are used to] eating each other." And in a
gaffe reminiscent of Trent Lott's unfortunate paean to Strom Thurmond,
Democratic Senator Christopher J. Dodd once said of Democratic Senator
Robert Byrd, a former Ku Klux Klan member and one of the leaders of the
filibuster against the passage of the Civil Rights Act of 1964 (and who has
since repented of those sins), that he "would have been a great Senator at
any moment" in American history.

IN THE FINAL ANALYSIS, when we closely examine liberalism and conservatism, it seems clear that in principle, at least, liberalism's central concern
for social justice and care for the poor are closer to the politics of Jesus
than conservatism's greater attention to the interests of the rich and well-
to-do. The heart of liberalism is empathy and care for the people's well-
being, as opposed to conservatism's emphasis on individualism, that is,
looking out for oneself. But it doesn't stop there. At liberalism's core also
resides a sense of responsibility to act on its empathy or, as George Lakoff

puts it, to "use the common wealth for the common good to better all our lives." Lakoff continues, "In short, promoting the common good is the central role of government."

Conservatives, on the other hand, seek to dismantle the federal government, which unfortunately includes its crucial protections of the poor and vulnerable from the rich and the strong. Grover Norquist, a former staffer in the Reagan White House, current head of the Americans for Tax Reform, and a major conservative strategist, explains the conservative view this way: "My goal is to cut government in half in twenty-five years to get it down to the size where we can drown it in the bathtub."

Still, to imply that liberalism is in some way synonymous with the politics of Jesus would be untrue, if not blasphemous. Liberalism is a modern phenomenon and a human philosophy. One cannot give liberalism divine sanction any more than conservatism can claim to be divinely ordained. Where liberalism does accord with the politics of Jesus is in its underlying sentiments of care for the weak and the needy, respect for human integrity, freedom of religion, and rejection of all forms of religious pretense and compulsion.

Ultimately, we must transcend the categories of liberal and conservative to reclaim the politics of Jesus. We must reject the aspects of each that contradict Jesus' politics and embrace those things that are in accord with his Gospel. We must embrace conservatism's willingness to speak its faith and the transformational power of that witness. And we must lay claim to liberalism's care for the poor and weak and its insistence on equity and justice.

We Christians must not let ourselves be deceived into either exclusive allegiance or exclusive opposition to either party. What must be opposed is valorization of the rich as if they have a natural right to rule. What must be opposed is moral laxity masquerading as liberation. What must be opposed is hunger and violence and exploitation and oppression, and mistreatment of anyone for any reason. We must oppose all these because they fly in the face of the politics of Jesus. To do otherwise is to dishonor his ministry, his mission, and the death he willingly died for our sakes.

✣

NINE

A Manifesto: Practicing the Politics of Jesus

The Principles of Jesus' Politics

Today's political landscape is rife with politicians proudly—and loudly—identifying themselves as Christians. Some of these imply—indeed, some even claim—that their political positions are inspired, if not fully guided, by the teachings of Jesus. Yet we have seen that the politics of Jesus are very different from the partisan politics of politicians. Partisan politics are characterized by self-serving deals, unethical compromises, and a thinly veiled selfishness in which all seem to seek only after the good of themselves and those they count as their own, while giving little thought to the well-being of others except as it benefits their personal agendas. Rather than "Love your neighbor as yourself," the mantra of to-day's political culture seems to be "Love yourself and those who are like you." And "*God's* will be done" has been replaced by "*Our* will be done," with the accompanying claim that our will is God's. Unfortunately, the politics of most politicians "of faith" have proven to be cut from that same cloth. However, the politics of Jesus have little to do with what one calls oneself or the faith one confesses. Jesus' politics is based upon principles, not slogans or self-serving rules.

Principles are directions or guides as to how we should live our lives and conduct our affairs. The principles of Jesus' politics are rooted in the most foundational ethics of the Bible, especially those that we shall revisit below.

The first is *mishpat*, "justice," the establishment or restoration of fair, equitable, and harmonious relationships in society. In its purest form this ethic holds that everyone has the same inalienable right as anyone else to life, liberty, and the pursuit of happiness and wholeness; the same right of freedom from exploitation and oppression and every form of victimization. *Mishpat* also means "judgment" in the sense of setting in balance— that is, resolving—conflicts in a just and equitable fashion with the full rights of all in mind, be they social, economic, political, or religious.

Then there is *sadiqah*, "righteousness," behavior that faithfully fulfills the responsibilities of relationship, both with God and with humanity. Or to put it another way, *sadiqah*/righteousness is the loving and just fulfillment of our responsibilities to others as the ultimate fulfillment of our responsibility to God.

A third foundational ethic of Jesus' politics is *hesed*, "steadfast love," which underlies his rearticulation of Deuteronomy 6:5 and Leviticus 19:18 in his seminal pronouncement of Matthew 22:37–40: "You shall love your lord your God with all your heart, and with all your soul, and with all your mind . . . And . . . [y]ou shall love your neighbor as yourself." Jesus considered these to be the greatest of all God's commandments and the epitome of "all the law and the prophets." *Hesed*, *mishpat*, and *sadiqah* are all implied and reflected in these commandments.

These are the base ethics of the politics of Jesus. However, they can be encapsulated in this one animating principle: Treat the people and their needs as holy.

POLITICS AND BIBLICAL LEGALISM

One cannot find specific guidance in the Bible for every detail of social and political life. Moreover, when rules and laws are found that appear to speak to particular situations, the myriad cultural changes and adaptations that have occurred over millennia make it unwise to apply specific biblical mandates uncritically to the complexities of life today. That is where principles come in: they can give guidance and perspective where appropriately applicable instructions are lacking.

The weakness of principles, however, is that it is not always clear how they should be applied in practice. And then there is always the danger of their being reduced to narrow laws that can ultimately contradict the very principles they claim to embody. It is for the very reason that principles are not hard-and-fast laws specifying how and when they should be applied that one must approach them with humility, with sincerity, and, for the followers of Jesus and all people of goodwill, also with love. In contrast, a legalistic attitude that reduces principles to inflexible laws requires no humility, sincerity, love, or even mercy. It requires only a spirit of compulsion. Jesus' reply to the Pharisees' contention that his disciples should go hungry rather than pick a few kernels of wheat on the Sabbath made it clear that this kind of inflexible legalism is misguided. "The Sabbath was made for humanity," he said, and not the other way around. In other words, Jesus' view is that laws are to serve us, not oppress us. That is why in our practice we must always stress the foundational principles of Jesus' politics—justice, righteousness, and steadfast love. Any laws that are not based on these principles are inconsistent with the politics of Jesus. Still, in recent years we have seen such reductionistic legalism employed by a number of fundamentalist Christians, with frightening results.

One example is theologian Kenneth L. Gentry's articulation of what he calls "elements of a theonomic approach to civic order." "Theonomy," which means "God's law," is the belief that every nonceremonial Old Testament law must be obeyed by all of humanity. Whether one agrees with them or not, some of Gentry's theonomic biblical interpretations appear to be reasonably mainstream, such as requiring a moral yardstick for electing public officials, punishing "malicious" lawsuits, and forbidding industrial pollution. Others seem to owe more to capitalism than to Christ, like Gentry's concern to specifically protect the rich from too much taxation. Still others can only be called drastic, such as abolishing prison systems in favor of a system of "just restitution" for noncapital crimes, and mandatory execution for everyone convicted of capital crimes. Women who have abortions or commit adultery or lie about their virginity, blasphemers, children who strike their parents, gay men, and witches are included in Gentry's category of those eligible for capital punishment.

Gary North is an economist who is well known in fundamentalist circles for his extensive efforts to reconcile economic theory with Old Testament passages. This excerpt from his explanation of wealth and poverty as divine reward and punishment is, in effect, also an exposition of "just restitution": "[T]he poor man who steals is eventually caught and sold into bondage under a successful person. His victim receives payment; he receives training; his buyer receives a stream of labor services. If the servant is successful and buys his way out of bondage, he re-enters society as a disciplined man, and presumably a self-disciplined man. He begins to accumulate wealth."

Neither Gentry nor North seems to have any sense of the human suffering such biblical interpretations could cause or the potential of such interpretations to foster real injustice. Gentry simply disregards Jesus' admonitions against those who hoard their own riches while the masses of God's children live in poverty. Worse, he outright ignores the rapidly mounting evidence that numerous innocent Americans have been condemned and executed for crimes they did not commit. And his judgment of abortion as a capital crime is on less-than-firm biblical footing.

For his part, North leaves completely unaddressed the question of what happens to the "servant" if he is not "successful," whatever that means. Nor does he seem to mind that his notion of divine "just restitution" reinstitutes the dastardly practice of state-sanctioned enslavement of human beings, despite the fact that the Jesus North confesses as his personal savior would undoubtedly find such a notion abhorrent and sinful. That is why legalistic interpretations of biblical meaning ultimately must be rejected: because they leave no room for the love, mercy, justice, and grace that undergird the Gospel at every turn. This Jesus pointedly affirmed in Matthew 23:23: "Woe to you, scribes and Pharisees, hypocrites! For you tithe mint, dill, and cummin, and have neglected the weightier matters of the law: justice and mercy and faith. It is these you ought to have practiced without neglecting the others."

The Yardstick of Justice

Rather than taking a literalistic or legalistic approach, the politics of Jesus calls for scrutinizing every political policy and policy proposal by this standard: Is it based upon the command to "love your neighbor as yourself"? That is, does it treat the people and their needs as holy? It is important that this principle not be treated as a law with layers of liturgical and organizational requirements. Rather, it is to be seen as a yardstick that at every point seeks to apply *mishpat*/justice, *sadiqah*/righteousness, and *hesed*/steadfast, continually demonstrated love for our neighbors to every public and private act of consequence. This is the way the politics of Jesus enjoins us to approach every question of politics and social policy.

The definition of "people" is crucial. As it is used here, "people" does not refer to any particular grouping; it means people in general. In the politics of Jesus there can be no seeking advantage for any one group over another, regardless of gender, race, class, creed, or religion. As the biblical witness points out, "there is no perversion of justice with the LORD our God, or partiality" (2 Chronicles 19:7). Jesus himself asks, "[I]f you love those who love you, what rewards do you have?" (Matthew 5:46). Indeed, each of the four Gospels tells us that Jesus ministered to the rich, the poor, women, men, the old, the young, Jew, pagan, the powerful, the powerless. But not only that. He also ministered to those considered to be enemies of the Jews, including Samaritans and Romans. In other words, this devout son of Israel refused to let his love and sense of responsibility to all of humanity be circumscribed by religious chauvinism or by a sense of national loyalty, what we today proudly call "patriotism."

PATRIOTISM AND THE POLITICS OF JESUS

It is important to discuss patriotism when considering the politics of Jesus because in the strange calculus of American political culture patriotism has come to be virtually equated with Christianity. Love of country is extolled in the same breath as love of God.

That is how patriotism is usually defined: as love of one's country. But patriotism can be destructive as well as constructive. *Constructive* American patriotism, or what Pastor James Forbes of the historic Riverside Church in New York City calls "prophetic patriotism," is the willingness to strive to ensure that this nation is healthy, whole, and secure and is conducting its affairs at home and abroad according to the political doctrines we claim to hold dear. But negative or *destructive* patriotism is more focused on discrediting or destroying those it perceives as opponents of America. In other words, its purview is "us" against "them," "them" being not only foreigners, but also any American who openly disagrees with the official actions of the political leaders of the United States, no matter if the policies espoused by those leaders contradict the politics of Jesus.

Yet good-faith criticism of government policies and practices is squarely in the tradition of the biblical prophets. It is also an underlying component of constructive patriotism. In this sense it is an important principle of the politics of Jesus. It is concerned with political affairs, but it is also concerned with the spiritual and moral health of America. In that it seeks to help the nation become its best and most righteous self, ongoing constructive prophetic oversight of the righteousness of America's deeds is the highest and healthiest form of patriotism. Thus a true patriot will welcome well-intentioned prophetic critiques of the United States government because they will make America more righteous and just. The true patriot will also reject uncritical abdications of our prophetic responsibility, as expressed in such slogans as "America—love it or leave it." Yet in today's political climate, those who engage in prophetic critique to help America be all that it can and should be—at home and abroad—too often are demonized, discredited, and subjected to scurrilous attacks on their character. Their livelihoods are threatened, their integrity is impugned, even their relationship with God is questioned and belittled.

To the degree that patriotism causes division and enmity between any of God's children, it is in opposition to the Gospel. But it is when patriotism seeks to silence prophetic criticism that patriotism becomes more than oppositional; for it is then that it has made an idol of its own beliefs and judgments, no matter how narrow or misguided or unbiblical they might be. Moreover, this blind patriotism is destructive because it values the welfare and even the humanity of some of God's children—that is, Americans, and not all of those, either—over the welfare and humanity of others, particularly those who look and speak and worship differently. Rather than engage in blind patriotism, followers of Jesus should keep in mind the question he posed in the Sermon on the Mount: "Why do you see the speck in your neighbor's eye, but do not notice the log in your own eye? . . . [F]irst take the log out of your own eye, and then you will see clearly to take the speck out of your neighbor's eye" (Matthew 7:3, 5).

Edith Cavell, a British nurse in World War I, was martyred by the Germans for helping Allied solders to escape to neutral Holland. Yet even in the face of those who declared themselves the enemy of all that she held dear, this devout Christian remembered to keep patriotism in Gospel perspective. "Patriotism is not enough," she declared. "I must have no hatred or enmity towards anybody."

In this way, patriotism that is truly guided by the Gospel will confess, like the apostle Peter, "I truly understand that God shows no partiality, but in every nation anyone who fears him and does what is right is acceptable to him" (Acts 10:34–35).

This must be the basis of our patriotism. Not hatred and enmity and the imperial will to exercise power over those who are different from us or who disagree with us. If we must have a patriotic slogan, it should not be some version of "America—love it or leave it." If we truly take seriously the Gospel of Jesus Christ, our patriotism must declare, "America, love your neighbor as yourself." Not only should we sing "God bless America" but, like the pure-hearted Tiny Tim in Charles Dickens's *A Christmas Carol*, we must lovingly pray, "God bless us, every one!" In the final analysis, this means that each day before we pledge allegiance to the flag and the republic for which it stands, we must first recommit our allegiance to the Gospel of Jesus and the justice of God and the love of neighbor it commands. We must remember that the flag doesn't supercede the cross. And if it is the Gospel that is truly the object of our faith and our allegiance, we must thank God for the faithful voices that, despite the derision and even the personal physical harm they risk, nonetheless speak out against every action, policy, and perspective of our leaders and our government that distances us from the politics of Jesus and the kingdom of God.

THE POLITICS OF JESUS AND THE KINGDOM OF GOD

In Luke 4:18–21 Jesus himself says that the good news to the poor and the liberation of the oppressed have been accomplished with the advent of his ministry: "Today this scripture has been fulfilled in your hearing." Yet, long after Jesus' crucifixion, hunger and poverty still persist in every corner of the world, and spirit-crushing oppression reigns over most of humanity. So how have Jesus' life, death, and Gospel teachings fulfilled his promise of economic, social, and political justice in our world?

A major feature of Mark's Gospel is its portrayal of Jesus as always *en te hodo*, "on the way," always moving from village to countryside to village and finally to city, spreading the good news of the kingdom of God to everyone he encountered. Jesus' movement was so incessant that one early-twentieth-century commentator concluded that Jesus suffered from a pathological need to wander! But Jesus' descriptions of the kingdom of God in both the parable of the sower and the parable of the mustard seed (see Mark 4:26–32) as kernels that are to be liberally strewn in every setting and at every opportunity offer a different explanation: Jesus' practice of sowing good news to the poor and oppressed in his every waking moment was an integral part of his strategy to establish God's kingdom of justice, a strategy brought to fruition by his courageous death and the power of his

resurrection, both of which affirmed for all time the truth and transform-
ative might of his message when it is rightly understood and practiced.

In other words, Jesus' words and deeds set the kingdom in motion.
Through his gospel ministry he sowed the seeds of God's kingdom of justice and peace and wholeness and love that we, his followers, must nurture. That was his mission, not to proclaim himself king or to bring
immediate, short-term results. His charge was to implant the seeds of
God's kingdom of liberation and to give his followers the spiritual food to
nourish their growth. Jesus held to his principles without wavering, secure
in his knowledge that bearing witness to truth and justice and love for
God and neighbor was the only lasting way to establish God's kingdom on
earth as in heaven.

Thus, Jesus' model for establishing his politics is for us to nurture his
political principles. That means sowing the seeds and the deeds of justice
that will grow into the kind of world Jesus seeks for us, not demonizing
those who oppose us or forcing our own perspectives on them like we are
modern-day Crusaders. Christianity that is truly based upon the teachings
of Jesus is a fellowship of faith, and true faith can never be coerced, only
lovingly tended. When the seeds of God's kingdom are nourished by deeds
of love and justice, gradually they will take root. The deeper their roots,
the stronger the stem or trunk, and the higher the plants will grow. The
higher their growth, the wider their reach and the greater the fruit they
will bear. If lovingly nurtured, they will pervade the fields into which they
are introduced, offering peace and shelter to all who need them. This is the
only way that the kingdom of God's justice will transform the governments of this world: through the sowing of seeds of truth, love, and mercy
by consistent words and consistent deeds.

If Jesus' imagery of the kingdom of God as seeds being sown does not
model this strategy clearly enough, he explained it another way, too. In
Matthew 13:33 he proclaimed, "The kingdom of heaven is like yeast,"
which, when introduced in even small measure, can leaven the whole
loaf. Or society. Or world.

Thus, if sown lovingly, courageously, and unstintingly, the seeds of
God's justice and mercy can change this world to a world of peace and jus-

tice and love and righteousness. That clearly seems to have been Jesus' meaning when he proclaimed, "Come to me, all you that are weary and are carrying heavy burdens, and I will give you rest" (Matthew 11:28). R. H. Tawney, the noted British economic historian, educator, and devout Christian, put it this way: "Granted that the Kingdom of God is something more than a Christian social system, we can hardly take the view that it is something less."

FOLLOWERS OF JESUS OR SIMPLY BEARERS OF HIS NAME?

The First Letter of Peter declares, "[I]f any of you suffers as a Christian . . . glorify God because you bear this name" (1 Peter 4:16). Nowadays it seems that many Christians take to heart only the last part of the verse: they simply bear the name. But calling oneself a Christian and actually following Jesus' teachings are not necessarily the same. Consider this statement by a well-known politician:

> The national government will maintain and defend the foundations on which the power of our nation rests. It will offer strong protection to Christianity as the very basis of our collective morality. Today Christians stand at the head of our country. We want to fill our culture again with the Christian spirit. We want to burn out all the recent immoral developments in literature, in the theater, and in the press—in short, we want to burn out the poison of immorality which has entered into our whole life and culture as a result of liberal excess during recent years.

This a clear example of a leader who calls himself a Christian and extols Christianity as the most important force in the nation, but who in actuality is anything but a follower of Jesus. How do we know? The speaker is Adolf Hitler.

Hitler's hypocrisy is sickening. What is frightening about his statement, however, is that it is virtually interchangeable with statements made by any number of self-avowed politicians "of faith" today. And because the statement uses the term "Christian," it would be embraced by many Americans without questioning the speaker's personal integrity or his real agenda, just as it was so easily accepted in Germany.

As followers of Jesus the Messiah we must make a distinction between "Christian" and "follower of Jesus." We must reconsider the faith claims of those in leadership positions. Not just on political grounds but, even more important, on biblical grounds. Christians and all people of goodwill must set aside religious and denominational loyalties, political partisanship, and personal affections to demand truthful and just actions from those leaders who so loudly trumpet Jesus' name. It is our duty. To continue to tolerate misrepresentations of the politics of Jesus is a sin.

When Jesus himself was confronted with the publicly pious leaders who shouted "Lord, Lord" while engaging in traditions and public practices that violated the justice of God, he paraphrased God's lament in Isaiah 29:13, saying, " 'This people honors me with their lips, but their hearts are far from me; in vain do they worship me, teaching human precepts as doctrines.' " Then he pronounced his own judgment: "You abandon the commandment of God and hold to human tradition . . . You have a fine way of rejecting the commandment of God in order to keep your tradition!" (Mark 7:6–9).

If we look honestly and unflinchingly at the political culture in America today, it becomes clear that Jesus' judgment against the religious and political leaders of his day (in reality, they were the same) is also his judgment against the leaders of our day. America's most vocal and self-described politicians "of faith" profess biblical beliefs while consistently acting in ways that contradict biblical justice. Worse, they portray themselves to the American masses as the definitive moral voice of America, the righteous, divinely ordained spokespersons for God to us all. Yet there is little question that if Jesus were walking among us now, he would stand against the political leaders of *our* day—and many of the religious leaders, too—as he stood against them in his own day.

When Jesus was asked, "What must we do to perform the works of

God?" He answered, "This is the work of God, that you believe in him whom he has sent" (John 6:28–29). That means much more than simply shouting "Lord, Lord" and proudly bearing Christ's name. It means following him by humbly and sincerely discharging our responsibility to feed the poor, clothe the naked, protect the vulnerable, and dismantle all structures of oppression and exploitation.

The prophetic ministry of Jesus has shown us that to believe in him is to bear witness to the justice of God in every season. Even the evangelist Billy Graham has come to realize this in the unfolding dusk of his days. "If I had my time again," he has said, "I would be stronger on social injustices."

A Manifesto

It is in this spirit, the spirit of Jesus the revolutionary, that we who follow him must call upon the religious and political leaders of America to reclaim our biblical mandate to act justly in our nation and in the world.

We call upon our government officials and elected representatives to turn from the greed and imperial ambitions of Caesar to embrace Christ's call for us to care for those in need of care: the weakest, the neediest, those in the twilight of their days.

We call upon the politicians of America to stop the crony capitalism that enriches the few and impoverishes the many.

We call for provision for all Americans of adequate health care, a livable minimum wage, and access to an education that can prepare them to be fruitful in the marketplace and to contribute to the common good of all.

We call upon our political leaders to stop their cynical misuse of religion and "faith" to support exclusionary policies, exploitative policies, policies that deal in killing and death.

We call upon our leaders to serve the justice of God rather than grasping for political power.

We call upon all who claim to be politicians "of faith" to return integrity to America's political culture by embracing the same humility that moved the psalmist to pray, "Search me, O God, and know my heart;/test me and know my thoughts./See if there is any wicked way in me,/and lead me in the way everlasting" (Psalm 139:23–24).

We call upon all who bear the name of Christian to reclaim the holistic spirituality that Jesus taught, not the one-dimensional imitation practiced by many in the Church that frees us from the responsibility to make justice roll down like waters and righteousness like a mighty stream.

Finally, we call upon our politicians to end their ceaseless drive for power and to begin to sincerely serve the needs of those entrusted to their leadership. For the politics of Jesus seeks not possession of worldly power, but to serve the justice of God.

JESUS DID NOT establish a bureaucratic institution, weekly social gatherings, or houses of religious entertainment. He started a movement that demands that rather than spend our time establishing ever more luxurious churches, we must strive to establish God's kingdom of love and justice on earth as in heaven. The Gospel he lived and died for summons us to treat all people and their needs as holy. This means instituting policies that fairly, equitably, and lovingly respond to the suffering and want of all people or, at the very least, of as much of humanity as possible. Yes, *lovingly*, because Jesus' entire Gospel is based on love. But note well that love as it is used here is not mere sentimentality; it is actively working to secure for one's neighbor what one wants for oneself. That is the difference between the politics of Jesus and the politics of politicians: Jesus' way acknowledges God as "our" Father, meaning that all are children of God, and thus the needs of all are holy. It is this standard that separates the politics of Jesus from the politics of politicians.

In the politics of Jesus, then, every policy and policy proposal must be judged by Jesus' yardstick of love and justice. We must ask: Do our social programs treat the people's needs as holy? Do our tax laws? Do our healthcare policies treat as holy all in need of coverage? Do our foreign policies treat all people as children of the same Creator? Or do we treat those outside our borders as children of a lesser god and, therefore, worthy of only inferior chances in life?

Treating the people and their needs as holy should be the perspective of everyone who purports to be a lover of God and humanity, but it must certainly be the perspective of every religious and political leader who claims to follow Jesus. In the politics of Jesus, there can be no "politicians" in the sense of "professional" politicians, whose dedication is to power and self-aggrandizement rather than to principles. There must only be servant leaders, just as the Son of Man came not to *be* served, but *to* serve.

THE GOAL OF JESUS' movement, ministry, and politics is a new creation: a political order that truly serves the good of all in equal measure. Those who strive to practice Jesus' politics must always keep that as the focus of our prayers and our compassion, of our love and our most faithful social action. It is not optional; it is required of every follower of Jesus. He declared as much in terms that left no doubt: "Whoever is not with me is against me" (Matthew 12:30). That is to say, if you do not work for, or in some real way support, the establishment of God's kingdom of love and justice, then your silence and inactivity ultimately serve the forces of injustice.

It will not be easy. It seems that every aspect of today's political culture militates against the Gospel's call for truth, honesty, and sincere service in the public square. But this is as Jesus foretold it: "I send you out as sheep in the midst of wolves; . . . you will be dragged before governors and kings for my sake, to bear testimony before them" (Matthew 10:16, 18 [RSV]). This means that in every political setting the true followers of Jesus will be called forth to speak truth to power and to find power in the truth. Even as many strut about proudly wearing their faith like crowns, the true followers of Jesus must hold dear his cross of self-sacrificial love.

All of this requires more than simply bearing his name. These things we must do if at the sunset of our lives we are to be counted among those who truly tried to love our neighbors as ourselves by living the politics of he who died so others might live: Jesus the Messiah, Jesus the lover of humanity, Jesus the political revolutionary.

EPILOGUE

Should not shepherds feed the sheep? You eat the fat, you clothe yourselves with the wool, you slaughter the fatlings; but you do not feed the sheep. You have not strengthened the weak, you have not healed the sick, you have not bound up the injured, you have not brought back the strayed, you have not sought the lost, but with force and harshness you have ruled them.

EZEKIEL 34:2–4

TODAY religion is a greater public issue in America than at any other time in this nation's modern history. Indeed, it is no longer enough to be a Christian. Now one must claim to be a particular kind of Christian with certain litmus-test beliefs, or one is treated as a nonbeliever. Even candidates for the nation's highest court are judged today as much by their publicly professed religious beliefs as by their judicial qualifications. In such a religiously charged atmosphere, no serious discussion of the politics of Jesus can close without assessing the impact made upon our society and its religious discourse by the "born-again" Christian who sits at the head of this nation.

President George W. Bush has been hailed as a man of devout Christian faith since the early days of his first presidential campaign. When he was asked in a 1999 debate to name his favorite philosopher, his response—"Jesus Christ, because he changed my life"—was for many a welcome injection of Christian faith into the public square. After what some considered Bill Clinton's disgrace of the presidency, Bush's profession of faith seemed to portend the return of the traditional biblical morality that Americans expected from the White House. His regular references to his faith on the campaign trail raised even greater expectations in a large number of Americans, especially evangelical Christians, who believed him to be God's choice to lead this nation. After the Supreme Court decision that allowed Bush to assume the presidency, many Christians rejoiced that "God's man" was now in the White House. Apparently, that remains the belief of many today.

I accept that President George W. Bush is a man of faith. I don't mean to imply otherwise. I can even accept that his faith is in the Gospel. Unfortunately, it appears that it is the Gospel according to Emperor Constantine that fuels Bush's faith. His faith certainly does not seem to be in the Gospel of Jesus Christ, for he has dismissed, distorted, and violated its teachings at every turn. Despite Jesus' admonition to care for the weak and the needy, Bush has been a scourge upon the poor. Despite Jesus' condemnation of the greedy rich, Bush has missed no opportunity to further enrich them. Despite Jesus' instructions to live honestly and peacefully, Bush's lies and warmongering have brought death and horrible injury to tens of thousands of innocent children of God. The sad and undeniable truth is that the faith George W. Bush *claims* is altogether different from the faith his actions *show*.

What *is* clear is that Bush and the right-wing religionists and politicians aligned with him have done more to misrepresent the teachings of Jesus in the public square than any leader or any movement in many generations. Along the way they have managed to make more acceptable than ever the elitism, militarism, and imperialism of the Constantinian Christianity that was a travesty even in its own day. Bush has played upon the heartfelt faith of millions of sincere Christians in order to mislead them into supporting an agenda of greed and uncaring and overt militarism that is condemned on virtually every page of the Gospels. In essence, George W. Bush and his political and religious cohorts have deceived the earnest Christians of America into endorsing what can only be called an anti-Gospel.

For these transgressions George W. Bush should be ashamed. If Matthew 25 is true, for his betrayal of the teachings of the one he calls his

Lord, George W. Bush will be judged. Unless he repents, changes his course, and begins to treat the people's needs as holy, there is no question that he will be found wanting by the standard of love and care, justice and truth that Jesus declared as God's truest measure of the deeds of us all: "Truly I tell you, just as you did not do it to the least of these, you did not do it to me."

And we, the American people who have been so painfully betrayed, must never again permit ourselves to be so grievously misled, by platitudes and seeming words of faith, from the message of Jesus, who gave his life so we might know the loving will of God more deeply in our own lives.

Notes

1. FROM THE RED SEA TO THE JORDAN RIVER: THE ROOTS OF JESUS' POLITICAL CONSCIOUSNESS

13 **holy days** For instance, Matthew 23:23; Luke 2:41–49; and John 5:1.

13 **references to Moses** As in Matthew 23:2 and John 3:14; 5:45–46; 6:32; among others.

13 **Torah as holy writ** Matthew 5:18.

15 **Hebrew/*hapiru*** See Norman K. Gottwald, *The Tribes of Yahweh* (Maryknoll, 1979), 401–9.

19 *malkuth shamayim*, **"sole sovereignty of God"** See Martin Hengel, *The Zealots* (Philadelphia, 1989), 90–145; and George V. Pixley, *God's Kingdom* (Maryknoll, 1981), 19–36.

21 **"Judas the Galilean"** Flavius Josephus, *Antiquities of the Jews* 18.1.6.

21 **"A long time ago"** Flavius Josephus, *History of the Jewish War* 7.323.

25 **from the time of Saul** See Hengel, *Zealots*, 290–302.

25 **several roles that the Messiah** See Geza Vermes, *The Dead Sea Scrolls*, rev. ed. (Philadelphia, 1977), 184–86.

31 **people of significant financial means** See Bruce V. Malchow, *Social Justice in the Hebrew Bible* (Collegeville, 1996), 33–34.

32 **"Jesus the prophet interpreted"** William R. Herzog II, *Jesus, Justice, and the Reign of God* (Louisville, 2000), 67.

34 **number of deportees** See John Bright, *A History of Israel* (Grand Rapids, 1997), 397.

34 **"high priest" was used prior to the exile** See Leviticus 21:10; Numbers 35:25, 28, 32; and 2 Chronicles 34:9.

36 **the physical center of their own faith and culture** See Nehemiah 2:19–20.

39 **Nicanor's Day** See Josephus, *Antiquities of the Jews* 12.10.5. Also see 1 Maccabees 7:39–50; and 2 Maccabees 14:31–33; 15:6–11.

40 **Pompey desecrated the Holy of Holies** See Josephus, *Antiquities of the Jews* 14.105.

41 **slow in raising an additional levy** See Josephus, *History of the Jewish War* 1.180, 219–20.

42 **Citing Josephus** See Josephus, *Antiquities of the Jews* 15.366–69.

42 **"Herod, in fact, instituted"** Richard A. Horsley, *The Liberation of Christmas* (New York, 1989), 71.

42 **"one can mention no suitable spot"** Josephus, *History of the Jewish War* 1.407.

42 **Herod would not kill a pig** See Macrobius, *Saturnalia* 2.4.2.

43 **What is the biblical notion of justice?** This discussion is based on Bruce V. Malchow's text *Social Justice in the Hebrew Bible*.

2. Birth of a Revolutionary: The Shaping of Jesus' Politics

50 **"produced terror and uncertainty"** Klaus Wengst, *Pax Romana and the Peace of Jesus* (Philadelphia, 1987), 13.

50 **Augustus kept up to 100,000 legionnaires** Martin Goodman, *The Roman World 44* B.C.–A.D. *180* (London, 1997), 82.

51 **"[We] have sought in vain"** Tacitus, *Agricola* 30.

51 **a time of numerous violent uprisings** See David M. Rhoads, *Israel in Revolution* (Philadelphia, 1976); and Richard Horsley and John S. Hanson, *Bandits, Prophets, and Messiahs* (Minneapolis, 1985).

51 **"Whenever we crucify the guilty"**   Quintilian, *Declamationes* 274, quoted in Martin Hengel, *The Crucifixion of Jesus* (Philadelphia, 1977), 50.

53 **"The increased Roman military presence"**   Richard Horsley, *Galilee: History, Politics, People* (Valley Forge, 1995), 131.

53 **"Yesua ben Pantera"**   See Jane Schaberg, *The Illegitimacy of Jesus* (New York, 1987), 157–58, 170–74. Although provocatively titled, this is a serious and respectful treatment of the questions surrounding Jesus' birth.

53 **enraged at his invasion of Israel**   See Martin Goodman, *The Ruling Class of Judaea* (Cambridge, 1987), 9.

54 **"reactionary psychoses"**   See Frantz Fanon, *The Wretched of the Earth*, trans. Constance Farrington (New York, 1963), 249–310.

54 **Latin military and economic terms**   These include *modios* ("peck measure," Mark 4:21), *legion* ("battalion," 5:9, 15), *spekoulator* ("executioner," 6:27), *denarion* ("silver Roman coin," 6:37, 12:15, 14:5), *xestes* (a corruption of *sextarius*, Latin for a liquid measure approximating a pint, 7:4), *kensos* ("tax," 12:14), *kodrantes* ("a penny," 12:42), *phragelloun* ("to flog," 15:15), and *kenturion* ("centurion," 15:39, 44). See Herman Waetjen, *A Reordering of Power* (Minneapolis, 1989), 13; and Werner H. Kelber, *The Kingdom in Mark* (Philadelphia, 1974), 129.

56 **nonpriestly "retainers"**   The term refers to those who serve a ruling elite and help it maintain and expand its wealth and power. The roles of the retainer can include military, judicial, and administrative functions, as well as priestly ones. See Gerhard Lenski, *Power and Privilege* (Chapel Hill, 1984), 243–48. Originally published in 1966.

59 **served only one day**   See Josephus, *Antiquities of the Jews* 17:166.

59 **Herod's last appointee**   Ibid., 17:207.

60 **priestly excess**   See Joachim Jeremias, *Jerusalem in the Time of Jesus* (Philadelphia, 1989), 92–99.

60 **bearing the emperor's image**   Josephus, *Antiquities of the Jews* 18.55–59, and *History of the Jewish War* 2.192–201.

60 **"the Jewish priestly aristocracy"**   Richard Horsley, "High Priests and the Politics of Roman Palestine," *Journal for the Study of Judaism* 17 (1986): 11.

60 **"found himself in the rather strange position"**   Sean Freyne, *Galilee, Jesus, and the Gospels* (Philadelphia, 1988), 199.

60 **"Woe unto me"**   Preserved in the Babylonian Talmud, Pes. 57a. Jeremias, *Jerusalem*, 195–96, dates it between A.D. 50 and 75. Also see Tessa Rajak, *Josephus: The Historian and His Society* (Philadelphia, 1984), 22–24.

61 **"presents two classes"**   A. N. Sherwin-White, *Roman Society and Roman Law in the New Testament* (Oxford, 1963), 139.

61 **bands of homeless poor**   See Peah 8:7 in the Mishnah, the second-century collection and codification of Jewish laws, which hereinafter will be signified by its conventional abbreviation "m."

61 **stampeded like cattle**   See m. Peah 4:2.

62 **"the daughters of Israel"**   m. Nedarim 9:10.

62 **"Peasants . . . were structured inferiors"**   John Dominic Crossan, "Peasantries in Anthropology and History," *Current Anthropology* 13 (1972): 385–415.

62 **less than 6 acres**   B. Golomb and Y. Kedar, in "Ancient Agriculture in the Galilee Mountains," *Israel Exploration Journal* (1971): 138, place the average acreage of an enclosed field in Galilee at about 4 acres. Martin Goodman, in *State and Society in Roman Galilee A.D. 132–212* (Totowa, 1983), extrapolates a figure of 6.175 acres (2.5 hectares) from a survey of farms in Western Samaria.

62 **hardly enough to support a family**   Douglas E. Oakman, *Jesus and the Economic Questions of His Day* (Lewiston, 1986), 64. Oakman's conclusions are based upon an extrapolation of the average caloric yield per acre in first-century Israel using the agricultural techniques of that time.

62 **one-half to two-thirds of the land in Galilee**   See Harold Hoehner, *Herod Antipas* (Cambridge, 1972), 52–53.

63 **"even according to Caesar's most friendly decree"**   Salo Wittmayer Baron, *A Social and Religious History of the Jews*, rev. ed., vol. 1 (New York, 1958), 279–80.

63 **"entered rich Syria poor"**   Quoted in ibid., 263–64.

64 **twelve different classes of tithes and offerings**   See Emil Schürer, *The History of the Jewish People in the Time of Jesus Christ*, rev. ed., vol. 2 (Edinburgh, 1973), 257–74.

64 **combination of secular and religious taxes**   See Jacob Neusner, *Judaism in the Beginning of Christianity* (Philadelphia, 1984), 22.

64 **"every year farmers had officials"**   E. P. Sanders, *Judaism: Practice and Belief 63 BCE–66 CE* (London, 1992), 149.

64 **Josephus places the number**   See Flavius Josephus, *Against Apion* 2.108.

64 **just two weeks per year**   This is reflected in 1 Chronicles 24:7–19 and Luke 1:5, as well as in Josephus, *Antiquities of the Jews* 7.366 and *Life* 2. Also see

M. Avi-Yonah, "A List of Priestly Courses from Caesarea," *Israel Exploration Journal* 12 (1962): 137–42; and Schürer, *History of the Jewish People,* vol. 2, 245–50.

65 **"delivered him to the torturers"**   The New Revised Standard Version (NRSV) correctly translates the sense of the Greek word *basanistais* in Matthew 18:34 as "to the torturers," in contrast to the translations "to the tormentors" of the King James Version (KJV) and "to the jailers" of the Revised Standard Version (RSV).

65 **a whole village was emptied in this way**   See Gerd Theissen, *The Shadow of the Galilean* (Philadelphia, 1987), 68–69 and 204n8.

65 **records of debts that were stored in the Temple**   Josephus, *History of the Jewish War* 2.426–27.

65 *opheleimata,* **which does not occur often**   For example, see Matthew 18:24–34; 23:16, 18; Luke 7:41; 13:4; 16:5, 7; 17:10; and Romans 4:4.

65 **also has "release" as a primary meaning**   For instance, Luke 4:18 uses *aphiemi* in this same sense: "He has sent me to proclaim *release* to the captives."

66 **Banditry is a classic symptom**   See Horsley and Hanson, *Bandits, Prophets, and Messiahs,* 48–87.

66 **Roman law counted it as a natural disaster**   See Brent D. Shaw, "Bandits in the Roman Empire," *Past & Present* 105 (November 1984): 9.

68 **"[were] not friendly"**   Ramsay MacMullen, *Roman Social Relations 50 B.C. to A.D. 284* (New Haven, 1974), 34.

68 *choritai,* **"country folk"**   See G.E.M. de Ste. Croix, *The Class Struggle in the Ancient Greek World* (Ithaca, 1981), 18.

68 **the superior gods live in the city**   Ibid.

69 **priests' role as absentee landlords**   Josephus, *Life* 63, 80, 422.

69 **mud-and-palm-thatched roofs**   The NRSV correctly renders Mark 2:4 "after having dug through it [i.e., the roof]," which refers to an earthen roof of mud, clay, and river reeds. Luke's version, "they let him down with his bed through the *tiles*" (Luke 5:19), reflects the urban social identity that most biblical scholars ascribe to Luke. Apparently unfamiliar with village architecture, Luke recounted the event in the terms and images he himself understood: images of the city.

70 **distinctively accented pronunciation of Hebrew**   See Geza Vermes, *Jesus the Jew* (Philadelphia, 1981), 52–53. Also see Alfred Edersheim, *The Life and Times of Jesus the Messiah* (Grand Rapids, 1971), 225–26.

70 **"Companion, butter devour you"**   See Edersheim, *Life and Times,* 226.

70 "Galilean fool!"   Ibid.

71 shorten Eleazar to "Lazar"   See W. F. Albright, *The Archaeology of Palestine* (Baltimore, 1961), 244. Also see Vermes, *Jesus the Jew*, 53–54, 190–91, and 261n144.

71 "Galilee, Galilee"   Quoted in Vermes, *Jesus the Jew*, 57. y. Shab. 15d.

71 *ammi ha-aretz*   See A'haron Oppenheimer, *The 'Am ha-Aretz: A Study in the Social History of the Jewish People in the Hellenistic-Roman Period*, trans. S. H. Levine (Leiden, 1977), 67–117.

72 "Who is an *am ha-aretz?*"   Babylonian Talmud 47B.

72 "A man . . . should not marry"   Quoted in Oppenheimer, *'Am ha-Aretz*, 175.

73 counterbalanced the priests' negative judgments   Because the Greek grammatical construction in John 15:1 emphasizes the pronoun "I," it can be read as contrasting Jesus with another. That "other" was the priestly aristocracy, whose role it traditionally was to purify or "cleanse" other Jews by conducting Temple sacrifices. In essence, here Jesus contrasts his own favorable assessment of the common Galilean people with the negative assessment they receive from the priests. In this way, Jesus invalidates the elitist judgments of the priests.

3. How Jesus the Revolutionary Became Jesus the Meek and Mild

82 a mere 1,400 calories   See Luise Schottroff and Wolfgang Stegemann, *Jesus and the Hope of the Poor* (Maryknoll, 1986), 41. Also see Oakman, *Jesus and the Economic Questions of His Day*, 64.

82 "a man standing permanently"   R. H. Tawney, *Land and Labor in China* (Boston, 1966), 77. Originally published in 1932.

83 "If a Roman soldier pushed Jesus"   Howard Thurman, *Jesus and the Disinherited* (Boston, 1976), 33. Originally published in 1949.

87 "the first totalitarian state in history"   A. N. Wilson, *Paul: The Mind of the Apostle* (New York, 1997), 6.

91 "Everybody sought membership"   Jesse Lyman Hurlbut, *The Story of the Christian Church*, rev. ed. (Grand Rapids, 1970), 62.

92 the New Testament letters known as 1 Timothy, 2 Timothy, and Titus   Many scholars believe these letters to have been written in Paul's name sometime in the second century—when the Church's assimilation had be-

gun in earnest—by a disciple of Paul who felt it necessary to address the cultural and moral issues of his own time as he sincerely believed Paul would have had he still been alive. This practice, called pseudonymity, was a widespread and accepted literary convention in late antiquity.

93 "[T]he post-Constantinian theological structures"   Thomas D. Hanks, "Why People Are Poor," *Sojourners*, January 1981.

93 "too often the weight"   Thurman, *Jesus and the Disinherited*, 31 [my emphasis].

4. MESSIAH AND TACTICIAN: THE POLITICAL STRATEGIES OF JESUS

109 "We are not Christ, but if we want to be Christians"   Dietrich Bonhoeffer, *Letters and Papers from Prison*, ed. Eberhard Bethge, rev. ed. (New York, 1997), 14.

110 "Their problems are our problems"   Quoted in Bruce Nolan, "A Wealth of Compassion," *New Orleans Times-Picayune*, November 11, 2005.

110 "The heart of [humanity]"   Ibid.

115 a portion of every Temple sacrifice and offering   See Leviticus 27. Also see Roland de Vaux, *Ancient Israel*, trans. John McHugh (New York, 1961), 417, 465–66.

116 "[T]he only logical reason to lend"   Goodman, *The Ruling Class of Judaea*, 56.

117 the price of doves eventually was lowered   See Jeremias, *Jerusalem in the Time of Jesus*, 33–34. Also see Ched Myers, *Binding the Strong Man* (Maryknoll, 1988).

119 Theudas   Josephus, *Antiquities of the Jews* 20:97–98. Also see Acts 5:36.

119 The unnamed "Egyptian"   Josephus, *History of the Jewish War* 2.261–63. Also see Acts 21:38.

119 scourged him until his bones showed   Josephus, *History of the Jewish War* 6:300–10.

119 "They carried the fire"   Ibid., 2:247.

119 "went so far"   Ibid., 4:139–41 [my emphasis].

119 "The high priest Ananias"   Josephus, *Antiquities of the Jews* 20:205, 207.

121 destruction of a fig tree is symbolic   The texts include Isaiah 28:1–4; Jeremiah 8:13; Hosea 9:10, 16; Joel 1:7, 12; and Micah 7:1. See Myers, *Binding the Strong Man*, 297–99.

128 "it would be impossible to bring more than a hundred thousand"

Meet the Press panelist Lawrence Spivak, quoted in Taylor Branch, *Parting the Waters: America in the King Years 1954–63* (New York, 1988), 871.

137 **"[W]e should not assume that the householder is God"**   Warren Carter, *Matthew and the Margins* (Maryknoll, 2139), 395.

139 **the number of unionized wage and salaried workers in the United States has dwindled**   United States Bureau of Labor Statistics, "Union Members Summary," January 20, 2006.

150 **some 200,000 homes in the greater New Orleans area**   "In New Orleans, Housing Sales Are Bright Spot," *New York Times*, January 1, 2006.

151 **"Well, why is that?"**   *The Rush Limbaugh Show*, September 1, 2005.

153 **"We have no official reports to document any murder"**   Quoted in "Storm and Crisis: Lawlessness: Fear Exceeded Crime's Reality in New Orleans," *New York Times*, September 29, 2005.

153 **"Is that fair, to blame the victims"**   "Paula Zahn Now," aired September 1, 2005.

153 **"To those who wonder"**   Wil Haygood, "Living Paycheck to Paycheck Made Leaving Impossible," *Washington Post*, September 4, 2005.

153 **"The aftermath of Hurricane Katrina"**   Cynthia Tucker, "Katrina Exposes Our Callous Treatment of the Poor," *Universal Press Syndicate*, September 6, 2005.

154 **"These people are being forced to live like animals"**   Chris Lawrence, "Stories of Heartbreak and Hope in Katrina's Wake," posted on CNN.com, September 1, 2005.

154 **"the poor and the vulnerable end up getting hit the hardest"**   Senator Barack Obama on *This Week with George Stephanopoulos*, aired September 11, 2005.

154 **"It's so strange"**   John Lewis, "This Is a National Disgrace," *Newsweek*, September 12, 2005.

155 **"If I were stuck in New Orleans"**   David Corn, "Hurricane Katrina: Blaming Bush, Being Pro-Looting and More," *The Nation*, September 1, 2005.

155 **"If I was down there"**   Quoted in "Etan Thomas Rises to the Occasion," *The Nation,* September 26, 2005.

156 **a man of "conservative political views"**   Arthur M. Schlesinger, Jr., *The Age of Jackson* (Old Saybrook, 1971), 132. Originally published in 1945.

157 **"every principle of honour"**   Mathew Carey, quoted in Schlesinger, *Age of Jackson,* 133.

157 "erroneous opinions"   Ibid.

157 "continued prevalence of irrational, anti-republican and unchristian opinions"   Quoted in ibid. Author's emphasis.

161 "it is easy to see why *orgistheis*"   Bruce Metzger, *A Textual Commentary on the Greek New Testament* (New York, 1971), 76.

162 the Greek word *embrimasamenos*   See Max Zerwick and Mary Grosvenor, *A Grammatical Analysis of the Greek New Testament*, 5th rev. ed. (Rome, 1996), 104.

164 Jesus' anger at the leprous man's plight   See Myers, *Binding the Strong Man*, 153.

164 some scholars prefer this translation   See, for example, Zerwick and Grosvenor, *Grammatical Analysis*, 104.

165 to be treated humanely again   The prescriptions for offerings after purification from leprosy are contained in Leviticus 14:1–32.

170 "Thank you. And now for the children"   Quoted in Walter Wink, *Engaging the Powers* (Minneapolis, 1992), 191. The discussion that follows owes much to Wink's brilliant insights on this passage.

170 "Coat" for Matthew   Ibid., 178.

172 Jesus "articulates . . . a way"   Ibid., 189.

172 "a commitment to respect"   Ibid., 217.

174 One of the most lucid treatments of this question   See ibid., 184–86.

175 "Coercion" as we use it here   Ibid., 192.

175 the elements of Jesus' nonviolent teaching   Ibid., 186–87.

186 "sometimes journey[ed] alone"   Andrew Levy, *The First Emancipator* (New York, 2005), 81–82.

186 "I . . . doubted, till very lately"   Robert Carter III, quoted in ibid., 82.

186 "I do now disclaim it"   Quoted in ibid., 90.

186 "I am informed that an Iron pott"   Quoted in ibid., 82.

187 his "present wish"   Quoted in ibid., 151.

187 "laid the primitive groundwork"   Ibid., xvii.

5. IN WORD OR IN DEED? THE POLITICS OF JESUS
AND THE POLITICS OF POLITICIANS I: THE CASE OF
RONALD REAGAN

193 "God wants me to run for president"   "When Religion and Politics Mix," *USA Today*, October 24, 2004.

193 **the right-wing scholar Kengor's**   Paul Kengor is a fellow at the Hoover Institution, a well-known conservative think tank.

194 **pushed into oblivion**   "Dose of Tenacity Wears Down an Ancient Horror," *New York Times*, March 26, 2006.

196 **Another prominent poll**   See James Taranto and Leonard Leo, eds., *Presidential Leadership* (New York, 2004), 11.

196 **"[I]'s pretty hard not to conclude"**   Wolf Blitzer, senior correspondent for CNN, quoted in Jay Tolson, *Newsweek*, June 21, 2004, 49.

197 **"I'm accused of being simplistic"**   Ronald Reagan, remarks at the Annual Conference of National Religious Broadcasters, January 1983.

197 **"My own prayer"**   Ronald Reagan, quoted in Paul Kengor, *God and Ronald Reagan* (New York, 2004), 165.

197 **" 'This is God's plan' "**   Don Moomaw, quoted in ibid., 160.

197 **"felt 'called' to lead the nation"**   Frank van der Linden, quoted in ibid., 160.

197 **"silent colloquies"**   Edmund Morris, *Dutch: A Memoir of Ronald Reagan* (New York, 1999), 427.

198 **"I think I basically stand for"**   Ronald Reagan, quoted in Lawrence E. Davis, "Reagan Assesses Political Future," *New York Times*, July 25, 1965.

199 **As a result of his attack on disability assistance**   See Michael B. Katz, *In the Shadow of the Poorhouse* (New York, 1986), 286.

200 **"only had the foggiest idea"**   David Stockman, quoted in Haynes Johnson, *Sleepwalking Through History* (New York, 1991), 109.

200 **a whopping 60 percent**   See Katz, *In the Shadow*, 288.

200 **Reagan's tax policies were so friendly**   See Citizens for Tax Justice, *Corporate Income Taxes in the Reagan Years* (Washington, DC, 1984).

200 **The poorest 20 percent of Americans**   See Sheila Collins, *Let Them Eat Ketchup!* (New York, 1996), 112.

201 **Reagan's attorney general**   See Howard Zinn, *Passionate Declarations: Essays on War and Justice* (New York, 2003), 149.

202 **declarations that racism was a "sin"**   See Kengor, *God and Ronald Reagan*, 179.

203 **"sand niggers"**   "Bell Tells a Sorry Story," *Time*, November 2, 1987.

204 **"immoral, evil, and totally un-Christian"**   Archbishop Desmond Tutu, quoted in "US Policy on S. Africa Is Immoral, Tutu Says," *Boston Globe*, December 5, 1984.

6. In Word or in Deed? The Politics of Jesus
and the Politics of Politicians 2: The Case of
George W. Bush

208 **"I believe God wants me to run for president** . . . God wants me to do it" George W. Bush, quoted in J. Lee Grady, "The Faith of George W. Bush," *Charisma & Christian Life*, November 2000.

208 **"He just wants God to use him"**   Rev. James Robison, quoted in ibid.

208 **"[I]t was obvious this man's heart"**   Quoted in ibid.

208 **"[But] I'm surely not going to justify war based on God"**   "Stranger Than Fiction," *New York Times*, May 9, 2005.

208 **"President Bush is God's man at this hour"**   Tim Goeglein, quoted in *World Magazine*, May 6, 2001.

208 **"Why is this man in the White House?"**   General William G. Boykin, quoted in David Rennie, "God Put Bush in Charge, Says the General Hunting bin Laden" *London Daily Telegraph*, October 17, 2003.

209 **"It's legislation that was passed before my time"**   George W. Bush, quoted in Mansfield, *The Faith of George Bush*, 118.

209 **Presidential speechwriter David Frum**   See ibid., 118.

210 **"The undeniable change in George W. Bush"**   Rev. James Robison, quoted in ibid., 163.

210 **"because they despise your Christ"**   Excerpt of letter from Bob Jones III to George W. Bush dated November 3, 2004. Quoted in "Dubya Saves: Bob Jones," *New York Daily News*, November 12, 2004.

211 **"could have cut tax rates across the board"**   Andrew Sullivan, "Why I Want to Vote for George Bush . . . but Why I Can't," *Esquire*, September 2004, 178.

211 **"One must be careful"**   Rich Cizik, quoted in Wes Allison, "Man of Faith," *St. Petersburg Times*, January 16, 2005.

212 **Yet the richest 0.5 percent of taxpayers**   *Citizens for Tax Justice*, "Analysis of Bush Plan Updated to 2001 Levels," February 27, 2001.

212 **The tax cut of 2003**   See Citizens for Tax Justice, "Most Taxpayers Get Little Help from Latest Bush Tax Plan," May 30, 2003.

213 **Less than three thousand, or about 1.9 percent**   See "Talk of Lost Farms Reflects Muddle of Estate Tax Debate," *New York Times*, April 8, 2001.

213 **"Mr. Bush hasn't yet gotten all he wants"**   Paul Krugman, "Bush's Own Goal," *New York Times*, August 13, 2004.

214 "If a working person has to pay taxes on every dollar"   Bill Press, *Bush Must Go* (New York, 2004), 109.

215 "the worst in two hundred years"   George A. Akerlof, quoted in "US Nobel Laureate Slams Bush Gov't as 'Worst' in American History," *Der Speigel*, July 29, 2003.

216 According to the *Austin Chronicle*   See Louis Dubose, "Read My Chips," *Austin Chronicle*, September 1, 2000.

216 "Bush took his time"   David Corn, *The Lies of George W. Bush* (New York 2003), 18.

217 "really does take the food from the mouths of babes"   Paul Krugman, "Bush's Class-War Budget," *New York Times*, February 11, 2005.

218 "affected by the reduction in services"   Lawrence A. McAndrews, quoted in "The President's Budget: Domestic Programs; Subject to Bush's Knife: Aid for Food and Heating," *New York Times*, February 8, 2005.

219 "as a result of [Bush's] faith commitment"   Rev. James Robison, quoted in Mansfield, *The Faith of George Bush*, 163.

219 "I don't understand how poor people think"   George Bush, quoted in "Political Memo; Bush 'Compassion' Agenda: An '04 Liability?" *New York Times*, August 26, 2003.

220 "The haves and the have-mores"   George Bush, quoted in "Bush and Gore Do New York," CBSNEWS.com, October 20, 2000.

221 "The supremacist ideology of the Bush Administration"   George Soros, *The Bubble of American Supremacy* (New York, 2004), 10.

221 "is built on two pillars"   Ibid., 11.

221 "a dark vision of eternal war"   Jim Winkler, quoted in Paul Kengor, *God and George W. Bush* (New York, 2004), 231.

222 "We're an empire now"   Quoted in Ron Suskind, "Without a Doubt," *New York Times*, October 17, 2004.

223 "If people want to say we're an imperial power, fine"   William Kristol, quoted in "American Empire, Not 'If' but 'What Kind,' " *New York Times*, May 10, 2003.

223 "God's blessing is on him"   Pat Robertson, quoted in Alan Cooperman, "Bush Predicted No Iraq Casualties, Robertson Says," *Washington Post*, November 21, 2004.

223 "Empire is about domination"   George F. Will, "No Flinching from the Facts," *Washington Post*, May 11, 2004.

224 **refusing to further engage in the longstanding symbolic practice**
Josephus, *History of the Jewish War* 2.197.

225 **"I like that law the way it is now"**   George Bush, quoted in the *Dallas Morning News*, May 19, 1999.

225 **"one bite of the apple"**   George Bush, quoted in Alan Berlow, "The Texas Clemency Memos," *Atlantic Monthly,* July/August 2003.

226 **"Please don't kill me"**   George W. Bush, quoted in Tucker Carlson, "Devil May Care," *Talk,* September 1999.

226 **"judgments about the heart and soul"**   George W. Bush, quoted in Kengor, *God and George W. Bush,* 39.

227 **"in high spirits"**   See Mike Allen, "In Private, Bush Seems Relaxed, Associates Say," *Washington Post,* March 8, 2003.

227 **"Feels good"**   George W. Bush, quoted in Martin Merzer, Ron Hutcheson, and Drew Brown, "War Begins in Iraq with Strikes Aimed at 'Leadership Targets,' " Knight-Ridder Newspapers, March 20, 2003.

227 **"a glimpse of the president's vulgar callousness"**   Paul Waldman, *Fraud: The Strategy Behind the Bush Lies and Why the Media Didn't Tell You* (Naperville, 2004), 8.

227 **"Those weapons of mass destruction have got to be somewhere"**
George Bush, quoted in "MIA WMDs—For Bush, It's a Joke," TheNation. com, March 25, 2004.

228 **"Instead of urgently focusing"**   Bob Herbert, "A Failure of Leadership," *New York Times,* September 5, 2005.

228 **"this is working very well for them"**   Barbara Bush, quoted in "Barbara Bush Calls Evacuees Better Off," *New York Times,* September 7, 2005.

229 **"I had other priorities in the 60s than military service"**   Richard B. Cheney, quoted in the *Washington Post,* April 5, 1989.

229 **"a man may be a patriot"**   Andrew W. Mellon, quoted in Howard Zinn, *A People's History of the United States* (New York, 2003), 255. The first edition of Zinn's book was published in 1980.

230 **"owe equal allegiance to their country"**   Colin Powell, *My American Journey* (New York, 1995), 148.

230 **"while others risked their lives"**   Glenn W. Smith, *Unfit Commander* (New York, 2004), 4.

231 **"African American males die sooner"**   George Bush, quoted in "Little Black Lies," *New York Times,* January 28, 2005.

232 "one of the cruelest things I have ever read"   Charles Rangel, quoted
     in "Bush Argues His Social Security Plan Aids Blacks," *Boston Globe*, January 30,
     2005.

232 "I frankly found the statement that the president made"   Barack
     Obama, quoted in "Obama Slams Bush for Linking Accounts to Blacks' Life
     Span," *Chicago Tribune*, March 11, 2005.

232 "I don't think when Bush approaches the issue"   Rich Cizik, quoted
     in "Man of Faith," *St. Petersburg Times*, January 16, 2005.

233 Bush's public profanity   See Jake Tapper, "A Major League Asshole,"
     Salon. com, November 4, 2000.

233 Bush routinely uses profanity   See Doug Thompson and Teresa Hamp-
     ton, "Bush's Erratic Behavior Worries White House Aides," CapitalHillBlue.
     com, June 4, 2004.

235 "Politicians will stretch the truth"   Ron Reagan, "The Case Against
     George W. Bush," *Esquire*, September 2004, 182.

235 "a dangerous national disease"   Bob Herbert, *New York Times*, November
     1, 2005.

235 "the dossier didn't correspond to the truth"   Quoted in "Italy: We
     Warned U.S. on WMD Docs," CBS/Associated Press, November 3, 2005.

236 no evidence linking the Iraqi regime of Saddam Hussein to the attacks
     "Bush Intelligence Briefing Kept from Hill Panel," Murray Waas, *National Jour-
     nal*, November 22, 2005.

237 "We have not seen such systematic distortion"   John B. Kiesling,
     quoted in Walter Clemens, Jr., *Bushed* (Skaneateles, N.Y., 2004), 183.

237 "God told me to strike at al Qaida"   George W. Bush, quoted in Arnon
     Regular, "Road Map Is a Life Saver for Us," *Haaretz*, June 26, 2003.

238 "had been 'coordinated' with the office of Vice President Cheney"
     "E-mail Links Cheney's Office, Contract," *Washington Post*, June 2, 2004.

239 *billions* of dollars of income   Bob Herbert, "The Halliburton Shuffle,"
     New York Times, January 30, 2004.

239 Bechtel Corporation . . . George P. Shultz   In his revealing book *Con-
     fessions of an Economic Hit Man* (San Francisco, 2004), former international econ-
     omist John Perkins names Shultz as the head of an International Monetary
     Fund–linked international network of cartels that Perkins claims is dedicated
     to the destruction and looting of targeted Third World nations by saddling
     them with impossible debts.

240 **In May 2003, Bush signed**   See Amy Goodman, *The Exception to the Rulers* (New York, 2004), 68.

240 **"In terms of legal liability"**   Tom Devine, quoted in Ruth Rosen, "As Ordered, It's About Oil," *San Francisco Chronicle*, August 8, 2003.

242 **"Companies come and go"**   Paul O'Neill, in interview by Tony Snow, *Fox News Sunday*, January 13, 2002.

244 **a sampling of his positions**   See John Nichols, *Dick: The Man Who Is President* (New York, 2004), 90–93.

245 **out of the 435 members**   Ibid., 77–78.

247 **"I am more fearful for the state of this nation than I have ever been"** Elmer Andersen, quoted in the *Minneapolis Star-Tribune*, November 13, 2004.

7. Reagan, Bush, the Politics of Jesus, and the Politics of the Church

250 **"Everyone takes our calls"**   Craig Unger, "American Rapture," *Vanity Fair*, December 2005.

254 **a popular book by a well-known minister**   Myles Munroe, *The Purpose and Power of Praise and Worship* (Shippensburg, 2000).

8. The Politics of Jesus: Conservative or Liberal?

256 **"Words like 'right wing' "**   Henri J. M. Nouwen, *In the Name of Jesus* (New York, 1989), 44–45.

257 **the vast majority are run by conservatives**   See Eric Alterman, *What Liberal Media?* (New York, 2003), 9–13.

257 **"I admit it"**   William Kristol, quoted in *The New Yorker*, May 22, 1995.

258 **their think tanks are America's best endowed**   See Jon B. Eisenberg, *Using Terri: The Religious Right's Conspiracy to Take Away Our Rights* (San Francisco, 2005), 94–108, for a sense of the extraordinary wealth that supports conservative think tanks.

258 **the John M. Olin Foundation**   "Goals Reached, Donor on Right Closes Shop," *New York Times*, May 29, 2005.

258 **"a lexicon of demonization"**   Bruce J. Miller, *Take Them at Their Words* (Chicago, 2004), xviii.

258 **pejorative words and phrases**   Ibid., xviii.

258 "Liberals hate America"   Ann Coulter, *Slander* (New York, 2002), 7.

258 "Liberals seek to destroy sexual differentiation"   Ibid., 36.

258 "Liberals . . . promote immoral destructive behavior . . . hate society"
     Ibid., 35.

258 "Even Islamic terrorists"   Ibid., 7.

259 "our battle is with Satan himself"   Jerry Falwell, quoted in *The Best Liberal Quotes Ever* (Naperville, IL: 2004), 264.

259 "Liberals hate all religions except Islam"   Coulter, *Slander*, 7.

259 "Liberals hate religion"   Ibid., 247.

259 "there is only one thing wrong with liberals"   "Battered Republican Syndrome," *Jewish World Review*, August 29, 2002.

260 "I want you to let a wave of hatred"   Randall Terry, Fort Wayne *News-Sentinel*, August 16, 1993.

260 "a few more bodyguards"   Dana Milbank, "And the Verdict on Justice Kennedy Is Guilty," *Washington Post*, April 9, 2005.

260 "Blow them away in the name of the Lord"   Jerry Falwell on CNN's *Late Edition with Wolf Blitzer*, aired October 24, 2004.

261 "We should invade their countries"   Ann Coulter, "This Is War," *National Review Online*, September 13, 2001.

261 "My only regret with Timothy McVeigh"   Ann Coulter, quoted in the *New York Observer*, August 23, 2002.

263 "Conservatives are most often found"   Jay M. Shafritz, *The HarperCollins Dictionary of American Government and Politics* (New York, 1992), 139.

268 Matrisciana also admitted   See Murray Waas, "The Falwell Connection," Salon.com, March 1998.

268 "The cities to which the soldiers returned"   Zinn, *People's History*, 240.

269 thirty-five to fifty cents per day   Ibid.

269 "22,000 railroad workers were killed or injured"   Ibid., 256.

269 "The present system has enabled capitalists"   Quoted in ibid., 244–45.

271 only 19 dealt with the rights of blacks   Ibid., 261.

271 "It is the unvarying law"   David J. Brewer, quoted in ibid., 261.

271 Ludlow Massacre   See ibid., 354–55.

272 "From the blazing tents"   Julia May Courtney, "Remember Ludlow!" quoted in Howard Zinn and Anthony Arnove, *Voices of a People's History United States* (New York, 2004), 281. Originally printed in *Mother Earth* 9, no. 3 (May 1914).

273 **"[W]e have you for your strength"**　　Frederick Taylor, quoted in George F. Will, review of *The One Best Way: Frederick Winslow Taylor and the Enigma of Efficiency* by Robert Kanigel, *New York Times Book Review*, June 15, 1997, 8.

274 **"With one book, Russell Kirk made conservatism"**　　Lee Edwards quoted in Scott McLemee, "A Conservative of the Old School," *Chronicle of Higher Education*, May 7, 2004.

275 **Kirk's six tenets**　　See Russell Kirk, *The Conservative Mind* (New York, 1953), 8–9.

276 **"In America, 'the rich'"**　　Robert Bork, quoted in Robert Reich, *Reason: Why Liberals Will Win the Battle for America* (New York, 2004), 118.

279 **"put the brakes on"**　　Billy Graham, quoted in Stewart Burns, *To the Mountaintop: Martin Luther King's Mission to Save America 1955–1968* (San Francisco, 2004), 180.

279 **"[T]ime is neutral"**　　Martin Luther King, Jr., "Letter from a Birmingham Jail," April 16, 1963.

282 **"derives its moral authority from God"**　　Antonin Scalia, "God's Justice and Ours," *First Things* 123 (May 2002): 17–21.

283 **"The time will come for the men responsible"**　　Tom DeLay, quoted in "DeLay Targets Legal System in Schiavo Case," Associated Press, March 31, 2005.

283 **"are making political decisions, yet are unaccountable"**　　John Cornyn, quoted in "Senator Links Violence to 'Political' Decisions," *Washington Post*, April 5, 2005.

284 **"The real villains in this matter"**　　DeWayne Wickham, "Schiavo Case Reminds Me of My Brother's Death," *USA Today*, March 29, 2005.

285 **Herbert Spencer**　　See Robert B. Reich, *The Resurgent Liberal* (New York, 1989), 236–38.

286 **"an electrifying effect"**　　Ibid., 236.

286 **"Making people struggle a bit"**　　Rick Sanctorum, quoted in "Tighter Rules for Welfare Families," *Los Angeles Times*, September 11, 2003.

287 **trying to "end poverty with the stroke of a pen"**　　Quoted in Collins, *Let Them Eat Ketchup*, 49.

287 **"We would like a less value-laden concept"**　　Quoted in Bill Kovach, "Federal Panel Considering Shift in the Definition of Who Is Poor," *New York Times*, April 7, 1973, 36.

288 "disinformation campaign"   Heritage Foundation, monograph, *How "Poor" Are America's Poor?*, September 21, 1990.

288 "Only 2.6 percent of those age sixteen"   Mona Charen, *Do-Gooders: How Liberals Hurt Those They Claim to Help (and The Rest of Us)* (New York, 2004), 108.

290 a clandestine arrangement with Mobutu   "Zaire Trip Criticized," *The Christian Century,* April 15, 1992; also "Jewels for Jesus," *Time,* February 27, 1995.

291 Robertson also denounced the United States government   See "Pat Robertson's Gold," *Washington Post,* September 22, 2001; also "Pat Robertson's Right-Wing Gold Mine," *Ms.* Fall 2003.

293 "The individual freedoms destroyed"   Arthur M. Schlesinger, Jr., "A Question of Power," *American Prospect,* April 23, 2001.

294 "Liberals and conservatives agree"   Robert Kuttner, "The Poverty of Neoliberalism," *American Prospect,* June 23, 1990.

294 "Liberalism in its most characteristic"   Alan Bullock and Oliver Stallybrass, *The Harpor Dictionary of Modern Thought* (New York, 1977), 347.

299 "If there is any one overall defining difference between liberalism and conservatism"   George McGovern, *The Essential America: Our Founders and the Liberal Tradition* (New York, 2004), 82.

300 "For the first time since the Jackson era"   Milton Viorst, *Liberalism: A Guide to Its Past, Present, and Future in America* (New York, 1963), 41–42.

301 Progressive Party   See McGovern, *Essential America,* 86–87.

303 "The New Deal was a revolution"   Herbert H. Lehman, quoted in Ted Rall, *Wake Up, You're Liberal!* (New York, 2004), 122–23.

304 "the best thing ever to hit Indian reservations"   Russell Means, *Where White Men Fear to Tread* (New York, 1995), 137.

306 the Second Bill of Rights   See Cass R. Sunstein, *The Second Bill of Rights* (New York, 2004), 13.

312 "Dear Reverend and Sir"   Letter from Franklin D. Roosevelt, from the personal archives of Rev. Emilee Whitehurst, Austin, Texas.

317 "potentates down from Africa"   Ernest "Fritz" Hollings, quoted in Christine Todd Whitman, *It's My Party, Too* (New York, 2005), 113.

318 "promoting the common good is the central role of government"   George Lakoff, "The Post-Katrina Era," *Huffington Post,* September 8, 2005.

318 "drown it in the bathtub"   Grover Norquist, quoted in Robert Dreyfuss, "Grover Norquist: 'Field Marshall' of the Bush Plan," *The Nation,* May 2001.

9. A Manifesto: Practicing the Politics of Jesus

321 **"elements of a theonomic approach to civic order"**   See Kenneth L. Gentry, *God's Law in the Modern World* (Phillipsburg, 1993).

322 **Gentry's category of "murderers"**   John Suggs, "One Nation Under God," *Mother Jones*, December 2005.

322 **"[T]he poor man who steals"**   Gary North, "The Covenantal Wealth of Nations," *Biblical Economics Today* 21, no. 2 (February/March 1999).

328 **"The national government will maintain"**   Adolf Hitler, *My New Order: The Speeches of Adolf Hitler*, vol. 1 (London, 1942), 871–72.

Scripture Index

The numbers indicate, respectively, the chapter, the verse, and then the page, which appears in parentheses. Psalm numbers are followed by line and page numbers in parentheses.

Subject Index

personal needs as absent from, 103–4
universal nature of, 105
"Your kingdom come" in, 104, 107–8, 184,
185, 263, 280
Lott, Trent, 228, 317
"love your neighbor as yourself," 31, 93–94,
102, 106, 109, 144, 182, 203, 230, 240,
296, 319, 323, 331
Ludlow Massacre, 271–72

McAndrews, Lawrence A., 218
Maccabean Revolt, 20–21, 22–23, 37–39
Antiochus IV's incitement of, 37–38
Jewish male children named for leaders
of, 38–39
subsequent commemoration of, 39
McCarthy, Joseph, 130–31, 257, 274, 293
McGovern, George, 299
MacMullen, Ramsay, 68
McVeigh, Timothy, 261
Madison, James, 191
malkuth shamayim ("sole sovereignty of God"),
19–23, 94
as heavenly destination, 25
in Jesus' ministry, 19, 39, 78, 107–8
Maccabean Revolt and, 20–21, 22–23,
37–38, 39
priests' betrayal of, 61
resistance movements based on, 20–23
in Shema, 20
strands of belief in, 19–20
Mandela, Nelson, 245
Mansfield, Stephen, 209, 233, 234
March on Washington, 125–28, 141
Martineau, Harriet, 267
Mary, Mother of Jesus, 61–62, 179
Masada, 21
mashiach ("anointed"), 23–24
Matrisciana, Pat, 268
Mattathias, 20, 38, 39, 40
Matthew, apostle, 39
Matthias, apostle, 39
Means, Russell, 129–30, 304
Medicaid, 218, 286, 295, 304
Medicare, 215, 244, 264, 286, 295, 304, 308
Meese, Edwin, 201
Meeting Point International, 110
Mellon, Andrew W., 229
Menahem, 21
Messiah, 23–27
anointing of, 23–24, 26–27, 28
as Christ, 24, 26, 86
David as, 24
expectation of, 24–25
Jesus as, 26–27, 61–62, 89
as military leader, 23, 24
as political liberator, 24, 25, 27
in Psalms of Solomon, 25, 26

roles of, 25–26
Samuel's warning against, 16–17, 23
Saul as, 24, 25
as spiritual office, 25
Zechariah's prophecy of, 26
Metzger, Bruce, 161
Micah, 29, 118
Midianites, 28
migrant workers, 141–44
Milbank, Dana, 260
military service, wealthy evaders of, 229–30
Miller, Bruce J., 258
ministers, Christian, *see* religious leaders
mishpat ("justice, judgment"), 17, 43–44, 49,
94, 111, 220, 320, 323
Mobutu Sese Seko, 290–91
monotheism, 15
Moomaw, Rev. Donn, 197
Moore, Michael, 315–16
Moral Majority, 6, 193
Morris, Edmund, 197
Moses, 13, 16, 19, 28, 57
Mount Zion, 122
mustard seed, parable of, 326–28
My American Journey (Powell), 229–30

nabi ("one commissioned"), 27
Naboth's vineyard, 28
National Council of Churches, 249
National Farm Workers Association
(NFWA), 142–44
National Guard, 230, 270, 272
National Labor Relations Board (NLRB), 201
National Security Strategy (NSS) (Bush
doctrine), 220–24
Native Americans, 87, 266
BIA taken over by, 128–30
and Johnson's antipoverty programs, 304
Wounded Knee besieged by, 129–30
Nazareth, 52
Neas, Ralph, 202
Nehemiah, 36
Neighborhood Youth Corps, 305
Nero, Emperor of Rome, 86
New Orleans, 150–56, 219, 220, 228–29
New York Times, 194, 222, 233, 249, 261, 287
Nicanor's Day, 39
Nixon, Richard M., 239, 274, 293, 305
poverty problem solved by, 287–88
nonviolent resistance (Strategy Six), 168–77
definition of, 172–73
"Do not resist an evildoer" in, 174–75
elements of, 176
examples of, 173–74, 176–77
"give your cloak as well" in, 170–71
goals of, 175
"go the second mile" in, 171–72
self-determination in, 169–72

OBERY M. HENDRICKS, JR., is Professor of Biblical Interpretation at the New York Theological Seminary, and Ordained Elder in the African Methodist Episcopal Church, and the author of *Living Water*. He has served as a professor at Drew University, as visiting scholar at Princeton Theological Seminary, and as president of Payne Theological Seminary, the oldest African American theological institution in the United States. He lives in New Jersey.